DATE		ISSUED TO

THE LAWS OF
CHOICE

Predicting Customer Behavior

ERIC MARDER

THE FREE PRESS

New York   London   Toronto   Sydney   Singapore

THE FREE PRESS
A Division of Simon & Schuster, Inc.
1230 Avenue of the Americas
New York, N.Y. 10020

THE FREE PRESS and colophon are trademarks
of Simon & Schuster Inc.

Designed by Michael Mendelsohn of MM Design 2000, Inc.

Manufactured in the United States of America

printing number
10 9 8 7 6 5 4 3 2 1

Library of Congress Cataloging-in-Publication Data

Marder, Eric
    The laws of choice: predicting customer behavior / Eric Marder.
      p.   cm.
    Includes index.
    ISBN 0-684-83545-2
    1. Consumer behavior.   2. Consumers—Attitudes.   3. Motivation
research (Marketing)   I. Title.
HF5415.3.M273   1997
658.8'342—dc21
                                          97–7041
                                            CIP

To the memory of
Richard C. Sheldon,
a colleague at International Research Associates, Inc.
in the early 1950s;
a friend who from the first made a generous distinction
between "ordinary research"
and "your kind of research";
a research director who in January 1960
became the first client of Eric Marder Associates, Inc.
Without his early support,
much of the work reported in this book
might never have been done.

CONTENTS

PART III: THE STRUCTURE OF CHOICE

PART IV: SYNTHESIZED OFFERS

PART V: MESSAGE DELIVERY

SUMMING UP

APPENDIX

PREFACE

For the past forty years, I have been doing marketing research surveys, initially in an advertising agency and since 1960 in my own company. This book is an account of that work. It presents a theory of choice behavior, supported by major, previously unpublished studies, drawing upon experience and data based on cumulative sample sizes of millions of interviews.

From the outset, I was as interested in the general as in the specific. I pondered such questions as: How many really different variables do we need to measure? How many really different problems are there? What do studies of automobiles and baby foods have in common? What is the connection between trying to improve the taste of an orange juice and trying to set the right price for an opera ticket? This led to some surprising conclusions. We need to measure only a few basic variables. There are only three basic problems, and these problems have a single common denominator. One way or another, marketing research boils down to measuring and predicting the choices people make. In spite of the fact that this is totally obvious, I did not understand it right away. The variables are treacherous. Unless one takes firm hold of them, they twist and turn, change form, and slip through one's grasp. But if one persists, one is led to a theory. That is what happened to me. I did not start with this theory in mind. The theory was born and grew up in the real world. The data that gave it sustenance came from the real world. I was driven to it inexorably by my desire to solve practical business problems.

Measurement played an indispensable role in the development of the theory. Without it, there would have been no theory, only a mélange of words—something that happens now and then in the social sciences. In my own mind, measurement always came first. The words—the labels attached to the measurements—came later. The theory came last, an after-the-fact synthesis in the domain of ideas of what had already been accomplished in the real world.

This duality is mirrored in the pages of this book. There are frequent changes of scale. On the one hand, there are sweeping generalizations that aspire to cover conceptual ground far beyond the commercial exchange of goods. On the other hand, there are painstaking accounts of specific techniques. And there are shifts from the forest to the trees, and back to the forest again. This is not happenstance. For better or worse, it reflects the fact that abstract theory and concrete measurement have gone hand in hand in my work. So I have presented them together.

At the core of the theory are three laws of choice behavior: the Law of Congruence, the Law of Primacy, and the Law of Persistence. These laws are both general and self-evident. At first glance, they are so self-evident that you might say, "I have known this all along." My reply is, "Of course you have known it all along. It probably wouldn't be true if you hadn't known it all along. But there is a difference between knowing and knowing, between the passive knowing that allows us to persist in actions that are inconsistent with what we know and the active knowing that helps us change the way we do things." I believe that knowing the laws of choice behavior—really knowing them—changes the way we do things. My crass but stringent criterion has been that a good theory should enable someone equipped with it to make more money than someone who isn't. I believe my theory has passed this test.

What kind of a book is it? Don't expect it to fall too readily into pre-defined categories. It is certainly a technical book in that it deals seriously with technical issues. But it is not written like a technical book. Theory, methods, and data are not presented in disembodied form. They are located in space and time, positioned in the institutional environment in which they arose, supplemented by anecdotes when appropriate. I simply do not believe that science needs to be treated as an abstract exercise, ethereally removed from human concerns. This is particularly true for an embryonic discipline. In such a discipline, the ideas one rejected, the path by which one got to where one is, may be as important as where one has arrived. For that reason, I have also provided the personal context, which makes parts of the book read like an autobiography.

The book is addressed to both the business and the academic communities, to businessmen and businesswomen who pose marketing questions, to my colleagues in marketing research who try to answer these questions, to the advertising community which is charged with implementing some of these answers, to teachers and students in business schools, to survey research practitioners, and to social scientists of all stripes. It may also be of interest to a broader audience that is curious about anything that has to do with human behavior and wants to get an inside glimpse into a small but intriguing corner of the business world.

Through the years, I refrained from publishing. I simply did not want to put in print work I knew to be incomplete. But my business interests

led me to promulgate every new insight far and wide, carrying it from company to company, from one prospective client to the next, talking to anyone who would listen and to many who wouldn't. In this process, I won acceptance of my point of view from the major companies that became my clients, and exercised indirect influence on the thinking of a wider circle of people in the field. In addition, I resolved privately to publish my work when it had progressed far enough to be presented as a coherent synthesis of theory and empirical evidence. Here it is: a technical book that freely straddles the technical and the personal, full of original data from massive real-life experiments, a summary of the thoughts I had and the results I obtained in many years of practicing my craft.

Eric Marder
New York
1996

ACKNOWLEDGMENTS

In the beginning, three people influenced the course of my career. Leo Bogart hired me for a summer job in survey research. Watching him work, I learned what it takes to direct a complex study effectively. On Leo's recommendation, Budd Wilson kept me on at International Research Associates when the summer was over. He taught me that a business can have a human face. Max Ule invited me to come to Kenyon & Eckhardt. He convinced me that business and the pursuit of knowledge did not have to be incompatible.

Marketing research is a collective enterprise. In my company, at least five professionals worked on every study, usually in collaboration with research and marketing people from the client organization. The ideas in this book were honed in the give and take of that work.

The colleagues with whom I worked most closely, and who contributed the most, were my four principal associates—Ira Potashner, Ira Lichtenstein, Hal Hendler, and Larry Gibson—and, in alphabetical order, Larry Brauner, Barry Cook, Glen Culbertson, Jim Drummey, Michael Geselowitz, Chris Hepburn, Larry Krauss, Sanjeev Luther, Jerry Milch, Malcolm Murphy, Joyce Pollitt, Peter Strear, Andrea Thompson, David Titus, Connie van Bommel, John Waldes, Simon Wardle, Sherwin Wasserman, and Judy Winzemer.

The clients with whom I worked most closely, and who contributed the most, were (in alphabetical order): from AT&T, Dave Carter and Dick Conrad; from the Newspaper Advertising Bureau, Leo Bogart and Stu Tolley; from Brown & Williamson, Brendan Ryan and Scott Wallace; from Chesebrough-Pond's, Andy Gerry, Shelly Newman, and Bob Stark; from CBS, Jay Eliasberg, Paul Kramer, and Phil Luttinger; from CPC International, Aaron Strauss; from Du Pont, Irv Gross and Mal McNiven; from General Foods, Jack Andrews, K. C. Blair, Jim Bueide, Rick DeSantis, Joel Levine, Donna Neal, Al Ossip, Fred Posner, Jack Shipman, and Sherm Schiller; from General Mills, Bill Etter, Larry Gibson, Heidi Hildreth, Gove Layborne, John Nylander, and John Urich; from the *Herald Tribune,* Dick Sheldon; from Hewlett-Packard, Bill BonDurant, Betty Sproule, and

Dave Welch; from Johnson & Johnson, Carol Panzer; from Lever, Bill Moran and Mike Naples; from Lipton, Vivian Bruno; from Merck, George Hamilton and Ed Neff; from NBC, Tom Coffin; from Olympia Brewing, Dennis Murphy; from the *Saturday Evening Post,* Charlie Swanson; from Scott Paper, Don Dietrich, Evan Frazer, Lee Griffith, Bobbie Harvey, Chuck Lamar, Laurie Neff, Neil Palmer, Doreen Rehrig, Barbara Rice, and Paul Schregel; from Standard Brands, Dave Graham, Ellen Marram, and Art Pearson; from Time-Life, Dick Ostheimer; and from Xerox, Arnold Cordts.

Four members of my staff helped directly in the preparation of the book. Connie van Bommel assembled the data, searching through mountains of files to locate materials from studies, some of which were more than thirty years old. She conformed the charts to the sources, proofed the entire text, and made many valuable suggestions. Larry Brauner did the computer work, consolidating studies and generating new analyses as required. He was my severest critic. I felt confident that if I could persuade Larry of something, I would be able to persuade just about anyone else. His contribution was invaluable. The manuscript was written entirely in longhand, in a handwriting rumored to be illegible, and was faithfully transcribed by María Hernández. For this feat, María earned the awed admiration of our staff as well as my heartfelt gratitude. I don't know what I would have done without her. Ben Thompson produced the charts, patiently recharting until the desired format was achieved.

I am grateful to my editor, Bob Wallace, for the generosity with which he responded to the manuscript, his help, and the consummate tact with which he extended that help.

Dick Conrad, Barry Cook, Ken Martin, Art Pearson, Betty Sproule, and many of my colleagues at Eric Marder Associates made valuable comments and suggestions. Additionally, five people with no connection to marketing research took the trouble to read the manuscript: my brother Herbert; my childhood friend Raul Hilberg; my daughter Eve Marder; my nephew Michael Marder; and my friend Bob Carballal. I was moved by the care with which they read and by the relevance of their comments. They helped me, and I thank them.

My wife, Barbara, was my gracious, steady source of support, always encouraging me even when every weekend and every vacation was devoted to the book. Her love enabled me to work in peace of mind.

TO THE READER

This book is addressed to both specialists and nonspecialists. I believe that the specialists—marketing research practitioners and teachers in business schools—will find the entire book relevant. For their purposes, the appendix is an integral part of the book. It has been separated from the text only to make the body of the text accessible to all readers. Nevertheless, I still don't expect all readers to be equally interested in everything in the body of the text.

Business executives, for example, may be most interested in substantive findings which can be applied directly to their business. Advertising people may be most interested in the final part of the book, which is devoted entirely to advertising. And social scientists, including survey research practitioners, may be most interested in the theory, the research methodology, the laws, and the substantiating evidence.

Mindful of this probable diversity of interests, I have written a brief introduction to each of the main parts of the book. These introductions—in effect, guides to the individual parts—are intended to orient you to what lies ahead and to help you identify material you may want to skim or skip altogether.

I believe, of course, that everything I have written is important and that any reader who is interested in any part of the book would benefit from reading all of it. But if you want to read selectively, I have tried to help you do so. My private hope is that if I direct you to the material you judge to be most relevant to you, you will go on from there to read more than you had planned to read, and will discover things of value throughout the book.

The book contains three types of technical terms: (1) everyday English words, such as *beliefs, accessibility,* and *effect,* that have been given special meaning; (2) compound terms, such as *price-sensitivity, customer satisfaction,* and *tie matrix;* and (3) acronyms, such as STEP, SUMM, and VEST. The pages on which these terms are defined or on which their meanings are explained are shown in boldface in the Index.

PART I

THE FOUNDATIONS

These four chapters introduce Choice Research.

Chapter 1 (Marketing and Choice) provides a succinct summary of a particular way of looking at marketing and defines the terms used in the theory of choice.

Chapter 2 (Defining Choice Research) defines Choice Research by contrasting it with other approaches.

Chapter 3 (First Principles of Choice Research) examines some widely held ideas and demonstrates that these take on a dramatically different aspect when viewed from the perspective of Choice Research.

Chapter 4 (The First Law: The Law of Congruence) is the cornerstone of the theory and of the entire book. It is the foundation for everything that follows—addressed to specialists, business executives, and social scientists alike.

CHAPTER 1

Marketing and Choice

A Personal Note

I came to marketing in a roundabout way. I was working in survey research. Superficially, surveys are a commonsense matter. One asks questions. One gets answers. One analyzes and reports the results. But my ambition went beyond that. I had an intuition that what happens in a survey, or what could be made to happen if one approached it in the right way, is of greater significance than meets the eye. If one thinks of every question as a stimulus, if one thinks of every answer as a response, if one focuses not on what is said, attributing literal meaning to it, but on the fact that it *is* said, then the response constitutes a special kind of behavior which should be psychologically meaningful.

My ambition was to open a path to those aspects of human nature that become most peculiarly accessible by examining what happens when questions are asked and answers are given. I was not concerned with how people felt about any particular subject, be it toilet paper or nuclear energy, an inquiry I held to be equally trivial in both cases, but with the universal pattern hidden in the responses, which would, at the appropriate level of generality, lead to principles and laws, not laws about toilet paper or nuclear energy, but laws about patterns of responses and hence about some aspects of human nature itself.

In 1951, I was contacted by the head of a prestigious graduate school and invited to join the faculty to attempt to develop a theory of marketing. I had hardly ever heard the word and thought of it more as having to do with getting my groceries home than as a serious field of study. After some soul-searching, I declined. Marketing, or what I thought it was, seemed frivolous to me. I wanted to continue to think about the embryonic science of questions and answers. Several years later, I went to work at Kenyon & Eckhardt, then one of the ten largest advertising agencies in the country. The understanding was that I would continue to think about questions and answers but, in the new environment of the advertising agency, would channel these efforts into measuring the effectiveness of advertising and helping the agency's clients sell their products.

In 1960 I left Kenyon & Eckhardt to found Eric Marder Associates, Inc. (called "EMA" throughout this book). By then I was submerged in marketing research. To be sure, the central tool was still the survey. I was still asking questions and collecting answers. I was still thinking about the structure of these questions and about the general principles that might be extracted from them. But the emphasis had shifted entirely to looking for better ways of helping clients market products. To do this effectively, it became imperative to understand the client's problem, not in the vague terms he was prone to use in articulating it, not even in the way he actually thought about it, but in the way he should have thought about it. This became dramatically clear to me when I met a high-ranking marketing executive who said expansively, "We want to do a study to find out why Mercury isn't selling this year."

"No," I replied.

He was half startled, half shocked.

"I damn well know what I want to do," he said.

"I believe you want to do a study to find out what you can do to sell more Mercurys this year."

"But that's the same thing."

"It's not quite the same thing," I replied. "If I took the assignment at face value, I would do a study among people who have just bought some other car. I might find out that they considered a Mercury but decided against it because they didn't like the look of the front end. This would give you the right answer to your question, but it wouldn't do you any good. If I want to give you a useful answer, I must study people who haven't bought a car and find out what, if anything, I could promise them or do for them to induce them to buy a Mercury in spite of the fact that they don't like the look of the front end."

It became clear to me that assignments could not be taken at face value. The important thing was not to listen to what the client said he wanted, but to what he really wanted, or to what he should have wanted, or to what he could be made to see he wanted if the issues were properly dissected for him. I also realized that much marketing research was doomed from the outset. For how could it hope to generate the right answer if it had not addressed the right question?

This led me to ponder what the right questions were, and so I began to think about marketing. Before long, a theory began to emerge, an orderly way of looking at the problems every marketer must face and solve one way or another. Given my temperament, I made every effort to think in general terms, so the theory would apply with equal force to the marketing of a paper towel, a computer, a presidential candidate, a religion, or anything else someone might attempt to induce people to choose. Ironically, I had come full circle. In the end, I was thinking about marketing after all and was thus carrying out the very assignment I had arrogantly rejected as a young man. Arrogantly indeed, though perhaps not foolishly. Because even though the theory I offer now is so elementary that I should have been able to articulate it after a little thought, I confess that it has taken many years before I was able to strip it of involutions and complications, of big words and technical jargon, and reduce it to the commonsense form in which it is presented below.

Nomenclature

What is marketing? There is, of course, no right answer. Definitions can be neither right nor wrong. But definitions do matter, for they are the tools we use in thinking about things. And some definitions can be more useful than others in helping us think clearly and arrive at answers we might have missed otherwise. In that spirit, I believe it is useful to think of marketing as a game played by N players (the marketers), each equipped with chips (their respective budgets). The players make moves on a board (the principles governing choice behavior) by adjusting eight dials (the eight tools of marketing). To understand the game, we need to understand the board on which it is played. So I begin by describing that board, using the terms *marketer, brand, customer,* and *choice.*

The initial meaning of these terms is self-evident. The *marketer* is the provider of goods or services, such as automobiles, soap, paging, coffee, or computers. The *brand* is whatever the marketer is trying to sell. The *choice* is the selection of one brand from a set of brands. And the *customer* is the person who makes the choice. The marketer may also be a campaign manager, the brand a political candidate, the choice an election, and the customer a voter. In general, these terms, as well as the principles and methods dealt with in this book, are intended to apply to any situation in which:

> Someone, anyone, (the *marketer*) is trying to induce someone, anyone (the *customer*) to make some selection, any selection (the *choice*) in favor of something, anything (the marketer's *brand*), often aided and abetted by a *researcher* whose job it is to subject the process to scientific scrutiny and to support it with empirical evidence.

Given the intrinsic limitations of the English language, which does not have gender-free pronouns, and being unwilling to use the awkward *he or she,* I am arbitrarily assigning genders to the cast of characters. The marketer shall be a *she*; the customer shall be a *she*; the researcher shall be a *he*. With some limited partiality, I am thus reserving my own gender for the actor with whom I identify most closely. I trust no one will take offense if the brand remains an *it,* even though it may on occasion be a political candidate.

A word of warning. This chapter consists of definitions, distinctions, and descriptions of commonplace events. I have taken pains to present these in the simplest terms possible. In doing so, I run the risk of losing you before we have gotten to the subject of the book. You are liable to say: "Why are you bothering to tell me things everybody knows?" If you bear with me, you will find that what I have to say may begin with definitions but will not end there. The basic variables will not only be described and defined. They will also be measured and used. And they will enable us to solve problems we didn't know how to solve until the obvious was articulated explicitly.

Desires and Beliefs

How does the customer choose among brands? She begins by assessing her options. Each brand promises her benefits. She evaluates these. In effect, she examines each offer and asks: What does this brand give me? And what does it require me to give up? The more she believes she gets, the more likely she is to choose the brand. The more she believes she must give up, the less likely she is to choose the brand. Her judgment of what she gets and what she must give up depends on her desires, on the value she places on the attributes of the brand. These desires are highly individual. One customer may consider the spiciness of a spaghetti sauce an asset; another may consider it a liability. One may consider an in-flight movie an asset; another may consider it a liability. It is less obvious that beliefs are individual. The commonsense expectation is that beliefs will not lag permanently behind objective facts. But this is not necessarily so. We therefore set aside objective facts. For our purposes, there are only desires and beliefs, and both are inside the head of the customer. If we measure them properly, they will help us predict what she will buy.

Desires and beliefs refer to the attributes of brands. These attributes can be organized into groups called *topics.* For a computer notebook, for example, the attributes "It weighs 1.5 pounds," "It weighs 2 pounds," and so on, can be grouped under a topic called "weight." Obviously such topics differ from product category to product category. A coffee has different topics than an airline or a fax machine or a life insurance policy. Nevertheless, these different topics can be grouped under some very broad headings that cut across product categories, that constitute common denominators. These are called the *primary topics*. They will help us understand how the customer chooses. Don't expect startling revelations. In one context or another, combined and rearranged in various ways, some or all of these factors have been mentioned by just about everyone who has thought about the subject. In this particular incarnation, they are *product, branding, price,* and *familiarity.*

The Primary Topics

Product attributes include attributes the customer can observe directly, as well as those she accepts on trust based on statements made to her. For example, the product attributes of an orange juice include the color and the sweetness, as well as the number of calories and the potassium content, which she may not be able to observe directly but which she accepts as factual, relying on government labeling regulations. The product attributes of a political candidate include his party and his voting record, as well as his marital status and the color of his eyes. In general, the product attributes comprise descriptions of the product and of the way it performs its principal functions.

By *branding* is meant collateral information that has been attached to the brand by external symbols: words, pictures, and music. This collateral information usually has two components: label and fable. The term *label* refers to the brand name together with the package graphics. The brand name is always part of the label, indeed its principal component by definition. Conversely, objective facts, such as $8\frac{1}{2}$ ounces or 320 mg of sodium per 100 grams, remain product attributes even if they appear on the label. But package graphics can belong either to the label or to the product. The graphics of a decorative facial tissue dispenser, for example, may be the very thing the customer is buying to decorate her bathroom, and hence an integral part of the product.

The following burlesque illustrates the role of label. A blue can with the name Nature-C and a red can with the name Vita-Life are filled from the same container of orange juice in the presence of a customer. We ask the customer to choose one of these "brands." She replies, "It makes absolutely no difference to me. Give me either one." But if we insist that she choose, her choice will not be random. One configuration of color and words will attract her more than the other, and that is the one she will choose. This is label at work in its purest form.

If labels are the intrinsic aspect of branding, because they consist of words and pictures that are permanently attached to the brand, fables are the extrinsic aspect of branding, because they are attached to the brand from the outside, most often by advertising. Typically, a brand is shown in close proximity to dogs, babies, boats, or undressed women, in the hope that the warm feelings customers have toward these objects will rub off on the brand and endow it with goodwill. Customers are also told overtly, ostensibly humorously, that if they buy this or that coffee, after-shave, or sailboat, they will become irresistible to the opposite sex. One particular type of fable has to do with social meanings. Buying a brand amounts to sending a message to the world, saying: "I am the kind of per-son who . . ." And this message is important to some people. We can imagine a customer who really does not like the seats, dashboard, styling, or handling of a Mercedes but buys one anyhow because she just has to have a Mercedes. Conversely, a multimillionaire might drive a beat-up pickup truck because he "wouldn't be caught dead" in his wife's Rolls-Royce. To be sure, the social meanings of brands are particularly perva-sive for major items, such as automobiles, homes, and jewelry, but they also operate, on a more modest scale, in the choice of coffee, toilet soap, and tennis racquets. A very special kind of fable comes into being when products are changed. For better or worse, some customers will continue to perceive products the way they were rather than the way they currently are, and they will hold beliefs about them they would not hold if they were unencumbered by associations with the past.

Everything has a price, and some brands have a higher price than oth-ers. We expect customers to prefer low prices. But like product and branding, price is individual and can have different value for different people. Upon learning that the price of a wine is five dollars per bottle, a customer asks whether the store carries anything "better," by which she means that she wants to pay more. One customer insists on buying a "real" diamond, even though neither she nor most jewelers (I am assured by a diamond dealer) can tell the difference between a diamond and a zir-con with the naked eye. Another customer wants a zircon because she takes pride in making a "rational" choice. There are also choice situations in which no money changes hands—voting for a candidate, for example. But the primary topics include price because they are intended to be com-prehensive. This does not preclude the possibility that a primary topic will vanish in a particular case or will simply become nonapplicable because it has the same value for all brands.

The fourth primary topic, familiarity, is fundamentally different from the others. Beliefs about product, branding, and price may be accurate, inaccurate, or totally fictitious, but they describe the brand. Familiarity, on the other hand, describes the customer, specifically, the customer's his-tory with respect to the brand. Provided this history is not too negative, high familiarity is an asset in its own right. The familiar takes on a positive aura, contributes comfort and security, and finally coalesces into habit. People simply don't respond the same way to things they don't know as to things they know. This became dramatically clear to me when I attempted to get respondents to tell me why they had switched from one brand to another. The sequence of questions was:

- What brand did you buy the time before last? Answer: Bounty.
- What brand did you buy last time? Answer: Viva.
- What brand are you going to buy next time? Answer: Bounty.
- You bought Bounty the time before last, but Viva last time. How come? Answer: It was on sale.
- You bought Viva last time, but you are going to buy Bounty next time. How come?

When the results were tabulated, the EMA project manager reported that this last question had "not worked." The respondents had not given their "real" reasons but had given stereotyped cliché responses instead. In particular, more than 70% had explained their intent to switch back to Bounty by saying, "I will buy it because I always buy Bounty."

I realized at once that this reason was neither a stereotype nor a cliché. The respondents were telling the literal truth. The most important reason for buying a brand is that one "always" buys it. If the decision is made by habit, it entails no effort. The converse is also true. If the brand has low familiarity, a measure of uncertainty, and hence risk, automatically attaches to it. It takes effort to examine the package, read the label, investigate the features. This is most patently obvious in the case of a major purchase. A salesman recommends that a business install a new computer system that will perform better and save money. But the very prospect of considering such an installation is so onerous that the decision maker elects to pass, not because he has concluded that the proposed system won't deliver, but because he is not prepared to spend the money, time, effort, and anxiety to find out whether it will or not. Thus high familiarity functions as an additional asset and low familiarity as an additional liability.

Taken together, branding, price, and familiarity add a positive or negative increment of value to what would otherwise be deserved by the product alone. This increment represents the value of the brand and will be called the brand's image. I am giving the term *image* a specific, narrow meaning for the purpose of distinguishing between attributes of the product itself and all other attributes that impact brand choice. Holding price constant, the relative importance of product and image varies from category to category and from customer to customer. As the product attributes of brands become more similar, the role of image increases. When the products become identical, the image becomes the sole determining factor. At the outer limits, we can imagine theoretical product-to-image ratios of 100-to-0 or 0-to-100, but in practice the ratio is usually somewhere in between and the customer almost always buys both product and image attributes. This idea of a product-to-image ratio is not just theoretical talk. It is measured specifically, as described in Chapter 10.

In general, we may say that a brand has many attributes derived from many sources. Some of these attributes have positive value and some have negative value. Consolidating the positive and negative values results in a net value which is called the *desirability* of the brand for the customer. The way this is done is dealt with in Chapters 16 through 18. And other things being equal, the customer chooses the brand with the highest desirability. But other things are not equal.

Accessibility

The choice the customer makes takes place in an environment. At the point of choice, situational factors make it easier to choose some brands than others. These enhancers or deterrents are not reflected in the desirability of the brands, but they affect the outcome. They are collectively called *accessibility* and function as a barrier that must be overcome before desirability can be consummated in choice.

Every choice involves some effort. Accessibility is the complement of that effort. Minimally, the customer must go to the store. If she is buying an automobile, the nearest Peugeot dealer may be twenty miles farther from her home than the nearest Ford dealer, clearly a differential expenditure of effort. In a supermarket, one brand may be on the bottom shelf while another one is within easy reach. In this case too, it takes more effort to choose one brand than another, a very tiny amount of additional effort, but if the brands are otherwise equivalent, this tiny amount may be decisive.

One might ask why I have not simply included this effort as one more attribute associated with a brand. The answer is that this type of effort is different. The confusion can be cleared up by distinguishing between use-effort and choice-effort. Use-effort is indeed a product attribute. If one car is more difficult to drive than another, if one hot cereal is more difficult to cook than another, these attributes are certainly product attributes that contribute to the overall desirability of the brand. Choice-effort, on the other hand, is the effort required at the point of choice. A brand's desirability will not change just because the brand happens to be stacked in an end display one day and unavailable on the shelf the next, but the amount of effort the customer will have to make to buy it will change, and her actual choice will change along with it. If the relative choice-effort (E)

required to buy a brand is represented as a number between 0 and 1, then the accessibility (A) of the brand can be defined as the complement of choice-effort, or $A = 1 - E$.

We can then imagine assigning a score to every brand. At the extremes there is little doubt about this score. A dominant brand with many shelf facings and supplementary end displays gets an accessibility of 1. A brand that is not distributed in the city gets an accessibility of 0. We can imagine intermediate values. A brand that is not available in a particular store might get an accessibility close to 0, but perhaps not quite, since the customer could go to another store. A brand that is not on the shelf but is available in the store might get some low accessibility, say .1 or .2, since the customer could ask for it. At the other end of the spectrum, a brand that is on the shelf but not displayed prominently might get an accessibility of .8 or .7 or .6, depending on the circumstances. Whether measured directly or crudely estimated from known distribution data, accessibility clearly plays an important part in determining what gets bought.

In addition to external accessibility, there is internal accessibility. The word *choice* actually encompasses two entirely different behaviors. Sometimes the customer chooses by selecting among alternatives. At other times, she chooses by selecting from an internal set. The distinction between these two types of choice is perhaps best exemplified by the customer's experience in a restaurant. She orders beer and the waiter asks, "Which brand do you want?" The customer must reach inside herself and locate a brand. Assuming that not all brands of beer have equal internal accessibility for her, she may be more likely to "find" Budweiser than Beck's and may order Budweiser. On the other hand, if the waiter hands her a menu that contains both Budweiser and Beck's and asks, "Which brand do you want?" the accessibility of all the brands on the list has now been equalized, and she may order Beck's. In this case, external accessibility, whether the brand is on the menu or not, becomes decisive.

Internal accessibility is measured by means of the question, "Please name a brand of beer. Just tell me the first one that comes to your mind." The percent mentioning a brand is defined as the *awareness* or the *internal accessibility* of the brand, a number between 0 and 100 percent. Awareness operates in situations in which the menu or shelf is not available. In prescribing a drug, a doctor does not ordinarily consult a list of available brands. She prescribes a brand, writing the prescription on the spot. In that situation, internal accessibility can be of substantial importance, augmented perhaps by the fact that her desk drawer is loaded with free samples of one of the brands. Without pursuing the distinction further, we may note that choice situations usually have both external and internal accessibility components. In the general case, accessibility is a weighted average of the two accessibilities, itself a number between 0 and 1. But though conceptual completeness requires giving equal billing to both accessibilities, external accessibility plays the dominant, if not the exclusive, role in the many practical market situations in which the choice is made from a menu, a catalog, a shelf, or an in-store display.

The Choice Process

The entire process can be summarized as follows: The customer examines each brand offered to her. Based on her desires, beliefs, and familiarity, she assigns a value to each brand. That value is defined as the desirability of the brand. Her actual choice then depends on

1. The desirability (D) of the brands; and
2. The accessibility (A) of the brands.

Defining brand strength (S) as $S = DA$, we can say concisely that she chooses the brand that has the highest brand strength at the moment of her choice.

Once she has bought the brand, she uses it. In the course of that use, she acquires information that may change her beliefs about the brand. She may have believed that the ready-to-eat cereal would stay crunchy but discovers that it gets soggy the instant it touches milk. She may have believed that her senator would vote for gun control but learns that he voted to repeal the ban on assault weapons. She may have believed that the personal computer would be difficult to use, but is pleasantly surprised to discover that it is user-friendly.

At the same time, the brand's image undergoes transformations and takes on new positive or negative values. Minimally, the brand becomes more familiar and more positive by virtue of that fact alone. But new fables also come into being. Some terrible thing may happen to her one morning immediately after eating the cereal, and she may thereafter superstitiously associate the brand with "bad luck." Good, bad, or indifferent, experience with the brand changes what she believes about it, and these new beliefs define the desirability of the brand the next time she has to make a choice, which may be after many years in the case of a business system, after two or three years in the case of an automobile, after two weeks in the case of a coffee or paper towel, and after a day or two in the case of a beer or cigarette.

The entire transaction is graphically summarized in Figure 1–1. In this figure, everything that happens inside the head of the customer is shown in circles. Everything that happens in the world outside is shown in rec-

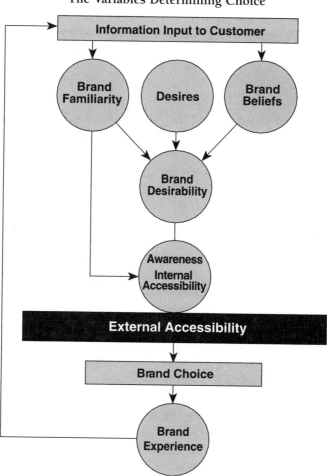

Figure 1–1
The Variables Determining Choice

tangles. Thus, we start with the rectangle on top, which represents information reaching the customer from the external world. This information has an effect on her beliefs and on her familiarity, which in turn affects her awareness or the internal accessibility of the brand. The combination of her desires, beliefs, and familiarity produces the desirability of the brand. This desirability, as well as the desirabilities of other brands, passes through the double screens of internal and external accessibility, resulting in a brand choice, which gives rise to experience with the brand, which is transformed into new information input, and the cycle repeats.

This structure does not merely define abstract concepts. Each variable is firmly grounded in the real world, independently measurable, capable of yielding data that can be checked for internal consistency and put to work in solving practical problems. The customer's desires, the values she attaches to various attributes, are directly measurable. Her beliefs about the various attributes of the brands are measurable. The desirabilities of the brands are measurable, either directly, or indirectly by way of their components. Familiarity and internal accessibility (brand awareness) are measurable. External accessibility is measurable, either directly or by inference from relationships in the data. And brand choice is measurable. Thus Figure 1–1 provides a practical map of the major variables at the interface between the marketer and the customer, a map that defines the ground to be covered. In due time, it will help orient us in solving practical marketing problems.

Marketing Strategy

Having looked at the process from the point of view of the customer, we turn the tables to look at it from the point of view of the marketer. If the marketer is playing a game on the "board" we have just described, what must she do to win? Since both she and her competitors are equipped with budgets and must compete for the same customers, her assignment boils down to using her resources efficiently. To do so, she develops a marketing strategy, which usually has three components: customer definition, selling strategy, and accessibility strategy.

First she identifies her prospective customer. This definition is often, though not always, self-evident. It may seem obvious at first glance that the prospective customers for a new brand of decaffeinated coffee should be decaffeinated coffee drinkers. And this may indeed be the most productive customer definition. But there is no intrinsic right or wrong in this matter. A particular new brand may have attributes that will also appeal to regular coffee drinkers, in which case the customer definition could be properly enlarged to include all coffee drinkers. It is also conceivable that the attributes of the new brand will appeal to people who don't drink coffee at all, in which case the customer definition could be enlarged to encompass all adults, perhaps all people. Thus customer definition can range from loose to tight. The trade-off is between the size of the customer base and efficiency in converting prospects into buyers.

The proper balance between these factors is important but a source of much confusion in practice. Some marketers define their customers too broadly and pursue the will-o'-the-wisp that their particular brand of soda pop will convert beer drinkers to soda pop, something that is possible but not probable. Other marketers, having been sensitized to the idea that their brand will probably appeal to a small number of people, are seduced by so-called segmentation studies into defining their prospective customers narrowly, for example, "Successful career women between the ages of twenty-one and thirty-five," a definition that is probably neither appropriate, since the appeal of brands is not likely to drop off sharply when a woman turns thirty-six, nor fully actionable, since efforts to market as selectively as that will inevitably exclude wanted people and include unwanted ones. This is not to condemn all narrowly drawn definitions outright. They may be appropriate in some instances. It is only to note in passing that prevailing fashion makes it more likely that the marketer will err on the side of defining the customer too narrowly than too broadly, at least for talking purposes. Such definitions have a way of looking properly scientific in the marketing plan.

Having defined the prospective customer, the marketer adopts a selling strategy. This is mandatory and inescapable. The strategy may be developed in a deliberate planning process or may evolve spontaneously. It may or may not be articulated explicitly. Occasionally, it may be incoherent. An incoherent strategy is usually the result of the way the business is organized. If R&D, marketing management, advertising, and promotion are linked to each other in a loose federation of separate fiefdoms, the selling strategy may be pulled in different directions as one or another organizational entity gains temporary ascendancy and compromises are struck, giving each party something and no one everything.

Whatever the circumstances, whether deliberately crafted, intuitively evolved, hammered out in compromise, or careening this way and that, underneath it all there is always a selling strategy, and this selling strategy always consists of three elements.

1. Brand attributes (A, B, C, . . .).
2. Customer desires (X, Y, Z, . . .).
3. A syllogism linking them.

Together, these three elements constitute the template embodied in the following principle.

THE SELLING STRATEGY PRINCIPLE
Explicitly or implicitly, every brand has a selling strategy that consists of the same universal syllogism: Because my brand has attributes A,B,C, . . . , it will satisfy your desires X,Y,Z, . . . better than any other brand.

A selling strategy is only as strong as its weakest link, so failure of any one of the elements results in failure of the whole. If the customer does not believe that the brand really has attributes A, B, and C, the strategy fails. If the customer believes that the brand has attributes A, B, and C, but does not desire X, Y, and Z, the strategy fails. And even if the customer believes that the brand has attributes A, B, and C and desires X, Y, and Z but does not believe that attributes A, B, and C will satisfy desires X, Y, and Z, or believes that some other brand will satisfy them better, the strategy fails. Keeping this in mind is vital. But marketers and researchers who may disdain to be reminded of the obvious often turn their backs on it, in deeds if not in words.

Finally, the marketer adopts an accessibility strategy. This involves selecting the channels through which the brand will be distributed. Everything else, the judicious definition of the customer and the adoption of an effective selling strategy, comes to naught if the customer who wants to buy the brand cannot get it. To the extent that the selected channels involve wholesalers or retailers, the marketer must induce them to carry, stock, and display the brand. For that purpose, the retailer becomes the customer, and the sale of the brand to the retailer is governed by the same principles that govern the sale of the brand to the user, except for one thing. The "brand" sold to the retailer has entirely different attributes than the brand sold to the user. For the user, the relevant attributes of a ready-to-eat cereal may be that it contains raisins, that it contains vitamin C, that it has no additives, and so on. For the retailer, the relevant attributes of the brand will be that it is easy to ship and stock, that it has a high margin, and that customers will buy it by the carload. Since it is imperative for the marketer to get the brand on the shelves, she may have to offer the retailer major initial incentives in the hope that once customers begin to buy it, more viable margins will become acceptable.

The Eight Tools of Marketing

The marketer has eight tools at her disposal to implement her strategy, or extending the metaphor of the marketing game, eight dials to manipulate in her effort to induce the customer to buy her brand. I shall call these the Eight Tools of Marketing:

1. *Product.* She makes the physical product, giving it specific, carefully selected attributes: an orange juice with 100 calories per glass, a pungent taste that is both sweet and tart, a container that is easy to open. A laptop computer with a fifteen-hour battery, a user-friendly keyboard, a weight of 1.5 pounds, etc.

2. *Label.* She develops the label, giving the product a name, package graphics, and a logo, thereby creating the skeleton of what we call the brand.

3. *Message.* She adopts a selling strategy and implements it with claims, promises, and advertising copy, to communicate information about the product attributes of the brand and to refine and articulate its image. By showing the laptop computer on the beach of a Caribbean island with a couple of beautiful, half-naked people coming out of the water, she may be telling us that the brand is so portable that it can be taken to a Caribbean beach. But she may also hope to attach to the brand the glow of the Caribbean sun. Whether such strategies work is an empirical question. They are cited without prejudice because they are part of the marketer's arsenal.

4. *Schedule.* She decides on the media through which she will reach and attempt to influence the customer, and on the frequency and patterns of those communications. She may employ personal sales calls, conferences, press releases, point-of-sale displays, direct mail, newspaper ads, magazine ads, television ads, and other means. She may employ different reach-frequency combinations. She may schedule these in continuous or intermittent patterns with flights of various duration.

. 5. *Price.* She selects the price at which the product will be offered. Price includes the amount, the pricing structure, and the terms. The price may be $1.99 for a twin pack of paper towels. It may be $11,900 for a computer, including a training seminar, a warranty, and a year's free service. Or it may be an initial fee of $50 plus an interest rate of 18 percent per annum on the unpaid balance of a credit card, with no interest for the first month after the purchase, and with free travel insurance for all tickets purchased through the card.

6. *Distribution.* She distributes her product to make it easily accessible to the customer. If the product is sold in stores, this may involve sending salespeople to call on the retailers to obtain distribution in as many outlets as possible. Sheer availability alone, however, is only part of it. Brands that are prominently displayed have substantial advantages over brands that are available only in some obscure corner of the store. If the brand (for instance, a business system) is sold to the customer directly through a sales force, she arranges for sales representatives to be within easy reach of the customer, to make the product as accessible to the customer as possible.

7. *Promotion.* She engages in auxiliary activities, which are usually dumped into the catch-all category of promotion. This includes price-off deals, premiums, coupons, point-of-sale displays, contests, lotteries, gifts with proof of purchase, etc. There are consumer promotions and trade promotions, but promotion really has no separate existence of its own. It all boils down to an indirect, and often not-so-indirect, price reduction or dis-

tribution-building mechanism. Putting products "on sale" is obviously only a price reduction. In effect, the marketer seeks the best of both worlds: the higher revenue from those customers to whom the price does not matter much, and the marginal revenue from those customers who insist on a lower price. A premium, self-liquidating or not, amounts to the same thing. With every three boxes of laundry detergent you get a free mug—in effect, a price reduction equal to the value the customer places on the mug. This value, incidentally, need not have any direct relation to its cost, and in the extreme case can exceed the combined cost of product and premium. If the box of cereal contains a free plastic dinosaur, which costs 5 cents, and if Johnny is determined to have the dinosaur, his mother may buy the $3.50 box of cereal just to satisfy Johnny's craving for the dinosaur. By the same token, a lottery for a free trip to Hawaii is a de facto price reduction to the tune of the psychological value of the lottery ticket, which may be substantially higher than the economic cost of the lottery ticket.

Trade promotions serve to increase accessibility. The retailer receives a so-called trade allowance of several dollars per case in exchange for his promise to build special end displays, giving the brand increased visibility in the store and making it just a trifle easier for the customer to buy it on impulse. If the customer likes Lay's Potato Chips and Wise Potato Chips about equally and is prepared to buy either, passing a huge pyramid of one at the front end of the aisle may be sufficient to induce her to take that one instead of searching for the other one in its usual place on the shelf. Thus, the financial inducements the marketer offers the retailer are designed to obtain extra display space, to make the brand more accessible to the customer.

8. *Sampling.* All of the other tools operate directly on the choice process of the customer, seeking to maximize the probability that she will choose the brand. Sampling bypasses the choice process by putting the brand directly into the customer's hands. To be sure, she may simply throw out the free sample. But this is not likely. Once in her hands, the product is likely to be used. Once used, it will affect her familiarity with and beliefs about the brand, which will govern her subsequent choices and may translate into long-term business for the marketer. Sampling is not limited to packaged goods. Pharmaceutical firms give samples of drugs to doctors for distribution to their patients. Automobile companies invite customers to take test drives or lend them automobiles, and publications offer money-back trial subscriptions.

Figure 1–2 summarizes the entire process in a single chart. It is possible to consider the eight marketing tools separately and to seek to optimize them independently. Each poses distinct empirical questions.

Figure 1–2
The Board of the Marketing Game

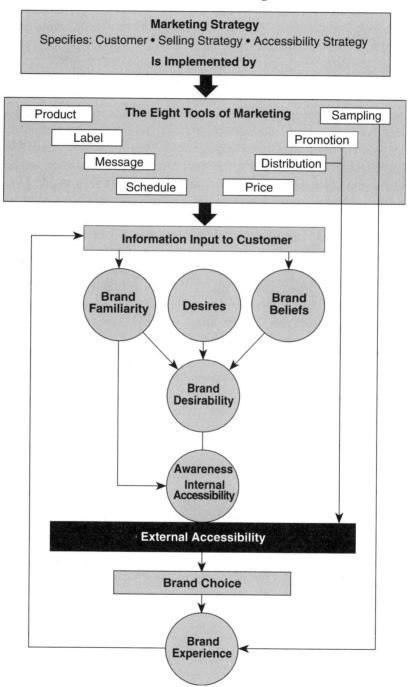

Should I make the product sweet or sour? Should I call it Svelta or Minima? Should I use a package with red stripes or green polka dots? Should my advertising use an attractive model or a cartoon character? Should I advertise in print or on television? Should I try to reach many people occasionally or a few people frequently? Should I sell the brand at $1,250 or at $1,450? Should I sell the brand in supermarkets or in fast food outlets? Should the premium be a bottle opener or a calorie counter? Should I distribute a coupon or a free sample?

In the end, all of these tactics interact and need to be considered and investigated in relation to each other. The different elements of the total strategy need to reinforce each other to create a single, coherent story providing an unambiguous image for the brand. Real intuition in deciding where to start is indispensable. No matter how good the intuition, however, the marketer cannot stop there. There are new pitfalls and new traps at every turn. The customer, more specifically the collection of customers, reacts in strange, often unanticipated ways. And if the marketer wants to improve her chances of being right, she needs to find out which strategies and tactics will work and which won't, which will work better and which will work worse. That is the function of marketing research. To the extent marketing research is asked to answer meaningful questions, and answers them meaningfully, it can help the marketer improve her odds of winning the game. How that is done is the subject of this book.

CHAPTER 2

Defining Choice Research

Operational responsibilities aside, the marketer's job has two strategic aspects:

1. Creative: To define objectives and potential options, say A, B, and C.
2. Evaluative: To decide which of those alternatives, A, B, or C, will produce the best results.

Marketing research is supposed to help by providing a framework for thinking about these problems, and the information necessary for solving them. This entails a range of diverse activities which can be classified under two broad headings: qualitative research, which generates stories and explanations, and quantitative research, which generates measurements and predictions. These two types of research differ fundamentally in objectives, philosophy, method, and style. But both are called marketing research, and people often lose sight of the distinction between them. This results in confusion about what marketing research really is and what it is trying to do. It is therefore important to spell out their proper roles.

The marketer has many tools to aid her in creating options. She receives input from her staff, her advertising agency, and her consultants. Someone, anyone, needs to think about her problem and come up with what may be loosely called "ideas." Depending on the temperament of the practitioner, this process varies from systematic orderly thought to intuitive flights of fancy. But neither the process nor the source matters. The purpose of the exercise is to generate options. And options can be neither right nor wrong, only more or less original, interesting, and worth exploring further. Accordingly, the marketer looks for help with ideas wherever she can get it, and that sometimes includes the marketing research community, which offers her descriptive surveys and qualitative research.

Descriptive surveys are represented as the starting point for the marketer's thinking. For how can she be expected to think about a category and to formulate options when she knows hardly anything about it? Qualitative research, consisting of what traveled under the buzz name of motivational research in the 1950s and of focus groups nowadays, is intended to put the marketer in direct touch with the customer, to allow her to hear the customer talk in her own language and thereby arrive at a deeper understanding of the problem. Qualitative research can serve that function. When it comes to inspiration, the end result is all. Anything goes. But it is necessary to use unmistakable labels to make a clear distinction between work that is done to think up options and work that is done to evaluate these options. As things stand, qualitative research drifts dangerously back and forth between the inspirational and the evaluative, and marketers often skim lightly over what appear to them to be unduly pedantic distinctions. They speak of how they discovered this or that truth in focus groups, and in doing so, stretch qualitative research way beyond its proper limits.

Evaluation calls for measurement and hence for quantitative research, but even this category is much too broad. It is necessary to distinguish further between two different kinds of quantitative research. The first is the traditional descriptive survey. Given the need to evaluate alternatives, the traditional survey starts by collecting data: Who does what, how often, in what manner, under what conditions, in whose presence, for what purpose, for what length of time, and so on. Anything that is relevant, or thought to have the possibility of becoming relevant, or if not relevant at least interesting, is included. The effort is to be exhaustive. The data are collected, tabulated, and analyzed. The analysis, a well-crafted work of art, is a hunt for patterns in the data, which may yield discoveries, conclusions, and, depending on the skill and intuition of the analyst, recommendations. I am calling this type of marketing research *Descriptive Research*.

The alternative starts from the other end and works backwards. Marketing research, it argues, is being undertaken to help the marketer decide on a course of action. Accordingly, we need only examine the marketer's options and ask: What is the minimum amount of information the marketer must have to decide whether to take action A or B or C? This, I believe, consists of measuring the extent to which doing A or B or C will influence what the customer will buy, the choices she will make. Accordingly, I am calling this type of marketing research *Choice Research*.

The debate between Descriptive Research and Choice Research is far from settled. There are many places where it has not even been joined yet. Each philosophy has partisans of varying degree of commitment and varying degree of tolerance for the other view. I declare myself from the outset an unabashed advocate of Choice Research. As such, I do not consider the schism between Descriptive Research and Choice Research to be a matter of style, but one of fundamental substance—a matter of right and wrong—and I see marketing research as a disparate collection of activities, from qualitative research to Descriptive Research to Choice Research, that have been gathered under a single banner and march uneasily side by side, guarding their respective domains and protecting their flank lest they be engulfed by their equally reluctant partners.

A few astute marketers, of course, use marketing research properly. Often enough, however, marketing research is rendered irrelevant not only by those who reject it, but also by many who embrace it. Marketers who are strongly committed to some particular course of action typically don't want any marketing research. They are convinced that they don't need any testing. They are going to bring their idea to market, come hell or high water. They may tolerate some marketing research if that is an institutional requirement. In that case, however, they prefer research that is as fuzzy as possible, that will provide many pages of unreadable output with lots of numbers from which they can extract predesignated conclusions while preserving their right to tell the management that everything they are proposing is supported by research. These marketers resist evaluative research in almost direct proportion to its ability to furnish unambiguous conclusions. From the other end of the spectrum, research is choked in the loving embrace of those who turn to it uncritically, willing to accept any method that is labeled "marketing research." These marketers base major business decisions on qualitative research or Descriptive Research, methods that may appear to them to enhance their understanding of the world but are inappropriate for predicting the consequences of potential actions.

In coining the label *Choice Research* and defining it as a coherent subset of the various activities that are loosely grouped under the heading of marketing research, I am separating Choice Research from those other activities, and am delineating the boundaries and proper concern of this work.

CHAPTER 3

First Principles of Choice Research

Choice Research differs from Descriptive Research in some important respects. Perhaps the best way to spotlight these differences is to consider two questions:

1. When should the analysis of a study be performed: before collecting the data or after collecting the data?
2. How many measures for a variable should the analysis use: as many as possible or only a single one?

Choice Research brings a nontraditional perspective to answering these questions.

Analysis

Presumably the need for an analysis arises from the fact that a study has been done, data have been generated, and conclusions are sought. But what does this process entail? Every conclusion is necessarily made up of three elements. First there are assumptions. This is unavoidable. No matter how much we know, the unknown remains a permanent horizon, always receding as we push further, so that when we have settled one issue empirically and no longer need to make assumptions about it, a new issue moves in to take its place. We simply cannot avoid making assumptions. Then there are data. And finally there is a logic, a process of reasoning—a set of permissible rules for the manipulation and transformation of the data. But if we accept the data as a fixed, immutable given, the analysis itself consists of only two elements: the assumptions and the logic. This means that the conclusions that can be drawn from any particular body of data are fully determined as soon as the assumptions and the logic have been specified. When that has been done, the analysis is complete; filling in the actual numbers is then just a mechanical detail.

Now suppose we have performed the analysis, have generated a conclusion, and don't like it. We may not like it for venal reasons, perhaps because it conflicts with the findings of a prior study or because it would displease our client. Or we may dislike it for honorable reasons. The conclusion does not make sense. We are convinced that it is wrong and we don't want to steer our client wrong. What can we do about it? One thing we can do is go into the back room, locate the questionnaires, erase some of the responses, and replace them with others. But this would be cheating, and quite apart from the fact that such cheating could have serious legal consequences, the idea of cheating is so onerous that it wouldn't even occur to us.

The irony is that if we want to change the conclusion, we don't need to change the questionnaires. There is an easier and totally respectable way. The conclusion depends on three elements. Changing any one of them will do. If we don't like the conclusion, we need only change one of the assumptions or the logic. Keep in mind that the assumptions are, by definition, unsupported, so it is not known whether they are true or false. It is therefore always possible to find some other, equally justifiable assumption or some new logic for operating on the data that will more nearly give us the conclusion we are eager to produce.

No matter how noble the motive, a change in assumptions or logic after the data have been examined is as lethal a case of cheating as changing the questionnaires. Yet perfectly honorable people routinely take pride in doing just that because, coming from the tradition of Descriptive Research, the complex manipulation of data is seen as a sign of thoroughness and sophistication, a process in which the researcher arranges, rearranges, computes, and recomputes until he succeeds in generating a conclusion that "makes sense." Then, and only then, does the process stop. This amounts to saying that it stops only when the researcher has finally persuaded the data to tell him what he wanted to hear.

When must the analysis be done? Before we see the data. Once we have seen the data it is too late. Actually, the analysis needs to be done even earlier than that, not merely before we see the data but before we collect them. For if we are prepared to do the analysis before seeing the data, we may as well do it before constructing the questionnaire. In that case, we can make certain that the questionnaire will contain everything needed and, incidentally, nothing else. This brings me to the second question: Is it better to have many measures for a variable or only a single measure? Traditional practice calls for many measures. That is judged to be the conservative position. What if the chosen measure should prove to be the wrong one? The whole study would be lost. So there is safety in numbers.

Additional measures are included to provide insurance. Can we sustain this line of thought?

Suppose we include two measures for a variable, say two different ways of asking the question. If the two measures agree, we don't need both. If they disagree, we must decide which one to use. If we examine the data first, we violate the requirement that the analysis be done before the data are examined. If we specify ahead of time which measure we will use if they should disagree, we don't need the other one. If, finally, we specify some function of the two measures, for example, their mean, or their product, or any other function, then we have really adopted a single measure. There is no objection to defining a measure as a function of many numbers provided the function has been specified in advance.

A corollary of this principle, in fact, its most pernicious special case, has to do with the utilization of multiple criteria in a study. Suppose we are called upon to evaluate three advertisements—A, B, and C—for a new low calorie beverage. We decide that what counts is whether the respondents are interested in drinking the new beverage, but we include further questions about whether the respondents would be willing to serve it to their guests, whether they know that the beverage has fewer than 10 calories per glass, and whether they remember the ad. The researcher likes Ad A best, the marketer likes Ad B, and the advertising agency likes Ad C. As it happens, more people exposed to Ad A say they are interested in drinking the beverage, and the researcher reports that Ad A has won. The marketer is unconvinced. She points out that more people exposed to Ad B indicate that they will serve the beverage to their guests, and that this is important because the selling strategy is "A beverage suitable for serving to guests." Accordingly, she judges that Ad B has won. The advertising agency does not agree. More people exposed to Ad C know that the beverage is low in calories, and more remember the ad. What is the point of running an ad if no one remembers either the ad or the brand's attributes? Accordingly, the agency judges that Ad C has won.

In the ensuing debate, the marketer concedes that there is some merit to each argument and that each of the four criteria should be taken into account, perhaps by averaging the four scores. But the researcher, who happens to have a good head for numbers, retorts that a simple average of the four numbers is not appropriate, since two of these numbers— whether the respondents know about the calories and remember the ad— are really aspects of the same variable. Accordingly, he proposes to combine those two into a single number and then average the remaining three. The marketer and the advertising agency agree. The computation is made and Ad A wins, as the researcher anticipated when he proposed this method of combining the measures. The point of the story is that once we have seen the data it is too late to do the analysis, too late to choose a criterion. Given enough measures and the freedom to select and combine them, we can generate almost any conclusion from almost any set of data, and there is no need to do the study. We might as well just negotiate the outcome.

There is only one way out of this predicament: not to get into it in the first place, to use only a single criterion. In the example, that criterion could have been any one of the four measures or any function of these four measures, provided that the function had been specified ahead of time. Thus Choice Research accepts rules that may appear overly rigorous, if not outright pedantic, to anyone raised in the tradition of Descriptive Research, but which are nevertheless essential if the value of the exercise is to be preserved. This is summarized in the first two principles of Choice Research.

THE INDEPENDENT ANALYSIS PRINCIPLE
The analysis must be completed before the data are collected.

THE SINGLE-CRITERION PRINCIPLE
The analysis must use only a single criterion, and only a single measure for any variable.

Interface with the Marketer

Now suppose the researcher has understood these principles and has obeyed them faithfully, but the marketer refuses to play by the rules. Must the marketer too be committed in advance? No. The researcher and the marketer are bound by different rules, which can be clarified by considering the roles of judgment and research in arriving at decisions.

Should business decisions be made on the basis of judgment or on the basis of research? I believe this question has a categorical answer: Every decision must be made on the basis of judgment. Assume you are called upon to decide whether to take a medication or not. This may be a life-and-death decision, but if the decision is yours, no amount of data or medical advice can make the decision for you. You must ultimately make it on the basis of what you believe. The role of the data is not to compete with your beliefs but to influence and change them. The subtle but important point is that just as the researcher must be bound by the rules of Choice Research, so the decision maker cannot be bound by these rules and must remain free to make her decision based on what she happens to believe at the time of making it.

Here is an example that illustrates this dynamic. The marketer has authorized a pricing test. She is considering raising the price of her product and is requesting an estimate of how much volume she will lose by taking a modest 5% price increase. The researcher designs a study, allows the marketer to review his method, and secures the marketer's agreement that the procedure is reasonable and that she will abide by its results. The data come in. The predesignated analysis is conducted, and the researcher is shocked to find that the relatively modest price increase results in a 30% loss of business. The researcher is deeply troubled by this result. Put bluntly, he does not believe it. He examines and reexamines the data, as well as the analysis plan, and finds that the plan provided for giving special weight to respondents who were designated as "price sensitives." On further thought, he now believes that this was a mistake. If he drops the price-sensitivity weight, the data become reasonable. The small price increase results in only a negligible loss of business.

He is seriously conflicted. What is his moral and professional duty in this case? Should he report the results of the study as a 30% drop, notwithstanding his personal conviction that this cannot be right? Should he quietly drop the price-sensitivity weight and report that the study showed no significant loss of business? Or should he tell his client that the original analysis had indeed produced a finding of a 30% drop, but that he, the researcher, had not stopped there. He was nobody's fool. He had not mechanically accepted a preposterous result. He had continued to analyze the data further, had discovered that the mistake lay in the notion of using a price-sensitivity weight, an idea that had seemed plausible, in fact brilliant, before the fact, but had now been unmasked as a serious blunder. He had been conscientious enough to discover his mistake, and honest enough to admit it and to excise it from the analysis.

The temptation to take the third option is overwhelming on all counts. But the researcher is familiar with the first two principles of Choice Research, understands the harsh discipline these principles impose on him, and even appreciates the wisdom of the rules. For wouldn't it be the ultimate irony if, having obtained and then abandoned the 30% result, that result turned out to be correct after all? So after churning and flirting with temptation, he decides with a heavy heart to abide by the principles of Choice Research, to follow through as planned and to report the outcome as an estimated 30% loss of volume.

The marketer is a reasonable person, but shakes her head in utter disbelief and says: "This is ridiculous. I just don't believe it."

"Nevertheless," replies the researcher, "this is the result we obtained. I have checked the numbers many times. I am convinced that there is no error in the tabulations or in the calculations. This is our finding. I can understand that you find it difficult to believe. I find it difficult to believe myself. It is conceivable that my method is in error. But insofar as this test is concerned, these are the rules of the game and we must abide by the them."

"This may be a game to you," replies the marketer, "but it is serious business to me. And I don't have to play by rules I don't like. The fact is I don't believe your findings, and I am going to ignore them and take my price increase."

This is the decision maker's prerogative and obligation. She cannot but act on what she believes about the price increase. But the researcher would defeat the purpose of the exercise if he acted on what *he* believes about the price increase. Is this reasonable? Why should we apply different yardsticks to the decision maker and to the researcher?

The paradox is only apparent. The rules are in fact complementary. The important thing to understand is the contract between the decision maker and the researcher. By implicit agreement, each is supposed to bring a different expertise to the process. The marketer has been hired because she presumably has good judgment about substantive marketing issues, about whether a price increase of 5% is likely to produce a 30% loss of business. The researcher has also been hired for his judgment, but judgment of an entirely different kind. He has been hired because he presumably has good judgment about how to do research. If the marketer's judgment is bad, she will make bad marketing decisions. If the researcher's judgment is bad, he will design bad studies.

As long as both stick to their lasts, as long as the researcher confines himself to making judgments about research design and the marketer confines herself to making judgments about marketing issues, the business can have the benefit of both. The moment the researcher abandons his primary role and allows his marketing judgment to intrude into the analysis, he deprives the business of the potential contribution that research could have made. The business is then reduced to relying exclusively on marketing judgment—the marketing judgment of the marketer who has been hired to provide it and the marketing judgment of the researcher who has not been hired to provide it but cannot restrain his impulse to take a hand at the marketing game. Ironically, the researcher owes it to his marketing client to keep his marketing judgments out of the analysis, lest the marketer be deprived of what she hired, or should have hired, him to do for her. This is summarized in the following principle.

THE JUDGMENT-SEPARATION PRINCIPLE
The researcher must adhere to the principles of Choice Research even if his client, the marketer, exercises her right to violate them.

CHAPTER 4

The First Law:
The Law of Congruence

Constructing Questions

Let us suppose now that the researcher understands the principles, is persuaded by them, and is prepared to adhere to them. He defines the analysis ahead of time, uses a single criterion, and vows to set aside his personal judgment about the marketing issues when reporting his findings. Such adherence is a good first step, a necessary condition, but far from sufficient for accomplishing his task. Suppose he has been given a concept for a potential new brand and has been asked to evaluate it. He is quite serious about eliminating irrelevancies and is ready to focus on the central issue, which he correctly identifies as the need to estimate how many people will buy the product. Accordingly, he decides to expose a group of respondents to the concept and to ask them whether they will buy the brand. The options on the checklist are:

- Will definitely buy
- Will probably buy
- Will probably not buy
- Will definitely not buy

He decides, before having seen the data, to be conservative and to count only responses to the two top boxes (will definitely buy and will probably buy) and to discount the latter by 50%, so that his estimate of how many people will buy the brand is defined as the percent saying they will definitely buy it plus one-half of the percent saying they will probably buy it. His conclusion after completion of the test is that 30% will buy the brand, a result he judges to be quite unlikely based on his intuition, his experience, and his feelings about the product, but he dutifully reports this finding to his marketing client and leaves it to her to discount it as judgment may dictate necessary.

Having done so, however, he has serious misgivings about the method he has used and is determined to behave responsibly. To have done the job inadequately once is one thing. To perpetuate a defective method is another. It is obvious that something is wrong. A little thought leads him to realize that if he were to ask the same question in the same format not about one product, but about many, say twenty, one hundred, or more, he would eventually accumulate so much reported buying that even if the respondents were to spend twenty-four hours a day doing nothing but consuming, they would not be able to use everything they had said they would buy.

Sophisticated researchers of the descriptive school are neither surprised nor daunted by this observation. Everyone knows, they will say, that respondents are inconsistent, irrational, emotional. They hardly know what they have done, let alone what they will do. They are yea-sayers and nay-sayers. So it is necessary to calibrate their responses against known empirical facts, sometimes known as norms. On closer examination, however, this turns out to be less satisfying than it seemed at first. To say that a report of 30% will be scaled down to 8% based on empirical evidence implicitly assumes that those respondents who over-report their probable future buying react to different products in approximately the same way as those who don't. Calibration will hold only if this is true.

Here is a stylized example, designed to illustrate this point. Say the population consists of two groups of people: fifty percent who report accurately what they will buy and fifty percent who report falsely that they will buy products they won't actually buy. Assume that 10% and 8% of the accurate reporters say that they will buy test products A and B, respectively, and that they actually buy these. Their buying will contribute 50% x 10% = 5% for Product A and 50% x 8% = 4% for Product B. Suppose, however, that the false reporters don't respond in the same proportions. Assume that 20% of them say they will buy Product A and 30% say they will buy Product B. Since we don't know which respondents are which, we have only the aggregate data, which are, for Product A, 50% x 10% + 50% x 20% = 15%, and for Product B, 50% x 8% + 50% x 30% = 19%. In this circumstance, calibration would provide small solace. We would recognize that both products' shares are overstated. But reducing both by a constant to eliminate the overstatement would preserve the false conclusion that Product B (19%) would outsell Product A (15%), whereas the opposite would be true: Product A = 5%, Product B = 4%. If the data contain false information, calibration will cure the problem only if the false reporters respond to different products in the same ratios as the accurate reporters, something that may happen but certainly cannot be counted on generally. Thus the dilemma remains.

In a sense it serves us right, for we have arrogantly assumed that the respondents are irrational and confused and that inconsistencies in the data are their fault. The fact is that the inconsistencies are not in the data but in the way we insist on reading and interpreting them. Going a step further, we may say that the respondents' answers are correct by definition, correct in the sense that the respondents answered this particular question in this particular way. This is a fact. What this fact means, however, is another matter. So it behooves us to take stock, to examine our assumptions, and to ask ourselves whether what we have been doing makes sense, whether it can stand closer scrutiny.

Well, what have we been doing? We asked a respondent whether she would buy a brand, and the respondent told us. What is there to examine or reexamine? It is perfectly straightforward, isn't it? Or is it? To explore this, let us look at the process more carefully. Just what is a question? And what is an answer? What would you say, for example, if you encountered the following "question" in a survey?

Long-Lifos is a product of Vitality Corporation, one of the oldest and most respected makers of life-prolongation products. Long-Lifos are delicious and particularly convenient because they need no refrigeration and remain permanently fresh. Will you buy Long-Lifos the next time you shop?

☐   Will definitely buy
☐   Will probably buy
☐   Will probably not buy
☐   Will definitely not buy

We can clearly identify two elements in this question:

1. A persuasive message addressed to the respondent.
2. A request that the respondent make a choice, in particular that she choose one of the four categories of the checklist.

A researcher from the descriptive research tradition might object on the ground that the question is biased. If the survey dealt with a political issue he might charge bad faith. In any event, he might insist that we rewrite the question to remove the bias. Suppose we rewrote it as follows:

Will you buy Long-Lifos the next time you shop?

- ☐ Will definitely buy
- ☐ Will probably buy
- ☐ Will probably not buy
- ☐ Will definitely not buy

The researcher might be satisfied, but the rewrite has changed nothing. The question still consists of the same elements as before: a persuasive message and a request that the respondent make a choice among the categories of the checklist. To be sure, the length and possibly the persuasiveness of the message have been reduced. But the question still reminds the respondent that Long-Lifos exist and induces her to think about Long-Lifos, something she might not have done otherwise. As long as we regard the message that is explicitly or implicitly inherent in the question as a bias, something bad to be extirpated at great cost, we are doomed to failure. Bias will haunt us wherever we go. The alternative is to accept it, not as the distorting nemesis of research, but as its central tool. In that view, there is nothing wrong with delivering a message in a question. On the contrary, that is the very purpose of a question. The only issue is whether we are delivering the right message, that is, the message that will properly serve the research purpose at hand. We must therefore rethink, refine, and redefine the concepts of question and answer insofar as these apply to Choice Research and, for that matter, to survey research generally. These definitions are contained in the following principle:

THE QUESTION-ANSWER PRINCIPLE
A question is a persuasive message, which triggers an answer, which is a choice.

If we want to understand the meaning of the responses, we must understand both the persuasive message in the question and the choice that is demanded of the respondent. Once we examine the question from this perspective, we can hardly be surprised that the answers obtained in response to questions of this sort yield patently absurd results. But the fault, dear Brutus, is not in the stars, or in the respondents, but in ourselves. Quite apart from the message, which may involve no more than a selective focusing of attention on the new brand (a considerable factor in its own right), the choice presented to the respondent, though apparently relevant, in fact has little relation to what we seek to investigate. In effect, we are inviting the respondent to choose between two options: to buy the new brand or not to buy the new brand. Are those the options the respondent faces in life?

Suppose respondents were asked the question:

Do you want to be subjected to three weeks of discomfort?

☐ Yes
☐ No

It would hardly surprise you if 99% answered no. On the other hand, suppose the same respondents were asked:

Which of the following would you prefer?

☐ To die.
☐ To suffer three months of excruciating torture.
☐ To be subjected to three weeks of discomfort (presumably by agreeing to an operation).

It would hardly surprise you if a substantial number now chose to have the operation, thus electing to be subjected to three weeks of discomfort. To be sure, this example magnifies the issue, but this magnification does not distort. It only helps us see more clearly. The psychological principle operating in the two questions:

Will you buy the Long-Lifos?

☐ Yes
☐ No

---

and

Will you "buy" three weeks of discomfort?

☐ Yes
☐ No

---

is in fact identical.

If the answer to a question is a choice, then the outcome of the choice must depend crucially on the options. And when these options are not spelled out fully, the respondent is invited, actually compelled, to apply a rule of reason, fill in the gaps, and supply options of her own, which may correspond neither to the options that normally exist in life, nor to the options the researcher intended when he drafted the question. If my choice is three weeks of discomfort or three weeks of comfort, I reject the discomfort. If my choice is three weeks of discomfort, or torture, or death, I accept the discomfort. There is nothing inconsistent or unreasonable about this. Analogously, if my choice is to buy the new brand or not to buy it, I may choose to buy. Given the ambiguous and nonspecific way the options have been stated, I may, in the extreme, take the options in their most literal sense, as asking whether I would buy the new brand or buy nothing. And, of course, the number of people who would buy the new brand in preference to nothing is larger than the number of people who would buy the new brand in preference to the real options that exist in the marketplace.

So the discrepancy between how the respondents answered the question in the survey and how they behave in the marketplace may not be attributable to the confusion of the respondents after all, but to the confusion of the researcher who failed to understand that responding to a question involves a choice. If the options in that choice are significantly different from those the respondent will confront in the marketplace, her responses will be commensurately different. It all boils down to the quip attributed to Maurice Chevalier who, on being asked how it felt to be eighty years old, replied, "It's all right, considering the alternative."

The Law

There is a debate in the social-psychological literature about the relationship between attitude and behavior: whether attitude causes behavior, or behavior causes attitude, or whether there is causation in both directions. From the perspective of Choice Research, this debate is moot. Whether a customer decides to attend one church or another, picks up this brand or that from a supermarket shelf, or checks one box or another in a questionnaire, she is making a choice in each instance. Checking a box in a questionnaire is as much a behavior as selecting an item from a supermarket shelf. Both are governed by the same laws. If we want to design studies that will produce meaningful predictions of customer behavior, we must be mindful of these laws. Accordingly, we proceed to take a closer look at choice itself, to construct more rigorous definitions, and to formulate the First Law.

First, a definition of the mathematical term *vector*. A vector is just a collection of numbers. For example, if a respondent buys the following number of packages of five brands,   10   3   0   5   12,   this collection of numbers, taken in its entirety, can be referred to as the *buying vector*. Any change in any of these numbers generates a new vector. Two vectors are equal only if every single number of the first vector is the same as the corresponding number of the second vector. Now to the substance. A *choice situation* arises whenever a customer is called upon to choose among brands. Collectively, the brands are called the *competitive frame*. The customer's total information about the various brands of the competitive frame is called the *information* of the choice situation. The customer's accessibilities to the various brands of the competitive frame are called the *accessibility* of the choice situation. The customer's probabilities of choosing the various brands of the competitive frame are called the *choice vector* of the choice situation. Two choice situations are said to be *congruent* if they have identical competitive frames, information, and accessibility.

THE FIRST LAW: THE LAW OF CONGRUENCE
Congruent choice situations have equal choice vectors.

This law is simply saying that it doesn't matter whether the choice consists of voting in a booth or voting in a survey. It doesn't matter whether it consists of selecting a brand from a shelf or selecting a brand while playing a game in a questionnaire. Provided we can keep the competitive frame, the information, and the accessibility the same in the questionnaire as in life, the choices in the questionnaire will also be the same as the choices in life. By saying that the information in the questionnaire is the same as the information in life, I mean that the totality of what the customer knows about the brands at the time of making choices in the questionnaire is the same as the totality of what she knows about the brands at the time of making choices in the supermarket. The central idea is simple enough, possibly self-evident. Have we then merely taken the obvious, elaborated it with fancy definitions, and stated it in formal language? Conceivably, but I believe not. The fact is that a full understanding of the First Law has some important consequences for how we design and conduct marketing research studies. It is certainly the pivotal axiom of Choice Research.

Returning to our point of departure, if the options offered the respondent had not been

- Will definitely buy
- Will probably buy

- Will probably not buy
- Will definitely not buy

but had instead conformed to the alternatives she faces in the supermarket, the results in the questionnaire would have appropriately conformed to her behavior in the supermarket. This is the First Law in action, and its application leads to the following principle.

THE CONGRUENCE PRINCIPLE
The main concern of Choice Research is the congruence between the choice situation in the questionnaire and the choice situation in the world.

And what if perchance we should design an appropriately crafted questionnaire, abiding by the First Law, and should nevertheless find a discrepancy between the behavior of the respondents in the questionnaire and their behavior in the marketplace? The First Law, being a proper law, has built-in tautological protections. If the data obtained in the questionnaire and in the marketplace should happen to disagree, this would, ipso facto, be evidence that unwittingly a discrepancy had crept in, a breakdown of congruence. Somehow, somewhere the competitive frame had become different, or accessibility had become different, or the respondents had acted on different information about one or another of the brands than the information on which they ordinarily act in the marketplace, and the law would have been preserved. But I have seen the data. I know what lies ahead. And I am comfortable in the knowledge that the law is not in jeopardy. The data will support the law well, even exceedingly well, and we will not need to summon tautology to the rescue.

PART II

INTEGRATED OFFERS

This part of the book deals with the market shares deserved by integrated offers—offers specified by brand name, description, and price.

Chapter 5 (Measuring Choice) introduces a method that puts the First Law to practical use and presents empirical support for it.

Chapter 6 (Price Testing) and Chapter 7 (Concept Testing) summarize substantive findings from studies conducted over the course of many years.

Chapter 8 (Product Testing) provides a generic classification scheme for comparing all possible product testing methods.

Chapter 9 (Paired Comparisons) demonstrates, by analysis and by empirical data, that the method of paired comparisons—which has been used by some of the most respected packaged goods manufacturers—is fundamentally flawed and capable of generating wrong results.

Chapter 10 (Deserved Share) deals with how product tests should be conducted. The section "What's in a Name" contains surprising results about the role of product and image.

Chapter 11 (What STEP Measures) is a nontechnical recap of the ideas (not the findings) in the previous chapters. Together with Chapter 5, this chapter provides an overview of the measurement of integrated offers.

Chapter 12 (Beyond Product Category Boundaries) examines the implications of the First Law for offers that don't appear to fit into definable product categories, and introduces a self-validating technique for dealing with such cases.

CHAPTER 5

Measuring Choice

The principles and laws presented in this book are general. The techniques I developed for applying them, on the other hand, are specific. Variations of these techniques, or other techniques that conform to the same principles and laws, might be equally acceptable or even preferable. Nevertheless, I must concentrate attention on the particular techniques I developed, not because these are the only way, but because the masses of data I am reporting were in fact collected that way. I begin with STEP, a technique that meets the requirements of the First Law. STEP stands for "Strategy Evaluation Program." It has been a tool of EMA since 1960. The original impetus for its development was the desire to test concepts for new products, and selling strategies for existing products. Since then, STEP has proliferated and has been applied to a wide range of problems, all of which, however, turn out on closer examination to be variations of a single ubiquitous problem.

Insofar as possible, STEP tests are self-administered, usually through the mail, though there is nothing sacred about mail. When mail is not practical, STEP tests are done by personal interviews in central locations or in the respondents' homes or places of business. In those cases, the interviewer functions as a messenger to deliver and retrieve the STEP booklet (the questionnaire) without intervening in the process. The STEP booklet is intended to speak for itself, to stand or fall on the way it is constructed. We may like the data it produces or we may dislike them, but we know what we have: one booklet from one respondent, just as the respondent filled it out, without regard for what she may have understood or what she may have meant. We know what she saw and we know what she *did*.

The Measuring Instrument

The first page of a STEP booklet is usually devoted to factual questions about the respondent's use of the brands in the product category. The next page has the general format illustrated in Figure 5–1. The upper portion

Figure 5–1
Sample STEP Product Page

$1.89
for 1 box

200 sheets

NO-ROLL
Available in assorted colors and white,
in a variety of decorator boxes.

No roll. No tearing, folding, or crumpling. Take one sheet at a time. You only need one sheet because each sheet is as thick and as strong as five sheets from a quality roll of tissue. Fits right on your bathroom tissue holder.

| STEP 1 | • Do you believe this product is worth the price shown above? ☐ YES ☐ NO ☐ NOT SURE
• Does the picture arouse your interest? ☐ YES ☐ NO ☐ NOT SURE
• Does the statement impress you favorably? ☐ YES ☐ NO ☐ NOT SURE |
| STEP 2 | |

of the page, called the strategy section, consists of three elements: a picture, a statement, and a price. It summarizes the selling strategy, in effect telling the respondent: Here is what you get (the picture); here is what it will do for you (the statement); and here is what you will have to pay (the price). Underneath this portion of the page are three sensitizing questions. The responses to these questions are not tabulated. They are used to induce the respondent to take note of the three elements of the selling strategy. At the bottom of the page is an empty space marked STEP 2; the respondent is instructed to ignore this space for the time being.

The respondent goes though the booklet from page to page, each page devoted to a different brand, each presented in the identical format, followed by the identical sensitizing questions. The number of brand pages in the booklet varies depending on the product category and ranges from as few as three to as many as forty, but usually around ten. After the last brand page there is a page with ten adhesive stickers, accompanied by instructions to the respondent to distribute these stickers among the brand pages of the booklet, based on her likelihood of buying the brands. This page is illustrated in Figure 5–2. By the nature of the task, the respondent must peel one sticker off at a time, paste it on some page, and repeat the process until she uses up the stickers. The share of stickers given to a brand is called the *STEP share* of the brand.

The process is embedded in a controlled experiment. The total sample of respondents is divided into N randomly equivalent groups. Each receives the same booklet, identical in all respects except that one strategy element is different on the test brand page: the statement, or the package graphics, or the product name, or the logo, or the price, or any other aspect of the selling strategy of the brand. If, under these circumstances, we obtain a test brand STEP share of, say, 12% in Group A exposed to Statement A, but of 16% in Group B exposed to Statement B, we may conclude categorically that, sampling error aside, we have measured the relative effectiveness of these two sets of words in biasing the respondents in favor of the test brand. Instead of complaining about bias and seeking to eliminate it, we have turned the tables on it. We have given it center stage. It has become the very thing we are measuring. This interviewing method does not rely on the meaning of words, or on what the respondents say, but on the choices they make, which is a behavior in its own right and, according to the First Law, as relevant a behavior as the one we are presumably interested in, namely their potential behavior in the marketplace.

Much has been said about the importance of unconscious motivations, an emphasis that has been pressed by advocates of qualitative work, particularly by those with a psychoanalytic bent. These analysts propose depth interviews and projective devices and usually offer the services of

Figure 5–2
Sample STEP Stickers Page

STEP 2

Here are 10 labels:

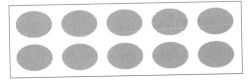

Please paste these labels on the various pages of this booklet (in the spaces marked STEP 2) to show how you feel about the products.

- The more likely it is that you will buy a product *(assuming it is available at the price shown in this booklet)*, the more labels you should paste under it.

- Please use all 10 labels.

- You may give any product all or none of the labels, or as many or as few as you want. But remember, you have only 10 labels for all the products in this booklet. And the more labels you give to one product, the fewer will be left for the others.

an interpreter-analyst who examines what the respondents said and tells us what they really meant. But if one believes in the unconscious, one must entertain the possibility, indeed the probability, that such interpretations will reflect not only the unconscious of the respondents but also the unconscious of the analyst. Ironically, the only surefire way of documenting unconscious forces in the marketplace is to use quantitative experiments like the one just described. If we observe different choices in groups exposed to different strategy elements, these can provide categorical evidence for the existence of motivations some of which may be unconscious.

In considering whether a STEP study is well designed, the key question is whether it has met the requirements of the First Law: Has the competitive frame been represented properly? Has appropriate congruence been established between the information in the STEP booklet and the information in the marketplace? In this respect, there is no absolute right or wrong. The competitive frame and the information elements can be only approximately right for a problem. If we design a study improperly, we will still get a right answer. It just won't be the answer to the question we were trying to answer, but the answer to another question instead.

The principal features of STEP are:

1. It uses a competitive frame suitable for observing choices congruent with those that occur in the market.
2. It uses a measuring device (the stickers) that compels the respondents to make choices among the brands of the competitive frame.
3. It uses a controlled experiment to evaluate the impact of various strategy elements on the choices of the respondents.

STEP Share and Market Share

Suppose we have chosen a product category and have created a STEP booklet to represent the major brands in that category. Suppose we have selected a sample of respondents, have sent them a STEP booklet and have computed the STEP shares for the various brands. What should we expect when we compare these STEP shares with market shares obtained from external sources? Under ideal conditions, assuming total congruence between the STEP booklet and the marketplace, we should expect perfect correspondence between the STEP shares and the market shares, as illustrated in Figure 5–3. All points should lie on the 45-degree line, $M = S$.

In practice, there are many reasons for discrepancies. Some are purely

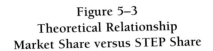

Figure 5–3
Theoretical Relationship
Market Share versus STEP Share

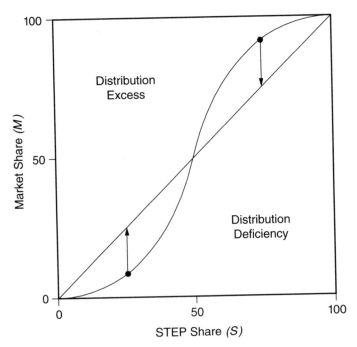

mechanical. The market share data are based on a sample of stores; the STEP data are based on a sample of respondents. These two populations are not necessarily the same. But even if the populations were identical, sampling error in both measurements would give rise to discrepancies.

In addition to these obvious mechanical factors, there are substantive discrepancies. The most important of these has to do with accessibility. In the STEP booklet, all brands are equally accessible, each having 100% distribution. This is not so in the marketplace. Consider a brand that is available in only half of the stores. Such a brand might receive stickers in the STEP booklet, but if the respondents who gave it stickers cannot find it in the store, they won't buy it. Such a brand would have a higher STEP share than market share and would lie below the line in Figure 5–3, somewhere in the region of distribution deficiency. Conversely, consider a brand that has higher distribution than other brands. Such a brand might do less well in the STEP booklet, where the competitors are available, than in the stores where they are not. It would therefore lie above the line on the chart, somewhere in the region of distribution excess.

The most extreme manifestation of this phenomenon occurs when the STEP booklet includes a page for a nonexisting brand. Such a brand must lie on the x-axis. It receives a share in the STEP booklet even though its market share is zero by definition. And it is precisely this discrepancy that allows us to use STEP to forecast the future share of currently nonexisting brands or the deserved share of currently unimplemented strategies. Turning the analysis around, we can use the same chart to measure accessibility differentials, covering not only whether the brand is available in the store, but also the extent and quality of its representation on the shelf.

Putting it all together, we expect a general relationship between STEP share and market share, and we expect deviations from the 45-degree line due to mechanical, statistical, and substantive factors, but we do not expect any particular brand or group of brands to deviate from the line in any systematic way. There is one deviation, however, that *is* systematic. If a brand has low distribution, it must necessarily have lower market share. People can't buy it if it isn't on the shelf. Conversely, if a brand has low market share, retailers will be reluctant to keep it on the shelf. In either case, the outcome will be the same: Brands with low market share will have distribution deficiency and brands with high market share will have distribution excess. This results in a systematic tendency for low-share brands to fall below the line, and for high-share brands to fall above the line. The theoretical relationship between market share and STEP share should therefore be an S-shaped curve with concave curvature in the lower section and convex curvature in the upper section.*

The data in Figures 5–4 to 5–6 show STEP share (S) on the x-axis and market share (M) on the y-axis for nine product categories, presented in scrambled order: baby wipes, cigarettes, frozen dinners, frozen pot pies, ground coffee, instant coffee, paper towels, sanitary protection, and toilet tissue. In each case, the STEP shares were generated in a control group in which no extraneous test strategy elements were used and in which all brands were represented, to the best of our ability, as they were positioned and priced at the time of the study. The market shares were furnished by the client, drawn from data provided by one or another of the services that measure and report market share by noninterview means, such as store audits or warehouse withdrawals. There can be no assurance that either

---

*This type of curve can be obtained from the function $M = aS + bS^2 + cS^3$, where M represents market share, S represents STEP share, and a, b, and c are constants, constrained to $a + b + c = 1$, which assumes that the curve passes through $M = 100\%$, $S = 100\%$. The absence of a stand-alone constant further constrains the curve to pass through $M = 0$, $S = 0$. The degree of the curvature is controlled by a, b, and c. In the limiting case, when $a = 1$ or very close to 1, and $b = c = 0$ or very close to 0, the curve becomes $M = S$ or very close to it.

Figure 5–4
Market Share versus STEP Share for Established Brands
Product Categories 1–3

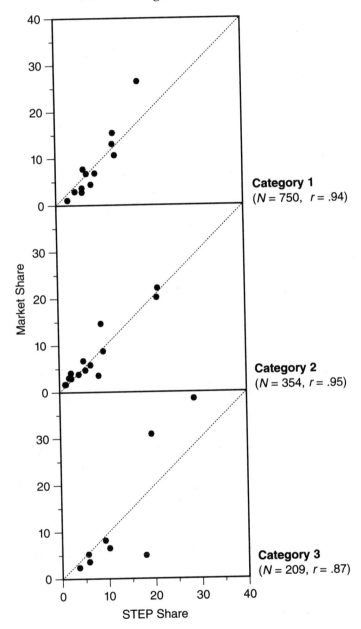

Category 1
($N = 750$, $r = .94$)

Category 2
($N = 354$, $r = .95$)

Category 3
($N = 209$, $r = .87$)

Figure 5–5
Market Share versus STEP Share for Established Brands
Product Categories 4–6

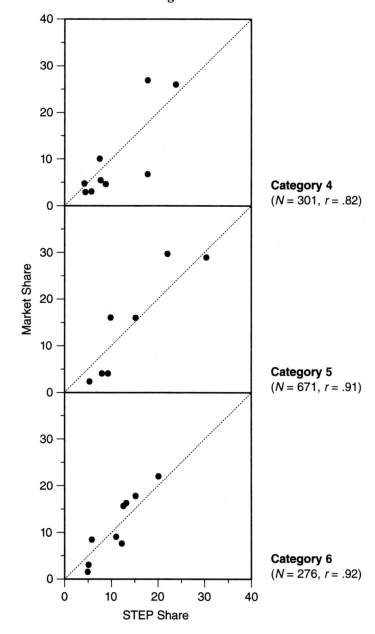

Category 4
(*N* = 301, *r* = .82)

Category 5
(*N* = 671, *r* = .91)

Category 6
(*N* = 276, *r* = .92)

Market Share

STEP Share

Figure 5–6
Market Share versus STEP Share for Established Brands
Product Categories 7–9

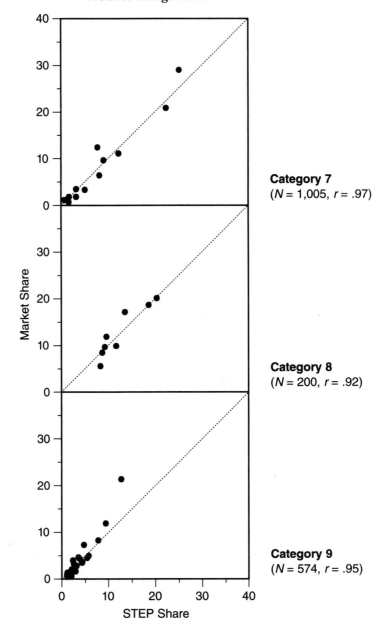

Category 7
($N = 1,005$, $r = .97$)

Category 8
($N = 200$, $r = .92$)

Category 9
($N = 574$, $r = .95$)

the time period or the geography matches precisely, but, given the extent of the correspondence between STEP share and market share, this point is largely moot. The correlations range from a low of .82 to a high of .97, with an average of .92. In examining these data, keep in mind that this particular test of the theory is a weak one at best. The theory postulates that, when accessibility is unusually low or unusually high, brands should move away from the 45-degree line, resulting in progressively lower correlations. Because we believe that most established brands in packaged-goods categories have high and approximately equivalent accessibility, we expect to see generally high correlations. But because we know that some brands have distribution deficiencies and others distribution excess, we expect these correlations to fall well below 1 on this conceptual count alone, quite apart from all the usual sources of measurement error.

The data for all nine categories are consolidated in a single chart in Figure 5–7, showing the best-fitting constrained cubic as well as the 45-

Figure 5–7
Market Share versus STEP Share
for 108 Brands in Nine Categories
$(N = 4,340, r = .92, M = -.000132S^3 + .0150S^2 + .828S)$

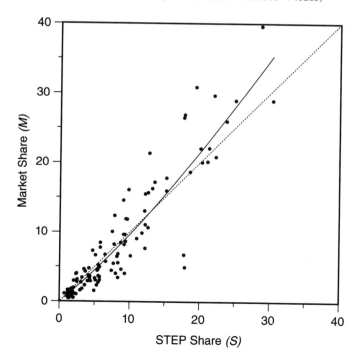

degree line $M = S$. In examining the data, note that the relationship between STEP share and market share is strong no matter which function is adopted. The best-fitting cubic is almost, but not quite, the same as the 45-degree line. Even if we insist that the 45-degree line is the only appropriate yardstick for testing the First Law, the average absolute deviation from that line is 3.45. The linear correlation coefficient is .92. We need not stop there, however. The S-curve does yield a slightly better fit, and certainly not a worse fit than the straight line.

The average absolute deviation is 3.31.* Thus the first cut of the data supports, or at least does not refute, the basic theory. This first cut, however, is a first cut only.

Aggregate and Individual Data

Correlation is a necessary but far from sufficient requirement for the usefulness of a method. The principal difficulty lies in the fact that a correlation, by itself, tells us nothing about the direction of causality. The possibility remains that STEP share may be no more than a reflection of market share. In that case, we might see the strong correlations we have observed, but the measurements would serve no useful purpose. Instead of predicting what customers will buy under different future conditions, they would merely reflect what customers have already bought. If this were so, of course, we would never observe any incremental shares for information elements that have not yet been introduced in the market, and STEP data would be flat from experimental group to experimental group. Chapters 6 and 7, which deal with price and concept testing, demonstrate beyond a doubt that this is not the case. STEP shares respond in dramatic and consistent ways to changes of information on the pages of the STEP booklet. We can therefore be certain that whatever STEP measures, it does not merely parrot buying behavior that has already taken place, holding in abeyance for the moment the further question of whether and to what extent the obverse is true: namely, that what STEP measures will manifest itself not only in STEP but in subsequent buying behavior as well.

So far, we have considered only the aggregate relationship between STEP share and market share. If this relationship holds dynamically, it may be sufficient for practical purposes. Nevertheless, the question remains whether the relationship between STEP share and market share is limited to the aggregate level or whether it extends to the individual level. An

---

*The data could have been fitted by a sigmoid of the form $M = a / (1 - e^{-b(S-C)}) + d$, but the constrained cubic does just as well.

Table 5–1
Sticker Allocation

| | Percent of Respondents Giving This Number of Stickers | | | | | | Average Number of Stickers | STEP Share |
	0	1	2	3	4	5		
Brand A	40	10	10	10	10	20	2.0	20%
Brand B	10	10	10	10	10	50	3.5	35
Brand C	0	5	5	5	5	80	4.5	45
Total							10.0	100%

example will help clarify the distinction between these two types of relationship. Tables 5–1 and 5–2 show a hypothetical set of data, constructed for the purpose of illustrating the point. Table 5–1 shows a sticker distribution for three brands. We see that 40% of the respondents gave Brand A zero stickers, 10% gave it one sticker, and so on. The average number of stickers given to Brand A is 2.0. Since each respondent has ten stickers to distribute, the averages for the three brands add up to ten. And since the STEP share of a brand is defined as the share of stickers given to that brand, the STEP shares for Brands A, B, and C are 20%, 35% and 45%, respectively.

Table 5–2 shows the average number of packages bought by these same respondents during a two-week period. Two data patterns, Case I and Case II, are illustrated. In Case I, all of the respondents bought the

Table 5–2
Purchasing

| | Average Number of Packages Bought by Respondents Giving This Number of Stickers | | | | | | Average Number of Packages Bought | Market Share |
	0	1	2	3	4	5		
Case I								
Brand A	2.0	2.0	2.0	2.0	2.0	2.0	2.0	20%
Brand B	3.5	3.5	3.5	3.5	3.5	3.5	3.5	35
Brand C	4.5	4.5	4.5	4.5	4.5	4.5	4.5	45
Case II								
Brand A	0.5	1.0	1.5	2.0	3.5	5.0	2.0	20
Brand B	0.5	1.0	2.0	3.5	4.5	4.7	3.5	35
Brand C	0.0	1.5	2.0	3.0	4.0	5.0	4.5	45

same number of packages of Brand A (2 packages), regardless of how many stickers they gave it. Similarly, all respondents bought 3.5 packages of Brand B and 4.5 packages of Brand C. Accordingly, the market shares of Brands A, B, and C were 20%, 35%, and 45%, respectively. The fact that there is no individual relationship between stickers and buying might suggest that the allocation of stickers is not predictive of market share, but there is a 1.0 correlation between STEP share and market share in the aggregate. This correlation tells us that even though it is not possible to use a respondent's stickers to predict what the particular respondent will buy, the respondents nevertheless tend in the aggregate to give Brand C more stickers than Brand A, just as they tend in the aggregate to buy more packages of Brand C than of Brand A. This is usually sufficient. It allows us, for example, to predict the potential of new brands, though we may still need to satisfy ourselves that actions that change the allocation of stickers also produce commensurate changes in the marketplace. This kind of relationship will be called an *aggregate relationship*.

Case II shows a different pattern of responses, culminating in the same average number of packages bought as above. In this case, there is a definite monotonically increasing relationship between stickers and packages. Taking each of the three brands separately, the number of stickers given a brand directly predicts how many packages of that brand the respondents are likely to buy, ranging from around .5 packages for respondents who give the brand no stickers to around 5.0 packages for respondents who give the brand five stickers. This stronger relationship, which holds not only in the aggregate but also on a respondent-by-respondent basis, will be called an *individual relationship*.

In practice, we cannot expect relationships to display the stark all-or-nothing patterns of the example and must expect varying degrees of aggregate and individual relationships. But given only aggregate data, Case I and Case II look the same, and we cannot infer from such data alone whether the relationship is aggregate or individual. To answer this question, we need information about the buying behavior of the particular respondents who answered the STEP booklet, information that is ordinarily unlikely to be collected because it is apt to be regarded as a luxury of greater theoretical than practical value. We do, however, have two studies for which just such data are available.

Individual STEP Scores and Buying

In 1972, one of EMA's clients was planning to introduce a new baby product. In anticipation of that introduction, a comprehensive research program was undertaken to evaluate the potential of the test brand and of various proposed marketing strategies for it. The testing program included a store test in Rochester, New York. Arrangements were made with a supermarket chain to keep the brand on its shelves for the duration of the test. A panel of mothers who shopped in the chain was recruited. The members of the panel agreed to participate in the test by completing an initial self-administered questionnaire, and by accepting a telephone call once every two weeks to report the number of packages of various baby products they had bought during the two weeks since the prior call. The baseline questionnaire consisted of three STEP booklets, covering baby foods, baby wipes, and baby lotions. Two of the categories had no role in the analysis and were included only to avoid focusing special attention on the test category. For the same reason, the biweekly purchase interviews covered brands in all three categories. In order to accelerate the respondents' exposure to the test brand, a free sample of the test brand was sent to them during Week 2. This sample was unrelated to their participation in the test and came to them directly from the manufacturer, indistinguishable from the general barrage of samples, coupons, and similar inducements mothers of new babies routinely receive from companies marketing baby products.

From a methodological point of view, the important feature of this test is that the respondents returned the STEP booklet before the test brand was on the shelves, before they could have known anything about it, before they had received the free sample, and before they had ever bought a single package of it. Accordingly, the causal and predictive direction is clear. The free sample doubtless contributed information about the test brand beyond that contained in the STEP booklet. It must have increased awareness and it certainly had an impact on the respondents' subsequent buying behavior. For that reason, it could easily have overridden, and conceivably totally wiped out, the information on which the initial sticker allocation was based. But this is not what happened. Figure 5–8 shows the average number of test brand packages bought by the respondents over the course of the twenty weeks after the test brand had become available on the shelves, as a function of the number of stickers they had originally given to it. The relationship between before-introduction STEP stickers and subsequent buying behavior is almost perfect. The correlation is .99. And most important, we are dealing not only with an aggregate relationship but with one that holds on the individual level—the strongest possible kind of relationship—which is the point of the chart.

An even more dramatic illustration of the same phenomenon arises in an entirely different context. The client was the provider of a subscription service, interested in a forecast of the rate at which subscribers would cancel the service. To facilitate this estimate, a calibration study was

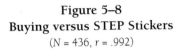

Figure 5–8
Buying versus STEP Stickers
($N = 436$, $r = .992$)

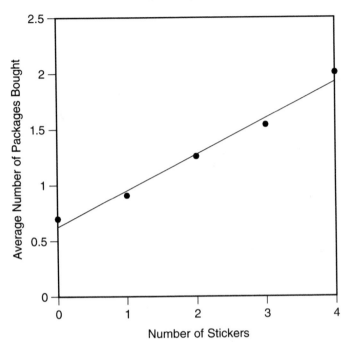

undertaken. STEP booklets were completed by over 11,000 known sub-scribers. In the STEP booklet, the respondent allocated stickers among eight "brands." One of these brands was "subscribing to the service." The other seven brands were products the respondent could buy to accom-plish the same objectives as subscribing. The idea was to find out whether and to what extent the STEP stickers allocated in the STEP booklet would enable us to predict the subsequent subscribing behavior.

At the time of planning the study, I had serious concerns that we might be demanding more from a single measurement than it could reasonably deliver. Accessibility was not the same in the booklet as in actuality. In the booklet, all options had equal accessibility. In the world, inertia made it easier to continue to subscribe than to cancel the subscription. In the ordinary course of events, respondents were expected to drop out of the subscriber ranks gradually under the influence of environmental factors. It was therefore going to be necessary to track respondent behavior for several years. Was it not a foregone conclusion that after two years or more had passed, most of the information contained in the original measure would have dissipated? To make matters worse, there was no assurance that the particular person in the household who had filled out the STEP booklet would be the one deciding whether or not to cancel the subscription a year or two later. All of these considerations raised doubts about whether a relationship between STEP stickers and subsequent behavior would be detectable this way, even if it existed. Nevertheless, we judged that the potential benefits outweighed the risks and that the test, though stringent, was worth conducting.

The client furnished the names of households who were still subscribing at various points in time. All respondents were classified by the number of stickers they had assigned to "subscribing" in November 1986 at a time when they were still subscribing. For each of these sticker groups, we determined the percentage still subscribing at several points in time: in March 1987 (three months after the STEP measurement), in April 1988 (one and one quarter years after the STEP measurement), and in July 1989 (two and a half years after the STEP measurement). The results are plotted in Figure 5–9. The data demonstrate a relationship between the number of

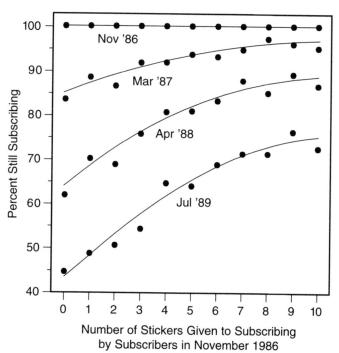

Figure 5–9
Subscriber Retention versus STEP Stickers
(N = 11,420)

STEP stickers assigned originally and the percent of respondents still subscribing at later points in time. Around 95% of those who had originally given ten stickers were still subscribing three months later, but only 83% of those who had originally given zero stickers were still subscribing, a significant result in its own right. More important, these rates diverged with the passage of time. By April 1988, 86% of those who had originally given ten stickers were still subscribing, but only 62% of those who had originally given zero stickers. And though more subscribers dropped out during the following year, the differential persisted. By July 1989, around 75% of those who had originally given ten stickers were still subscribing, but only 45% of those who had originally given zero stickers. Thus, a single STEP measurement, obtained from a single household member at a single point in time in November 1986, was still predicting the behavior of these households a full two and one half years later.

As in the case of the baby product study, we see evidence of an individual relationship between STEP stickers and subsequent behavior. Once again we can be confident of the direction of the causality. In the baby product case, purchasing could not have caused the sticker assignment because that assignment was made before the brand was available in the stores. In the case of the subscription study, canceling the subscription could not have caused the sticker assignment because the respondents were still subscribers at the time the STEP data were collected. Taken together, these findings, based on more than 11,000 respondents, provide empirical evidence for the operation of the First Law and substantiation of the power of STEP in predicting choices that have not yet been made in the market place.

CHAPTER 6

Price Testing

The fact that the First Law operates, that responses in STEP predict subsequent behavior, is of methodological interest to the theorist but of only passing interest to the marketer, who properly sees theory as just a means to an end, a tool to help answer practical business questions. These questions often call for concept tests—tests designed to measure the potential of some aspect of an offer, for example, the promise, the package graphics, the price. Although a price test can thus be thought of as just another concept test, price occupies a special place among concept tests and warrants special attention. Because price is quantitative, there is an implicit expectation that the price-demand relationship will prove to be a simple mathematical function and that the coherence of price tests will be easily demonstrable. At the same time, price is crucial from a marketing perspective. Of all the variables at the marketer's disposal, it is the one most likely to have an immediate dramatic impact on the bottom line, the one that simply cannot be ignored.

Pricing policies vary widely. Some marketers charge a percentage above cost. Some charge a percentage above or below the highest, lowest, or average competitor. Some believe that there is a simple inverse relationship between price and volume. Some are aware that they don't know, but believe that it is their job to guess, the polite phrase being to use "judgment." And a few, here and there, appreciate the importance of the question and look for an opportunity to answer it empirically. When they do, they are offered surveys, analytic techniques, or test market designs. Some marketers who have been dissatisfied with those options have used STEP.

STEP price tests have been conducted for a broad spectrum of products, ranging from packaged goods that were sold for under one dollar to business computer systems that were sold for hundreds of thousands of dollars. Some of these studies have focused on price points, that is, have sought to distinguish among specific, designated prices. Others have focused on price-demand curves, that is, on the entire price continuum, recognizing that particular points might be unstable, but that all points, taken together, could generate a curve defining the relationship between price and share.

In the course of this testing, we have learned that the accepted wisdom is true: When price goes up, share goes down—some of the time, that is. We can quantify the relationship empirically for particular products at particular times, answering by how much share goes down when price goes up. From time to time, however, unexpected findings turn up. In the end, I have concluded that although the price-demand relationship is often orderly, coherent, and persuasive, it does not conform to any single overriding pattern and must be studied on a case-by-case basis. I therefore begin by examining a few specific studies to give you a sense of what price data can look like.

Some Specific Studies

In 1986, EMA conducted a study of a product in the $1,000 price range. The assignment was to assess the potential share of the test brand at three price levels (high, medium, and low) when the test brand was offered with and without a certain feature. The total sample size was 1,583, divided into six groups of approximately 264 each. Figure 6–1 shows the results. Without the test feature, the test brand share drops from 17% to 13% as the price is increased from low to high. That is 4 share points, or 4/17 = 24%. When the test feature is added, an analogous result is obtained. All test brand shares are higher with the feature than without. But the price-demand relationship is about the same. The test brand share drops from around 20 to around 15 (5 share points or 5/20 = 25%) as the price is increased from low to high, an almost perfect replication of the first result.

Putting it together, we may say that the price increase results in a loss of approximately 4.5 share points, or approximately 25%. At the same time, we have three separate estimates of the value of the test feature. At the low price, that value is 2.5 share points (19.8 - 17.3 = 2.5, or 2.5/17.3 = 14%). At the medium price, the value is 1.2 share points (17.9 - 16.7 = 1.2, or 1.2/16.7 = 7%). And at the high price, the value is 1.9 share points (14.8 - 12.9 = 1.9, or 1.9/12.9 = 15%). Taking all of the data into account, we estimate that the feature increases the potential share of the brand by around 12%, offsetting approximately half the share lost by the price increase from low to high.

The test has confirmed our expectations. We would certainly have expected a higher share at the lower price, and we would certainly have expected a higher share for the test brand with the feature than without it. We would not, however, have known how many share points the price increase would lose, or how many share points the feature would be

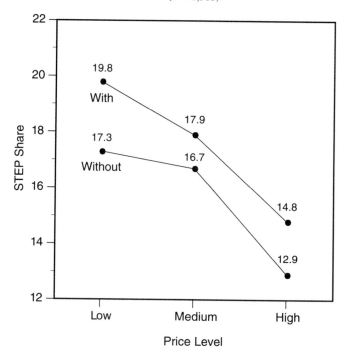

Figure 6–1
STEP Share versus Price
With and Without Special Feature
(*N* = 1,583)

worth, and we certainly would not have known the relationship between the two. The test has quantified all of these.

Results of this sort are not limited to high-ticket items and can be observed at low price levels as well. In 1987, EMA conducted a major study to construct a price-demand curve for a service in the $2 to $10 range. The total sample size was 5,967, divided into nine groups of approximately 663 each. The study was confined to current buyers of the test brand. The objective of the study was to estimate the losses that could be expected at various price levels above the then current level. The first panel of Figure 6–2 shows the price-demand curve. The STEP shares are in the 50% range because the study was confined to buyers of the test brand. Again the curve conforms to expectation. STEP share drops as price increases; in fact, it drops to a little over half its level (from a share of around 50% to a share of around 30%) as price is increased from around $2 to around $8.

This study was repeated in essentially identical form in 1989, 1991, and 1993, except that the test brand's current price was higher in each succes-

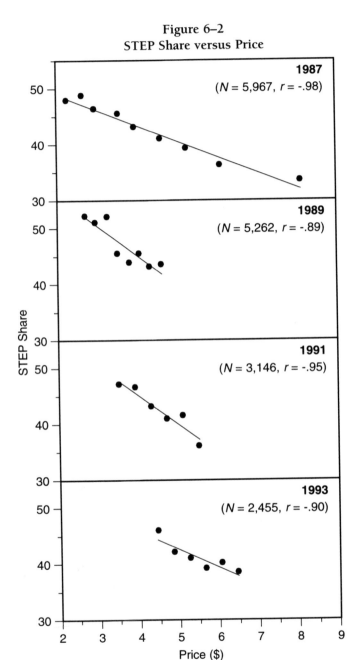

Figure 6–2
STEP Share versus Price

sive study, because the data had shown that price increases would be profitable, as indeed they turned out to be. The total sample sizes were 5,262, 3,146, and 2,455 for the 1989, 1991, and 1993 studies, respectively. The last two studies covered only five price points above the current price. The second, third, and fourth panels of Figure 6–2 show the price-demand curves for these studies. Apart from the fact that the absolute STEP-share levels changed somewhat from study to study due to general changes in market conditions, the four studies, done over a six-year period, replicate and supplement each other remarkably. The price-demand curve is monotonically decreasing with approximately the same slope in all four studies, and the wider price span covered by the 1987 study fits well with the narrower price bands covered by the other three studies.

For practical purposes, it is of course proper to take the most current data as the best estimate of the price-demand curve under prevailing market conditions. From a methodological perspective, however, it may be more interesting to ask whether all of the data, taken together, yield a single coherent price-demand curve. The answer is yes, as demonstrated in Figure 6–3, in which the data points from the four studies have been combined into a single data set represented by a single least-squares line.

The 1989 and 1991 studies provide an additional opportunity to examine a replication. They addressed the further question of what would

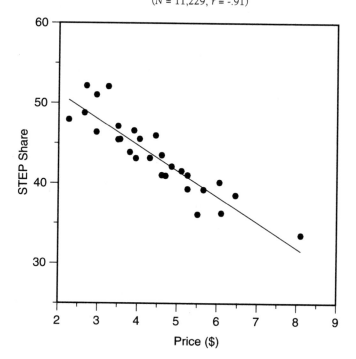

Figure 6–3
STEP Share versus Price
Four Studies Combined: 1987–1993
($N = 11,229, r = -.91$)

Figure 6–4
STEP Share versus Price
1989 and 1991 Studies and Additional Price Critique Cells
(N = 13,207)

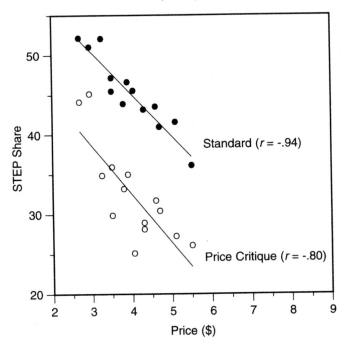

happen if customers were actively alerted to a price increase—for example, by way of competitive advertising. To investigate this question, parallel sets of "price critique" test groups were created. These were identical to the standard groups, except that no mention of a guarantee was made and the pricing policy of the test brand was spotlighted critically. Figure 6–4 contrasts the two price-demand curves, the standard curve and the price critique curve, consolidated across the two studies. The price critique was clearly effective. All STEP shares in these groups are lower than the STEP shares in the corresponding standard groups. The price-demand relationship, however, remains essentially the same, generating two parallel curves that diverge slightly with increasing price, indicating that the price critique becomes progressively more damaging as price is raised.

Seeing this succession of charts and the orderly pattern in them, one could lose sight of the character of these data. These are not survey results. We are not asking people how they feel about different price levels. Each respondent saw only one price for the test product. Every little point on every single chart represents a separate experimental group of several hundred different respondents, and shows how these respondents allocated stickers to the test brand in a constant competitive frame. This is real behavior. And we know from Chapter 5 that it is relevant behavior. The more stickers respondents allocate to a brand, the more likely they are to buy that brand subsequently. It is therefore persuasive to find both sensitivity and constancy in the data.

The experiment is sensitive in detecting the impact of different prices, as well as the impact of words that call attention to these prices, and the relative contribution of each. At the same time, it documents the constancy of the price-demand curve. The adverse message does not eliminate or even drastically change this curve; it merely lowers it in its entirety. Taken together, the four studies illustrate that the same price-demand curve can manifest itself repeatedly, at different current prices, at different points in time, and in different message contexts. Supported by this amount of replication, we can feel confident that what we have measured is real. But we might also be tempted to generalize and to assume that all price-demand relationships look the same. And that would be a mistake.

In January 1969, EMA conducted a test of three price levels—59¢, 63¢, and 69¢—for a snack product. The total sample size was 1,831, divided into three groups of approximately 610 each. The results are shown by the solid line in the top panel of Figure 6–5. They did not make sense. The highest price, 69¢, got the highest STEP share (20.4%) and the middle price, 63¢, got the lowest share (17.2%). Setting aside the 18.9% share at 59¢, the most troubling aspect of the data was the 3.2 share point advantage of 69¢ over 63¢. How could that be, the client demanded. I did not know. Statistical aberrations can produce weird results. The only way to find out was to repeat the test. This suggestion is not ordinarily received kindly, but in this instance, the two offending price levels were retested in May 1969. The results are shown as the dotted line in the top panel of Figure 6–5. Once again, 69¢ produced a higher share (this time 1.8 share points higher) than the 63¢ price. The puzzlement deepened.

We were done with replications for the time being, but several years later, in June 1973, EMA was asked to do still another price test for the same brand, testing 69¢, 71¢, 75¢ and 79¢. The results are shown in the second panel of Figure 6–5. This time the STEP shares were well behaved, more or less. They dropped dutifully as the price rose from 69¢ to 71¢ to 75¢. But the demon reappeared at the final point. The STEP share at 79¢ was higher than at 75¢. Again I did not know what to make of it. As the years passed, the price levels inched up. By 1977, EMA was asked to test 89¢ and 99¢. These results were well behaved. STEP share dropped by 1.1 share points (from 23.7 to 22.6) when price was increased from 89¢ to 99¢. In 1978, EMA did the final test in the series,

Figure 6–5
STEP Share versus Price
Snack Product

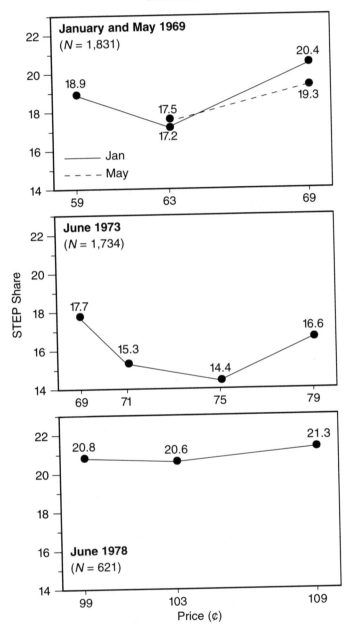

shown in the bottom panel of Figure 6–5. It yielded flat results, but did produce a slight increase in STEP share from $1.03 to $1.09.

Examining this series of tests as a whole, one is struck by the fact that, sampling fluctuations aside, two separate things appear to be going on in the data. First, there is a relatively modest monotonically decreasing relationship between price and STEP share. Second, the respondents seem to have a special affinity for price points with a 9 in last place. In particular, 69¢ produced a higher STEP share than 63¢ in two separate tests; 79¢ produced a higher STEP share than either 71¢ or 75¢; and finally $1.09 produced a marginally higher STEP share than $1.03. To be sure, the last of these is well within sampling error, but it is in the same direction. Putting the data together and considering only the directional pattern, the price point with a 9 in last place produced a higher share than the corresponding lower prices in four out of four comparisons. This may not be definitive, but it is certainly suggestive.

When a different client requested a price-demand curve for a household product in 1982, we saw an opportunity to test the "9" hypothesis experimentally. The full study was analyzed separately for two regions of the country, the East and the Central-South. This means that we have in effect two separate studies for the same brand, conducted at the same time, but otherwise independent of each other. The total sample size was 2,566, divided into twenty groups of approximately 128 each. Ten price points were tested in each of these studies: 65¢, 69¢, 75¢, 79¢ and so on, all the way to $1.09. Figure 6–6 shows the results. There is a 27% decline from 69¢ to $1.09 ((14.3 - 10.4) / 14.3 = 27%) in the East and a corresponding 26% decline ((11.0 - 8.1) / 11.0 = 26%) in the Central-South. Thus the data once again show substantial internal consistency, this time across regions. And once again we see the "9" phenomenon. In the East, the "9" price point is higher than the "5" price point in three out of five comparisons. In the Central-South, it is higher in five out of five comparisons. Altogether, it is higher in eight out of ten comparisons or, if we consider these data in conjunction with the snack data, twelve out of fourteen comparisons. The probability of having obtained this result by chance is less than .007.

The STEP Database

The separate studies just presented are important in their own right. They produced internally consistent findings, supported by replication. But I presented them for illustrative purposes only. I now turn to the larger question: What have we learned? What generalizations are appropriate?

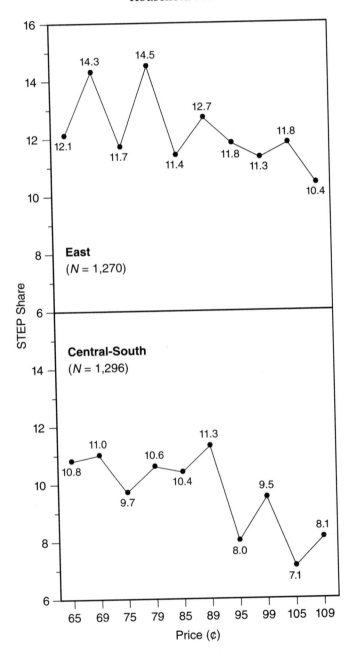

Figure 6–6
STEP Share versus Price
Household Product

To address this question, we need some way to summarize a large body of heterogenous data. And this creates a dilemma.

Which studies should be included in the summary? STEP tests have been done for many years. Some of them, especially the older ones, were lost or partially destroyed. I could have limited myself to presenting "representative" studies, but this would have required some unpalatable selections. We see, remember, and select what we want to see, remember, and select. I really wanted to present a census, which was not practically feasible. After struggling with this for a while, I decided to use a limited census, consisting of the last 1,000 STEP studies EMA completed before the end of 1994. This collection of studies—including not only STEP studies dealing with price, but all STEP studies regardless of subject—will be called the STEP Database. It is the universe for summaries of STEP data in this book.

For purposes of inclusion in the STEP Database, every replication is counted as a separate study. For example, if a study was conducted separately in two regions of the country, each is counted as a separate study. If a study covered price under two different concept scenarios, each is counted as a separate study. But each group of respondents is allocated to only one study and is counted only once. For factorial studies, covering both price and concept variations, price is given priority. In other words, four price points at each of two concepts are treated as two price studies rather than as four concept studies.

One thousand studies is an arbitrary number, but it has the virtue of objectively defining a block of data, a substantial block at that, consisting of an average 2.7 groups per study with an average sample size of 331 respondents per group, and an aggregate sample size of 886,842. The studies comprising the STEP Database hardly constitute a sample of what goes on in the world. All were conducted for clients of EMA and dealt with whatever the marketers in these organizations elected to test. Subject to this limitation, however, no further selection was made. For better or worse, whether the findings were consistent or inconsistent, coherent or preposterous, *all* of the last 1,000 studies completed before the end of 1994 are included. One point of clarification may be in order. The STEP Database is intended for summaries of large bodies of data. Where specific one-of-a-kind methodological experiments exist, I will report them even if they are older and are not included in the STEP Database.

The Price-Demand Relationship

The STEP Database contains 167 pricing studies, covering a wide range of brands, product categories, and price levels. These studies have been classified into two major categories, durables and consumables. When the product is a service, it was classified as either durable or consumable depending on whether it is purchased rarely for continuing use or routinely requires frequent new purchase decisions. The aggregate sample size is 188,276, divided into 626 groups, 3.8 groups per study, 301 respondents per group on the average.

How to present this mountain of data? To begin with, we need to consolidate data across huge price ranges. In some cases, we are dealing with price variations between 59¢ and 69¢; in other cases, with price variations between $400,000 and $500,000. For that reason, all studies are normalized around the average price of the test brand. For example, if a study tested three price levels, $1.60, $2.00, and $2.40, the average price level ($2.00) is represented as 0%, and $1.60 and $2.40 are represented as -20% and 20%, respectively. By the same token, the shares of the test brand are expressed as percent deviations from the average share. Continuing with the example, if the test brand obtained shares of 40%, 38%, and 30% in the three test groups, the average share (36%) is represented as 0, and the shares generated by the three price levels become +11.1% (4/36), +5.6% (2/36), and -16.7% (-6/36), respectively. This method of representing the data allows us to show studies for brands of widely different price levels and with widely different share levels in the same format, on the same chart.

The hypothetical three-group data are graphically illustrated in Figure 6–7. On this chart, the points are connected with dotted lines. If we choose to take the data at face value, they represent share levels for three discrete price points. Alternatively, we may consider the three points to be reflections of an underlying linear price-demand relationship, in which case we may calculate the best-fitting least-squares line for the points. This is the solid line on the chart. Even if the underlying relationship is not linear, the slope of this line provides a measure of the *price-sensitivity* of the data taken in their entirety. In particular, we define price-sensitivity (P) as the negative of the slope (m) of the least-squares line, $P = -m$. For these data, the slope is -.7. Accordingly, the price-sensitivity is .7. This means that we should expect a loss of 7 percent of share for every 10 percent of price increase.

Let us begin by looking at the price-demand relationship for durables. The STEP Database contains 101 price studies in this category. To help with the overview, these 101 studies have been divided into two groups, based on outcome:

1. *Monotonic studies:* studies that generate curves in which each point is equal to or lower than the preceding point. In order to include studies that are essentially monotonic but for which isolated

Figure 6–7
Hypothetical Price-Demand Relationship

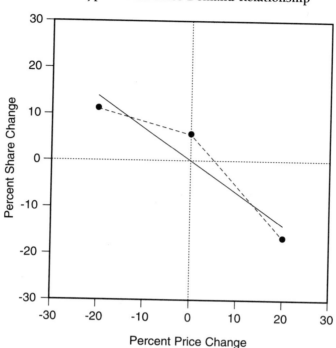

points show minor fluctuations, studies have been classified as monotonic if their last point is lower than their first point and no point is more than half an absolute percentage point higher than any preceding point. Thus, studies with approximately flat but orderly arrangements of points qualify as monotonic.

2. *Discrete studies:* all other studies, including those in which shares increase with increasing price and those in which shares fluctuate irregularly from price point to price point.

Given these definitions, the 101 price studies for durables break into 51 monotonic and 50 discrete studies. Figure 6–8 shows the results for the monotonic and discrete studies. On these charts, each point represents one group of respondents. The points of each study are connected by lines, forming one curve (of sorts) per study. Each of the charts summarizes a large amount of data, making it impossible to identify specific points of specific studies. The purpose of these charts, however, is not to present the particular but the general, to provide a sweeping overview of the patterns in the data. Obviously, the curves of the monotonic studies

Figure 6–8
Price-Demand Curves
Durables

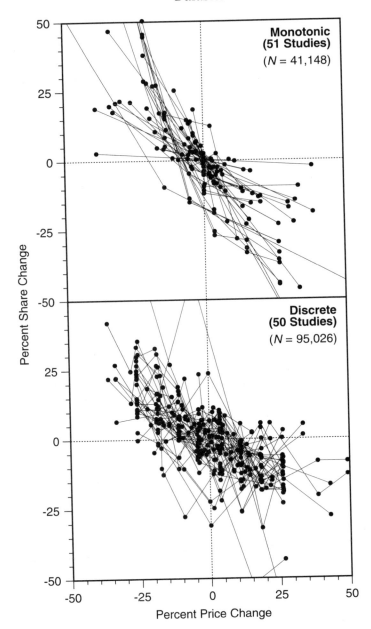

decrease monotonically by definition, though there is considerable variability in price-sensitivity. This variability will be examined in greater detail below. For the moment, it is sufficient to note that even the discrete studies reveal a decreasing pattern. To be sure there is a jumble of points in the midregion of the chart, but the general drift is downward from the upper left to the lower right and there are substantially fewer points in the other two quadrants.

The STEP Database contains 66 pricing studies for consumables. Of these, 49 are monotonic and 17 are discrete, summarized in Figure 6–9. There are some important differences between the durables and the consumables. The consumable studies generally cover fewer price points per study, and these points tend to be confined to a narrower price range. This is purely artifactual. It has nothing to do with price-demand and is a manifestation of the different behavior of EMA's durables and consumables clients. The marketers of durables were more frequently interested in generating broad price-demand relationships, willing to study many price points along a continuum to obtain a picture of the price-sensitivity of their brand under various conditions. The marketers of consumables were more frequently focusing on a relatively small number of specific price points. Should they increase their price by five or ten cents? This distinction between the interests of the marketers of durables and consumables holds only in a general way. The data certainly include price-point studies for durables and wide-ranging price-demand curves for consumables.

Going beyond what was studied to what was found, we may say by way of a preliminary conclusion that although there are instances of low and high price-sensitivity for both durables and consumables, price-sensitivity is generally more variable for consumables. Let us quantify this more specifically. Each study can be characterized by a single number, its price-sensitivity, which is the negative of the slope of the least-squares line, expressed as the percent share loss per percent price increase. Figure 6–10 shows the distribution of price-sensitivity for the 101 durables studies and for the 66 consumables studies. The average price-sensitivity is approximately the same for both: .92 and .96, respectively (around a 9% share loss per 10% price increase). But the standard deviation of the price-sensitivity of the consumables is more than double that of the durables (1.93 compared to .89).

Only 14% of the durables studies have a price-sensitivity of 0 or below, compared to around 33% of the consumables studies. But those of the consumables studies that are price sensitive have higher price-sensitivity than the durables studies. In particular, 23% of the consumables studies

Figure 6–9
Price-Demand Curves
Consumables

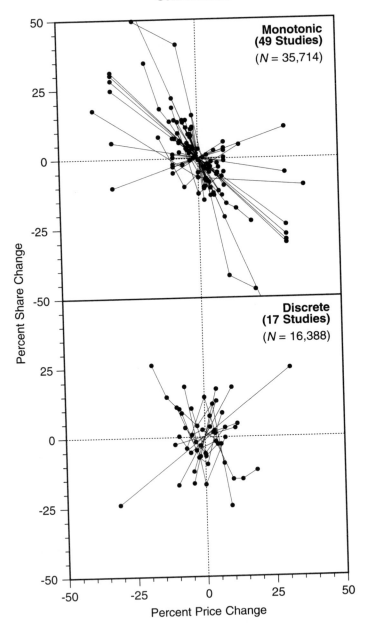

Figure 6–10
Percent Distribution of Price-Sensitivity

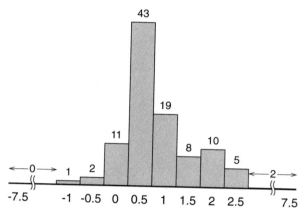

Durables
101 Studies
($N = 136,174$, $\bar{x} = .92$,
$SD = .89$)

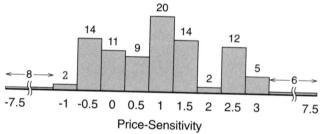

Price-Sensitivity

Consumables
66 Studies
($N = 52,102$, $\bar{x} = .96$,
$SD = 1.93$)

have a price-sensitivity of 2.5 or higher, compared to only 7% of the durables studies. What this amounts to is that, for the durables, price makes a difference most of the time. Increases in price consistently result in losses of share. In only a relatively small number of cases was a durable capable of increasing price with impunity. For the consumables, this happened more often. In one-third of the cases, a consumable managed to raise prices and get away with it, or even come out ahead. When this was not the case, however, the penalties of a price increase were generally more severe for the consumables than for the durables.

Durables and consumables do pose different marketing problems. The focus of durables is usually on a one-time purchase, whereas consumables live or die by their steady-state repurchase rate. Durables are also generally, though not exclusively, big ticket items, while consumables have modest prices. This raises the question whether the differences we have

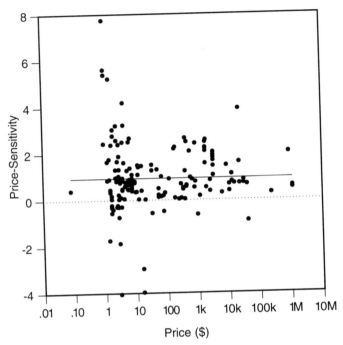

Figure 6–11
Price-Sensitivity versus Log of Price
for 167 Studies
($N = 188,276, r = .000$)

seen flow from the intrinsic differences between these product types, or whether they are mainly due to differences in absolute price levels. To address this question, we examine the more general relationship between price-sensitivity and price level. This is shown in Figure 6–11. The chart has 167 points, each representing the price-sensitivity of one study, plotted against the price of the test brand in that study. Since the price levels range from below $1 to above $1,000,000, the x-axis uses a logarithmic scale. The line is the least-squares line fitted to the points. This line is horizontal, the correlation being zero ($r = .000$), indicating that there is no change in price-sensitivity as price increases. This is summarized in the following principle.

THE PRICE-SENSITIVITY PRINCIPLE
Price-sensitivity is independent of price level. On the average, price-sensitivity is the same whether we are dealing with a $1 item or a $1,000,000 item.

Figure 6–12
Percent Distribution of Price-Sensitivity
167 Studies
($N = 188,276, \bar{x} = .93, SD = 1.39$)

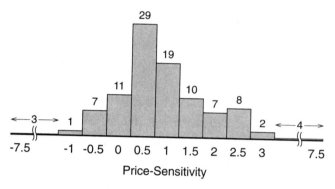

Price-Sensitivity

Accordingly, we return to an examination of the frequency distribution of price-sensitivity, consolidating the data of all 167 studies this time, as shown in Figure 6–12.

Approximately 20% of all studies show essentially no price-sensitivity, approximately 30% show price-sensitivity of around .5, and the remaining 50% of all studies show price-sensitivity of 1.0 or larger, around 20% being 2.0 or larger. The grand average price-sensitivity is .93. Thus, our conclusion is: Yes, what you have always known is true. Increase your price, and you will lose share. Based on the grand average, you may expect to lose approximately 9 percent of your share when you increase your price by 10 percent, and you may expect to lose at least this much approximately half of the time. This average, however, is like the proverbial lake whose average depth is one foot, but which has many spots in which one can drown. One time in five you will lose a lot more than 9 percent per 10 percent increase. And approximately one time in five you will get away with increasing your price and lose nothing, or even gain. The general pattern is certainly there. But in the end it depends on the competitive context, the particular brand, and the particular situation in which the price change is contemplated. All of this is summarized in the following principle.

THE PRICE EFFECT PRINCIPLE

On the average, a price increase of ten percent will produce a share decrease of around nine percent, but there is a great deal of variability in this result. One time in five the loss will be much larger, and one time in five there will be no loss at all.

CHAPTER 7

Concept Testing

Whereas price is a continuous variable, permitting a definitive ordering of different price levels, other concept tests are usually discrete by their very nature. There is no a priori reason to expect any set of words to capture a higher or lower share than any other set of words. If we want to estimate the difference a concept change is likely to produce, we must be prepared to compare every test group in a study with every other test group in that study. In doing so, we can obtain what amounts to an average difference between any two concepts.*

The STEP Database contains 329 concept studies, utilizing 3.2 groups per study on the average, with an average sample size of 320 per group and an aggregate total of 1,060 groups and 339,392 respondents. Of these, 115 studies were for durables and 214 for packaged goods.

It bears emphasizing that there is no such thing as an average concept, or for that matter an average difference between two concepts. A concept is simply a collection of information elements, objective or subjective, designed to present a brand in its best light. No matter how similar the effects produced by a large number of concepts may be, the possibility always remains that some other, unthought-of concept might produce a better result. But even if this reservation is set aside, the concepts in our studies don't begin to cover the theoretical distribution of concepts, because they constitute a subset drawn from the positive end of the continuum. These concepts were not produced by an academic effort to construct a

---

*Defining such an average requires some rules for combining differences from different studies to make sure that each is weighted properly. Consider one study in which n different concepts were tested. The difference between the STEP shares of any two concepts in that study is called a *concept difference*, or *score* for short. The study allows us to construct $n(n-1)/2$ such scores (n things taken two at a time). But these scores stem from only $n-1$ independent observations. Accordingly, the total information derived from this study should receive a weight of only $n-1$. If we multiply each score by $n-1$ and divide it by the number of scores contributed by the study, we obtain $2(n-1)/n(n-1)$ = $2/n$. Applying this weight to each of the scores allows us to add the scores from all of the studies while ensuring that each study is counted only in proportion to the number of independent observations it has contributed to the total.

broad array, ranging from the worst thing one might be able to say about a brand to the best. The marketers who conceived them and submitted them for testing were attempting to put their best foot forward and to submit, insofar as they could, alternatives that would produce large positive shares for their brands. This alone should have reduced the range of the tested concepts, except for the fact that judgment will often produce wider disparities among candidate concepts than intended. We must allow further that not all product categories, and beyond that not all brands within a product category, may be equally amenable to concept-induced changes.

Because I will use the term *standard error* (SE) in the following discussion, I am providing a brief explanation for readers who may be unacquainted with statistical terminology. Standard error is a measure of the amount by which a result obtained from a sample of respondents is likely to differ from the value that would have been obtained if the same measurement had been made on a census of the whole population. In general, we want the standard error to be as small as possible, but we are limited by budget considerations. To reduce a standard error to half its value, we need four times the sample size; to reduce it to one-third its value, we need nine times the sample size. Nature gives up its truths only to the extent we are willing to pay for them.

In an experiment in which two groups are compared (for example, respondents exposed to two different concepts), the effect— the share difference between the groups—also has a standard error. We usually divide this effect by its standard error because, once it has been expressed in standard error units, we can rely on a general mathematical law to tell us the probability of having gotten this effect by chance. For example, the probability of having gotten at least .5 standard errors by chance is 61%; at least 1 standard error, 32%. We do not ordinarily have much confidence in results of this magnitude. On the other hand, the probability of having gotten at least 2 standard errors by chance is only 5%; at least 3 standard errors, .2%; at least 4 standard errors, .04%; and beyond that essentially zero. As the effect, expressed in standard errors, increases, we become increasingly confident that whatever the data may mean, they mean something real and are not just statistical noise.

Durables

We can now proceed to summarize the concept differences we found. Figure 7–1 shows the frequency distribution of the concept test differences for durables generated by studies in the STEP Database. Approximately one-third of these differences were less than 1 share point, meaning that the con-

Figure 7–1
Distribution of Concept Differences for Durables
278 Comparisons
($N = 146,226, \bar{x} = 2.87, SE = .11$, normal $\bar{x} = 1.41$)

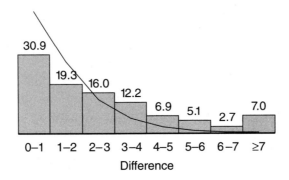

cepts tested were in effect equivalent. Approximately one-third were between 1 and 3 share points, indicating a small difference. And one-third were over 3 share points, approximately 10% being over 6 share points. Thus, there were major differences among at least some of the concepts EMA was asked to test. To get some sense of the significance of this distribution, we compare it to the distribution we would have expected to get by chance. If we had tested the identical concept over and over again, we would have expected to get differences that were normally distributed around 0. The curve superimposed on the bars in Figure 7–1 shows the distribution of differences we would have expected in this null case, that is, if the data had been generated by chance from a single concept and if the true difference had been 0.

The average of this expected null distribution is 1.41; the average of the observed distribution is 2.87. The difference between these averages, 1.46, will be called the *net difference*. This means that the average difference between two concepts is 1.46 share points larger than the average difference that would have been expected by chance alone. Since the standard error of this net difference is .11, the probability of having obtained the observed result by chance is essentially zero. We can be confident that the result is real. Putting a 95% confidence interval around the estimate of the net difference, we can say that the probability is 95% that the interval 1.46±.22 covers the true (unknown) average net difference.

The test concepts can be classified into three broad categories:

1. *Specific features* (165 concepts), tests that compared verbal specifications of verifiable, objective characteristics (for example, numbers of pages per minute printed by a fax machine, horsepower ratings of an automobile).

2. *General promises* (162 concepts), tests that compared slogans, promises of benefits—words used in describing and positioning the brand.
3. *Name* (66 concepts), tests that compared brand names, model names, manufacturer's identification, and so on.

Figure 7–2 shows the frequency distributions of the differences produced by tests in each of these categories. The results are highly signifi-

Figure 7–2
Distribution of Concept Differences for Durables

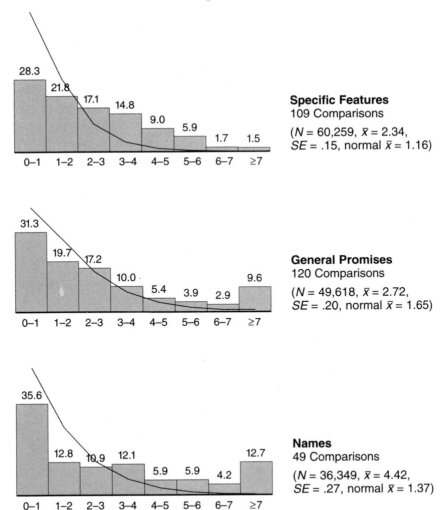

Specific Features
109 Comparisons

($N = 60,259$, $\bar{x} = 2.34$, $SE = .15$, normal $\bar{x} = 1.16$)

General Promises
120 Comparisons

($N = 49,618$, $\bar{x} = 2.72$, $SE = .20$, normal $\bar{x} = 1.65$)

Names
49 Comparisons

($N = 36,349$, $\bar{x} = 4.42$, $SE = .27$, normal $\bar{x} = 1.37$)

cant for each of the three categories taken separately. For the specific features, the net difference is 2.34 - 1.16 = 1.18, or 7.9 standard errors. For the general promises, the net difference is 2.72 - 1.65 = 1.07, or 5.4 standard errors. And for the names, the net difference is 4.42 - 1.37 = 3.05, or 11.3 standard errors. Thus, the probability that any of these net differences is spurious is essentially zero.

The net differences for the specific features and for the general promises are around 1 share point. For the names, the net difference is around 3 share points. For the durable variants EMA was asked to test, at any rate, brand name or corporate identification thus proved to be critical; it made a greater difference than either specific features or general promises. Around 40% of the differences between names were worth more than 3 share points, and around 20% were worth more than 5 share points.

Consumables

The pattern of results for consumables is different from that for durables. The three panels of Figure 7–3 show the frequency distributions of differences for specific features, general promises, and names for consumables. In general, the average differences for the consumables are smaller than the average differences for the durables. This is true for all three categories. Nevertheless, the net difference for specific features, shown in the top panel, is substantial (2.07 - 1.33 = .74, or 4.4 standard errors), high enough to make the probability of having obtained the result by chance essentially zero. We can be confident that we are dealing with a real result. On the other hand, in the aggregate there were no differences among the general promises for consumables. The net difference was 1.54 - 1.52 = .02, conforming almost precisely to what one would have expected under the null hypothesis. On a test-by-test basis, the general promises EMA was asked to test simply were not different. The consumer didn't care one way or the other and responded accordingly.

The objection might be raised that perhaps this result merely demonstrates that the method is not sensitive, but this is not the case. We have seen overwhelming evidence that what is put on the page of the STEP booklet matters. First, there were hundreds of price tests which demonstrated that the respondents react differentially to what is on the page. Second, we saw three separate categories of tests for durables which demonstrated the sensitivity of the instrument in distinguishing among statements. Finally, the specific features for the consumables showed a net difference of over 4 standard errors. The probability of having obtained that result by chance alone is less than .000006. The data therefore clearly

Figure 7–3
Distribution of Concept Differences for Consumables

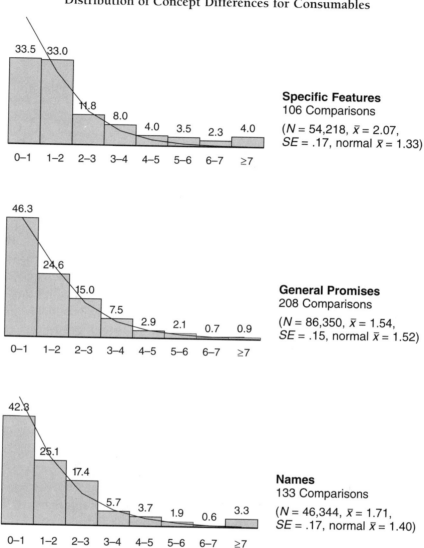

Specific Features
106 Comparisons

(N = 54,218, $\bar{x}$ = 2.07,
SE = .17, normal $\bar{x}$ = 1.33)

General Promises
208 Comparisons

(N = 86,350, $\bar{x}$ = 1.54,
SE = .15, normal $\bar{x}$ = 1.52)

Names
133 Comparisons

(N = 46,344, $\bar{x}$ = 1.71,
SE = .17, normal $\bar{x}$ = 1.40)

are not an artifact of the measuring instrument. They tell us something real. But what?

First, I must reiterate the basic qualification made at the beginning of this chapter. We are not dealing with a sample of all possible concepts, only those concepts EMA clients chose to test. If these clients were skillful enough to craft only good general promises, statements that focused on different aspects of the brand but were all equally effective, the consequence would have been precisely what we observed. The general promises would have proved to be interchangeable. Whatever the explanation, however, the fact remains that the specific features and the general promises produced different results. When the words tested dealt with specific features, these words generated a net difference of .74 share points, but when the words consisted of general promises, the net difference was zero (.02).

Is it possible that customers of consumable products have been so inundated by superlatives that they have become largely impervious to them? This finding appears to contradict one of the shibboleths of advertising: "Sell the sizzle, not the steak." In these data, at least, the sizzle has not done well. For consumables, which customers buy and use continually and with which they have continual direct experience, all general promises produced about the same results. Perhaps people are neither as gullible nor as stupid as the marketing community sometimes expects them to be. They have seen the claims and have used the products. To the extent they have found the claims at variance with their experience, they have learned to trust the evidence of their eyes and to discount general promises. Durables, on the other hand, are bought less frequently. People have less experience with brands they don't happen to own and may therefore be more prone to rely on what they are told by a manufacturer, especially one they are inclined to trust based on reputation.

For consumables, many of the names EMA tested proved to be effectively interchangeable. A handful of name tests, however, produced differences that were so large (7 share points or more) that they could not have come about by chance, even taking into account the number of trials. To this extent, the consumables support the broader finding for the durables that names can be of major importance.

The net differences generated by all of the concept tests are summarized in Figure 7–4. The most striking aspect of this summary is the extent to which the concept results for the consumables differ from those for the durables, as expressed in the following principle.

THE PROMISES PRINCIPLE
For consumables, only specific features are likely to matter. General promises won't. For durables, both specific features and general promises are of major importance.

For the name tests too, the results for the durables and the consumables are different. Looking at all of the name tests from another perspective, we can compare them to what we found in the price tests. The

Figure 7–4
STEP Concept Test Differences
Net Difference for Three Concept Categories
(N = 333,138)

	Mean	Expected	Net Difference (Share Points)
Durables			
Specific features	2.34	1.16	1.18
General promises	2.72	1.65	1.06
Name	4.42	1.37	3.05
Consumables			
Specific features	2.07	1.33	0.74
General promises	1.54	1.52	0.02
Name	1.71	1.40	0.31
Average durables	**3.16**	**1.39**	1.77
Average consumables	**1.77**	**1.42**	0.35

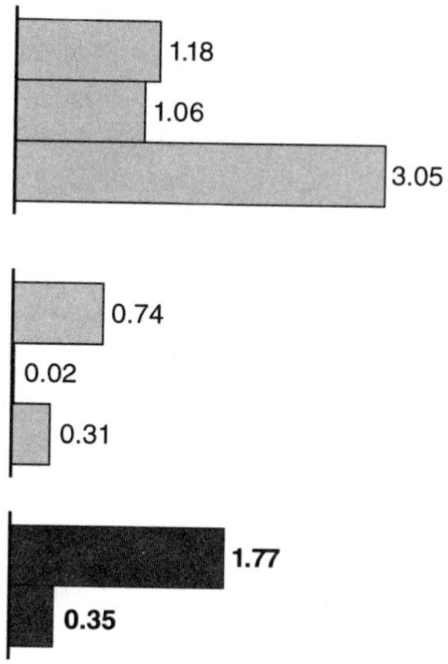

average durables name, and at least a small number of the consumables names, produced net differences of 3 share points, and in some instances as large as 7 share points. It happens that 3 share points corresponds to an average price change of approximately 20%. This leads to the following principle.

THE NAME PRINCIPLE
A name is worth money. For durables, a good name may permit charging as much as twenty percent more for the brand, on the average; in some cases, as much as fifty percent more. It can also be of comparable value for consumables, but only rarely.

Line Extensions and Cannibalization

The STEP Database contains 271 tests of line extensions, 117 for durables and 154 for consumables. The principal feature of a line-extension test is that the offer is presented to the respondent on a separate page of the STEP booklet. Typically, the control booklet contains the current competitive frame, including one or more varieties of a parent brand. The test booklet contains the additional page. The potential of the line extension is its net contribution. For example, if the current line has a STEP share of 22% in the control group and 20% in the test group (indicating a cannibalization of 2%), and if the line extension has a share of 8%, the net value of the line extension, after cannibalization, is 20 + 8 - 22 = 6.

The upper panel of Figure 7–5 shows the percent distribution of the line-extension effects for durables; the lower panel shows the distribution for consumables. The curve on each panel shows the effects expected by chance if the true value of the line extensions were zero. For the durables, the average line extension received a share of 4.85 with a 95% confidence interval of ±.40. The comparable average for the consumables was 3.88±.34.

Although these findings are obviously limited by the particular line extensions EMA was asked to test, they demonstrate that some line extensions can have negligible effects while others produce large effects. Half or more of the line extensions tested produced no effects or only small ones, but close to half of the durables line extensions and approximately one-third of the consumables line extensions produced effects of over 5 share points, in some instances, over 10 share points. For the durables, two exceptional line extensions may have thrown an adverse light on the entire line, thereby reducing its total appeal. For the consumables, the negative effects are totally within the bounds of chance.

The extra page used in the line extension tests may partially account for the magnitude of the effects. But we know that a page for a completely unknown brand will ordinarily command no more than 1 to 2 share points. The high shares obtained in the line-extension tests cannot, therefore, be dismissed as an artifact. What is on the page matters. The page does, however, give the test brand an advantage. It increases its accessibility relative to the control group. Accordingly, we must consider whether the line extension is likely to receive comparable treatment in the market. This amounts to asking how much space the line extension is likely to get in the store and whether that space is likely to be incremental or taken from one or more of the other items of the line. If it is anticipated that the latter will happen, the most conservative thing is to replace the lowest-share item of the line with the line extension. This keeps the total number of pages—presumably the total space available in the store—equal in the test and control groups, and measures by how much the proposed line extension would increase the total line share of the brand if accessibility for the entire line remained constant.

Focusing on the most positive findings, around 25% of the line extensions for the durables and around 10% of the line extensions for the consumables produced line-share increments of 10 points or more, effects

Figure 7–5
Percent Distribution of Line-Extension Effects

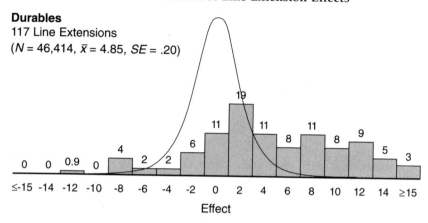

Durables
117 Line Extensions
($N = 46,414$, $\bar{x} = 4.85$, $SE = .20$)

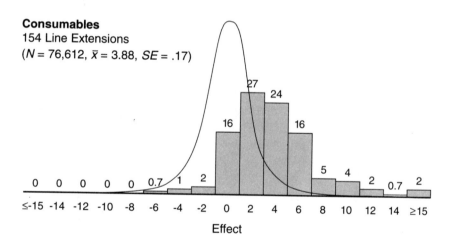

Consumables
154 Line Extensions
($N = 76,612$, $\bar{x} = 3.88$, $SE = .17$)

that are substantially higher than the largest effects we observed for simple concept differences. This says that whereas it may be difficult to come up with a good line extension, doing so can win big. This is expressed in the following principle.

THE LINE-EXTENSION PRINCIPLE
Provided you can get your line extension into the stores, a good line extension is likely to do more for you than a positioning change in one of your brands.

CHAPTER 8

Product Testing

A comment I hear over and over again in talking with researchers in major corporations is: "We don't really need sophisticated research here. All we do is ordinary product tests." No matter how often I hear this, it never ceases to amaze me. Product tests deal with the life-blood of the business, the very thing the marketer is seeking to sell. If there is any area in which research cannot afford to be wrong, it is product testing. Furthermore, I have never found product testing ordinary or unchallenging. Pitfalls and traps lurk at every turn. Nevertheless, researchers, marketers, and sometimes top managements of major companies take strong positions and occasionally issue edicts that can do much damage if taken literally.

It may be helpful to put our approach to product testing in perspective by comparing it with the methods that are most widely used. This, however, is not a simple matter. Every major manufacturer and every marketing research organization, large or small, conducts product tests. These amount to endless variations on a theme. And no matter how one might describe a particular approach, some researcher will complain that his point of view has not been represented properly, that what he does is totally different, and that it is precisely this difference that makes the difference. One can, however, take another approach to the description of methods. One can construct a classification grid that will make it possible to place all product tests, those we know about and those we don't, those that currently exist and those that no one has even thought of yet, into some box on the grid and will allow the proponents of the various methods to seek their proper places in the sun.

The Product Testing Grid

At the highest level of generality, every product test involves two things.

1. Some respondents must be exposed to one or more products; and
2. Some measurements must be performed on those respondents.

We can therefore classify all product tests on the basis of the type of exposure and the type of measurement they employ.

The exposure can be either artificial or real-life. By *artificial exposure* is meant that the respondent is recruited to participate in a product test and agrees to use the test products. This may lead her to use the products in a special way and to respond to the subsequent measurements in a special way. By *real-life exposure* is meant that the respondent does not know at the time of exposure that she is participating in a test, and does not know at the time of the measurement that the measurement is related to the prior exposure.

The respondent may be exposed to two or more products (*multiple exposure*) or to one product (*single exposure*). The difference between these tests often reflects fundamentally different approaches to measurement. Single-exposure tests imply experiments of some kind, one group receiving Product A, the other receiving Product B, followed by analytic comparisons across groups. An experiment is implied even when only one test product is being measured. In that case, the data are interpreted relative to some known yardstick that implicitly provides the missing cells of the controlled experiment. Multiple-exposure tests give the respondent two or more products and invite her to compare the products directly or rate them sequentially, which amounts to about the same thing since it generates implicit comparisons of the products. One particular variation of multiple exposure, which may be called a *benchmark exposure,* can be either multiple or single, depending on how it is used. In this type of test, one group of respondents receives Products A and C, and another group receives B and C. If the test is designed to measure A versus C and separately B versus C, it qualifies as a multiple. But if Product C is excluded from the analysis and is used only as a smokescreen to facilitate data collection, then this type of test is analytically equivalent to a single-exposure test that happens to employ Product C as part of the environment in which the measurement takes place.

Turning to measurements, the number of different questions that have been used or could be used as criterion variables is legion. But if we employ classification categories that are sufficiently broad, we can accommodate most, if not all, instruments that are likely to turn up. In particular, we can distinguish three types of measurements with respect to the test product(s).

1. *Absolute.* Measurements applied to one product at a time. For example: "How well did you like this product?" (Very much, somewhat, a little, not at all). "How likely is it that you will buy

this product?" (Will definitely buy, will probably buy, will probably not buy, will definitely not buy). "Use a scale from 0 to 10 to tell me how likely it is that you will buy this product."

2. *Relative.* Measurements asking the respondent to compare two or more test products. For example: "Which of the two products did you like better?" . . . "Which are you more likely to buy?" . . . "Divide 10 points between them."

3. *Share.* Measurements asking the respondent to choose among all brands of a competitive frame including the test product(s). For example: "Which of the brands on this list do you like best?" . . . "Which of the brands on this list are you most likely to buy?" . . . "Divide ten stickers among the brands on this list."

The question might be raised whether there is some ambiguity between relative and share measurements. That ambiguity arises when the test products being compared constitute the entire competitive frame. In that special case only, relative measurements between the test products are also share measurements.

The classification grid is summarized in Figure 8–1, which shows the intersection of four exposure types (real-life and artificial) x (single and multiple) and three measurement types (absolute, relative, and share) resulting in twelve combinations. Of these, two cells are logically impossible and have been struck from the table. A respondent who has received only a single test product cannot be asked to provide a relative measurement comparing two test products. The remaining ten cells have been consolidated into six types. The labels used for these types are arbitrary, have been chosen for convenience, and may not correspond to the way some of the terms have been used in other contexts. In case of doubt, the definitions govern and the labels can be abandoned and replaced by type number.

Type 1: Paired comparison. This category includes all tests in which the respondent receives multiple products with artificial exposure and is asked for a relative rating. A test also qualifies as a paired comparison if the respondent is asked for sequential absolute ratings, in which case the comparison is implicit.

Type 2: Pseudo response. This category includes all tests in which the respondent receives a single product, with artificial exposure, and is asked for an absolute rating.

Type 3: Pseudo share. This category includes all tests in which the respondent receives single or multiple products, with artificial exposure, and is asked for a share rating.

Figure 8–1
The Product Testing Grid

Measurement

		Absolute	Relative	Share
Artificial Exposure	Multiple	**Paired Comparison**		**Pseudo Share**
	Single	**Pseudo Response**		
Real-Life Exposure	Multiple	**Retrospective Comparison**		**Deserved Share**
	Single	**Deserved Response**		

Type 4: Retrospective comparison. This category includes all tests in which the respondent receives multiple products, with real-life exposure, and is contacted after product use and asked for either absolute or relative retrospective ratings.

Type 5: Deserved response. This category includes all tests in which the respondent receives a single product, with real-life exposure, and is contacted after product use and asked for absolute ratings. The ratings need not be confined to answers to questions and can consist of objective measurements.

Type 6: Deserved share. This category includes all tests in which the respondent receives single or multiple products, with real-life exposure, and is contacted after product use and asked for a share rating. If the respondent receives a product with real-life exposure and the subsequent measurement consists of an objective count of what the respondent bought, the test is a deserved share test provided the actual buying took place in a full competitive frame.

These six product test types coalesce into three pairs, the first member of which involves artificial exposure and the second real-life exposure. These pairs are:

1: paired comparison
4: retrospective comparison

2: pseudo response
5: deserved response

3: pseudo share
6: deserved share

Whereas this classification grid is certainly objective in that analysts holding different opinions should be able to classify most, if not all, product testing methods with reasonable consensus, the scheme is far from neutral. It employs labels some of which, for example pseudo response, might be considered nondescriptive and inflammatory. But even if we abandon these nicknames and respectfully refer to the methods by their proper formal names—Type 1, Type 2 and so on—the classification itself reflects a point of view. There is nothing impartial in the distinction between artificial and real-life exposure. The very words convey my belief that real-life exposure is better. Similarly, I hardly regard all types of measurement—absolute, relative, and share—as equally appropriate criterion variables. Everything I have said in the previous chapters reflects my belief that only share measurements are likely to be consistent with the First Law (the Law of Congruence).

Thus the classification promotes an implicit gold standard. The most desirable tests—those that provide for real-life exposure with share measurements—occupy the lower right-hand corner of the grid. Such tests may be difficult, if not impossible, to implement in practice, in which case one may be compelled to depart from the lower right-hand corner and to move either left or up or both left and up on the grid. To the extent one does, however, one should accept the dual burden of proof: that the move is indeed necessary for practical reasons, and that the gain in practical feasibility is not offset by a loss in data quality. The grid should help assess these trade-offs.

Blind and Identified Tests

There is one further aspect of product testing which has been held in abeyance so far, not because it is unimportant, but because it applies uniformly to all of the six types. Each can be either identified or blind. A test is designated as *identified* when the test product the respondent receives is packaged conventionally under its current or intended brand name. A test is considered *blind* when the respondent receives test products that are not identifiable. Often, test products are packaged in plain white packages with code designations such as "Test Product EW." Given this tradition, it might seem at first blush that real-life and blind exposure are incompatible conditions. However, this is too narrow a view of what it takes for a test to be blind.

Setting aside the more fundamental question whether blind tests should be employed at all, and if so for what purpose, and focusing on the *how* rather than on the *whether,* there is a better way to construct a blind test than to use the usual antiseptic package, labeled "Distributed by Research Company XYZ." The advocates of blind testing argue that they want to obtain a pure test of the product, divorced from the image that attaches to the brand. But the effort to separate the test product from an image altogether is futile. A plain white hospital-style wrapper, marked "Distributed by Research Company XYZ," also has an image, even a substantial image. Minimally, it signals caution. Here is something, it says, that may be experimental, untried, perhaps unsafe. Or it may say, here is something that is new and therefore wonderful.

To sidestep this issue, I have adopted a different way of accomplishing the objective. The test product is packaged in a standard testing label, using a standard testing brand name that does not exist in the market. This label is called the *decoy label.* Packaged this way, the test product is indistinguishable from a product the respondent might expect to see on the shelf of a supermarket. But the test is *blind* because the brand's image has been replaced by the image of the decoy label, which can be empirically demonstrated to be negligibly small. Blind and real-life testing are therefore no longer incompatible. To be sure, the decoy label requires additional expense in preparing test materials, but the expense is well worth it, as some of the data reported subsequently will demonstrate. Thus, the device of the decoy label allows us to split each of the six basic product testing types into two subcategories, blind and identified.

Which way of testing is better, blind or identified? Which gives the right answer? If the test is properly conducted, both do. The issue is not which answer is right, but which of two equally right and probably different answers is relevant to the particular problem at hand. And thereby hangs a tale we shall pursue in Chapter 10.

CHAPTER 9

Paired Comparisons

The president of a major corporation issued a directive to make one of the company's brands, let me call it Ours, better than one of its principal competitors, let me call it Theirs. This directive filtered down through the organization and was translated into the demand to determine whether Ours beat Theirs in blind paired-comparison tests, and if not, to modify it until it did. In this, as in so many other instances, my discussion with the issuer of the edict began with what could easily have been taken as quibbling over trivial distinctions.

"There is no such thing as a better brand," I said.

He was startled because he had spent his business life trying to improve brands.

"What does that mean?"

"The goodness or the badness of the brand does not reside in the brand but in the minds of the customers. If one brand is sweet and the other is sour, it is not meaningful to say that the sweet one is better than the sour one. The sweet one may be preferred by people who like sweet things. The sour one may be preferred by people who like sour things."

"Then the sweet one is better if more people want it sweet."

"Not at all. Even if 90% want it sweet and only 10% want it sour, it is still misleading to designate the sweet brand as the better one. The critical issue is not whether the brand is better but whether it is, if you must think of it that way, good enough; whether it can attract a sufficient share to maintain a profitable business, and what, if anything, you may be able to do to increase its share."

"But you are just playing with words. That's exactly what I meant."

Perhaps that is what he meant, but that is not what he said. That is not what his organization heard. And most important, that is not how either he or his researchers translated either what he said or what he meant into a research design. For the design they proposed was a blind paired-comparison test, which is still one of the most popular product testing methods in use.

What could be more self-evident and reasonable? Put two products into unlabeled packages. That way, the respondents won't know which product is which. They won't be biased by label or image and will be forced to respond to the product and to the product alone. Rotate the order. Give half of them Product A first, the other half Product B first. This washes out order effects, if any. Allow the respondents to use both products and find out which one they like better, which one they are more likely to buy. Obviously right, isn't it? Not necessarily.

Theoretical Considerations

The error in the design of paired-comparison tests, blind or otherwise, usually boils down to a violation of the congruence principle. The following is an exaggerated example of this error. Suppose the marketer is considering introducing a new brand. She can make it either sweet or sour. She calls for a paired-comparison test. The researcher may propose such a test at various levels of sophistication. The simplest thing is to test the sweet product directly against the sour product. In that test he finds that the sweet product beats the sour product 80:20. In the world of paired-comparison tests, this is an overwhelmingly skewed result, so he reports the finding with great enthusiasm. Never in his many years of experience in testing has he found such an extreme difference. It is statistically significant at the .000001 level. The sample is representative. There can be no question of chance. We have a real result. Nevertheless, he adds a conservative word of caution:

"Because we have so much at stake, you might want to consider an additional test. Why don't we check how each of our new products would do in a paired-comparison test against the leading competitive brand, and just to be safe, let us also check how it would do in a paired-comparison test against a few other brands. No, let's go for broke, let's see how each of our products would do against each of the nine competitive brands on the market (Brands A, B, C, D, E, F, G, H, and I)."

The marketer is taken aback by the researcher's voracious appetite for tests.

"That means doing eighteen paired-comparison tests," she says plaintively.

"True," the researcher replies, "but the problem is important. Many millions are at stake. This is not the time to save on testing."

So the marketer authorizes the tests proposed by the researcher—not just one or two of them, but all eighteen of them, because she wants to be sure. The tests are conducted and come back with the results shown in Table 9–1. The sweet product wins up and down the line. Not only has it won the first hurdle, the direct head-on comparison with the sour product,

Table 9–1
Results of Eighteen Hypothetical
Paired-Comparison Tests

Competitive Product	Percent Preferring Test Product over Competitive Product When Test Product Is	
	Sweet	Sour
Brand A	43%	14%
Brand B	45	12
Brand C	44	23
Brand D	50	17
Brand E	41	19
Brand F	52	20
Brand G	45	16
Brand H	44	22
Brand I	47	24

but it wins in separate tests against each of the competing brands in the market. In every instance, it does substantially better than the sour product. There can be no question about the outcome or the recommendation. Let us stipulate further that the study was conducted with meticulous care, and no errors have occurred. Every statement in the report is true—every statement, that is, except the conclusion and the recommendation.

Suppose it happens that all of the competitive brands (Brands A, B, C, D, E, F, G, H, and I) are sweet. This, incidentally, is not unlikely because each brand's marketer conducted research before launching her brand. Each did a paired-comparison test. Each discovered the unquestionable truth that more people like sweet products than sour products. And each acted on that truth in launching her brand. But this very same truth will now produce the precise opposite result in the marketplace where the full competitive frame operates, as shown in Table 9–2. There, the sour product will beat the sweet product by a wide margin. Why?

The sweet product, if launched, would simply be one more sweet product. To be sure, far more people like sweet products than sour products, but these people can and do distribute their choices among the ten sweet products, giving each approximately one-tenth of the votes, or a 10% share, give or take. The sour product, on the other hand, stands alone and lays claim to the full 20% minority that likes sour products. Consider the notorious change of the Coca-Cola formula. I have no personal knowledge of the circumstances of that change, beyond reports in

Table 9–2
Results of Two Hypothetical
Market Outcomes

	Market Shares When New Product Is	
	Sweet	*Sour*
Brand A	13	11
Brand B	12	10
Brand C	8	8
Brand D	10	9
Brand E	7	6
Brand F	11	10
Brand G	12	11
Brand H	8	7
Brand I	9	8
Test Product	10	20

the press that it was based on extensive paired-comparison tests, but I was not surprised by the outcome. Paired-comparison tests can easily produce the right answer and the wrong conclusion. Thus, my initial critique of paired-comparison tests is not that they measure things wrongly but that they measure the wrong things. This should be sufficient for the moment, without prejudice to the possibility that we may, on further evidence, conclude later that paired-comparison tests not only measure the wrong things but measure them wrongly to boot.

An Experiment

The discussion so far has focused entirely on theoretical considerations and on hypothetical data. I have shown that it is theoretically possible for reversals to occur. But is that likely? What happens when real tests are conducted with real products among real people?

In 1983, EMA conducted a methodological experiment using two proposed product formulations of a brand of cigarettes to investigate various ramifications of product testing. The experiment was designed to make it possible to extract two independent analyses from a single body of data, one equivalent to a paired-comparison test, the other equivalent to a controlled experiment in which different respondents rate different product formulations against the entire competitive frame. Respondents were over twenty-one years of age, approximately half men, half women, all regular smokers of nonmentholated cigarettes. They were recruited in central locations in thirteen cities and initially filled out a self-administered questionnaire that measured the desirability to them of fifteen characteristics of cigarettes, as well as their beliefs about these characteristics for major brands of cigarettes, including the test brand and the brands they usually smoked most. These data allowed us to construct a desirability score for each of the brands in the competitive frame, based on data obtained before the respondents were recruited into the product test.

For purposes of the product test, each respondent received three packs of the test brand in the same regular label, distinguished only by small stickers bearing the code letters OG, MI, or EW. They were instructed to smoke these three packs in the order OG, MI, EW and to fill out the appropriate section of the questionnaire, recording their perceptions of test brand OG, test brand MI, and test brand EW, respectively, after smoking each pack, using the same measurement instrument with which they had recorded their beliefs about the various characteristics of the competitive brands of cigarettes in the preliminary interview. Thus, we now had, in addition to the desirability scores obtained initially, one post-product-use desirability score from each respondent for each of three identically branded test cigarettes labeled OG, MI, and EW.

Actually only two different formulations of the test brand were tested, Formulation A and Formulation B. Each respondent received, unknown to him or her, two A's and one B or two B's and one A. The total sample consisted of 481 respondents, divided into six randomly equivalent rotation groups:

Group 1: ABB
Group 2: BAA
Group 3: ABA
Group 4: BAB
Group 5: AAB
Group 6: BBA

This represents all six permutations of two things (A, B) among three positions. Since each group yielded three desirability scores (two for one of the formulations and one for the other), the design yields a total of 6 x 3 = 18 scores, 9 scores for A and 9 scores for B. This design enables us to extract from the results one subset of scores equivalent to what we might have obtained from a conventional paired-comparison test of A versus B, as well as a second subset of scores equivalent to what we might have obtained from a controlled experiment in which all factors except the test product (A and B) had been held constant. It also allows us to draw conclusions about the role of product sequence in the test.

The first step in the analysis was to extract from the data the equivalent of a paired-comparison test of A versus B. For that purpose, we used all data that were obtained when the same respondents were rating both A and B, making proper provision for rotating the sequence. In each instance, the percent preferring A or B, respectively (that is, the percent who had given either A or B a higher desirability score), was tabulated. From a paired-comparison perspective, the design provided twelve opportunities to compare A versus B—six in which A came first and six in which B came first—resulting in six comparisons if the two orders are combined to average out order effects, as is usually done in paired-comparison tests.

Figure 9–1 shows the A-versus-B preference for each of these combinations, arranged in balanced sequence. Since we have two products (A and B) but three observations from each respondent, it is possible to extract two separate pairwise comparisons of A and B from each respon-

Figure 9–1
Cigarette Product Test
Paired-Comparison Analysis
($N = 481$)

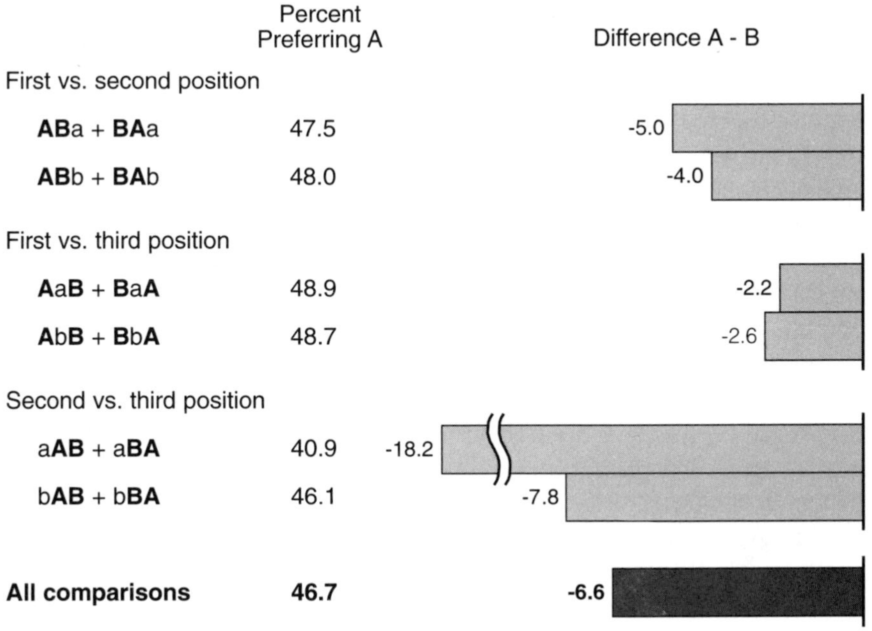

	Percent Preferring A	Difference A - B
First vs. second position		
ABa + **BA**a	47.5	-5.0
ABb + **BA**b	48.0	-4.0
First vs. third position		
Aa**B** + **B**a**A**	48.9	-2.2
Ab**B** + **B**b**A**	48.7	-2.6
Second vs. third position		
a**AB** + a**BA**	40.9	-18.2
b**AB** + b**BA**	46.1	-7.8
All comparisons	**46.7**	**-6.6**

dent. The particular scores A and B involved in the comparison are designated in capital letters. The unused score is shown in lowercase letters.
Thus, we start on line 1 with a comparison of AB and BA. In each case an
additional score "a" is left over. Don't worry, it will be used momentarily.
Line 2 provides the same comparisons, with a "b" left over. The next two
lines compare A versus B, using the previously left-over scores, again bal-
ancing the rotation, and so on until every possible pairwise comparison
has been exhausted, all balanced by position and by what was "left out"
in which place. Examining the results we find that Product A loses to
Product B by approximately 47 to 53, the difference being 6.6%, a result
that is most particularly relevant because it is replicated directionally in
six out of the six pairwise comparisons afforded by the data.

Let us now look at the same data and regroup them to construct the
equivalent of a controlled experiment in which each comparison consists of
using the score for Product A relative to the entire competitive frame and
compare it to the equivalent score for Product B, holding everything else
constant, that is, all product experience, except for the A-versus-B difference. In this case, the responses have been tabulated to count the percent
of respondents who give the test product (be it A *or* B) a higher score than
they gave to any of the other products in the competitive frame, thus yielding the percentage or share of cases in which the test product wins, or is
chosen over all other products. These are presented in Figure 9–2. Once
again the capital letters designate the scores used in the comparison and the
lowercase letters represent the scores temporarily set aside. The first three
lines represent comparisons in which respondents used and rated Product
A first in one set of groups (Abb, Aba, Aab) and Product B first in the other
set of groups (Baa, Bab, Bba). This is exactly what the test would have
looked like if the total sample had simply been divided into two randomly
equivalent groups, one of which had received only Product A and the other
only Product B. The next four lines show comparisons contrasting the
scores obtained by Products A and B when these were used *second,* holding
constant what was used first. Thus, these comparisons too hold everything
constant except that one set of groups used A in second position and the
other used B. Finally, the third set compares A in third position with B in
third position, holding constant the patterns that preceded it.

Altogether, there are seven comparisons: three in which the test product occupied first place, two in which it occupied second place, and two
in which it occupied third place. The results in this case indicate that
Product A beats Product B with a share of 12.4% for A compared to 9.4%
for B, with substantial internal consistency. Six out of the seven comparisons are in the same direction. Taken together, the data provide a dramatic illustration of an instance in which a head-on paired comparison of

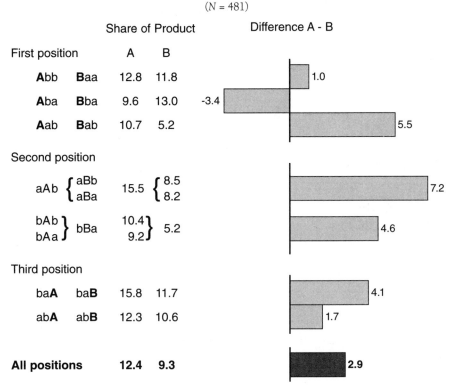

Figure 9–2
Cigarette Product Test
Share in Competitive Frame Analysis
(N = 481)

Product A versus Product B would have led to the conclusion that B is better than A, but in which A would have captured a higher share than B if each had been placed independently into the entire competitive frame. This illustration is particularly significant because it is constructed by taking the data used in the paired comparison, combining them only with additional data about competing brands, and obtaining an out-and-out reversal of the result.

The Antecedent Effect

So-called order effects are well known in paired-comparison tests and are usually corrected by rotation, that is, by requiring half of the respondents to use A before B, and half B before A. This study, however, allows us to examine the data from still another perspective. Is the score given to a product affected by what has gone before it? I will call this type of effect an *antecedent effect*. The distinction between order effect and antecedent effect is subtle but important. We are dealing with an order effect if the mere fact that the product is in second place gives it a different score from that which it would have received in first place. We may debate whether the second-place score should or should not be included in the data, but if we are really dealing only with an order bias, we can correct for it by rotation. Each product then has the same opportunity to be in first and second place, and the bias is eliminated.

An antecedent effect is an entirely different kind of animal. It implies that the score the product receives in second place measures not only what the product itself deserves, but also measures to some degree what the product that has preceded it deserves. If such an effect exists, it cannot be removed or averaged out by rotation, because we no longer know what portion of the second-place score is attributable to the second-place product and what portion is attributable to the product that has preceded it, and because we have no reason to believe that the antecedent effect will be the same for different products.

To examine the data for possible antecedent effects, we rearrange the scores once again. This time, we compare scores for Product A in second place with other scores for Product A in second place, holding everything constant except the product that preceded it. Similarly, we compare scores for Product A in third place with other scores for Product A in third place, again varying only what has preceded it. And we do the same for Product B. Once again the comparison is based on the share captured by the test product in the entire competitive frame, and once again we are designating the scores that are used in the analysis by capital letters and the ones that are temporarily set aside by lowercase letters. Figure 9–3 shows the results: a large antecedent effect, uniformly in the same direction. When we are measuring Product A, it receives a higher share when it was preceded by Product A than when it was preceded by Product B. When we are measuring Product B, it too receives a higher share when it was preceded by Product A than when it was preceded by Product B. This effect is large and uniform in all groups. Thus the data are saying that when we measure the product in second position, its score, far from being pure, is actually a partial measure of the product that was in first position. If the study had been confined to a two-product paired-comparison test, we would not have known this and would not have been able to sort it out. We would have mistakenly believed that our second score for Product B was attributable to the desirability of Product B, when it was in fact in considerable degree attributable to the desirability of Product A which had preceded it. All of this is summarized in the following principle.

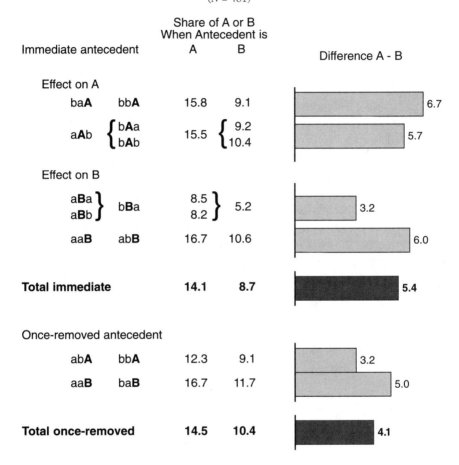

Figure 9–3
Cigarette Product Test
Antecedent Effect
(N = 481)

THE ANTECEDENT EFFECT PRINCIPLE

When two products are measured in succession, the measurement of the second product contains a component that is an additional measurement of the first product, an effect that cannot be removed by rotation.

Obviously many variations of paired-comparison tests are possible, some of which may at least partially cure the problems I have discussed. Most prominent among these is a design I employed in the 1960s in which respondents were prescreened for current product use, were given pairs of products always consisting of their current product and the test product, and were finally recombined analytically to compute the deserved share of the test product. This design is cumbersome, is predicated on our ability to predesignate different respondents as unique users of the various competitive brands (often difficult to do because respondents use more than one brand), and requires some constricting assumptions for the computation of the deserved shares. But even assuming that we could construct a viable rescue, the more fundamental question is: Why try in the first place?

Other things being equal, we should prefer real-life exposure to artificial exposure. This consideration alone should tilt the scale in favor of controlled experiment tests, but in conjunction with the risk of antecedent effects, it should probably be sufficient to eliminate paired-comparison tests altogether.

There is hardly a contest between tests that employ an absolute criterion and tests that employ a share criterion. The extensive discussion in Chapter 3, and the contrast between the kind of questions that obey the congruence principle and those that do not, should eliminate absolute designs. This leaves the lower right-hand corner of the grid, deserved share, as the tentative optimum design. But I suspend judgment for the moment about whether a pseudo-share test, a test that uses artificial exposure with a share measurement, might perhaps yield equally acceptable data. I also suspend judgment about whether such a test, or any other test, should be blind or identified.

CHAPTER 10

Deserved Share

One way or another, the difficulties with paired-comparison tests stem from the fact that they are usually inconsistent with the First Law (The Law of Congruence). But if we keep the First Law firmly in mind and follow it to its logical conclusion, the proper product testing method practically forces itself on us.

What should we expect from a product test? Setting aside the demand for diagnostics, which will be dealt with in Chapter 15, a product test should tell us how well a product will perform in the market, and whether it will capture a larger or smaller share than the current product. This is the same problem STEP has dealt with all along, except that in this case the strategy element is product experience. We need only give the respondents a product, allow them to use it, and observe the resulting STEP share. The design is called Product-STEP.

Product-STEP

Product-STEP is a real-life test. The respondents receive a free sample of the test product. The product is in full commercial regalia, packaged as one would expect to find it on the shelf, and appears to come directly from the manufacturer, ostensibly as part of a conventional sampling program. The recipient has no reason to treat the product with special consideration. She uses it as she judges appropriate, gives it to the children or feeds it to the dog, as though she had obtained it through sampling or by buying it in a store. After a few weeks, she receives a STEP booklet. The booklet contains pages for most, if not all, of the brands in the category, the test brand among them. Her choices in the booklet now reflect her experience with the test product. The resulting STEP share is a measure of that experience.

The question arises whether we are creating asymmetry. The STEP booklet ordinarily contains one page for every brand. Does it not follow, by analogy, that we should give the respondent every product in the category? This is obviously not feasible in practice. But suppose the practical problems could be overcome, would we give the respondent all the products in the category or only the test brand?

There is an overriding reason for giving the respondent only the test brand, even if it were mechanically feasible to give her all. Once again, the reason has to do with the principle of congruence. We are attempting to assess the potential consequences of some change, either a change in an existing brand or the introduction of a new brand. If we assume that the competitive environment the test brand will eventually face is best characterized by the current steady state, we don't want to give the respondent new information about competitive brands or subject her to special messages for those brands. She is continuously bombarded by such messages anyhow. Whatever the competitive brands can reasonably be expected to do, they have presumably done already. We are not trying to find out what would happen if every brand in the category embarked on a massive marketing program, but what would happen if every brand continued on its merry way and our brand, and ours alone, made some changes. And though we might not be able to afford a marketing effort as intensive as that measured in Product-STEP, it is one that could, in principle, be implemented. And it is precisely that potential that Product-STEP is designed to assess quantitatively.

Uncoupling

Since Product-STEP requires that respondents receive a free sample followed by a STEP booklet, the question arises whether the amount of time between the sample and the booklet matters. Time serves a dual role in this case. It provides an opportunity for the respondents to accumulate product experience, and it keeps the product experience real-life. If STEP share depended materially on the time interval, time would have to be dealt with routinely in every test. Conversely, if STEP share is relatively stable over time, it will be sufficient to select a reasonable time interval, taking into account the purchase cycle of the product category.

To throw light on this question, EMA conducted a methodological experiment in July 1973, using a national sample of telephone-listed households in one hundred market areas. The study used a recently introduced brand. Four randomly equivalent groups, of at least 500 respondents each, received a sample of the test product, followed by a STEP booklet containing eight to ten competing brands. All groups received identical booklets, except that the four test groups received the booklets two weeks, three weeks, four weeks, and five weeks, respectively, after the product. The results, shown in Figure 10–1, indicate that STEP share was

Figure 10–1
Product-STEP Share versus Elapsed Time
Weeks 2–5
(*N* = 1,920)

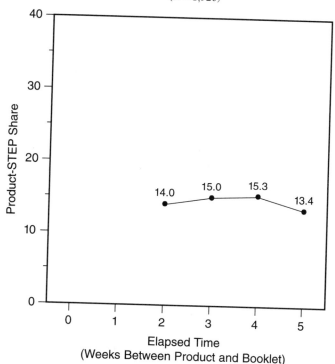

essentially flat over the two- to five-week period of the test, varying within 1 share point around an average share of 14.4, with a possible small fall-off in Week 5. Thus it appears that the time interval does not matter. But could we have gone all the way and eliminated it altogether?

Product-STEP achieves its real-life status by uncoupling the product experience from the test instrument. Sending the STEP booklet along with the product would have turned Product-STEP into an artificial-exposure test. Other things being equal, we prefer real-life tests over artificial-exposure tests. But other things are not equal. The real-life test is less efficient in that it requires two separate contacts with the respondent: the product delivery and the subsequent delivery of the questionnaire. So we pay a price for the uncoupling of product experience from the questionnaire, which raises the question whether the uncoupling is worth the price. Could we have obtained substantially the same result by abandoning the uncoupling and converting Product-STEP into an artificial exposure test?

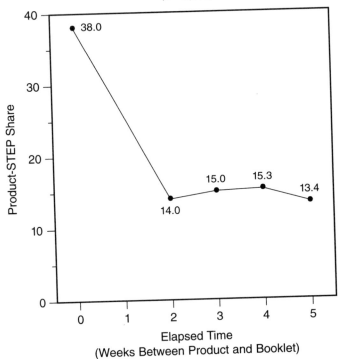

Figure 10–2
Product-STEP Share versus Elapsed Time
Weeks 0–5
($N = 2,341$)

Product-STEP Share

Elapsed Time
(Weeks Between Product and Booklet)

To investigate this question, a fifth group of approximately 500 respondents was included in the experiment. This group received the same product sample and STEP booklet as the other groups, but received both together in the same mailing, accompanied by a request to use the product and then return the booklet. As shown in Figure 10–2, the STEP share in this group was more than double the approximately flat level in the other four groups, clear evidence of a test effect. Once you tell people that they are participating in a test, they simply don't respond the same way anymore, either in how they use the product or in how they perceive its characteristics. Thus, we can draw a definitive conclusion: Yes, the uncoupling is necessary. Whether it is also sufficient, or, putting it more precisely, whether the particular procedure we employ accomplishes sufficient uncoupling to eliminate all or most test effects, is another matter. The results of this study do not answer this question definitively. They do, however, shed some light on it.

If a test effect exists, the observed STEP share would be made up of two components: the respondents' true choice (the STEP share we would have observed if there had been no coupling between the product experience and the measurement) and the test effect (the incremental share attributable solely to the fact that at least some of the respondents realized that there was a connection between the sample and the STEP booklet and gave the test brand more stickers than they would have given it otherwise). We would then expect to obtain a curve similar to the hypothetical one in Figure 10–3, in which both the true effect and the test effect decline after product experience, and the total effect approaches the true effect asymptotically.

Examining the results of the experiment against this model, we are led to hypothesize that either the test effect exists only in the artificial exposure cell and there is no test effect in the other cells because the uncoupling has eliminated it—our original hypothesis—or that by the time two to five weeks have passed, the test effect has decayed sufficiently to bring the STEP share very close to the limiting true effect—our fallback hypothesis. In either case, we would conclude that the experiment demonstrates that the uncoupling is necessary and lends at least indirect support to the hypothesis that it is also sufficient, or at any rate sufficient within reasonable bounds.

Figure 10–3
Hypothetical Relationship Between
True Effect and Test Effect

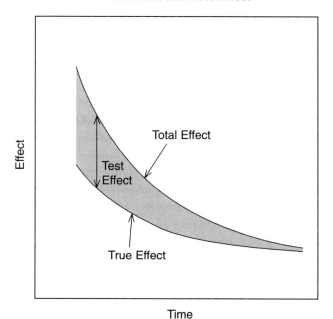

A proponent of paired-comparison tests might protest indignantly: "It should hardly surprise you that giving people a single product generates test effects. We have known this all along. It is called reward. That is why we do paired-comparison tests. By asking respondents to compare two products, blind ones at that, we make it impossible for them to reward the test product." This is true, but it misses the point. Giving the respondent two products does prevent reward, which is indeed a benefit, perhaps the only benefit, of paired comparisons. But to achieve this benefit, the paired-comparisons advocate pays the intolerable price of using an artificial test, using a competitive frame that violates the principle of congruence, and surrendering to the deadly antecedent effect, which blurs the distinction between that portion of the measurement attributable to the test product and that attributable to the other product of the pair.

By contrast, our desire to eliminate or reduce test effects in Product-STEP amounts to fine-tuning. Even if it were necessary to tolerate some residual test effects, these would have relatively little impact on the comparison of groups, beyond adding some increments to the absolute levels of the observed shares. Finally, we can draw on the results of other experiments that were not designed to deal with uncoupling or with Product-STEP but which, as it happens, throw important light on the question of uncoupling and indeed on the most fundamental assumptions underlying the use and interpretation of Product-STEP results. These are presented in Chapter 26 under the heading of "Decay and Persistence" and generally support the conclusions drawn here.

The Case for Blind versus Identified Tests

Once the decision has been made that a product test is in order, the question arises whether the test is to be blind or identified. In the real-life Product-STEP environment, blind testing implies use of a decoy label. But identified labels and decoy labels are interchangeable for new products, which have not been advertised yet. Their labels are still unknown and unencumbered, or unsupported as the case may be, by extrinsic image elements. Tests of new products are therefore governed by mechanical rather than by conceptual considerations. If the new product has not been named yet, if the ultimate package graphics are not available yet, the preliminary tests can be conducted with a decoy label, to be followed by identified tests later.

For established brands, the considerations are quite different and far from trivial. Two arguments are advanced in favor of blind testing, one having to do with measurement issues, the other with the way the marketer poses the question and her insistence that this question be answered literally. Both of these, as it turns out, revolve around sensitivity. Give the respondent a blind, unidentified product, it is argued, and she will approach it with an open mind. She will allow the characteristics of the product to shape her perceptions and to influence her reactions, undistorted by prior experience and expectations. The result will be a sensitive measure of the product and the product alone. If the respondent receives the product in branded form, the product experience will be only a small additional element in a sea of prior experience. She will not pay sufficient attention to the product, resulting in a loss of sensitivity. And even if she does pay attention to the product, the one experience will not be sufficient to override long-established judgments about the brand, and her subsequent choices in the STEP booklet will reflect primarily prior expectations, and only marginally her experience with the test product, again resulting in a loss of sensitivity.

For the researcher, the issue of sensitivity is a perpetual source of anxiety and defensiveness. Let him report that two products are different, and he is a hero. His method "works." He has produced a difference. Before the test, we did not know which was better, A or B. Now we know. But let him report that he did not find a difference, and eyebrows will be raised. If the marketer had not expected a difference, she probably would never have authorized the test to begin with, so this finding conflicts with her expectation at the least. In most instances, it is also frustrating in its own right, because we still don't know what to do. This gives rise to a fundamental conceptual problem. One can prove that a difference exists. If the difference is large enough, one can prove it categorically. But one cannot prove that a difference does *not* exist. One can only demonstrate one's inability to find one, which often gives rise to the comment, "Your measurement device has been too crude to pick up the difference. And that is precisely why I did not want to do the test in the first place. I suspected all along that you would generate nothing but random numbers."

For all these reasons, the researcher will go to great lengths in pursuit of "sensitivity," often sacrificing relevance and even common sense for its sake. I do not separate myself from my colleagues in this respect. I too have pursued sensitivity, eager to find differences. But I am aware of the critical need to strike a proper balance between the researcher's vested interest in finding and reporting differences and his ultimate obligation to find and report only differences that make a difference. Thus there is a substantial bias on the part of the researcher in favor of blind testing.

The marketer is motivated by analogous considerations. Measurement instruments are usually irrelevant to her, but she is perpetually pursuing the next product improvement that will turn the brand's downward slide around, pump new life into a flat brand, or skyrocket a growing brand, allowing her to reap benefits of fame and fortune. She believes that advertising, image, and positioning are her domain. "Don't worry about those," she tells the researcher. "Just tell me how the product itself is doing, and I will take care of the rest." So she too feels more comfortable with a blind test, which is supposed to measure the contribution of the product in its most pristine form, all image aside.

Against this lies the case for identified testing. Except when dealing with a new product, the established brand has an image that is not to be taken lightly or trifled with, not merely because of the associations that have been built up around it but, more important, because, having been around for some time, it has developed loyal buyers, self-selected for a host of different reasons, which, consciously or unconsciously, has culminated in high brand familiarity. This familiarity may be the most valuable aspect of the brand's strength. It is sometimes known as "goodwill," sometimes as the brand's "franchise," and constitutes a capital asset that must be nurtured and protected. It follows that if a product test is to be done for an established brand, we need to know not whether Variant A is better than Variant B in the abstract, but what impact each would have on the share of the brand for which it is intended. We therefore face a tradeoff between the blind test, which promises greater sensitivity, and the identified test, which promises greater relevance.

Two Experiments

How do the two methods, blind and identified, compare in practice? To make that comparison in a clean way requires experiments in which the same product variants are tested both blind and identified. Such experiments are rare. For the most part, the clients who pay for the research opt for one or another testing mode and are reluctant to support both. I do, however, have two cases in which two product variants were tested both blind and identified. One contrasted two product variants of a paper product, the other two product variants of a dessert.

The paper product study was conducted in September 1973, using a national sample of telephone-listed households in one hundred market areas. The total sample consisted of approximately 1,800 interviews, divided into four randomly equivalent groups of approximately 450. Groups 1 and 2 received the test product fully identified but labeled "new improved"; Group 1 received product Variant A; Group 2 received product Variant B. Groups 3 and 4 received Variants A and B, respectively, in a decoy label. Two weeks later, STEP booklets were mailed to all respondents. Each booklet contained one test page (either for the identified brand or for the decoy brand) and one page for each competitive brand. Figure 10–4 shows the results.

Figure 10–4
Blind and Identified Product-STEP Share
for Two Variants of a Paper Product
(N = 1,783)

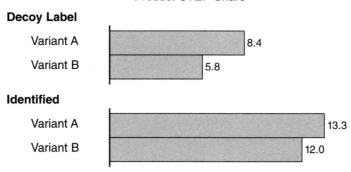

Product-STEP Share

Decoy Label

Variant A — 8.4
Variant B — 5.8

Identified

Variant A — 13.3
Variant B — 12.0

The experiment is inconclusive but contains nothing that should disturb the proponents of either blind or identified testing. Both comparisons yield the conclusion that Variant A has greater potential than Variant B. The proponents of blind testing may find some satisfaction in the fact that the blind difference is larger. The proponents of identified testing may reply that the differences were small in any case and within the bounds of reasonable chance fluctuation. Call it a draw, or almost a draw, and leave both in the running. A by-product of the experiment is the observation that otherwise identical products captured much larger shares identified than blind, an important point that will be developed later in this chapter.

The dessert experiment was a larger, more comprehensive study, designed to assess the role of two product variants, the "current" product and a "reformulated" product, and two themes (I and II) for positioning the brand. Each of these was tested both blind and identified. The blind portion of the test was further split into groups employing two different decoy labels (A and B). This resulted in a study of twelve groups (about 200 respondents per group). The STEP booklets were mailed approximately three weeks after delivery of the product samples and were completed during the middle of July 1979.

In order to focus on the practical implications of the data, we begin by asking, "Suppose we had conducted the entire test solely as a product-theme test using Decoy A, what conclusions would we have drawn?" The results for the Decoy A groups are shown in the top section of Table 10–1. On the basis of these data, we would have concluded that the current

Table 10–1
Decoy Product-STEP Share for a Dessert Product

| | Product Variant | | |
	Current	Reformul.	Average
Decoy A			
Theme I	9.7	10.7	10.2
Theme II	16.5	12.8	14.7
Average	**13.1**	**11.7**	**12.4**
Decoy B			
Theme I	13.4	9.6	11.5
Theme II	11.7	12.4	12.1
Average	**12.6**	**11.0**	**11.8**
Both decoys combined			
Theme I	11.6	10.2	10.8
Theme II	14.1	12.6	13.3
Average	**12.9**	**11.4**	**12.1**

product has a potential 1.4 share points higher than the reformulated product (13.1 - 11.7). That is not a very large difference and is attributable entirely to the fact that the current product outperformed the reformulated product by a wide margin (3.7 share points) among the respondents who were exposed to Theme II. But the sample size in each cell was only a little over 200, and we had determined in advance to read the data "marginally," meaning that we would look at product differences for the average of both themes and at theme differences for the average of both products. Accordingly, we would have concluded that the current product had somewhat higher potential than the reformulated product and that Theme II had substantially higher potential than Theme I (the difference was 4.5 share points).

For practical purposes, we would have sidestepped the question whether there really was an interaction between theme and product, because the conclusion, based on the marginals, that the current product outperformed the reformulated product and that Theme II outperformed Theme I, would have been confirmed in that the individual cell with the current product and Theme II also obtained the largest STEP share of the four cells. Thus, looking for the winning product-theme combination, either in terms of the marginals or in terms of the individual cells, would have yielded the same conclusion: the winning combination was the current product plus Theme II. (We are examining these data in this way solely for methodological purposes. At the time the study was done, the operational decision criterion for marketing purposes was defined in advance; it specified that the results of the identified test would govern, and that the decoy groups would be used only for methodological learning and possibly to break ties in the identified test.)

The cells using Decoy B provide an independent replication of the Decoy A test, the only difference being that a different decoy label was employed. This refinement was introduced into the design to explore, at least in a limited way, whether the particular decoy label used is likely to make much difference in a decoy test. The middle section of Table 10–1 shows the results for the Decoy B cells. The first thing to notice is that the aggregate shares in the cells using Decoy A and in the cells using Decoy B are similar, 12.4 and 11.8, respectively. Thus, the change from Decoy A to Decoy B did not have any substantial impact on the level of the shares earned by the test product.

Analyzing the Decoy B experiment independently, we would have concluded from the marginals that the current product has a potential 1.6 share points larger than the reformulated product and that Theme II outperforms Theme I by a negligible amount (.6 share points). On balance, we would have been well pleased with the outcome of the replication. To be sure, Theme II had won by a wide margin in the first test and by only a trifling amount in the second test, but the results were directionally the same and the product results were almost identical—1.4 share points and 1.6 share points, respectively—in favor of the current product.

Putting the two replications together, as shown in the bottom section of Table 10–1, yields the best estimate of the results of the test. The conclusions are unequivocal. All the comparisons are consistent. The current product beats the reformulated product by 1.4 share points with Theme I and by 1.5 share points with Theme II, in two independent comparisons, yielding an average difference of 1.5 share points. Concurrently, Theme II beats Theme I by 2.5 share points when used with the current product; it beats Theme I by 2.4 share points when used with the reformulated product. These comparisons too are independent, resulting in an average difference of 2.5 share points. No matter how the data are examined, all elements in the table yield the same result. We have the marginal conclusions, based on results from two groups of 800 respondents each. And if we insist on examining individual cells, limiting ourselves to a comparison of four cells of 400 respondents each, we obtain precisely the same result. The current product with Theme II is the winner; the reformulated product with Theme I is the loser. The other two combinations occupy commensurate intermediate positions. The outcome is about as convincing as we could reasonably have hoped for. The decoy test is sensitive and internally consistent, and it gives us a clear mandate for action.

Table 10–2
Identified Product-STEP Share for a Dessert Product

	Product Variant		
	Current	*Reformul.*	**Average**
Theme I	21.1	26.0	23.6
Theme II	18.2	21.2	19.7
Average	**19.6**	**23.6**	**21.6**

Let us now turn to the results obtained in the remaining four cells, in which the same two product variants and the same two themes were tested in identified form. The results are shown in Table 10–2. The first thing to note is that, just as in the paper product case, the identified STEP shares are substantially higher than the decoy shares—in this case, almost twice as high. In order not to be sidetracked from the main issue, we shall simply accept this fact for the moment and defer the discussion of its significance to later in this chapter. Going on, we note that the principal concern about identified tests, namely that they might not be sensitive, is allayed. All differences in the identified test are larger, indeed substantially larger, than the corresponding differences in the decoy test. They are equally coherent, unequivocal, internally consistent, and statistically significant, except for one small matter: They yield diametrically opposite conclusions, as illustrated in Figure 10–5.

Tested identified, in conjunction with Theme I, the reformulated product beats the current product by 4.9 share points. In conjunction with Theme II, it beats the current product by 3.0 share points. These are independent comparisons. Averaging them, we obtain the result that the reformulated product beats the current product by 4 share points. Examining the same data in the other direction, we see that Theme I beats Theme II by 2.9 share points with the current product and by 4.8 share points with the reformulated product. These are also two independent comparisons, resulting in an average difference of 3.9 share points in favor of Theme I. Thus the reformulated product with Theme I, the loser in the decoy test, wins. The current product with Theme II, the winner in the decoy test, loses. The other two combinations occupy intermediate positions. Taken as a whole, the results for the decoy and identified cells are about as perfectly reversed as possible. Winners become losers, losers become winners, and in a coherent and internally consistent fashion at that.

The implications of this experiment are far-reaching. If the results had been consistent, as in the paper product experiment, they would have

Figure 10–5
Blind and Identified Product-STEP Share
for Two Variants and Two Themes for a Dessert
(N = 2,709)

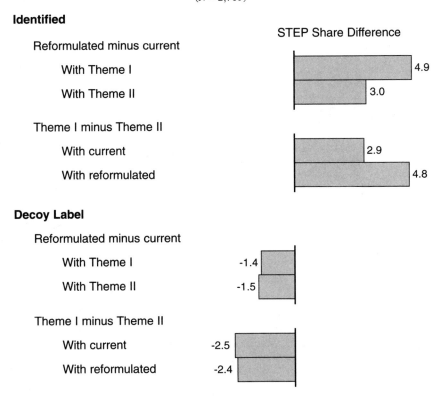

proved little. Even if we had seen three, five, or ten cases in which the decoy and the identified tests had yielded identical conclusions, we would not have been able to lay to rest the concerns of a skeptic who might have argued that an inconsistent case was right around the corner. A definitive reversal, on the other hand, raises fundamental issues that bear not only on the design of Product-STEP tests, but on product testing generally.

Let us therefore ask the more fundamental question: Which of these results is right? The answer, of course, is that both are right. Once again we have encountered the First Law. Each of the tests gives a true answer to a specific question. But it is important to understand the question and not to assume that it is what it is not. The results of the dessert experiment underscore the point that a brand is a synthesis of product and image. The product is here and now, but the image has a long history. Over time, the image has attracted customers with specific desires, beliefs, and expectations, and these customers will not, in general, respond in the same way as some new subset of the population that might be attracted by a hitherto unknown decoy brand. This means that if we are planning to sell an established brand, we had better test it in its proper clothes, properly identified by its real name. For this reason, almost all of the product-variant tests in the STEP Database were tested in fully identified form. Blind tests, conducted for other purposes, are discussed in a later section of this chapter.

Product Differences

How big is big? What order of magnitude of effect is likely to be produced by a change in a physical product? The STEP Database contains 82 Product-STEP studies, utilizing 2.6 groups per study on the average, with an average sample size of 429 per group and an aggregate total of 216 groups and 92,652 respondents. These studies afford 138 independent comparisons between products, generated the same way as the concept differences. All the reservations and qualifications made in connection with those tests apply equally to the product tests. The tests do not constitute a representative sample of product variants, only an aggregation of those variants EMA was asked to test. A further limitation is that the Product-STEP tests involved giving a product to the respondents, ostensibly as part of a routine sampling program, and as such are confined to consumables.

Figure 10–6 shows the observed distribution of differences, as well as the distribution that would have been expected by chance in the null case, that is, if there had been no real differences among the product variants. The observed average difference is 1.84; the null average difference is 1.32. Accordingly, the net difference is 1.84 - 1.32 = .52, or 3.46 standard errors, an effect that would have been expected by chance with a probability of less than 1 in 1,000. Once again, however, the average obscures much. Although many product pairs showed only small differences, a small but important number produced large and, in some instances, very large differences. One in thirteen differences was larger than 5 share points.

Minimally, this result must make us sit up and take notice. Apparently it is possible to produce a product variant that will make a big difference. But it is difficult and it doesn't happen often. We are not talking about the development of new products, only about efforts to change existing brands. But major R&D budgets are allocated to efforts to do just that. This raises some fundamental questions. How important are product differences anyhow? What portion of the total acceptance of a brand is attributable to product and what portion to image? Which brings us to

Figure 10–6
Percent Distribution of Product-STEP Share Differences
for 138 Product Variants
$(N = 92,652, \bar{x} = 1.84, SE = .15, \text{normal} = 1.32, \text{net} = .52)$

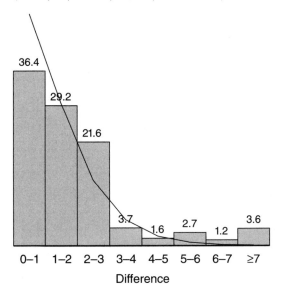

Difference

the principal use of decoy testing: the assessment of the relative role of product and image.

What's in a Name

Although the dessert experiment raises serious concerns about the propriety of blind product tests, there is one assignment blind tests are uniquely equipped to tackle, which cannot be addressed in any other way: namely, to measure the relative contributions of product and image. This is done by conducting concurrent blind and identified Product-STEPs. If respondents react solely to the product itself, the STEP shares in the two groups should be identical. The rose by any other name should smell as sweet. Conversely, as familiarity and the symbols that have come to be associated with the product become increasingly important, there should be a commensurate difference between the identified and the decoy shares. And we can use this difference to estimate the relative contributions of product and image.

The fully identified cell yields the total effect of the product plus its image. The decoy cell yields the effect of the product plus the decoy label's image. The decoy label's image can be measured directly by means of a control group that receives a STEP booklet containing a page for the

decoy brand. If such a control group is not available, we can estimate the
image of the decoy label conservatively as 2 share points. Given this
adjustment, we can quantify the relative contributions of product and
image. In particular, if the brand's identified share is S and its blind or
decoy share is D, and the image contribution of the decoy label is i, then
the contribution of the brand's product to its share is $D-i$, and the relative
percent contribution (I) of the brand's image to its share is

$$I = 100\% \; \frac{S - (D - i)}{S}$$

Reexamining the data for the paper product and dessert studies from
this perspective, we can consolidate all groups and compare only the
Product-STEP shares in the decoy cells with the Product-STEP shares in
the identified cells, holding the other variables constant. This comparison
is shown in Figure 10–7. In each case, the identified share is substantially
larger than the decoy share. Crediting an estimated 2 share points to the
image of the decoy label, the relative image contribution of the paper
product brand is 100% x (12.7 - 7.1 + 2) / 12.7 = 60%, and the relative
image contribution of the dessert brand is 53%.

Figure 10–7
Product-STEP Share for Two Products
Concurrently Tested Both Blind and Identified
($N = 4{,}492$)

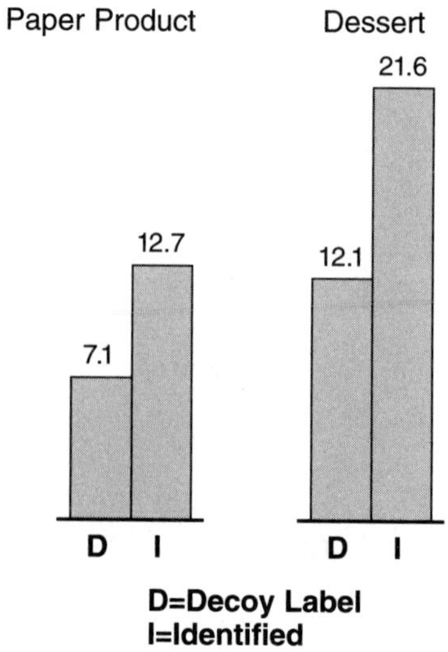

Paper Product   Dessert

D=Decoy Label
I=Identified

Is this a general pattern? Is the relative image contribution of all brands approximately 50 to 60%? This seems hardly likely, especially since we would expect the product contribution of newer brands to be higher than that of older brands. Fortunately, we can throw some empirical light on this question. Whereas we have only two studies in which different product variants of the same brand were compared concurrently in both identified and blind form, we have a larger number of cases, going back over many years, in which a single variant of a brand was concurrently measured both blind and identified. Before turning to a general summary of these cases, let us look at one particularly dramatic set of data from a study in which three different brands in the same product category (Brands A, B, and C) were measured concurrently both blind and identified.

The study was conducted in January 1986 in the central United States. The data are shown in Figure 10–8. In a decoy label, Brand A is the strongest of the three brands, capturing a share of 10.3 compared to shares of 7.4 and 3.4 for Brands B and C, respectively. These results are presumably based principally on the actual product. Once the products have been identified, the story changes. Brand A, the brand with the strongest product, has the lowest potential share, 15.9, compared to 23.8 and 19.9 for Brands B and C, respectively. This is particularly significant when we remember that the identified shares themselves are deserved shares rather than actuals. All of the respondents received a sample of the

Figure 10–8
Product-STEP Share for Three Brands
Concurrently Tested Both Blind and Identified
(N = 2,499)

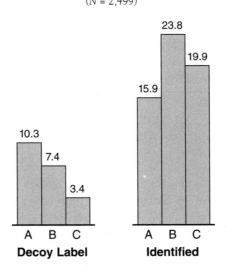

product. All had an opportunity to examine and use the product afresh. The intervention certainly raised shares substantially. Nevertheless, the image continued to play a dominant role in how the respondents reacted, either because their expectations governed what they perceived or because the identified label appealed selectively to respondents who were willing to approach the brand in a positive frame of mind. The relative contributions of product and image, moreover, were brand-specific. Calculating the relative image contributions, we obtain for Brand A (15.9 - (10.3 - 2)) / 15.9 = 48%, for Brand B 77%, and for Brand C 93%.

We now turn to a broader summary of studies in which the same brand was concurrently tested both blind and identified. Because the number of these studies is relatively small, I have gone back as far as possible. This search has yielded twenty-three studies, covering fourteen different brands. To the best of my knowledge, these represent a census of all studies of this type, mainly devoted to paper and food products. They are summarized in Figure 10–9, arranged in order of relative image contribution. For each brand, the first column shows the Product-STEP share for the product in a decoy label. The second column shows the Product-STEP share for the identical product when the brand was fully identified. Considering the first line, the brand's Product-STEP share was 3.4 in the decoy label and 19.9 identified (Product B of the prior example). Subtracting 2 share points leaves a product contribution of 3.4 - 2 = 1.4. Accordingly, the image contribution is (19.9 - 1.4) / 19.9 = 93%, represented by the horizontal bar. Scanning the figure, we see that the image contributions of different brands vary widely, from a high of 93% to a low of 35%.

It may seem surprising that the image contributions are so large. Do the data really say that the product itself is relatively unimportant? I don't believe so. I believe the product is more important than it appears to be. But the interpretation requires a bit more subtlety. The key lies in the role of familiarity. When a brand is introduced, it is in the same position as the decoy brand; the image has not developed yet. This is a critical time for the success or failure of the brand. If the product experience is favorable, the brand may attract a following. Its potential may be enhanced by advertising and other support, but must start from the product. As time passes and the image becomes more solidly established, the brand acquires a life of its own, governed by inertia, not unmovable, but strongly resistant to change. And it is this persistence of earlier responses to the product that results in the large image contributions we observe.

Like the early years in the life of a person, the early years of a brand are crucial. That is when the foundations for the future are laid. If the brand can develop a reputation, based on solid product performance, supported by name and label, it will acquire a following which can

Figure 10–9
Image Contributions of Fourteen Different Brands
(N = 17,399)

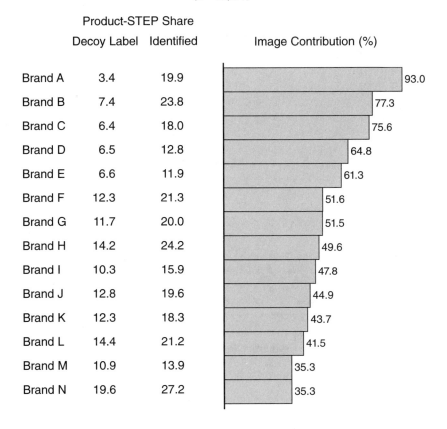

Product-STEP Share

	Decoy Label	Identified	Image Contribution (%)
Brand A	3.4	19.9	93.0
Brand B	7.4	23.8	77.3
Brand C	6.4	18.0	75.6
Brand D	6.5	12.8	64.8
Brand E	6.6	11.9	61.3
Brand F	12.3	21.3	51.6
Brand G	11.7	20.0	51.5
Brand H	14.2	24.2	49.6
Brand I	10.3	15.9	47.8
Brand J	12.8	19.6	44.9
Brand K	12.3	18.3	43.7
Brand L	14.4	21.2	41.5
Brand M	10.9	13.9	35.3
Brand N	19.6	27.2	35.3

become the basis of a long-term business. All of this is summarized in the following principle.

THE IMAGE PRINCIPLE
A brand's future is built on its past. It is easier to give a brand the right image in the first place than to change a wrong image once it has taken hold.

If this is so, the role of product should be particularly relevant in the case of new products, and I believe that it is. Figure 10–10 shows twenty-one new products in five product categories that were tested in Product-STEP between 1979 and 1989. They received Product-STEP shares ranging from 6 to 30. All of these products were subsequently introduced into test

Figure 10–10
Test Market Share versus Prior Product-STEP Share for
Twenty-one New Products in Five Product Categories
$(N = 9{,}271, M = .026S^2, r = .93)$

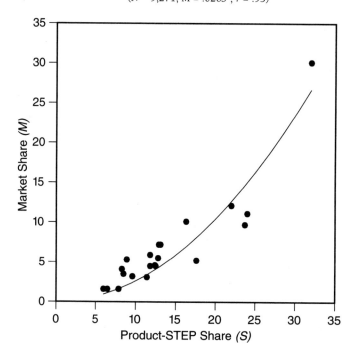

markets. The chart shows the plot of Product-STEP share versus test-market share of these products at the end of one year. The market shares were furnished by the client. With one exception, the products achieved market shares of approximately half their Product-STEP potentials, the differences being attributable, I believe, to the way the products were supported and promoted. One of the products achieved its full potential, perhaps because it received massive support. Overall, the Product-STEP versus market share correlation is .93.

CHAPTER 11

What STEP Measures

We have talked about the application of STEP to price testing, concept testing, and product testing. But just what does STEP actually measure? My answer to this question has evolved over the years. Here is its current version, expressed in a hypothetical conversation with a marketing client, the composite of many such.

The client asks, "Suppose you insert a page describing my product in your STEP booklet. Will that give me the market share of my product?"

"Not necessarily. In fact, not even likely."

"It won't? Why not?"

"To say that the STEP share alone will forecast your market share amounts to telling you that the information you are putting in the strategy portion of the STEP booklet is all that matters. Clearly this cannot be the case. Surely the physical product will influence the success or failure of your brand. The marketing support you put behind it—the distribution, promotion, and advertising—will make a difference."

"Then what will the STEP share give me?"

"It will tell you the share deserved by this piece of paper," and I point at the strategy portion of the STEP booklet. My marketing friend shows signs of exasperation.

"But what good is that? I am not going to sell pieces of paper. I am going to sell my product, a real product, to real people for real money. Don't you see?"

"Of course I see. But I was not the one who advised you to test your product in this preliminary form. You came to me. You showed me your concept statement and you asked: 'Can you test this?' My answer was, 'Yes, I can test it.' But I can test only what you give me. Give me a piece of paper, and I'll tell you the share deserved by the piece of paper. Give me a product, and I'll tell you the share deserved by the product. Though determining the share deserved by the piece of paper may not be as silly as it sounds. It may be of considerable value to you to know ahead of time that this particular paper deserves a larger or smaller share than some other piece of paper you could have given me instead."

"But that is not what I want to know," my marketing friend insists. "I am going to market a real product, and I would like to estimate the share it will get in the market."

"All right. In that case, we will send a free sample of your product to a group of respondents, not as part of a testing program but as part of a sampling operation. A few weeks later, we will send them a STEP booklet. The respondents won't know they are participating in a test. They will use the product, eat it, feed it to the children, or throw it out. When the STEP booklet arrives, their responses in the booklet will be shaped not only by what is on the relevant product page but also by their prior experience with the product—good, bad, or indifferent—and by the impressions, distinct or otherwise, that experience left behind. This is not materially different from what happens in the marketplace. A customer is exposed to a product by buying it, by seeing it in a friend's house, by seeing an ad, or in some other way. This exposure leaves an impression, and this impression governs her choice the next time she sees the product in the store. After product experience, the STEP booklet measures not only what is on a piece of paper but also the sum of all the impressions produced by exposure to the product. You can see that this is a direct extension of STEP. For obvious reasons, we call it Product-STEP."

"So this Product-STEP will give me the share I will achieve in the marketplace?"

"Oh no. Not necessarily."

"Not necessarily? What now? All you offer is excuses and alibis, one after another. Won't you ever put yourself on the line and say yes or no and make a simple prediction so I know where I stand?"

"I will make a prediction, all right, but it is important that you understand just what I am predicting and what I am not predicting. If we conduct the Product-STEP test I described, we will find out what share your product deserves, assuming that you market it in such a way that a hundred percent of the customers in the market get approximately the same exposure to your product as the exposure we created when we sent them the sample."

"But that is not practical."

"I am aware of that. It may not be practical, but this does not matter. In principle, at least, you could sample the whole country, or some section of the country, or some selected markets or submarkets, but that is not the point. Product-STEP is not designed to measure the effectiveness of sampling as a marketing device, nor do I necessarily recommend that you use sampling at all. The sample in Product-STEP is used solely for the purpose of generating a state of mind that will sooner or later have to exist among some customers in the marketplace if your product is to be viable. Sooner or later some customers will have to come away from experiencing your product with sufficiently favorable impressions to want to choose it again—in the STEP booklet for openers.

"In practice, you may conclude that sampling is inefficient, impractical, and will not pay out for you. But one way or another you will have to bring about conditions similar to those we created in the test. And Product-STEP tells you what share of market that will get you.

"To be sure, you also need to make some judgments about the level of product exposure your marketing plan will achieve. A Product-STEP share of thirty percent, for example, means that if you launched your product with a saturation marketing effort, you would achieve a market share of around thirty percent, give or take a few points. But if you expect to run an introductory campaign that will expose no more than twenty percent of the population to your product, your probable market share will be more nearly twenty percent of thirty percent, or six percent. The data I give you therefore have a very precise meaning. They are the *potential* of your product against the defined benchmark of total exposure. And they insistently remind you that there is no free lunch. Go light on the marketing plan, produce less than total exposure in the marketplace, and you will achieve commensurately lower market shares."

I can now answer the question, "What does STEP measure?" with greater precision. STEP measures the deserved share of an offer.

THE DESERVED SHARE PRINCIPLE
Measuring the deserved share of an offer amounts to measuring
the value of a collection of information elements.

From this general perspective, it does not matter how the information is delivered. It may be delivered on the page of a STEP booklet. It may be delivered in a print ad or a TV commercial shown to the respondents before they receive the booklet. Or it may be delivered by a product that can be touched, felt, used, smelled, or eaten. Concept statement, TV commercial, physical product—all are collections of information elements, and STEP assigns a deserved share (an incremental deserved share when compared to a control group) to each of them. This means that many "problems" that marketing research has traditionally dealt with coalesce into a single general problem, amenable to a single solution with a single measuring device.

It does not matter whether we are conducting a concept test, a name test, a logo test, a copy test, a price test, or a product test. All of them require the measurement of collections of information elements and pose the same question: "How many incremental share points would I get if I used this theme or that one, this brand name or that one, this product formulation or that one?" In each case, the answer is given in comparable terms. Relative to a control group, this product name is worth +2 share points, that price level is worth -3 share points, this product formulation is worth +4 share points, and so on. And though there are problems that cannot be dealt with by STEP, notably problems that deal with the relative efficiency of different information delivery systems (discussed in Part V of this book), a close examination of the stream of problems confronting the researcher reveals that a large number are concerned with evaluating the incremental value of collections of information elements.

This generality is by no means an unalloyed blessing, which was brought home to me painfully when I met with a researcher to talk about marketing research and STEP.

"I know all about STEP," he said to me confidently. "We have used it for a name test, and it worked very well. And we will certainly use it again as soon as we need to do another name test."

I expressed surprise. "I could understand if you told me that you don't like STEP, don't agree with it, won't use it. That would be a coherent position. But STEP measures the deserved share of information elements. The page in the STEP booklet does not care whether you are varying the name, the logo, or the theme. So it seems to me that if you believe the technique is appropriate for measuring the value of any particular collection of information elements, it should be equally appropriate for measuring the value of any other collection of information elements."

At that, he drew back and exclaimed, "Do you realize what you are saying?"

"What?"

"You are saying that I could dispose of eighty-five percent of all the problems that cross my desk with a single technique."

"That's right," I said happily, well pleased that he had understood the implications.

"But that would be terrible," he exclaimed in dead earnest.

"Terrible?" I said surprised.

"Yes," he said, "what would happen to me? Right now my marketing people come to me with their problems. I use this technique for this problem, that technique for that problem, a different technique for every problem. If one could handle every problem with a single technique, what would happen to me?"

I attempted to show him that there would be a great deal left to do, but he was not convinced. In the corporate environment of this researcher, generality was no blessing.

Although STEP has been around for over thirty years, it is far from having found wide acceptance. It has been presented, talked about, copied, embraced by some, ignored by many, seen as too subtle by some and too obvious, even trivially obvious, by others. But when you come right down to it, it is no more and no less than the simplest possible application of the First Law.

CHAPTER 12

Beyond Product Category Boundaries

Although it may be downright meaningless to speak of choice except in the context of a competitive frame, challenges to the very idea of competitive frames have cropped up regularly through the years. Some products are so new that they appear to have no competitive frame. My standing reply to this objection was that the so-called new products were merely new ways of addressing previously existing needs and that these needs were already addressed in other ways. A typical example I liked to give was the "travel belt." You push a button, lift off, and fly to your destination. Such a product may seem new, but it serves existing needs. As a means of transportation, it may compete with an automobile, a motorcycle, a bicycle. As a sport, it may compete with scuba diving, sky diving, downhill skiing. And it could be placed in some competitive frame.

Related to the new product problem was the category expansion argument. "My product," the brand manager would say, "is so special that it will not only capture share from existing brands but will also expand the category itself." For example, a new brand of fresh fruit ice cream might aspire to attract customers who currently do not eat ice cream. My remedy for this problem was to expand the competitive frame to include sorbets and yogurt, and beyond that berries and fruit.

For the most part, STEP studies have covered well-defined product categories with well-defined competitive frames. But competitive frames come in all shapes and sizes, ranging from unambiguous, tightly defined categories, such as toilet soap, notebook computers, or toothpaste, to vague, ill-defined frames for accommodating, say, an electronic babysitter or a housecleaning robot. As the competitive frame becomes vague, studies run increasing risks of surprises and breakdowns. Ironically, we need a precise definition of vagueness. We may say that a competitive frame is well defined when all items in the frame are unambiguously substitutable for each other and that it becomes vague to the extent that this assumption of substitutability becomes less supportable with respect to some and eventually with respect to many or all of the items in the frame. One consequence of vagueness is that the shares lose concrete meaning. A share of 18% in a well-defined frame usually represents a market of known size and is directly translatable into potential unit or dollar sales. Such translations become precarious as the boundaries blur. Nevertheless, my purist position for many years was that, vague or not, some implicit underlying frame was always appropriate.

In the back of my mind, of course, I knew that as the frame broadens, it must in the end include everything, which is tantamount to saying that it is no longer a competitive frame at all, for to paraphrase Gilbert and Sullivan, "When everything competes with everything, nothing competes with anything." But I began to rethink my position in earnest only when confronted by a particularly troublesome case. The assignment was to estimate the potential penetration of a new electronics product. As soon as I attempted to construct a competitive frame for this product, I ran into difficulties. The most important "competitive" item consisted of accomplishing the test product's function without recourse to a commercial product. I had grave misgivings about using "buy nothing" as an item in a competitive frame. I understood that this was merely a semantic trick, pretending to remain within the boundaries of the theory even though the theory had been abandoned implicitly. Given the differences in price, awareness, and accessibility between this non-item and any item that required the purchase of a commercial product, I had to concede that its inclusion was equivalent to asking people outright whether they would buy the new product and was subject to the troublesome consequences inherent in that procedure. I certainly knew and had demonstrated empirically (as reported in Chapter 13) that the aggregate number of items respondents say they will "definitely" buy can add to many times the number they could possibly buy. This questioning procedure was therefore structurally wrong. But was it necessarily wrong all the time?

I turned back to basics. My critique of the direct question had been that, expressed in choice terms, it was tantamount to asking, "Will you buy this brand or nothing?" When we deal with brands in established product categories, this question does indeed fail to correspond to the choice the respondent faces in the marketplace. Her choice is not whether to buy this brand or nothing, but whether to buy this brand or some other one. I now realized, under duress, that this critique had been correct but incomplete. The question, "Will you buy a Panasonic VCR?" generates distorted responses because it implies the unrealistic alternative "buy nothing." The question, "Will you buy a VCR?" on the other hand, may not generate distorted responses because, in this case, the implicit alternative "buy nothing" may in fact correspond accurately to the actual choice the customer makes in the marketplace. Generalizing, I concluded that in dealing with brands, the choice is usually which of several brands to buy, whereas in dealing with product categories, the choice is usually whether to buy the category or nothing.

Next I considered the measurement problem. Should we simply ask, "Will you buy a VCR?" a question I knew to be subject to other distortions, or could we construct a measurement device that would extract better information from the respondents? We ordinarily accept the respondents' reports of what they own as reasonably accurate. If they say they own a cellular phone, they probably really own one. Accordingly, it should be possible to measure the desirability of different product categories relative to a reference frame and to calibrate these measurements against what the respondents report they own. I called this technique VEST, an acronym for *Volume Estimation Test.* In the case of consumable products, mainly packaged goods, VEST estimates potential volume. For durables, VEST estimates *penetration,* that is, the percent of respondents who will own the product.

STEP and VEST complement each other. VEST deals with product categories; STEP deals with brands. VEST measures the primary choice, whether the respondents will buy the category at all. STEP measures the subsidiary choice, whether the respondents will buy a particular brand in the category. When a product is so new that it effectively defines a category, VEST is used to assess the potential of that category. As long as the penetration of the category remains small, VEST generally continues to be the more appropriate measuring instrument, because the marketer has little to gain from attempting to capture share from tiny competing brands and must focus on building the category. Once the category achieves high penetration, there is progressively less to gain from further efforts to build the category, and the emphasis shifts to the more conventional steady-state problem of capturing share from competing brands. And there are intermediate stages when the marketer may validly hope to capture business from competing brands, while at the same time enlarging the penetration of the category. In those cases, a combination of VEST and STEP may be in order, VEST to measure potential gains in category penetration, STEP to measure potential gains in brand share.

A word of caution is in order. Knowing that it is difficult to capture incremental share in well-established categories, marketers sometimes fall back on the consolation that their strategy will do wonders because it will expand the category. Most of the time, this hope is illusory. It is usually more difficult to win new converts than to capture share from existing brands. Category expansion strategies are realistic only for genuine, substantive innovations that can overcome critical psychological thresholds. A new hand-held voice-controlled PC, for example, might attract business not only from current PC owners but also from current nonowners. Innovations of this scope, however, happen rarely. Most of the time, problems can be classified with reasonable precision into primarily VEST problems (category penetration) or primarily STEP problems (brand choice).

VEST For Durables

A *reference frame* is a collection of product categories, in effect an elaborate yardstick, for measuring the potential penetration of a product category. Whereas STEP is predicated on choosing among items within a competitive frame, so that each choice of a brand takes place at the expense of one or more of the other brands comprising the frame, VEST is predicated on estimating the probable choice of a product category by comparing it to unrelated, noncompeting product categories. The items of the reference frame do not interact with the test category. They neither lose nor gain when the test category is chosen or rejected. They function as a stable, fixed scale against which the test category is measured. For simplicity's sake, I will use the term *category* as a shorthand for *product category* throughout the discussion of VEST.

We begin by constructing the reference frame. This frame consists of a collection of existing categories ranging from almost total penetration, such as a color television set, to very low penetration, such as desktop video conferencing. Approximately twenty categories are selected. Ideally they cover actual current penetration in approximately equal steps from penetrations close to 100% to penetrations close to 0%. There are no conceptual limitations, except that the categories should be independent of each other and of the test category, meaning they should be nonsubstitutable, coexisting categories, for example, vacuum cleaners and cellular phones. There is also no conceptual barrier to including an automobile and an electric toothbrush in the same reference frame. In practice, however, we prefer to construct the reference frame out of categories of similar type and price range in order to make the task easier for the respondent.

The categories comprising the reference frame, including the test category, are presented to the respondent on descriptive cards, which may include pictures. The respondent provides two pieces of information: She arranges the categories of the reference frame, including the test category, in rank order on the basis of how much she wants to own each, and she reports whether she currently owns each of the reference categories. The logic of the analysis and the detailed computations are in Appendix A. When the computations are performed, they yield two percentages for each of the reference categories in the frame: *actual penetration* (the per-

Table 12–1
Correlation between Actual and VEST Penetration
for Eight Durables Studies

	Correlation
Study 1	.950
Study 2	.834
Study 3	.686
Study 4	.938
Study 5	.913
Study 6	.940
Study 7	.815
Study 8	.820
Total	.89

centage of households or business units reporting that they own the category) and *VEST penetration* (an estimate of the percentage of households or business units that should own the category based on the VEST analysis). Since VEST is a relatively new technique, and since genuine category innovations that call for VEST are relatively rare, especially in consumables, EMA has done only nine VEST studies, eight for durables and one for consumables, the former divided equally between durables for household products and durables for business products. Table 12–1 shows the correlations between actual penetration and VEST penetration for the reference categories of the eight durables studies. Figure 12–1 shows a consolidated scattergram of actual penetration versus VEST penetration for the same studies. The consolidated correlation is .89.

Notwithstanding the high correlation between VEST penetration and actual penetration, many individual points are far from the line. This raises a further question. Are the deviations of individual reference categories from the line just a matter of sampling and measurement error, or do they convey information in their own right? Altogether, the VEST studies used 22 different reference categories in the household products reference frames and 32 different reference categories in the business products reference frames. Averaging the data for these categories for all studies in which they were used, we can calculate a VEST potential for each of the reference categories, defined as its VEST penetration minus its actual penetration. A positive VEST potential implies that the category is still in a growth phase; more people want it than have it. A negative VEST

Figure 12–1
Actual Penetration versus VEST Penetration
Durables
($N = 11,865, r = .89$)

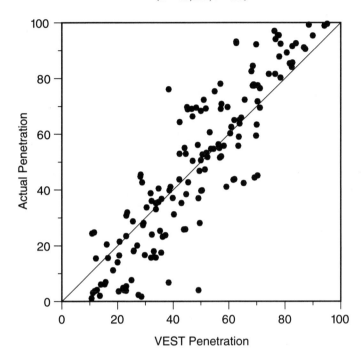

potential implies that the category has reached maturity and may be in a stable or declining phase; more people have it than want it.

Negative VEST potential does not necessarily mean that absolute sales of the category are declining. If the population base happens to be growing and the replacement market is substantial, sales could be stable or even increasing. The negative potential does indicate, however, that we cannot expect to obtain new customers from the existing population base. Conversely, a positive potential implies that we can expect further growth of penetration from the same population base. By the same token, high positive or negative potential may be attributable to accessibility differentials. In the general case, we expect categories with positive potential to have accessibility deficiencies, and categories with negative potential to have accessibility excesses.

Figures 12–2 and 12–3 show the VEST potentials for the 22 household categories and the 32 business categories, respectively. Among the house-

Figure 12–2
VEST Potential for Products in Four Studies
Household Products Reference Frame
(N = 4,698)

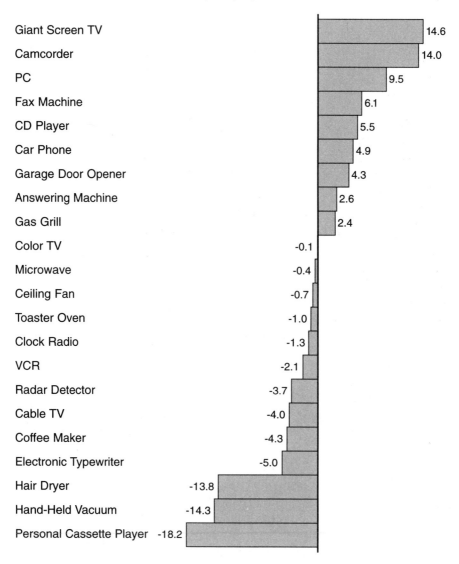

hold categories, the four with the highest positive potentials are: giant screen TV, camcorder, PC, and fax machine. The four categories with the highest negative potentials are: personal cassette player, hand-held vacuum, hair dryer, and electronic typewriter. For the business categories,

Figure 12–3
VEST Potential for Products in Four Studies
Business Products Reference Frame
(*N* = 7,167)

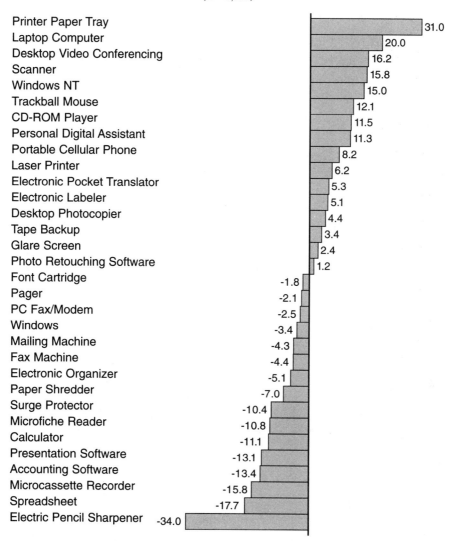

Product	Value
Printer Paper Tray	31.0
Laptop Computer	20.0
Desktop Video Conferencing	16.2
Scanner	15.8
Windows NT	15.0
Trackball Mouse	12.1
CD-ROM Player	11.5
Personal Digital Assistant	11.3
Portable Cellular Phone	8.2
Laser Printer	6.2
Electronic Pocket Translator	5.3
Electronic Labeler	5.1
Desktop Photocopier	4.4
Tape Backup	3.4
Glare Screen	2.4
Photo Retouching Software	1.2
Font Cartridge	-1.8
Pager	-2.1
PC Fax/Modem	-2.5
Windows	-3.4
Mailing Machine	-4.3
Fax Machine	-4.4
Electronic Organizer	-5.1
Paper Shredder	-7.0
Surge Protector	-10.4
Microfiche Reader	-10.8
Calculator	-11.1
Presentation Software	-13.1
Accounting Software	-13.4
Microcassette Recorder	-15.8
Spreadsheet	-17.7
Electric Pencil Sharpener	-34.0

the four with the highest positive potentials are: printer paper tray, laptop computer, desktop video conferencing, and scanner. The four with the highest negative potentials are: electric pencil sharpener, spreadsheet, microcassette recorder, and accounting software.

An important qualification must be kept in mind. Although the household sample may be reasonably representative of households, the business samples are definitely not representative of the business community at large. Depending on the particular test category that was investigated, special highly skewed segments of business respondents were chosen. I include the business products data, however, for the sake of completeness and also because they illustrate possible outcomes.

VEST for Consumables

There is a basic difference between durables and consumables. In the case of durables, we are primarily concerned with a single purchase, with whether the respondent owns or will own the category. In the case of consumables, we are primarily concerned with consumption volume, how much of the category the respondent uses or will come to use in some period of time. The previous section dealt with VEST for durable categories. There is an analogous form for consumables.

For this purpose, we need a yardstick of consumption volume that can span different product categories and can be applied meaningfully to all. The number of usage occasions serves as such a yardstick. We may ask a respondent to report usage occasions per month. On how many separate occasions does she usually drink coffee? On how many separate occasions does she usually take aspirin? On how many separate occasions does she usually use eyedrops? As in the durables case, a reference frame is constructed, including categories ranging from high usage-occasion rates to low rates. The respondent is asked to rank all categories, including the test category, putting the one she thinks she will want to use most frequently first and ordering the other categories from high to low based on intended usage occasions. In addition, the respondent is asked to report actual usage occasions for each of the categories in the reference frame (see Appendix A).

Figure 12–4 shows the relationship between the actual number of usage occasions and the VEST usage occasions for a reference frame consisting of the following categories: analgesics, antacids, breath fresheners, caffeine tablets, chewing gums, cold remedies, cough remedies, smokers' toothpastes, and vitamins.

VEST-STEP

Most of the time, problems can be assigned relatively unambiguously to either VEST or STEP depending on whether the marketer is primarily interested in winning new customers for the product category or capturing brand share within the category. But sometimes both of these objec-

Figure 12–4
Actual Usage Occasions versus VEST Usage Occasions
Consumables
(N = 2,100, r = .98)

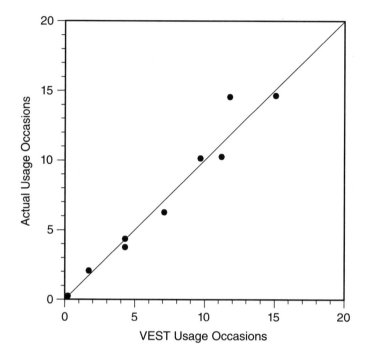

tives need to be addressed simultaneously. VEST-STEP is the synthesis of VEST and STEP that makes this possible.

The respondent begins with the STEP portion of the questionnaire, which can differ from test group to test group. The booklet contains a page for the test brand, appropriately featuring those special attributes that will presumably make it irresistible both to current category users and to prospective converts to the category. The stickers given to the test brand measure the test brand's share among the brands of the category. The respondent then goes on to the VEST portion of the questionnaire. Here she is confronted by a set of product categories, including the test product category. She has already been exposed to the fact that the test brand exists, so the test category itself is now endowed with hitherto unexpected features and benefits. She ranks the test category with that knowledge in mind. This generates a VEST score. Multiplying this VEST score by the STEP score yields a measure of the probability that she will buy the test brand.

If the control group sees the brand without the innovation and the test group sees the brand with it, the STEP difference can be used to estimate the extent to which the innovation will increase the brand's share; the VEST difference can be used to estimate the extent to which the innovation will increase the category's penetration; and the product of the two can be used to estimate the net effect. Viewed from the perspective of STEP, the VEST score is a number by which the STEP shares are weighted. Viewed from the perspective of VEST, the STEP score is a factor by which the category penetration of each respondent is multiplied to obtain the penetration of the brand for that respondent.

PART III

THE
STRUCTURE
OF CHOICE

This part of the book is the centerpiece of the theory. It should be of particular interest to social scientists and survey research practitioners. Business executives may find it theoretical. But at least three sections in these chapters contain practical advice on business strategy ("Desirability" and "An Interjection about Improving Brands" in Chapter 13, and "Product Category Differentiation" in Chapter 14).

Chapter 13 (The Anatomy of Questions) presents a general taxonomy of survey questions. It introduces the unbounded write-in scale, an original instrument for measuring desirability. It makes distinctions among the basic variables of the theory. And it demonstrates the importance of these distinctions by means of methodological analyses of large bodies of data.

Chapter 14 (The Second Law: The Law of Primacy) explores in depth the relationship between desirability and choice. This leads to the Second Law, which in turn leads to the tie matrix, with major implications for measurement theory and practice.

CHAPTER 13

The Anatomy of Questions

Having dealt with practical applications, we now turn to a more basic conceptual problem. How do the measurements examined so far fit into the set of all questions a respondent could be asked about a brand? Can the helter-skelter of such questions be classified in some coherent way? At first glance, one would say no. Surely the total number of questions must be unlimited in form and substance. On closer scrutiny, however, we discover common threads. Researchers think they are constructing new questions all the time, but they are actually asking the same ones over and over again.

When we come right down to it, there are only five generic questions. These constitute a template, the building blocks for the theory of choice. I believe that this template may apply to all survey research, but I am confining it to one particular subset of questions: those intended to measure how a customer relates to a brand (keeping in mind that the terms *customer* and *brand* are used in the encompassing sense given them in Chapter 1). Here are the basic five questions:

1. We can ask a customer what she *believes* (Beliefs).
2. We can ask her what she *wants* (Desires).
3. We can ask her to *choose* something (Choice).
4. We can ask her to *name* something (Awareness).
5. We can ask her to *report* something (Factual Reports).

Distinctions among these variables can be subtle. Semantic traps are everywhere. There is confusion between factual reports and beliefs, between beliefs and desires, and between desires and choice. This can lead to the failure of measurements that would have worked if they had been implemented properly. Accordingly, it is necessary to take a closer look at the basic variables and to draw boundaries around them.

Beliefs

The term *beliefs* is used here in a narrow technical sense. It has nothing to do with the colloquial distinction between knowing and believing. It refers only to statements that assign attributes to a brand. Statements about things that happened, things the respondent experienced, saw, heard or did, are *factual reports,* without prejudice to whether they happen to be accurate or not. Thus, the statement, "Coca-Cola has 140 calories per 8-ounce glass," is a belief. The statement, "Last Tuesday I bought three bottles of Coca-Cola," is a factual report. Even the statement, "I saw a TV commercial that said Coca-Cola has 140 calories per 8-ounce glass," is a factual report, a report about exposure to a television commercial.

At the boundaries, the distinction between beliefs and factual reports becomes so fine that it may appear to have little practical consequence. But conceptual coherence demands that the line be drawn. In this spirit, I distinguish between the statement, "Dannon Yogurt has no fat," which is a belief, and the statements "Last year Dannon Yogurt had no fat" and "Last year I believed that Dannon Yogurt has no fat," which are factual reports, the latter a factual report about a previously held belief.

In case of doubt, tense can be a clue. By definition, beliefs are held and asserted in the present. If the statement refers to something past, it is not a belief as the term is used here. The converse is not true. Factual reports usually deal with events that took place in the past, but they can extend into the present. The statement "I own a Jeep" is a factual report. Splitting hairs even finer, a belief must describe the brand generically rather than some particular instance of the brand. Thus "Jeeps are difficult to handle" is a belief, but "My Jeep is difficult to handle" is a factual report.

Beliefs about a brand are usually expressed as declarative statements: "BMW cars accelerate from 0 to 60 mph in 10 seconds." "ScotTissue has 1,000 sheets per roll." "A Rolls-Royce has a price of $100,000." We measure beliefs by asking the respondent to designate these statements as true or false. But a statement's truth, an absolute matter in mathematics, is never absolute in the real world, which leads to the idea of degrees of truth. This has three separate but related aspects.

First, there are varying degrees of certainty, which can be expressed as subjective probabilities. I believe that Coca-Cola has 140 calories per 8-ounce glass, but I am not quite sure. As a betting man, I can express my relative certainty by assigning a number between 0 and 1 to the statement. And because people find decimals awkward, we may ask them to express this probability on a scale from 0 to 10, which amounts to the same thing. When the respondent gives the statement an 8, she is presumably estimating that, upon objective check, approximately 80% of all statements she makes with comparable certainty will turn out to be true. Second, the statement has contextual ambiguities. The statement may be true in some situations but not in others. I may believe that the statement is true for Coca-Cola in bottles but not for Coca-Cola in cans, that it is true for factory-made Coca-Cola but not for Coca-Cola at soda fountains. This leads to the judgment that the statement is sometimes true and sometimes false, which can be captured with the same kind of scale, asking the respondent to rate how true she believes the statement to be. Finally, the statement has some degree of precision. Consider the sequence:

- Coca-Cola has a lot of calories.
- Coca-Cola has around 150 calories per glass.
- Coca-Cola has 140.3 calories per 8-ounce glass.

In this sequence, the first form of the statement is vague. It may mean one thing to one person, something else to another. But the progressively greater precision of the statements does not necessarily eliminate vagueness. How were the calories measured? Do the laboratory measurements apply to the specific beverage I purchased in the supermarket?

Thus the respondent has at least three kinds of doubt: doubt about the accuracy of the information, doubt about its context, and doubt about its precision. The measurement system evolves correspondingly. We start by asking the respondent to check True or False. We elaborate by adding a third category: True, False, Not Sure. We elaborate further by inserting intermediate categories: True, Probably True, Neither True nor False, Probably False, and False. We go on to the numeric scale, requesting the respondent to report her certainty by assigning a number from 0 to 10. But no matter how much we refine the response gradations, intrinsic ambiguities remain. This leaves the risk that the measurement will tell us more about how the respondent uses the scale than about what she believes about the subject.

Once again, both our understanding and the quality of the measurement can be enhanced by employing the principles of Choice Research. But we are not dealing with choice here, are we? Surely the respondent can believe different things simultaneously and does not have to choose among them. That is true up to a point. But we can clarify what the respondent believes by compelling her to choose among mutually exclusive statements. Instead of asking her to make an absolute judgment about the truth or degree of truth of the statement, "Coca-Cola has 140 calories per 8-ounce glass," we can ask her to indicate which of the following statements is "most nearly true" or "best describes" Coca-Cola:

- It has 120 calories per 8-ounce glass.
- It has 130 calories per 8-ounce glass.
- It has 140 calories per 8-ounce glass.
- It has 150 calories per 8-ounce glass.
- It has 160 calories per 8-ounce glass.

This question is a shortcut for five separate questions:

- How certain are you that Coca-Cola has 120 calories per 8-ounce glass? . . .130? . . . 140? . . . 150? . . . 160?

from which the single item that received the highest certainty score is selected analytically. This shortcut is largely independent of response tendencies. It measures, as closely as possible, what the respondent believes about the subject matter in the checklist.

Desirability

The distinction between desires and beliefs is fundamental. But the English language provides many grammatical conventions that are a source of confusion. These cause problems in two ways. They confound the thinking of some who are innocently caught in semantic webs. And they serve as tools for others who use them deliberately to distort and mislead. One difference between desires and beliefs is particularly important. When I express a belief, I am saying something about the world external to myself, something that may be true or false, perhaps difficult or even impossible to verify, but which is theoretically subject to objective verification. When I express a desire, I am telling you something about myself, something important, in fact crucial for the work we do, but something about myself, not something about the brand. "Coca-Cola has 140 calories per 8-ounce glass" is a belief. "I want to drink Coca-Cola" is a desire. In this case, the distinction is self-evident. But it isn't always that easy. How about the statement, "Coca-Cola tastes good"? Is this a belief or a desire? Before replying, let me explore the boundaries between beliefs and desires.

The English language provides several forms for expressing a desire. Each of these has different nuances, but at the core they all amount to the same thing.

1. *Direct.* "I want a BMW." This is the simplest and most elementary way of expressing a desire.
2. *Imperative.* "Give me a BMW." This is perhaps equally simple, though the desire is not expressed overtly. It must be inferred.
3. *Affective.* "I like a BMW." This is a more general form. It conveys

the idea that I am in some state of wanting with respect to BMW, without specifying the precise nature of the want. This may be self-evident from the context, or it may allow the speaker to remain fluid, leaving the precise meaning vague not only to the listener but perhaps to the speaker as well. Thus, "I like a BMW" may mean: "I *want* to own a BMW," "I *want* to drive a BMW," "I *want* to ride in a BMW," "I *want* to look at a BMW," or all of the above. Whatever it means, it implies some form of wanting.

4. *Projective.* "BMW is a good car." This is the most insidious of the forms. In the ordinary course of events, the language employs verbs to express desires and adjectives to express descriptions. When I say, "I like a BMW," my statement may be vague, my want may not be fully defined, but it is clear from the structure of the sentence that I am speaking about myself, not about BMW. There are times, however, when I want to disassociate myself from the personal aspects of my want and project it into the external world, obscuring the fact that I am speaking for and of myself, and insinuating that my private want is somehow an objective characteristic of the external world and, by implication, shared by all reasonable people. The language provides value adjectives for accomplishing this purpose, indispensable tools of the proselytizer and propagandist who uses them to project his personal desires into the outside world, only to discover them there, and to exhort others to join with him in their pursuit. They are also traps for people who embrace them in innocence, not quite realizing what they are doing, and then fall victim to their own propaganda.

This does not mean that it is improper to use any of these forms in the questioning of respondents. For this purpose, it does not matter which form is used. All forms will yield about the same answer. The way the response categories are constructed, however, will make a difference, in fact a crucial difference.

An Interjection About "Improving" Brands

The semantic structure of "I want," the various forms in which it is expressed and the projective form in particular, is dealt with in this chapter mainly for the purpose of identifying explicitly the variables employed in questioning respondents. The use of the projective form, however, spreads confusion more widely, sometimes in marketing thinking. I cannot pass this point without interrupting the main thrust of the chapter to comment on one particular manifestation of the projective form, the improvement of established brands.

Suppose a marketer approaches management with this proposal: "I need a budget of ten million dollars to improve my brand." The budget may be allocated or refused. But what management will not be sympathetic to "improving" a brand, to making it even "better" than it is already? But if the value language is excised, we are left with a request for ten million dollars to change the brand. If the matter is put this way, warning flags go up. Quite apart from the fact that money is requested, do we really want to change our brand? Recognizing that value adjectives, such as *good* and *beautiful,* convey information about the desires of the speaker rather than about the characteristics of the brand, we can avoid needless pain by translating sentences that contain them into their equivalent direct form.

Taken out of context, offered without explanation, simply stated affirmatively, the idea that it is meaningless to talk about product improvement is totally alien to the way most marketers think. In crassest form, it amounts to asserting that product quality itself, the currently fashionable obsession of so many companies, resides not in the brand but in the eyes of the beholder. This offends most people's common sense. They may concede that some things, such as whether consumers want a product to be chocolate or vanilla, are a matter of taste. But beyond matters of taste, there is objective reality. There is product quality. Some products are simply made better than others. They are more convenient. They are more accurate. They are more durable. Surely this is not merely a matter of taste. Everyone wants a product to be more convenient, more accurate, more durable. Don't they?

It isn't that simple. Just because a desire happens to be held universally does not change its essential character. In a place where one hundred percent of the people prefer chocolate to vanilla ice cream, the desire for chocolate would be universal, but it would still be a desire. By the same token, one hundred percent of the population might want a product to be more convenient, more accurate, and more durable, but this would not transform these desires into objective aspects of the world. Finally, even these desires are not nearly as universal as one might suppose.

When automatic cameras first came on the market, they were identified as more convenient. But professional photographers resisted that convenience. They had learned the skill of using a light meter, of controlling speed and aperture, skills that set them apart from the uninitiated, and they were unwilling to concede that their skills could be matched, duplicated, or even surpassed by a piece of equipment. They argued that the external light meter gave better readings, hardly a supportable position in the case of action shots, but the bottom line was that they simply did not want a camera that was more convenient in this respect. I might not want my car to have a maximum speed of 500 miles per hour. I might not want my watch to show time to the nearest 1/10,000 of a second. And I might not want my house to be built to last a thousand years. Thus the idea that products can somehow be made objectively or intrinsically "better" breaks down on closer scrutiny. We mean "change," don't we? Then let us call a spade a spade and avoid traps of our own making. This is summarized in the following principle.

THE IMPROVEMENT PRINCIPLE
Excise the word *improvement* from your vocabulary. Think instead of whether you want to *change* your established brand.

"All right," you say. "Have it your way. Call it what you will. So I won't talk about improving my brand. I'll just talk about changing my brand instead. What difference does that make?"

It makes a difference. If you really have a successful brand, you had better think twice, maybe three times, before you decide to change it. Your brand has been around a long time. This means some customers like it. Whether it makes sense to you or not, they like it the way it is, as evidenced by the fact that they have been buying it the way it is. And habit is important. It may be the most important thing of all. Make a change, any change, and it's a cinch you'll upset some of them, even if only a handful. Remember Coke. You may be willing to do this in order to get all those new customers. But keep this in mind. It's a lot easier to lose old customers than to gain new ones. And it's a lot faster, because your old customers will know about the change the moment you make it. If it turns them off, it'll turn them off right away.

The chances are that the new customers you hope to attract also know your brand, also have opinions about it, generally negative opinions. They have probably tried your brand in the past and have decided they did not like it. That's why they don't buy it. Now you propose to say to them, "Sure, I disappointed you before, but I have changed. Give me another chance." Eventually, some of them may do just that, but it'll take a lot longer. This means that you'll risk losing some current customers right away in the hope of winning some new customers, presumably more of them, later on. Are you sure this is a good idea? If you really think that your innovation has great potential, you don't need to change your current brand. Bring out the innovation as a new brand or as a line extension. If its potential is as high as you say it is, you can put all your marketing support behind it and allow the old brand to die of natural causes. The chances are it will refuse to die, and you'll come out ahead. But if you happen to be wrong, you will not have put your bread and butter on the line. All of this is summarized in the following principle.

THE CHANGING PRINCIPLE
Don't change a successful brand unless you are absolutely sure.
The chances are you'll lose more than you'll gain.

The Numeric Scale

My early attempts to measure the desirability of brands and characteristics of brands focused on problems of scaling. It seemed to me self-evident that people want some things and do not want others, that they like some brands and do not like others, and that the relative degree of their wanting or liking is a fundamental variable that must be defined in terms of a practical measurement device. Such a device had to have a natural zero point, a point of neutrality or indifference. People can tell whether they like something, dislike it, or are balanced in between, not caring one way or the other. And since wanting or liking is a matter of degree, a bipolar scale seemed appropriate.

One could, of course, ask people how much they like or dislike various characteristics of brands by means of verbal questions—such as

- I like it a lot.
- I like it somewhat.
- I just barely like it.
- I neither like nor dislike it.
- I just barely dislike it.
- I dislike it somewhat.
- I dislike it a lot.

But assuming that people can count on the fingers of one hand, and that they have some minimal appreciation of the relationship of small integers to each other, it seemed more flexible to use a numeric scale, which they were both able and willing to handle in all kinds of interviews, conducted in person, by telephone, or self-administered through the mail. The instruction was:

Please use a scale from +5 to -5 to tell me how you feel about each of the following things. If you like it, give it a plus number. If you dislike it, give it a minus number. The more you like it, the bigger the plus number. The more you dislike it, the bigger the minus number. If you neither like nor dislike it, that is, if you are indifferent, give it a 0.

This instruction was followed by a list of miscellaneous things—baseball, milk, boxing bouts, and so on—followed by collections of product categories, brands, and/or characteristics of brands.

When I started working with this scale in the 1950s, I had great hopes for it. It seemed to me to be simple, universally understandable, and universally applicable, using only the respondents' ability to count to five and their intuitive appreciation of the relative magnitude of the numbers 0 through 5. I also believed that the respondents would be able to look inside themselves, experience the relative magnitude of the wanting-liking tension there, and report it coherently.

This turned out to be true, to a point. The respondents had no difficulty using the scale. It was administered successfully to people from all walks of life, including children, and yielded systematic orderly patterns. It discriminated among product attributes and different brands, and it enabled us to observe differences among different groups of people. Figures 13–1 and 13–2 show some typical frequency distributions obtained with the scale. Average desirability of orange juice was 4.18; of a cheese sandwich, 2.90. Average desirability of Ford was 2.79; of Pontiac, 1.99. *Better Homes and Gardens* magazine received 3.21 from women, 1.54 from men. And cereal box prizes received 2.79 from children, -.64 from mothers. The frequency distributions, however, showed substantial percentages of respondents clustered at the extremes of the scale. Seventy-six percent of women gave orange juice a +5. Thirty percent of mothers gave cereal box prizes a -5. Forty-seven percent of women gave *Better Homes and Gardens* magazine a +5.

These concentrations of scores troubled me for two reasons, one conceptual and one practical. On a conceptual plane, it appeared that I had failed to accomplish what I had set out to do: to measure the degree of wanting or liking. I simply did not believe that the true underlying metric could be concentrated at extreme endpoints. This conceptual concern had a practical corollary. The scale was intended to measure the impact of messages. But there was a major objection to its use for this purpose. Taken at face value, the measurement was saying that close to 50% of all women already liked *Better Homes and Gardens* magazine as much as it was possible for them to like it and that nothing that could be said to these respondents could improve that desirability further, a conclusion that seemed patently absurd and therefore raised serious questions about the measure, and certainly about its use as a criterion variable in message experiments.

This was both a source of concern and a challenge to me for a number of years, during which I made unsuccessful efforts to extricate myself from the trap. My initial thought was that the scale did not extend far enough and that the pattern might change if we added more categories,

Figure 13–1
Percent Distribution of Desirability for Products
Numeric Scale

Foods
(N = 3,163)

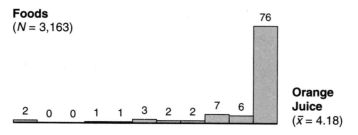

Orange Juice
$(\bar{x} = 4.18)$

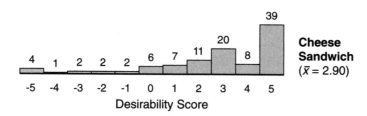

Cheese Sandwich
$(\bar{x} = 2.90)$

1957 Automobiles
(N = 2,426)

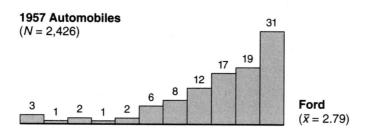

Ford
$(\bar{x} = 2.79)$

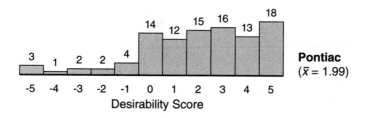

Pontiac
$(\bar{x} = 1.99)$

Figure 13–2
Percent Distribution of Desirability for Subgroups
Numeric Scale

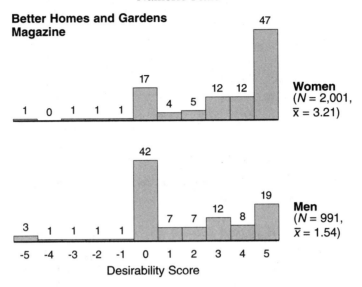

Better Homes and Gardens Magazine

Women ($N = 2{,}001$, $\bar{x} = 3.21$)

Men ($N = 991$, $\bar{x} = 1.54$)

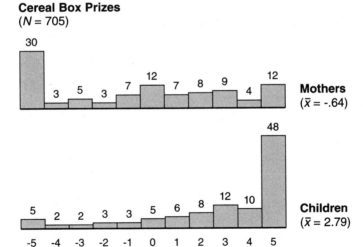

Cereal Box Prizes ($N = 705$)

Mothers ($\bar{x} = -.64$)

Children ($\bar{x} = 2.79$)

for example, allowing the scale to range from +10 to -10. This did not, of course, change anything. Now the respondents clustered heavily on +10. I then attempted to drive the respondents away from the extremes. If we could not take the scale out to infinity, we would bring infinity in to the ends of the scale. In this spirit, I labeled the two ends of the scale, "Like it more than anything else in the world," and "Dislike it more than anything else in the world," and gave the respondents a set of practice ratings that included such items as, "A long and successful life," "Dying of cancer," etc. After these practice items, the respondents were asked, "Now please use the same rating scale to tell me how you feel about each of the following TV programs. Start with The Ed Sullivan Show." To my chagrin, a substantial number of the respondents once again replied, "+10." This experience led me to formulate what I later called the Organic Response Principle.

Respondents have organic tendencies to perform tasks in certain ways, and no external instructions are likely to override those tendencies. Such instructions are equivalent to asking a right-handed person, "Please use your left hand." If a respondent, confronted by a bounded numeric scale, has the organic tendency to go to the ends of the scale, nothing will deter her for long. She will quickly revert to what comes naturally. Accordingly, it is a mistake for the researcher to attempt to shape a pattern of responses by instructions, explanations, or examples. These will be, if not forgotten, simply set aside when she answers further questions. This is summarized in the following principle.

THE ORGANIC RESPONSE PRINCIPLE
Responses to questions are largely impervious to instructions designed to override the organic way respondents approach tasks.

Carrying this principle to the extreme, we may say that instructions and explanations in the design of questionnaires accomplish nothing. The researcher's problem is not to explain to the respondent what he wants her to do, but to invent a task that will induce her to give him the information he seeks.

A clarification is in order. Instructions are certainly necessary to define the physical aspects of a task. If we want the respondent to write numbers between +5 and -5 in the boxes on the bottom of a page, we must tell her unambiguously where these boxes are located, how many numbers are to be written into the boxes, and so on. These instructions define the task. Once the task has been defined, however, instructions and explanations concerning the *meanings* she is to attach, and the special considerations she is to keep in mind in carrying out the task, will probably prove irrelevant. If we don't like the outcome we must change the task, not the instructions.

This principle finds an echo in the related concept of user-friendly appliances. Give people an appliance without an instruction booklet and they will complain. But give them the instruction booklet, and many will ignore it and start to push buttons. If the right things happen, they will praise the equipment. Otherwise, they will complain that the equipment is complicated and difficult to understand. It never ceases to amuse me how many executives, including computer professionals, complain that they have not been able to master the buttons on their office telephones and that they need assistance to transfer a call or to set up a conference call. To be sure, they have not bothered to read the manual. But it is also true that many telephone instruments are not receptive to intuitive button pushing. So the impasse continues.

It was out of my dissatisfaction with the properties of the +5 to -5 scale that I turned to an allocation of points among brands. The early studies in the late 1950s used personal interviews. The respondents were given ten poker chips to divide among brands displayed on a board. With this instrument, very few respondents clustered at the "10" extreme. In purely technical terms, it seemed the problem had been solved. But I adopted the tool with considerable reluctance. Desirability had to be bipolar, either positive or negative, because people could or should have been able to tell us how much they liked or disliked something. Accordingly, I felt that I had not really solved the problem but had merely evaded it. I had shifted conceptual ground. Having been unsuccessful in measuring adequately what I had intended to measure, namely desirability, I had turned to measuring something altogether different, for no other reason than that it had seemed more amenable to being measured.

In the beginning I understood the implications of this shift in only the vaguest way. Thus, I stumbled on the variable *choice* and started using it, long before I realized its full significance, long before I realized explicitly that choice is not only a different variable, but actually the crucial one. To be sure, desirability comes first, but choice is the consequence, and as it turns out, it is this consequence that manifests itself in behavior in the world. Theoretically, desirability is the more elementary of the variables, but desirability is transformed into choice once we enter the arena of the physical world in which, alas, two things can't be in the same place at the same time.

The Unbounded Write-In Scale

It was many years before I returned to a consideration of the measurement problem that had so stumped me. I was satisfied with the work that had grown around the measurement of choice, and was confident that it was sound both theoretically and practically. But in the back of my mind the old issue continued to nag me. I had never totally abandoned the conviction that we ought to be able to measure desirability directly and that, even though my various attempts to do so had been unsuccessful, someday a more coherent way would be found.

Pondering this issue one day, the obvious thought struck me that all measurement is comparative. We measure a physical length by lining it up with a yardstick. We measure a physical weight by putting it on a scale where it is compared either to a set of standard weights or to the resistance of a spring. If we want to measure how much the respondents like or dislike something, we need to give them something to push against, a device that will require them to make some expenditure of effort, however slight, to convey higher desirability. This effort would have to be large enough to deter them from going out to infinity and small enough for them to be willing to make the effort for the purpose of conveying gradations in their feelings. This led directly to the idea of basing a desirability scale on tiny amounts of work. I called it the *unbounded write-in scale* for measuring desirability.

The respondent is given the following instruction:

This section lists some brands. Please tell us how you feel about these brands by writing *L*'s or *D*'s or an *N* into the boxes next to them.
- If you like a brand, write *L* or *LL* or *LLL* or as many *L*'s as you want (the more you like it, the more *L*'s you should write next to it).
- If you dislike a brand, write *D* or *DD* or *DDD* or as many *D*'s as you want (the more you dislike it, the more *D*'s you should write next to it).
- Please don't leave any box blank. If you are neutral or don't care about a brand, that is, if you neither like nor dislike it, write *N*.

The scale has the following features:

1. It has a natural zero point to indicate indifference and extends outward from there in both directions to indicate increasing positive feelings (like) in one direction, and increasing negative feelings (dislike) in the other direction.
2. It does not require the respondent to use numbers, particularly not negative numbers, which some respondents find troublesome, but allows her to give direct behavioral expression to the quantitative aspects of her feelings.
3. It is unbounded, that is, open-ended in both directions, so there is no particular ceiling of like or dislike. No matter how much a

respondent reports liking or disliking something, she can always like or dislike something else more.

4. It is constructed out of tiny increments of effort that restrain the respondent from indiscriminate excesses and keep the responses within reasonable bounds.

The hypothesis in designing this scale was that it would generate distributions more nearly like what one would expect, namely, more nearly normal distributions. To test this hypothesis, EMA conducted a small methodological study. Two randomly equivalent samples, drawn from telephone-listed households in Nassau County, New York, received mail questionnaires asking them to rate fourteen political leaders with either the unbounded write-in scale (N = 137) or the +5 to -5 numeric scale (N = 170). Figure 13–3 shows the average scores obtained by the fourteen leaders with the two scales.

Figure 13–3
Average Scores for Political Leaders
Numeric Scale and Unbounded Write-In Scale
(N_N = 170, N_U = 137)

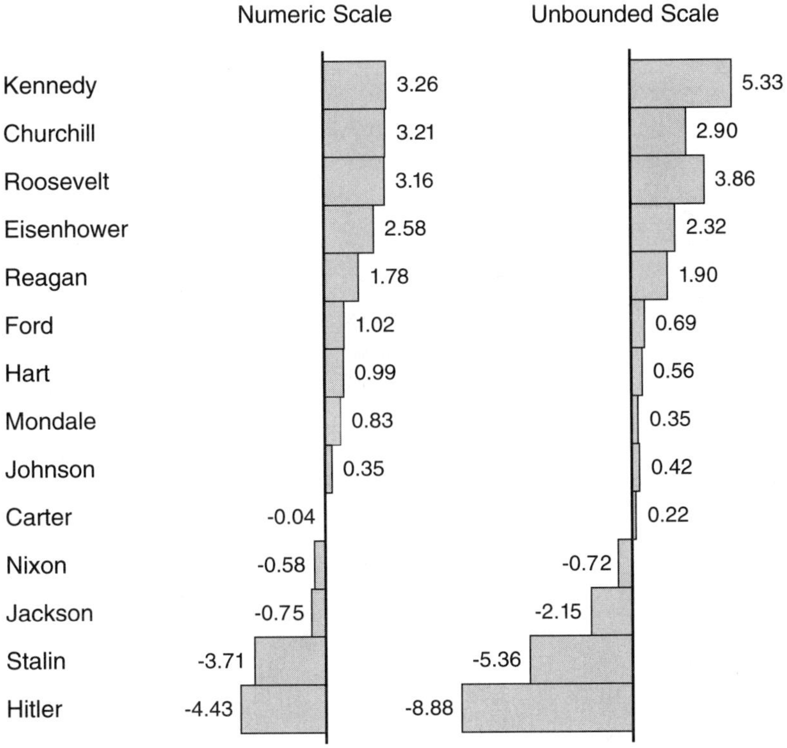

	Numeric Scale	Unbounded Scale
Kennedy	3.26	5.33
Churchill	3.21	2.90
Roosevelt	3.16	3.86
Eisenhower	2.58	2.32
Reagan	1.78	1.90
Ford	1.02	0.69
Hart	0.99	0.56
Mondale	0.83	0.35
Johnson	0.35	0.42
Carter	-0.04	0.22
Nixon	-0.58	-0.72
Jackson	-0.75	-2.15
Stalin	-3.71	-5.36
Hitler	-4.43	-8.88

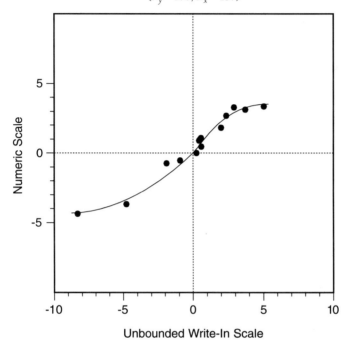

Figure 13–4
Numeric Scale versus Unbounded Scale
Average Scores for Fourteen Political Leaders
$(N_y = 170, N_x = 137)$

John F. Kennedy received the highest positive score on both scales; Adolf Hitler received the highest negative score on both scales. The ordering of the leaders was about the same for both scales.

As shown in Figure 13–4, there is a strong correlation between the two scales. The +5 to -5 numeric scale, however, levels off at both ends. The unbounded write-in scale allows distinctions, especially at the ends, that might have been damped or eliminated altogether by the numeric scale.

The distributions of the scores produced by the two scales were dramatically different. Figure 13–5 shows percent distributions for the numeric scale for Kennedy (mean = 3.26), Ronald Reagan (mean = 1.78), Jesse Jackson (mean = -.75), and Hitler (mean = -4.43). These distributions have heavy concentrations at the end points. Forty-six percent rate Kennedy +5, as high as possible on the scale; 89% rate Hitler -5, as low as possible on the scale. Even the two leaders who receive intermediate ratings have substantial concentrations at the endpoints: 27% +5 for Reagan and 25% -5 for Jackson. Figure 13–6 shows the distributions of scores for the same

Figure 13–5
Percent Distributions of Scores for Political Leaders
Numeric Scale
(N = 170)

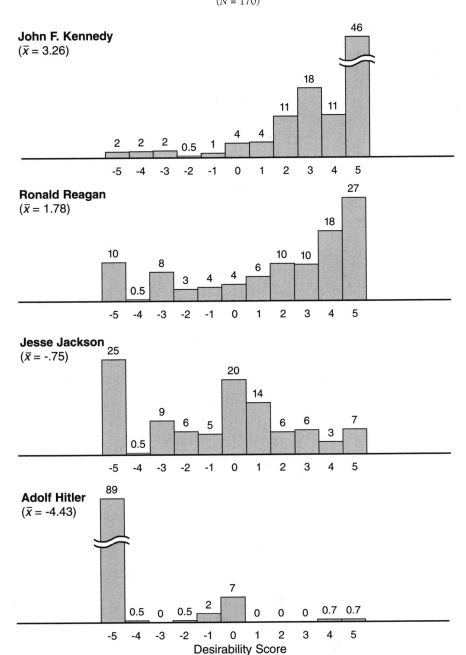

John F. Kennedy
($\bar{x}$ = 3.26)

Ronald Reagan
($\bar{x}$ = 1.78)

Jesse Jackson
($\bar{x}$ = -.75)

Adolf Hitler
($\bar{x}$ = -4.43)

Desirability Score

Figure 13–6
Percent Distributions of Scores for Political Leaders
Unbounded Write-In Scale
(N = 137)

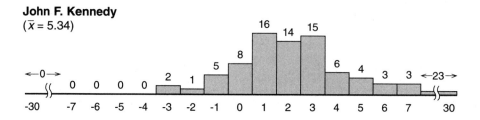

John F. Kennedy
($\bar{x}$ = 5.34)

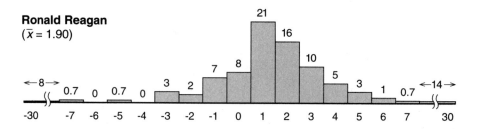

Ronald Reagan
($\bar{x}$ = 1.90)

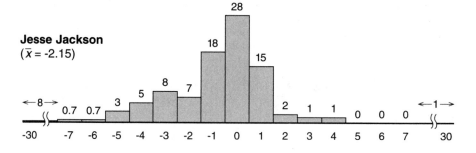

Jesse Jackson
($\bar{x}$ = -2.15)

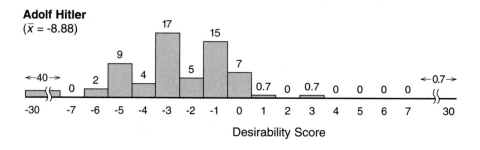

Adolf Hitler
($\bar{x}$ = -8.88)

Desirability Score

Figure 13–7
Percent Distribution of Maximum Number of *L*'s and *D*'s
Given to Brands of Bathroom Tissue
($N = 8{,}291$)

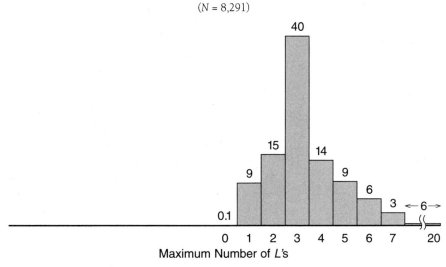

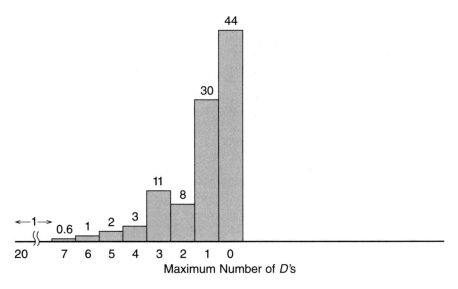

four leaders measured with the unbounded write-in scale. The bunching at the ends is gone. The general shape of the distributions conforms to what one would have expected on a priori grounds: peaks that fall off in both directions. This is true for all leaders, even Hitler.

The question arises whether respondents are willing to take the trou-

Figure 13–8
Percent Distribution of Desirability
Unbounded Write-In Scale

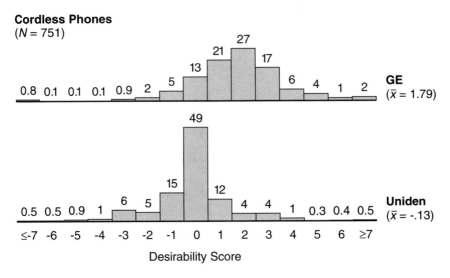

Cordless Phones
($N = 751$)

Attributes of Peanut Butter
($N = 197$)

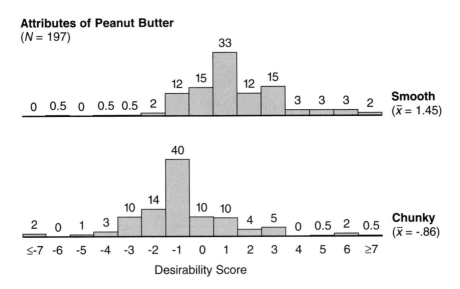

ble to write more than one *L* or *D* not only when rating high-interest political leaders, but also when rating ordinary low-romance products. Figure 13–7 shows a frequency distribution of the maximum number of *L*'s and the maximum number of *D*'s used by respondents in rating brands of bathroom tissue. Ninety percent of the respondents used at least two

L's for at least one of the brands; 75% used at least three *L*'s, and 35% used at least four *L*'s. At the same time, 56% used at least one *D*. Thus the respondents used the scale as intended.

The approximately normal shape of the distributions generated by the unbounded write-in scale is not limited to political leaders. It holds equally for brands and for attributes of brands. Figure 13–8 shows the distribution of desirability for two brands of cordless telephones, GE (mean = 1.79) and Uniden (mean = -.13), and for two attributes of peanut butter, smooth (mean = 1.45) and chunky (mean = -.86). These data illustrate that the unbounded write-in scale discriminates among brands and among attributes of brands, while curing the major defect of the +5 to -5 numeric scale, the bunching at the extremes. I prefer it on this count alone, but it also has another important feature. The scores generated by it have a stability that is not readily biased by context.

In one study, 32 different randomly equivalent groups (of 200 respondents each) received different product variants in the same decoy label. The respondents rated nine brands—eight existing brands in the category and the decoy brand—by means of the unbounded write-in scale. If we want to use the scale to measure the desirability of different product variants relative to the desirability of other brands, we don't want the fact that the respondents received different products to influence the way they rate the other brands. In this study, the average desirability of the decoy brand ranged from a low of 0 to a high of around 2.3, a huge range. For example, an average score of 0 might be produced if 100% of the respondents gave the test brand zero *L*'s, while an average score of 2.3 might be produced if 70% of the respondents gave the decoy brand two *L*'s and 30% gave it three *L*'s. Notwithstanding these differences in the desirability scores of the test product, the respondents' ratings of the current brands were unaffected by the test product, as illustrated in Figure 13–9. The average desirability scores given to the highest and lowest brands remained approximately the same, regardless of whether the respondents had received a high-scoring or a low-scoring test product. This suggests that the scale was functioning "absolutely," that is, making major discriminations among the test products while leaving the ratings of the existing brands essentially unaffected. Whether the data the scale generated are also useful remains an open question, which will be addressed in Chapter 19.

Is it possible to draw a sharp line between brand desirability and brand choice? Clearly the two are related. Brand choice flows from desirability. Is the distinction between them therefore largely semantic and technical, without real substantive import? Not at all. The variables are truly different, and the difference between them is important. This difference is totally obvious

Figure 13–9
Average Desirability of Highest and Lowest Brand
versus Average Desirability of Thirty-Two Variants of Decoy Brand
(N = 6,633)

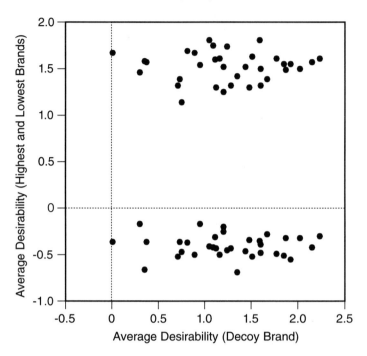

some of the time and more subtle on other occasions. But we can apply a simple test to determine at a glance whether we are dealing with a measure of desirability or with a measure of choice. If the task given the respondent allows her to rate each brand separately without knowing which other brands are to be rated subsequently, we are dealing with a measurement of desirability. If the task requires the respondent to consider all brands simultaneously, so that the subsequent introduction of any additional brand would render all prior ratings moot, we are dealing with a measurement of choice. Consider this measurement in which respondents are asked to estimate their probability of buying a particular brand. The question is:

Please give me a number from 0 to 10 to tell me how likely it is that you will buy Brand X the next time you shop. The more likely it is that you will buy Brand X, the bigger the number you should give. If you are certain that you will buy it, give it a 10. If you are certain that you will not buy it, give it a 0. And if you are not sure one way or the other, you may give it any number in between.

Figure 13–10
Percent of Respondents Assigning a Purchase Probability Score of 10
Fifty-Seven Styles
(N = 2,052, Total Will Buy = 959%)

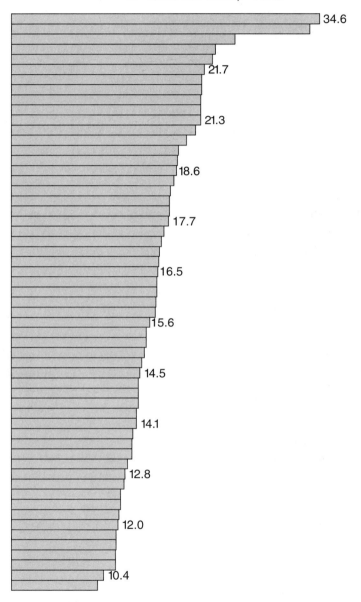

We might be tempted to think of this question, which resembles the STEP measurement in many respects, including the actual language employed, as a variation of the STEP measurement that can be used interchangeably with it. Nothing could be further from the truth. Regardless of the words used, the respondent is called upon to express a reaction to one brand at a time rather than to choose among brands. No matter how many such ratings the respondent has already given, she can always rate still another brand and another. These new ratings do not invalidate the scores collected previously. Accordingly, this purchase probability is just another measurement of desirability. This is summarized in the following principle.

THE VARIABLE-IDENTIFICATION PRINCIPLE
The measured variable is defined not by the words in the questionnaire, but by the task the respondent is asked to perform.

If we administer the purchase probability question with respect to a possible style of a product and ask the respondents how likely they are to buy it, a substantial percentage, between 10 and 35%, answer affirmatively. They like the style; they want to buy it. If we show them another style, the same is true. The respondents are neither irrational nor unreasonable. They like this one too; they want to buy this one too. Figure 13–10 shows what happens when we ask the same question for 57 candidate styles for the same brand. The aggregate percent who give a 10, meaning that they will definitely buy the style, adds to over 900%. In the world of desirability, this is not unreasonable. I may like nine different styles, I may even want to buy nine different styles, or fifteen, or one hundred. Once I confront the physical world, however, it is not possible for me to buy nine different styles when I have only one or two physical products in my home. In that circumstance, I am compelled to choose, and though my choice may flow from the relative desirability of different objects, it must be understood and studied in its own right. All of this is captured in the following principle.

THE DESIRABILITY PRINCIPLE
Desires are unlimited; choices are finite.

Brand Choice

Choice can be measured by asking the respondent to select a brand from a list of brands—in particular, the brand she wants most, likes most, or will buy next. This is called the *first-choice* measurement. The percentage of respondents who choose a brand in such a choice is called the *first-choice share* of the brand. This is the purest measurement of choice, most

closely congruent with the task the customer faces in the world when she confronts a shelf, a menu, a catalog, or a voting booth. But it can be developed further.

Many of the choices we make in life are made repeatedly, and we know that such choices are not always consistent, partly because of changes in the environment but also because we feel different at different times, which leads, in the general case, to the concept of probabilities of choosing different brands. This holds even for major, considered purchases like automobiles, computers, or homes, which presumably we buy so infrequently that the concept of a succession of purchases over time has no meaning. These choices, however, are accompanied by uncertainty, and this uncertainty is expressed by assigning odds to the outcome. This amounts to estimating that if we had to make the decision repeatedly, we would probably choose Brand A six times, Brand B three times, and Brand C once out of ten such choosing opportunities. Thus, the idea of repeated choices has meaning not only for consumables, for which the respondent literally makes repeated choices, but also for durables for which repeated choices, even if made only on paper, may elicit better predictions of the respondent's future behavior than a single choice.

This, of course, is what STEP does. More specifically, STEP can be thought of as an orderly replication of the measurement, equivalent to asking the respondent: "Please make this choice for us, not once, not twice, but ten times in a row." In doing so, the respondent gives us additional information that the cruder first-choice measure would have obscured, since it would have thrown together into the same category respondents who were completely committed to a brand and respondents who were teetering on the edge and finally chose the brand only because they had to choose something.

To investigate whether and to what extent this is so, we need studies in which both first-choice and STEP share were obtained. A number of such studies are available. Figure 13–11 shows the relationship between first-choice share and STEP shares for brands in ten product categories: answering machines, baby wipes, bathroom tissue, frozen dinners, laptop computers, paper towels, personal computers, soups, telephones, and teletype for the deaf. The linear correlation is .93. Notwithstanding the strong relationship between STEP share and first-choice share, the relationship flattens out at the ends. For low-share brands, STEP shares tend to be higher than first-choice; for high-share brands, they tend to be lower than first-choice. This phenomenon may reflect some real underlying differences in the way the two measures function at the ends, or merely artifactual rounding, or a combination of both. It is possible that while many respondents are willing to give a brand one sticker, dispro-

portionately fewer respondents are willing to choose the same brand outright when they have only a single opportunity to express their choice.
Some of these respondents may have the impulse to choose the low-share
brand at the particular moment of the interview, but may suppress this
impulse because it would do violence to what they know to be the larger
ebb and flow of their feelings over time. Related to such substantive considerations are purely artifactual rounding tendencies. If we view every
measurement as an approximation that rounds to the nearest available
unit, then the first-choice measure requires rounding to either 0% or
100%. STEP allows finer discriminations, enabling the respondent to
round to the nearest sticker, that is, to the nearest 10%. This also tends to
render very low shares lower in first-choice than in STEP, and high shares
higher.

Because the ten categories consolidated in Figure 13–11 include several giant categories, in particular soups (145 brands), frozen dinners
(102 brands), and paper towels (51 brands), the chart necessarily con-

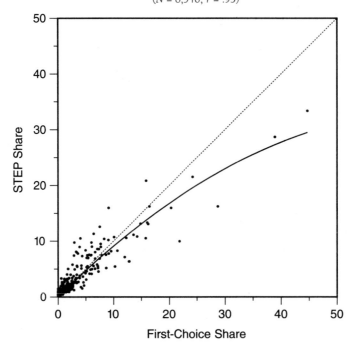

Figure 13–11
STEP Share versus First-Choice Share for
392 Brands in Ten Different Product Categories
($N = 8{,}546$, $r = .93$)

Figure 13–12
STEP Share versus First-Choice Share for
Low-Share Brands
(*N* = 8,546, *r* = .74)

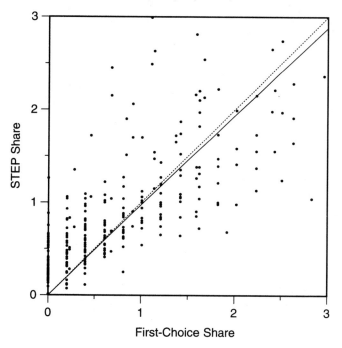

tains a large number of low-share brands. This accounts for the dark cloud of points in the region below share 3. Apart from the fact that the points in this region are obviously subject to proportionately larger variability, they are fully consistent with the relationship observed over the extended share range. Figure 13–12 is an enlargement of the 3 x 3 section of Figure 13–11. It does not contain new data. It merely replots the data in the low-share region on a scale that allows us to see what is happening there. Even confined to that region, that is for brands with shares of 3 or less, the correlation is still in evidence (*r* = .74). The chart, however, also illustrates the rounding phenomenon. Fifty-seven brands with first-choice shares of 0 have STEP shares ranging from .1 to 1.3. More generally, there are more points above the 45-degree line than below it, indicating that at low shares STEP is more likely to discriminate among brands than first-choice. (The statistical variability and the sensitivity of the two measures are discussed in Appendix B.)

Direct Rank

One way of expanding the first-choice measurement is to ask the respondents to provide a complete ranking of the brands. What information does such a ranking provide, and how should that information relate to STEP share? If we consider the task given to the respondent, we note that just as STEP requires the respondent to make a number of choices (ten choices if there are ten stickers), so the ranking task requires the respondent to make a number of choices (ten choices if there happen to be eleven brands). There is, however, an important difference between the two tasks. In the STEP measurement the competitive frame remains constant. The respondent is free to give each sticker to any one of the brands and may duplicate assignments to her heart's content, right down to giving all ten stickers to the same brand. In the ranking measurement the competitive frame changes continuously. After the first choice, the chosen brand is removed from the competitive frame. The respondent repeats the task, assuming that the chosen brand is no longer available, and so on down the line. This yields a rank for each brand, a score ranging from 1 to N, where N is the total number of brands.

There is another important difference between the two measures. Whereas STEP allows the respondent to assign equal numbers of stickers to different brands, so that three or four or more brands can each receive one sticker, and an unlimited number of brands can each receive zero stickers, ranking forces discrimination among brands whether such discrimination exists or not. This means that if there are real or de facto ties among the brands, meaning that the respondent is essentially indifferent to choices among those brands, the structure of the ranking task forces the respondent to place one brand ahead of another in some serial order whether that order happens to have meaning or not. There are good reasons for structuring the ranking task this way. True ties will not distort the data since each of the tied brands will be placed ahead of the others approximately equally often by chance, and even small real differences should be picked up probabilistically. Nevertheless, this is an essential feature of the ranking task and must be kept in mind in interpreting the results. The score obtained by a brand in an explicit ranking of brands will be called the *direct rank*, or just the *rank*, of that brand. Of course, the percentage of respondents who give a brand Rank 1 is precisely what we have called the first-choice share of that brand. The two terms are used interchangeably.

CHAPTER 14

The Second Law: The Law of Primacy

The previous chapter dealt with the distinction between desirability and choice and the various problems that attend efforts to measure each. We have looked at different measurement instruments, most notably the unbounded write-in scale for measuring desirability, and first-choice share and STEP share for measuring choice. We have been mindful of the fact that desirability and choice are so intimately related that there is a perpetual risk of confusing one with the other. And we have gone to considerable lengths to make distinctions between them in an effort to avoid such confusion. We are now ready to consider the precise relationship between them.

Desirability and Choice

Let us assume that we have measured the desirability of the brands comprising a competitive frame, all having equal accessibility. What can we say about the direction of the causality and the nature of the relationship between desirability and choice? To begin with, it is clear that desirability is the primary variable. I may like various brands in varying degree, and may be able to express such liking long before I am called upon to make a choice among the brands. And if the choice situation consists of being told, "Here is a list. Pick the brand you want most," I will choose the brand I want most, namely the brand with the highest desirability, by definition. To be sure, a customer does not always choose the same brand. But if the customer buys Brand A on one occasion and Brand B on another, we may take this as evidence that her desires have changed in the interim. And even if she buys several brands or flavors simultaneously, we may say that her choices are not independent and that, having picked up three pints of chocolate ice cream, her desire to add a fourth pint of chocolate is now lower than her desire to add a pint of vanilla. Provided we consider one decision at a time, we may continue to insist that she always buys the brand she likes best at each moment, in each situation, all things considered, and that this is true by definition.

That is not all there is to it, however, and in any event that is not what we set out to do. The definitional considerations may help us think more clearly, but we are not merely interested in formulating principles that are true by definition, but in constructing a theory that relates real variables to each other, variables that can be defined operationally and measured independently.

As was discussed extensively in the previous chapter, we can measure the desirability of brands by means of different instruments, including, in particular, the unbounded write-in scale, which we selected as the preferred instrument. And we can measure choice by different instruments, such as purchasing, first-choice share, or STEP share. Although it may appear that purchasing is the most relevant of the choice measures, it is not necessarily the most appropriate and certainly not the most practical for the purpose at hand. In the first place, purchasing will be influenced not only by desirability but also by accessibility, which we want to hold constant. Second, it is difficult, if not impossible, to obtain substantially contemporaneous measurements of desirability and purchasing. We do, however, have studies in which measurements of desirability and STEP share were obtained in the course of the same interview. Most prominent among these is the study I drew on to illustrate the stability of the unbounded write-in scale.

The study was conducted in 1994. It is described in Chapter 19. For the moment, it is sufficient to note that its aggregate sample size was over 6,600 respondents, and that it provided for measuring the full spectrum of the variables that play a part in the theory of choice, including some measures that were added for methodological purposes. It is the most comprehensive single reservoir of data available to me for studying the relationships among the variables of the theory, and I will use it as a major source for that purpose. Because of its breadth and large sample size, I call it the *Spectrum* study. In examining various relationships between variables, I will usually begin by drawing on the Spectrum study. That way, many analyses will refer back to a single data set. In addition, the conclusions drawn from the Spectrum study will be supplemented, insofar as data are available, by aggregating evidence from other studies.

Figure 14–1 shows the distributions of the desirability scores for the brand with the highest average desirability (1.53) and the brand with the lowest average desirability (-.43) in the Spectrum study. Even the highest brand received some negative ratings, though fewer than 7%, and even the lowest brand received some positive ratings, though fewer than 18%. Both brands received a substantial number of zero ratings. The difference in desirability between the brands is not limited to any particular region

Figure 14–1
Percent Distributions of Desirability
(N = 6,633)

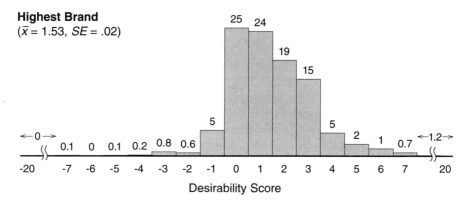

Highest Brand
($\bar{x}$ = 1.53, *SE* = .02)

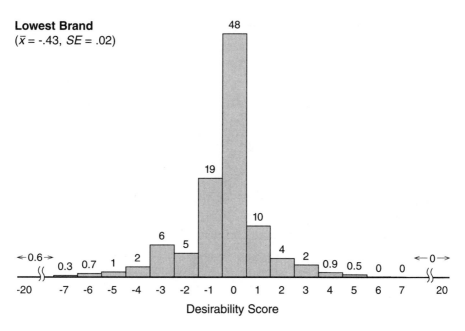

Lowest Brand
($\bar{x}$ = -.43, *SE* = .02)

of the scale, but manifests itself in a general upward shift of the scores all along the scale.

Since we believe that, other things being equal, respondents should have a greater tendency to choose brands they like than brands they don't like, the average desirability scores of the brands should be related to the STEP shares of the brands. This is indeed the case, as shown in Figure 14–2, but the result is far from satisfying. The correlation is .73, and there

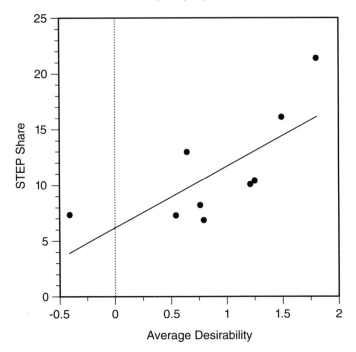

Figure 14–2
STEP Share versus Average Desirability for Nine Brands
Spectrum Study
($N = 6,633, r = .73$)

is a substantial amount of variability among the brands. In particular, some brands that differ in average desirability receive approximately the same STEP shares. Nevertheless we believe, reasoning from first principles, that a relationship is there and that it is stronger than the scattergram of Figure 14–2 suggests. So we suspend judgment while we go on from the aggregate to the individual level.

Figure 14–3 shows the average STEP shares associated with desirability scores ranging from -6 to 10. Examining this chart, we see that desirability is highly predictive of STEP share in the region between desirability = 0 and desirability = 7, and is essentially unrelated to STEP share for desirabilities below 0 and above 7. This result need not surprise us. The odds are that whether we dislike a brand a little or a lot, we won't buy it in either event. Conversely, if we like it sufficiently to buy it, it may not matter how much we like it. But examining the relationship between desirability and STEP share in its raw form really masks what is going on. Even a brand with low desirability may be chosen if the desirability of the

Figure 14–3
STEP Share versus Desirability Score
Spectrum Study
(N = 6,633)

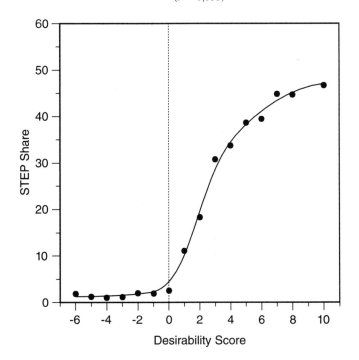

other brands is still lower. Even a brand with high desirability may not be chosen if the desirability of the other brands is still higher. And even the clean linear relationship between STEP share and desirability in the 1–7 desirability region may not necessarily mean that the increasing level of desirability itself is responsible for the higher STEP shares, but merely that as desirability increases, it is progressively more likely to exceed the desirability of the other brands. If that is so, what counts is not the absolute level of desirability but the brand's desirability relative to the other brands in the competitive frame.

The chart in Figure 14–4 illustrates the relative role of desirability and desirability-rank. It indicates that rank plays by far the more decisive role. For example, given a desirability score of 6, if the brand is liked most (Rank 1), it receives a STEP share of around 50; if it is liked second best, it receives around a 30; if it is liked third best, it receives around a 20. On the other hand, provided the brand is liked most, there is only a difference of around 3 STEP share points between desirability 6 and desirabil-

Figure 14–4
STEP Share versus Desirability Score at Various Ranks
Spectrum Study
(N = 6,633)

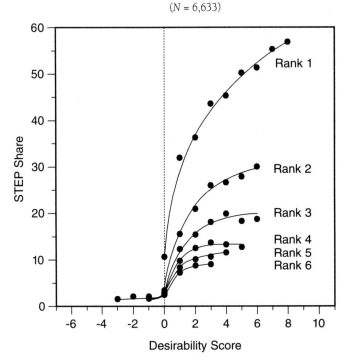

ity 5. The same is true at Rank 2 and at Rank 3. In each case, a change in absolute desirability score is associated with a much smaller STEP share change than is a change in desirability-rank. STEP share does drop substantially as Rank 1 desirability approaches 1, but this too probably reflects the relative levels of the brands. When the winning brand has a desirability score of 1, all the other brands must have 0 or negative scores, and respondents simply do not choose a brand to which they are not willing to give at least one L. This leads us right back to the commonsense proposition with which we started. Other things being equal, people choose the brand they like most at the moment of their choice. In case of a single choice, this is a truism; they must choose the brand they like most. If they chose another brand, we would doubtless say that in that particular instance at that moment, they had really liked the other brand better, or they would not have chosen it.

I said "other things being equal." Specifically, "other things" means accessibility. If the brand is not available, not there to be chosen, the respondents clearly cannot choose it. So accessibility must be taken into account. If we define brand strength (S) as the product of desirability (D) and accessibility (A), or $S = DA$, we may say that people choose the brand with the highest brand strength at the moment of their choice. This amounts to saying that if all brands have equal accessibility, people choose the brand with the highest desirability, but that any brand that has zero accessibility vanishes from the competitive frame. In STEP, of course, we go out of our way to make all brands equal in accessibility. Accordingly, we should expect respondents to give all ten stickers to the brand with the highest desirability at the time of their choice. But we know that, far from doing so, respondents generally distribute stickers among several brands. How come?

There is one circumstance in which the commonsense view can prevail in spite of the fact that respondents do not give all their stickers to a single brand: if two or more brands are tied for Desirability-Rank 1, literally or de facto. We may speak of a de facto tie if several brands receive scores that differ only due to chance fluctuations below the threshold of the respondents' ability to discriminate. In that case, we would expect all sticker allocations among two or more brands to be confined to ties for first place. In particular, we would expect that if two brands were tied for first place, each would receive half the stickers; if three brands were tied for first place, each would receive one-third of the stickers, and so on. We shall speak of brands tied for first place in brand strength as *strong* brands, and of all other brands as *weak* brands. All of this is summarized as the Second Law of Choice Behavior.

THE SECOND LAW: THE LAW OF PRIMACY
An individual for whom, at the moment of choice, *n* brands are tied for first place in brand strength, chooses each of these *n* brands with probability 1/*n*.

In the special case in which all brands have equal accessibility, this boils down to saying that on any single-choice occasion, individuals choose the brand they like most, and if they happen to like several brands most, they choose each of these with equal probability.

At first reading, the Second Law may appear to be unduly narrow, but it is not. Given the assumption that all choice grows out of desirability, the crucial theoretical need is to describe how this happens, and the Second Law does just that. This description is not tautological. Desirability and choice are subject to independent empirical measurement. And although the law states an elementary, largely self-evident proposition, as a good law should, it is subject to empirical verification and, as we shall see, gives rise to surprising, unforeseen consequences, empowering us to solve some elusive practical problems in simple and elegant ways.

Let us take a closer look at some of the implications of the Second Law. Given equal accessibility, the law attributes choice to desirability-rank. This implies intervention by the researcher. Choice is measured directly. Desirability is measured directly. But desirability-rank is a derived variable, a function, albeit a very simple one, rightly or wrongly—rightly according to the Second Law—imposed on the data by the researcher. By simple extension, the law applies to the entire ranking task. Asking the respondent to rank brands calls for successive choices in a chain of steadily shrinking competitive frames. If the law is applied successively at each of these stages, it follows that, for any competitive frame in which accessibility is held constant, the choice-rank vector (R_c) and the desirability-rank vector (R_d) should be the same: $R_c = R_d$. This amounts to saying that it does not matter whether the customer makes a choice directly by one of the means available to her—buying, selecting a brand from a list, distributing stickers among brands—or whether she makes the choice implicitly by supplying desirability scores for the brands and leaving it to the researcher to infer her choices. Once her desirability scores are converted into ranks, the result should be the same.

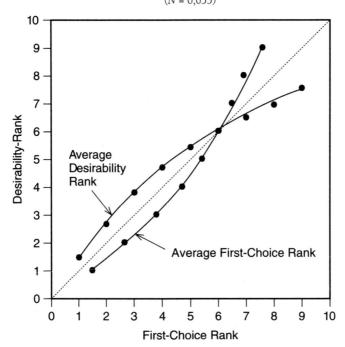

Figure 14–5
Desirability-Rank versus First-Choice Rank
Spectrum Study
($N = 6,633$)

Figure 14–5 demonstrates that this is indeed the case, subject to inevitable measurement error. The chart shows the average desirability-rank corresponding to different choice-ranks and the average choice-rank corresponding to different desirability-ranks for the nine brands of the Spectrum study. We expect that the correspondence should be good for the numerically lower ranks. As the ranking continues, however, the respondents should eventually become less able to distinguish among the brands, and their ratings, both direct choice and the implicitly obtained desirability-rank, should become erratic. This should manifest itself in a curve that is close to a 45-degree angle for the early ranks and flattens progressively as rank increases. Plotting the curve in both directions graphically illustrates both the intrinsic consistency of the measurements and the increasing error at the highest ranks.

The Tie Matrix

Before discussing some of the other implications of the Second Law, we should distinguish between two ways of thinking about STEP stickers. We may regard them as either probabilistic or discrete. According to the *probabilistic* model, STEP stickers measure probabilities of choosing brands. Implicit in this view is the idea that the respondents are psycho-logically simulating the passage of time, making successive choices in their imagination, not literally but de facto. The Second Law does not apply to this type of behavior because the Second Law deals only with a single choice, in particular with the relationship between that single choice and the desirabilities of the brands at the moment of that choice.

According to the *discrete* model, STEP stickers are ten choices made at one discrete point in time. From this perspective, the sticker allocation should be the direct consequence of the brands' desirabilities at the moment of the choice, and the Second Law should apply. It may appear that the discrete model is in blatant conflict with some of the things we have said and have empirically demonstrated about the assignment of STEP stickers. If we adopt the discrete model, the Second Law asserts baldly that each respondent should assign her stickers equally among her strong brands. This implies that out of the large number of ways in which respondents can in principle distribute stickers among brands, only n pure patterns should exist, where n is the number of brands—n being nine in the Spectrum study. On the face of it, this is simply not so. But the proposition warrants further exploration.

The following nomenclature, and the computational structure shown in Figure 14–6, will help us examine the problem in greater detail. Let us designate respondents with a single brand in first place as belonging to Tie-Type 1, respondents with two brands tied for first place as belonging

Figure 14–6
Tie Matrix

Tie-Type	F	Desirability-Rank						
		1	2	3	4	5	....	n
1	f_1	10	0	0	0	0	....	0
2	f_2	5	5	0	0	0	....	0
3	f_3	3.3	3.3	3.3	0	0	....	0
4	f_4	2.5	2.5	2.5	2.5	0	....	0
5	f_5	2	2	2	2	2	....	0
⋮	⋮	⋮	⋮	⋮	⋮	⋮		⋮
n	f_n	10/n	10/n	10/n	10/n	10/n	....	10/n

100%

Tie-Score share	x_1	x_2	x_3	x_4	x_5	....	x_n
STEP share	s_1	s_2	s_3	s_4	s_5	....	s_n

to Tie-Type 2, and so on. Let the percentage of Tie-Type 1 respondents be the tie-1 frequency (f_1), the percentage of Tie-Type 2 respondents the tie-2 frequency (f_2), and so on. These tie frequencies are shown in the column headed F and are the elements of the frequency vector (F). The tie frequencies add to 100%.

The arrangement of numbers in the body of the figure is called the *tie matrix* (T), and the elements of the tie matrix are the *tie scores*. The tie scores are numerical equivalents of stickers, simulations of stickers. Unlike actual stickers, which are assigned empirically, the tie scores are theoretical stickers, predictions of how stickers should be assigned under the discrete model, governed by the Second Law. The columns of the tie matrix represent Desirability-Ranks 1, 2, . . . , n. The tie scores in each row of the tie matrix add to ten hypothetical stickers. These rows represent the only response patterns that are theoretically permissible under the provisions of the Second Law. Thus, for respondents of Tie-Type 1, all tie scores (stickers) must be given to the brand with Desirability-Rank 1 (the brand in column 1), and all other brands must receive tie scores of 0. For Tie-Type 2 respondents, the brands with Desirability-Ranks 1 and 2 are tied, either literally or de facto. Accordingly, each of these two brands receives half of the available tie scores (stickers), all other brands receiving 0. And so on. Given this structure, we can add the tie scores in each column and divide through by the sum of all the tie scores in the tie matrix, to obtain the *tie-score shares,* x_1 being the tie-score share for Desirability-Rank 1, x_2 being the tie-score share for Desirability-Rank 2, and so on. Collectively, these shares will be called the *tie-share vector* (*X*). The elements of the tie-share vector add to 100%. Given the tie-share vector, we can directly compute the frequency vector and vice versa, as described in Appendix C.

These relationships hold only if the tie matrix in fact properly describes the behavior of the respondents, that is, if respondents really use only the nine tie-type patterns in distributing stickers among the brands. Once again we know, even before considering the issue, that this is not so. We know that all sorts of response patterns other than the nine ideal ones— for example, 8 1 1 0, 4 2 2 2, etc.—are routinely used. In fact, given the limitation of ten stickers, it is physically impossible for the respondents to employ the 3-tie, 4-tie, 6-tie, 7-tie, 8-tie, and 9-tie patterns precisely. Thus, even if the theory held absolutely, we would necessarily face deviations from the ideal tie-types due to rounding alone. The matter does not end there, however. We must expect a certain amount of measurement error, equivalent to shifting one or two stickers from the brand that ought to have gotten them to some other brand. And we must expect a certain amount of error in the measurement of desirability which will result in some improperly classified desirability-ranks. If the Second Law is valid, all of these discrepancies should be random. They may distort individual results but should leave the aggregate structure of the data intact. Accordingly, we can propose the following nontrivial test of the Second Law.

We begin by classifying each respondent's pattern of stickers into one of nine tie-types—the one that is "closest" to the observed one in the sense of least squares. For each respondent, the nine brands are arranged in order of their desirability-ranks from highest desirability to lowest desirability. Table 14–1 shows the data for one hypothetical respondent. This respondent gave the nine brands the sequence of stickers 2 3 1 3 0 1 0 0 0, shown in row 1 of the table. We now ask to which tie-type (3, 4, or 5) these scores are "closest." The tie scores for Tie-Types 3, 4, and 5 are shown in the next three rows of the table. To calculate the error resulting from assigning the respondent to Tie-Type 3, we sum the squares of all the differences between the actual number of stickers and the Tie-Type 3 tie scores: $(2 - 3.3)^2 + (3 - 3.3)^2 + (1 - 3.3)^2 + (3 - 0)^2 + (0 - 0)^2 + (1 - 0)^2 = 17$.

Table 14–1
Computing the "Closest" Tie-Type

| | Desirability Rank | | | | | | | | | Sum of |
	1	2	3	4	5	6	7	8	9	Squares
STEP score	2	3	1	3	0	1	0	0	0	
Tie-Type 3	3.3	3.3	3.3	0	0	0	0	0	0	17
Tie-Type 4	2.5	2.5	2.5	2.5	0	0	0	0	0	4
Tie-Type 5	2	2	2	2	2	0	0	0	0	8

For Tie-Type 5, this sum is equal to 8. For Tie-Type 4, it is equal to 4. Since Tie-Type 4 has the lowest sum of squares, it is "closest," and we assign the respondent to Tie-Type 4.

This means that, consistent with the Second Law, we have transformed the STEP scores from   2   3   1   3   0   1   0   0   0   into the tie scores   2.5   2.5   2.5   2.5   0   0   0   0   0. If the Second Law holds and respondents are largely allocating stickers in accordance with the pattern dictated by the tie matrix, then the tie-score shares for the various desirability-ranks should be reasonably close to the empirically observed STEP shares. The upper panel of Figure 14–7 shows a plot of the actual STEP shares versus the tie-score shares for the nine desirability-ranks. The correlation is practically 1.0, and the points lie almost perfectly on a 45-degree line.

We can carry the test one step further. We have transformed the empirically observed STEP scores into the tie scores, subject to the assumptions of the Second Law. If both the Second Law and the discrete model apply, this transformation should have done no violence to the data and should yield shares for each of the nine brands similar to the original STEP shares. The lower panel of Figure 14–7 shows the plot of STEP share versus tie-score share for the various brands. The correlation is .99. The points lie almost perfectly on the 45-degree line.

Thus the data are completely consistent with the tie matrix and the Second Law. There is no incompatibility between the probabilistic and the discrete models. They are interchangeable. We may think of STEP sticker assignment as a probabilistic measurement. But when appropriate, we may also think of STEP sticker assignment as a discrete measurement at a single point in time. From this perspective, the sticker assignment will deviate from the ideal patterns decreed by the tie matrix, but when large numbers of such measurements are aggregated, they will generate the same result as

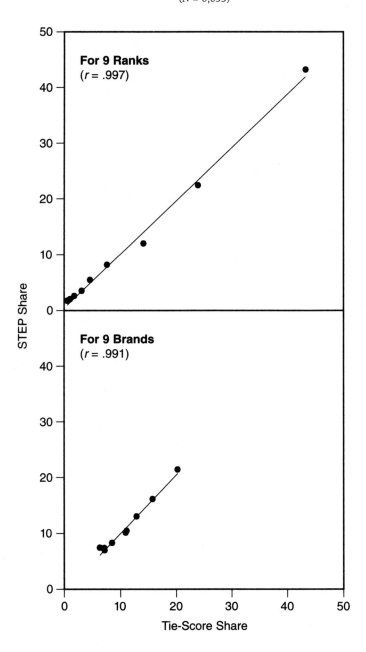

Figure 14–7
STEP Share versus Tie-Score Share
Spectrum Study
(N = 6,633)

when the STEP stickers are left alone and are treated as probabilities. If the data are internally consistent, this is precisely what one should expect, since summing the choices of a large number of respondents at different single points in time should conform to the choices of these same respondents over the course of time. All of this may seem abstract, but will turn out to have practical applications, explored in Chapter 20.

Can the tie model contribute to our understanding of the relationship between first-choice and STEP? I said in the previous chapter that first-choice is the most elemental measure of choice and that STEP is equivalent to ten first-choice measurements made in rapid succession. First-choice share and STEP share should therefore be highly related. We saw that this is indeed the case, but we also saw that the relationship is not linear. The upper panel of Figure 14–8 shows a plot of first-choice share versus stickers for the Spectrum data. The relationship is strong throughout the middle range, but first-choice share is about the same for eight, nine, and ten stickers. This observation immediately triggers the thought that this could be a manifestation of the tie model at work. Could the real relationship between first-choice and STEP lie in the tie scores that are, as it were, hidden in the STEP scores? What would happen if we computed tie scores, based entirely on the STEP scores, without using desirability-ranks at all?

Such tie scores will be called *internal tie scores,* internal because they use only the STEP stickers and transform these in accordance with the tie model into the "closest" ideal tie scores. Thus, the STEP sticker patterns 9 1 0 0 0, 8 2 0 0 0, and 8 1 1 0 0 are "closest" to the ideal tie-score pattern 10 0 0 0 0 in the sense of least squares and are transformed accordingly. Patterns 7 3 0 0 0, 6 4 0 0 0, and 5 4 1 0 0 are closest to 5 5 0 0 0 and so on. The resulting relationship between first-choice share and the internal tie scores is shown in the bottom panel of Figure 14–8. It is about as perfect as possible. First-choice and STEP contain precisely the same information, and the internal tie score is the device for extracting the common denominator, which, incidentally, constitutes further support for the Second Law.

Desirability-Rank and Choice

I have said that choice does not depend on the absolute level of desirability but on relative desirability. What kind of relationship should we then expect between desirability-rank and STEP share? Minimally, we expect STEP share to be a monotonically decreasing function of desirability-rank. That is, we expect fewer stickers to be given to brands that are liked less well. This much is a direct consequence of the tie matrix,

Figure 14–8
First-Choice Share versus STEP Stickers/Internal Tie Score
Spectrum Study
($N = 6,633$)

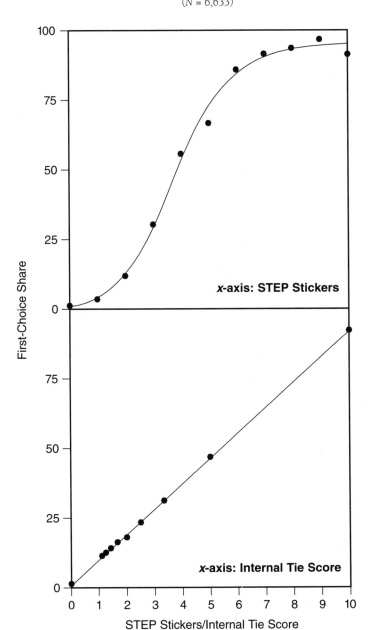

Figure 14–9
STEP Share versus Rank
Spectrum Study
(N = 6,633)

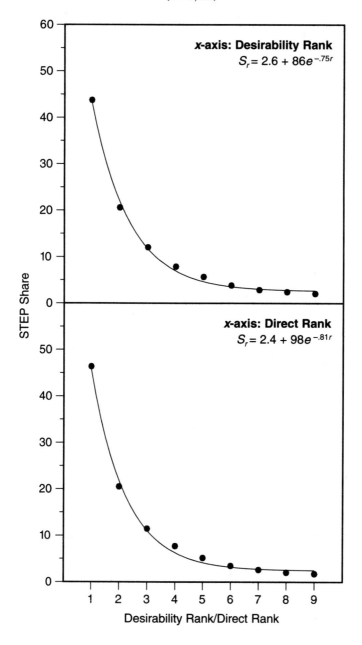

since each column of that matrix contains the same elements as the preceding column less one, so that each sum of elements must be smaller or, at most, equal to the sum of the elements in the preceding column.

The relationship, however, is not merely a monotonically decreasing function. It is a particular monotonically decreasing function, specifically a negative exponential.* The points in the upper panel of Figure 14–9 represent the empirical data for the Spectrum study. The curve is the best-fitting negative exponential. It fits the empirical points almost perfectly. Since the Spectrum study also collected direct ranks, we can examine the same relationship for direct rank. This is shown in the lower panel of Figure 14–9. It does not matter whether we use direct rank or desirability-rank (which is analytically constructed from the desirability scores), the result is about the same.

When I first saw this relationship, I felt that it was too good to be true. I thought that it had to reflect an artifact of some kind. If you arrange brands in order of their desirability and if people are more likely to give stickers to brands they like than to brands they don't like, then obviously each rank will receive fewer stickers than the rank before it. But the number of stickers diminishes in a consistent, orderly way. This is not an inevitable consequence of the Second Law alone. Even if the tie matrix applies, the particular function obtained depends on the distribution of tie-types. And though it is true that many possible distributions of tie-types generate tie-score shares that are approximately exponential, this is not a mathematical requirement. For example, the upper panel of Figure 14–10 shows the tie-score shares that would be generated by the frequency vector (the frequency distribution of the tie-types) 3 5 12 20 30 15 8 5 2 0. The lower panel shows the tie-score shares that would be generated by the frequency vector 0 0 0 30 40 30 0 0 0 0. The points represent the tie-score shares. The curves are the best-fitting exponentials. These data sets do not fit the exponential at all. But the distributions obtained from the real data *do* fit it, in fact fit it very well, not only for the Spectrum study but for many different product categories, as illustrated in Figures 14–11 through 14–13. Thus the data constitute a general empirical finding, which is summarized in the following principle.

THE EXPONENTIAL PRINCIPLE
Share of choice decreases exponentially with increasing desirability-rank.

---

*The form is $S_r = A_0 + A_1 e^{-dr}$ where r is desirability-rank, S_r is the STEP share given to the brand with desirability-rank r, d is the principal parameter of the function, A_0 is the asymptote, and A_1 is a normalizing constant.

Figure 14–10
Tie-Score Share versus Rank
Hypothetical Data, Demonstrating Poor Fit

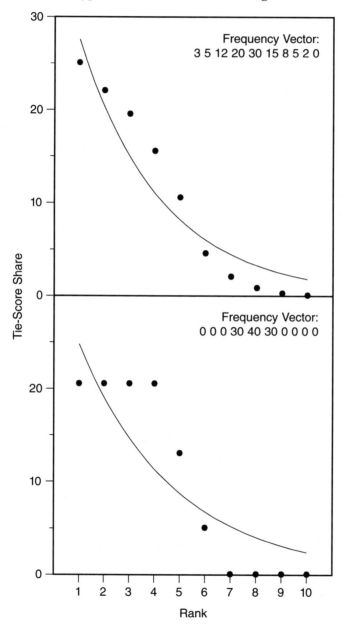

Figure 14–11
STEP Share versus Desirability-Rank

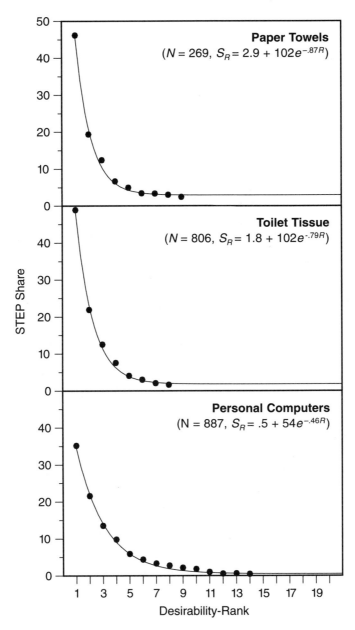

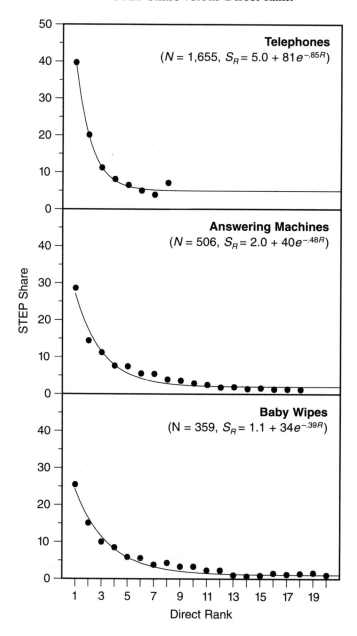

Figure 14–12
STEP Share versus Direct Rank

Figure 14–13
STEP Share versus Direct Rank

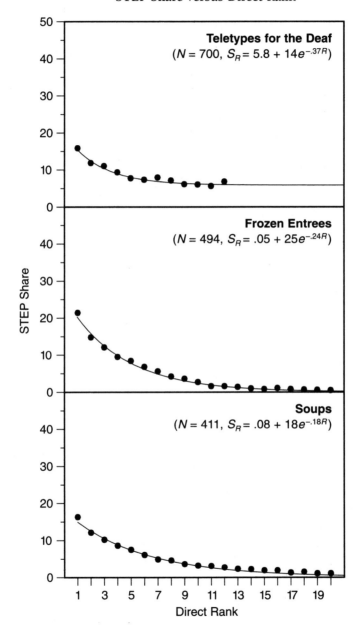

Product Category Differentiation

Although each of the curves in Figures 14–11 to 14–13 is a negative exponential of the same form, each curve has its own constant *d,* which reflects the steepness of the curve, the rate at which share of choice declines with increasing rank. This constant is related to an important characteristic of the category, its differentiation.

Category differentiation starts with the individual. One respondent, a wine connoisseur, can tell the difference between two vintages of the same label and is willing to pay hundreds of dollars for a single bottle. For her, wine is the quintessentially differentiated category. Another respondent cannot tell a Burgundy from a Bordeaux and cannot distinguish between a prestigious and an ordinary label. For her, wine is an undifferentiated category. If a category has *b* brands and a respondent's tie-type is *t,* there are *t* brands tied for first place (strong brands), and *b - t* remaining brands (weak brands). Since differentiation must become smaller as more brands are tied for first place, it can be defined in terms of the ratio of weak to strong brands, $(b - t)/t$. The maximum value this ratio can take occurs when $t = 1$, that is when there is only a single strong brand. In that case, the ratio is $(b - 1)/1 = b - 1$. Dividing through by this maximum possible value puts differentiation on a 0 to 100% basis and generates the definition of differentiation (D):

$$D = \left(\frac{1}{t}\right)\left(\frac{b - t}{b - 1}\right)$$

Given this definition, a Tie-Type 1 respondent in a category of *b* brands has a differentiation of $D = (1/1)(b - 1)/(b - 1) = 100\%$ and a Tie-Type b respondent in that same category has a differentiation of $D = (1/b)(b - b)/(b - 1) = 0\%$. By the same token, we define the differentiation of the product category as the average of the individual respondent differentiations.

One way of visualizing the implications of category differentiation is to consider two extremes. At one end of the continuum are categories that have 100% differentiation. These categories are composed of brands that are perceived to be uniquely different from each other. Some respondents prefer one brand; others prefer another brand. But no respondent considers two or more brands to be interchangeable, or even equally desirable. Setting aside the question of whether 100%-differentiation categories actually exist, or whether they are only a theoretical boundary condition, it follows from the definition that there are no ties in a category of 100% differentiation. At the other extreme are categories with 0% differentiation. Again it does not matter whether such categories actually exist or are only a theoretical boundary condition. We can say that such categories are made up of brands that respondents perceive to be interchangeable, or at least equal in desirability. For such a category, all scores are tied. Between these theoretical extremes are real categories with intermediate degrees of differentiation.

You may say, "All right, but so what?" It happens that these concepts have highly practical implications. Differentiation is directly measurable for different product categories and for different populations. And differentiated and undifferentiated product categories call for different marketing strategies. In a highly differentiated category, the marketer must select a selling strategy which, according to the Selling Strategy Principle discussed in Chapter 1, will persuade the customer that her brand has the characteristics that will satisfy the customer's desires better than any other brand. As the products offered by the various brands become more and more similar, however, the differentiation of the category, if any, becomes increasingly attributable to image alone. In that case, the best course of action is to focus on image and to proliferate brands.

This is illustrated by the following stylized example. Imagine an undifferentiated category that has four approximately equivalent and, insofar as the customer is concerned, interchangeable brands, each with a share of 25%. If the marketer simply repackages her brand, gives it a different label, and somehow induces the retailer to stock it, there will be five interchangeable brands on the shelf, each of which will, after the steady state has been reached, command a share of 20%. The marketer's total share will have risen from 25% to 40%. In that kind of market, name and label are of quintessential importance, because no matter how interchangeable the products may be, the one thing about a brand that always remains unique is its name and label. This is summarized in the following principle.

THE DIFFERENTIATION PRINCIPLE
In a differentiated product category, the optimal strategy is to develop unique product offers. In an undifferentiated product category, the optimal strategy is to focus on image and to proliferate brand names and labels.

PART IV

SYNTHESIZED OFFERS

This part of the book deals with the market shares of synthesized offers, that is, offers constructed by modeling.

Chapter 15 (Struggling to See the Obvious) describes two problems—the strategy planning problem and the diagnostic problem—that once seemed intractable, and tells how an effort to deal with these problems led to the development of SUMM (Single-Unit Marketing Model).

Chapter 16 (The Partitioning of Choice) describes SUMM, a choice model, and the view of marketing on which SUMM is based. This culminates in the definition of the universal marketing problem—the one problem every marketer must confront.

Chapter 17 (Constructing the Map) and Chapter 18 (Twists and Turns in Measuring the Desirability of Attributes) describe the measurement tools used in SUMM.

Chapter 19 (Dynamic Assessments) and Chapter 20 (The Synthesis of STEP and SUMM) demonstrate the predictive power of SUMM and its relation to STEP.

Chapter 21 (Brand Positioning) deals with the positioning of new brands, the repositioning of established brands, and the collection and interpretation of customer satisfaction data.

CHAPTER 15

Struggling to See the Obvious

Choice has been dealt with as a self-contained event, irreducible and discrete. It happens or it doesn't, and it cannot be partitioned into components, broken apart, and reconstituted. Yet that is precisely what we will do now. Today this seems the logical next step, but this was not always so. For the longest time, I was confounded by what I perceived to be two intractable problems. I called them the strategy planning problem and the diagnostic problem. I believed that I understood these problems sufficiently to appreciate why various proposed solutions to them were unacceptable. But I did not understand them sufficiently to see the solution that was staring me in the face, or sufficiently to realize that these apparently different problems were in fact one and the same and that a valid solution to one would automatically dispose of the other as well, something I grasped finally one day when the picture suddenly fell in place for me under the duress of a challenge from a prospective client. Let me tell you what these problems looked like in the mid-1950s and early 1960s and how I came to turn a critical corner in thinking about them.

The Strategy Planning Problem

The strategy planning problem was my first concern when I started to work in marketing research. It cropped up in various guises. Typically, the marketer would make a broad request: "We are marketing widgies and want to do a study to develop a deep understanding of the widgies market. We want to find out everything about widgie customers: when they get up in the morning, what they eat for breakfast, how long they have used widgies, how many widgies they use, how often they shop for widgies, which brands of widgies they buy," and on and on. Initially, I took these requests at face value. If the purpose was to find out everything about widgies, superior performance would surely consist of finding out not only everything you always wanted to know about widgies, but also everything you could conceivably have wanted to know about widgies. In that enterprise, the skill lay in generating several telephone books of tables, which, in the days when data were tabulated on counter-sorters and typed manually, was intrinsic evidence of the scope and hence excellence of the work.

In the beginning, I was full of enthusiasm. My studies were going to cover more ground than any done elsewhere. My enthusiasm did not last long. I found out soon enough that most of the information I collected was destined to be ignored. The vast bulk of the tables remained in appendixes that were never read. The written text usually received warm commendations like "very interesting," but did not, as far as I could tell, have any impact on what the people who had commissioned the studies actually did.

The studies served principally psychological, institutional, and occasionally ceremonial functions. The marketer could usually find solace somewhere in the report, if not in Chapter 1, then in Chapter 2 or 3 or 4, and could embrace its findings joyfully as evidence that she had been right all along, which seemed well worth the money that had been spent. The institutional benefit arose from the fact that it was chic in some organizations to assure management that extensive research had been done, and that recommendations were based on research. Finally, a research presentation could be scheduled that brought various echelons of corporate management together in one room, giving different players an opportunity to comment on findings and to demonstrate publicly that they were on top of their jobs. The mega-studies rarely had further impact on the business. This troubled me and I began to ponder how to correct it.

My first step was to shift from trying to find out everything to trying to find out only what the marketer actually needed to know. Stripped of extraneous considerations, this turned into what I came to call the strategy planning problem, epitomized by the question: "What must I promise my customer to maximize the probability that she will choose (buy) my brand?" The term *promise* referred not only to what was to be said to the customer in words, pictures, or music but also, by implication, to what changes in the product were to be made to support the promise. Once the strategy planning problem was formulated this way, it called for measuring what the customer wanted and to what extent she believed that the various available brands were giving her what she wanted.

I began to design strategy planning studies around the measurement of desires and beliefs. The respondents were asked to use scales, mainly +5 to -5 or 0 to 10 scales, to rate how much they liked various attributes of brands (the desires), and to indicate to what extent they judged that various brands possessed these attributes (the beliefs). My initial thought was that the best strategy for a brand would be to concentrate on attributes that the respondents desired and did not already attribute to the brand. Typically, the data were summarized in a desires and beliefs chart.

It did not take long before I became uncomfortably aware of fatal flaws in the logic. First, there were some conceptually trivial but practically serious concerns. How high was up? How high did the desires have to be to warrant consideration? If Attribute A with an average desire score of 4.5 was at the top of the list, could we safely go one-third of the way down the list and focus on Attribute F with an average desire score of 4.1? From the other end, how low did the customers' current belief about the brand need to be? Starting with Attribute W, which reflected the test brand's severest weakness (belief score 1.8), how high could we move up in an effort to find a proper balance between a high desire and a low belief?

These technical issues were only a hint of the more fundamental problem behind them. How would this analysis ever yield a recommendation to swim against the current, to pursue a strategy that might appeal to relatively few people but sufficiently to convert them into buyers? For a while, the idea of classifying respondents into segments seemed a possible solution. This approach appealed to me until I examined actual data. Empirically, it turned out that in varying degree all or almost all respondents wanted all or almost all attributes. And even if some respondents were a bit more concerned with the styling of an automobile, others with its performance, and still others with the comfort of the seats, none or hardly any of them were indifferent to any of these attributes. It was therefore difficult to classify respondents definitively into two or three or nine clean types. When they were forced into such procrustean beds, respondents belonging to a particular type usually proved to be almost as different from each other as from respondents belonging to other types. The data seemed to say that if we were really intent on classifying, we had to pursue the classification until the number of segments became so large that we needed a separate segment for each individual respondent. This seemed utterly absurd. It amounted to reading raw data, which, from the perspective of that time, would have been abandoning the analysis.

Stuck in this quagmire, I felt the need to go back to fundamentals. Stripped of all irrelevancies, we were trying to help the marketer decide what promises to make to induce the customer to buy the marketer's product. If that was the purpose, why not attack the problem head on? Why not construct an experiment, actually make different promises in the interview, and observe what happened? And so the precursor of STEP was born. To be sure, the mechanics were different in those days. The studies were done by means of personal interviews. Strategy statements were bound into portfolios. The criterion questions consisted of bounded numerical scales of desirability or purchase probability. But the critical elements were there. Randomly equivalent groups of respondents were exposed to different messages and were asked questions designed to ascertain their likelihood of buying various brands. I was out of the business of "analyzing" surveys. I had embraced the experiment, a critical transition that seemed so inevitable to me that it commanded my total commitment, left no room for turning back, and led to an obstinate insistence that this was the only way to approach the problem. It was better to reject assignments altogether than to tackle them with the strategy planning survey, which I had now come to regard as an inappropriate method.

I had founded EMA by then and was often approached by prospective clients who wanted to do what were called attitude and usage studies. When that happened, I usually launched into my tirade. The survey would not give them what they needed. The correct course of action was to define potential strategies, divide a total sample into randomly equivalent groups, and conduct an experiment that would tell them whether any of these strategies were effective, and if so which ones.

These speeches were received with intellectual appreciation, but most of the time my recommendations were rejected. The prospective client, usually a researcher, wanted to do a "major" study, not an experiment. He wanted to do that which had been done before, that which was then familiar, that which was expected of him, that which he would be able to sell to his marketing people and to his management. I came to dread the familiar phrase, "What you say is perfectly logical, but . . ." Once in a long while, my exposition produced a sudden insight, an appreciation of how beautifully simple and self-evident my recommendation was and an assignment to do the project. This was so rare that I came to take it for granted that insisting on my approach was tantamount to turning business away. I felt that this could not be helped, and I was resigned to it. There the matter stood for close to ten years.

The Diagnostic Problem

Separate from the strategy planning problem was the demand for diagnostics. No sooner had I begun to do controlled experiments than I encountered requests to add questions for "diagnostic" purposes. These requests were usually expressed in the form, "We want to know not only which message is best but also why." I resisted on the ground that I did not know how to do this, an admission that was received with raised eyebrows. My resistance was taken as evidence of arrogance, obstinacy, and unwillingness to play ball.

A common point of view was that whereas evaluation was quantitative, requiring large sample sizes and rigorous controls, diagnosis could be tackled qualitatively with small sample sizes and with just about any questions. I argued in vain that the controlled experiment provided the ultimate diagnosis par excellence. The observed result was directly attributable to the test message. If that message consisted of a single variable, we knew precisely what had produced the observed result: the test message. If the test message was made up of several components, separate experimental groups could be created to determine empirically which components were the critical ones and whether there were synergies among them. This reply was seen as theoretical. "Why can't you just ask them one or two or ten additional questions, so we will know not only what happened but also why?"

On occasion, I yielded under duress and agreed to tolerate add-ons if they did not interfere with the integrity of the experiment. I assuaged my conscience by putting my client on notice that in my judgment these add-ons were not worth the paper they were printed on. For the most part, however, EMA studies remained clean, single-criterion experiments, which was not seen as a virtue and was often held against me as a major shortcoming. The quintessential criticism reportedly leveled against EMA by a highly respected research director at a meeting of research directors was: "The trouble with STEP is it only gives you the answer," to which the research director who told me the story, an EMA client, laconically replied "Oh? It *only* gives you the answer?"

Sometime in the mid-1960s I gave a talk at a meeting of the American Association of Public Opinion Research in which I summarized my views on diagnosis. I said that I had thought about diagnosis at length and that I simply did not have an answer. I did believe, however, that I understood the problem. The balance of my talk consisted of defining the problem from the most general methodological perspective, which still summarizes my view today.

The term *diagnosis* implies an effort to explain a result, which in turn implies a criterion variable to be explained. This criterion variable can be purchasing, or voting, or STEP share, or any other measure used to evaluate a test message. If the criterion variable is Y, we cannot conduct a diagnosis by simply adding additional variables $Y_1, Y_2, \ldots$, parallel to the criterion variable. Such additions would lead either to a multiple-criteria analysis in which the researcher is free to select whichever scores he likes, an infraction of the Single-Criterion Principle discussed in Chapter 3, or to a redefinition of the criterion variable, asserting, for example, that the criterion should be changed to the largest of Y, Y_1, Y_2, or the mean of Y, Y_1, Y_2, or to some other function of the measures. Such a redefinition would evade the issue. The objective was not to abandon the criterion variable but to explain it in terms of something other than itself.

In the general case, we must select some variables, X_1, X_2, . . . , presumably variables over which we can exercise control, and express the criterion variable Y as a function of the X's. This amounts to thinking of the test message as made up of elements defined by the X's, and attempting to find out how much each of these elements contributes to the criterion variable. Suppose, for example, that the test message is a print ad and that the criterion variable (Y) is the incremental share of STEP stickers received by the test brand in a group exposed to the test ad compared to a control group not so exposed. Say this incremental share (Y) happens to be 2.5%. The demand for a diagnosis would be expressed colloquially by the question, "I understand that you got a 2.5%. But why was it 2.5% and not 4% or 5%?" Although the person asking this question hardly ever thinks of it that way, this implicitly demands that we partition the test message, in this case the ad, and then attribute this or that portion of the effect to this or that aspect of the ad. But even if we succeeded in doing that, the exercise would still fall short of the mark, as illustrated in the following dialogue.

The marketer has demanded to know "why" the test ad got a low score. The researcher is exploring the meaning of the request: "Why do you want to know?"

"Because I want to understand it."

"And why do you want to understand it?"

"As things stand, I don't know what to do next. But if you tell me why the ad scored poorly, I will be able to fix it and make a better ad."

"So you don't really want to know why the ad isn't working. You want to know how to make a better ad."

"If I knew why the ad isn't working I would be able to make a better ad."

This inference simply does not hold. Even if we could tell the marketer precisely "why" the ad wasn't working, this would not necessarily enable her to make a more effective ad. The marketer's commonsense request is a front for another, more stringent demand that is rarely articulated explicitly. Uncovering this hidden demand leads to the following formulation of the "diagnostic problem":

"Here is a test message. Tell me (a) how this particular test message scores on the criterion variable, and (b) how an unlimited number of alternative messages that have not yet been created would score if they were created and tested. You don't have to tell me how every possible message would score, and your prediction does not need to be very precise. But you must give me a reasonable broad-stroke prediction of how a large number of test messages would score if they were created and tested."

Such a prediction is the minimum information a method would have to generate before it could be thought of as a genuine "diagnostic" method. I concluded my remarks by saying that I did not know how to do this, that I did not even know whether it could be done, but that I believed that I had at least understood the problem.

Both the strategy planning problem and the diagnostic problem remained in my repertoire as unsolved, possibly unsolvable, problems. But I was not unduly troubled by this. I felt that the marketer could get all the answers she wanted provided she was willing to take the high road, do it the hard way, fall back on controlled experiments, and proliferate the number of groups as her taste for answers, explanations, and diagnoses escalated. My self-righteous bottom line was that those who wanted answers could get them by experiments and that those who did not want the pain of experiments did not deserve answers. I knew that this position was alienating prospective clients but consoled myself with the thought that this was the price of intellectual integrity, and that it was in any event more fun to work with people who could see the logic of the argument than with those who could not or would not.

A New Look at an Old Problem

Sometime around 1967, I received a call from a stranger who identified himself as a prospective client. We met for lunch. He explained that he wanted to do a major strategy planning study for his brand. My heart sank. I had been around this track many times and thought I could predict the exchange that would follow. I took a deep breath and launched into my exposition, explaining that general studies of this type did not yield actionable results, that the only way I knew of attacking the problem was to define alternative strategies and to evaluate those experimentally. He listened thoughtfully. When I had finished, he surprised me.

"I agree with you," he said, "but this leaves me with a dilemma. We know very little about the category. We don't even know where to begin. As we think about it, we can easily enumerate a large number of possible strategies, say one thousand. Now you are not really recommending that I run a controlled experiment using one thousand separate groups to evaluate these options?"

I flinched.

"OK," he continued, "then you must mean that I should first judgmentally select a relatively small number of strategies, say ten, out of the large list of possibles, and that you will do a study to help me pick the best of those ten, which may all be bad to begin with."

I shifted uneasily.

"I cannot believe," he concluded, "that this is the best that research can do for me. There must be some better way to select options from a large list than by judgment alone."

This appeal stopped me. He was right. His request had to be taken seriously. I replied: "I have never been able to figure out a good way of doing what you are asking, and I don't want to recommend a study if, in the end, I will have less confidence in my data than in your judgment. But your request is reasonable. I'll think about it."

I began to think about it as soon as I started to walk back to my office. I had not actively dealt with the problem for years. Now I looked at it with fresh eyes, looked at it on the merits, and suddenly a thought struck me, a thought so obvious that I found it difficult to comprehend why it had eluded me so long. Every effort I had ever made to deal with the problem had, by force of long habit, involved a resort to summary statistics, perhaps averages or medians or correlations or other measures, but always statistics predicated on aggregating data from different individuals. I suddenly realized that this had been fundamentally wrong. Brand choice has a different structure. Choices are made by individuals, not by collections of individuals. Any attempt to explain choice based on aggregations of individuals was doomed to failure. The problem had to be turned around. Instead of asking what was desired on the average, the interplay of attributes had to be examined one respondent at a time. For the purpose of predicting what a respondent would choose, only that particular respondent's desires and beliefs counted. The data from all the other respondents were irrelevant.

By the time I reached my office, I saw what we had to do. I went to the blackboard and wrote out the basic framework of the new technique. I subsequently named it SUMM (Single-Unit Marketing Model) in recognition of the fact that it analyzes data in terms of single units, that is one respondent at a time. SUMM has grown into a major tool since then. The measuring instruments, the scope of the applications, and our understanding of how to use them in practice, have evolved over the course of the years, but the basic idea remains the same today as when I first wrote it on my blackboard over twenty-five years ago.

It is ironic that the man who had posed the problem so cogently did not become the first user of SUMM. By the time I called him several days later to offer him my answer, he had lost interest in the question. But I remain grateful to him for having challenged me to take a new look at an old problem.

CHAPTER 16

The Partitioning of Choice

Taking one respondent at a time, the partitioning of choice turns out to be a process that follows directly from the Second Law. The individual customer wants things: product attributes, image attributes, price, and familiarity. These wants are not necessarily consistent. She may want a car that will carry twenty people because she has a large family, and she may want the car to be ten feet long in order to fit two of them into her one-car garage. There is no law against wanting. In the real world, however, she cannot get everything she wants, so she adopts what we may think of as a second line of defense: "If I can't get what I want, let me see what I can get." She examines her options and evaluates these. This evaluation may be implicit, as when she picks up a package of paper towels from the shelf of a supermarket, apparently without giving the matter much thought, or explicit, as when she makes a detailed list of the advantages and disadvantages of cars, houses, or jobs. Explicitly or implicitly, she always makes such an evaluation. Then she chooses the brand that gives her more of the things she wants than any other brand. More precisely, according to the Second Law, if t brands are effectively tied for first-place desirability, she chooses any of these t brands with probability $1/t$.

When I first articulated SUMM, I did not understand all of this in a formal way. The rational structure, the relationship between STEP and SUMM, and particularly the formal statement of the Second Law, all came later. But the one thing I grasped right away was that the moment the problem was approached one respondent at a time, everything that had previously seemed difficult became simple. Accordingly, I will begin with the partitioning of the choice of a single respondent.

Topics and Attributes

A *map* is constructed. This is a list of characteristics that could play a part in the customer's choice. SUMM maps are made up of *attributes*, which are grouped into *topics*. In selecting and organizing the attributes, two rules apply:

205

1. The attributes of any single topic must be mutually exclusive.
2. The attributes of different topics are not allowed to be mutually exclusive or to duplicate each other.

Actual maps typically consist of fifty to two hundred attributes, grouped into five to forty topics. For simplicity's sake, I will use a stylized product category, widgies. Widgies are easy to work with. They can be represented by only twelve attributes, organized into only four topics:

Topic	Attribute
1. Height	1: 2 feet
	2: 3 feet
	3: 4 feet
	4: 5 feet
2. Shape	1: round
	2: oval
	3: square
3. Appearance	1: beautiful
	2: attractive
	3: ordinary
4. Class	1: upper class
	2: middle class
	3: lower class

The topic names are used solely as convenient labels. The topics are actually defined by the attributes that comprise them. Widgies come in discrete heights: 2 feet, 3 feet, and so on. If their height varied continuously, we could have used intervals like "between 4 feet and 4.9 feet high." Widgies come in three shapes: round, oval, square. If combinations of shapes were the rule, we could have created such attributes as: "completely round," "partly round and partly square," and so on.

The widgies map illustrates topic types: quantitative variables such as height, qualitative variables such as shape, subjective variables such as appearance, and image variables such as social class. We need not take a position on whether it is meaningful to speak of the "social class" of a widgie. Such questions could certainly trigger a debate in a study design meeting, but the system is structurally indifferent to them. If the words can be used, the system can accommodate them, relevant or not. If they happen to be irrelevant, they will introduce some noise, which will not be fatal.

The map is the qualitative representation of the product category, the structural skeleton on which the measurements are built. Its construction is important and will be discussed in Chapter 17. One point, however, should be noted immediately: A map is simply a collection of attributes. It is neither right nor wrong, only more or less useful for a particular purpose. And even a poorly crafted map can yield valuable information, though it may not be focused on the problem at hand.

Insofar as the brands are concerned, the map functions as a descriptor. More specifically, a map of t topics is a t-dimensional descriptor. This means that, within the system, each brand of widgies is fully described by t attributes, one from each topic. In the example at hand, $t = 4$. Therefore, a brand of widgies is completely described by four attributes, for example: 5 feet long, round, attractive, and upper class.

Desires and Beliefs

Once the map has been defined, we can construct the questionnaire. This involves measuring the desirability of the attributes, and the beliefs about the brands. To avoid losing sight of the forest for the trees, a full discussion of the measurement process is deferred to Chapter 18. I am assuming for the moment that we are able, within reasonable bounds, to generate attribute desirability scores that are comparable within and across topics, and are additive across topics.

We begin by examining the data obtained from Alice, shown in Table 16–1. The first column shows the desirability of the various attributes. We see that Alice wants small widgies rather than large ones. She wants them to be square, beautiful, and middle class. It may not be quite clear just what Alice means when she expresses that preference, but we surmise that she is a down-to-earth lady and doesn't like widgies that are fancy. The data provide specific quantitative elaborations. Alice wants widgies to be beautiful, but beauty is worth only 5 points to her. On the other hand, it is very important to her that a widgie should not take up too much space. She assigns a full 60 points to a 2-foot widgie, compared to 25 and 20 points to 3-foot and 4-foot widgies, respectively, and 0 points to a 5-foot widgie. Taken as a whole, the column measures what Alice wants in a widgie. It is known as her *desires profile*.

We turn next to Alice's beliefs about the various brands available to her: Brands A, B, and C. We employ the map to measure what Alice believes about these brands. For each topic, she tells us which attribute best describes each brand. She believes that Brand A is 5 feet high and that Brands B and C are 3 feet high. She also believes that Brand A is round. Our engineers say that Alice is wrong, but we believe that the customer is always right. The distinction between "round" and "oval" may, in any event, be a metaphysical one. Even our engineers may have to concede

Table 16–1
Desirability of Attributes
and Beliefs about Three Brands of Widgies

Attribute	Desirability of the Attribute (d)	Beliefs about Brands			Desirability Contribution (c) for Brand		
		A	B	C	A	B	C
2 feet	60						
3 feet	25		x	x		25	25
4 feet	20						
5 feet	0	x			0		
Square	20		x	x		20	20
Oval	5						
Round	0	x			0		
Beautiful	5			x			5
Attractive	3	x	x		3	3	
Ordinary	0						
Upper class	0		x			0	
Middle class	15			x			15
Lower class	12	x			12		
SUMM score (U_k) of Brand k					15	48	65
Chosen brand							C
SUMM share (U_k) of Brand k					0	0	100%

grudgingly that some "ovals" can appear to be dangerously "round." Alice may also be using language in a looser but perhaps more psychologically meaningful way than the engineers. In any event, if Alice says Brand A is round, it is round for purposes of the system. Taken together, Alice's beliefs about the brands, A, B, and C, are called Alice's *beliefs profile* for widgies. Apart from background classification, the desires profile and the beliefs profile are all the information we collect from Alice.

Over and above what we have learned overtly, the data contain implicit information about how Alice relates to widgies. This information needs to be extracted in a formal way, which is done in the three right-most columns of the table. Alice has told us that a 5-foot widgie has a desirability of 0 to her, while a 3-foot widgie has a desirability of 25. She has also told us that she believes that Brand A is 5 feet high and that Brands B and C are 3 feet high. Accordingly, we credit Brand A with 0 points and Brands B and C with 25 points each. These numbers are called *desirabil-*

ity contributions, or *contributions* for short. In general, the contribution of a topic to a brand is equal to the desirability of the one attribute of the topic the respondent believes best describes the brand. It is 0 for all other attributes. Crediting each brand with one contribution for each of t topics, we obtain t contributions per brand. The SUMM score of a brand is defined as the sum of its t contributions.

The SUMM scores of Brands A, B, and C are 15, 48, and 65, respectively, as shown at the bottom of the table. None of the three brands gives Alice everything she wants. If a brand had done that, it would have had a SUMM score of 100. But Brand C has come closer to giving Alice more of the things she wants, as evidenced by the fact that its SUMM score is higher than the SUMM scores of the other brands. Accordingly, we call Alice a *chooser* of Brand C, and we call Brand C her *chosen brand.* Under actual market conditions, Alice may buy some other brand on account of accessibility, but holding accessibility constant, she should, in accordance with the Second Law, choose the brand with the highest desirability (SUMM score) within the error band of the map and the measurement devices.

An Illustrative Three-Person Market

We return to our point of departure. The measurements were undertaken in order to address the strategy planning problem. Our client's brand, Brand A, is in trouble, and the client has requested that we generate recommendations. If we were concerned only with Alice, the answer would be clear by inspection. We would propose to change Brand A to give Alice everything she wants. We would make Brand A 2 feet high, square, beautiful, and middle class. This would capture her as a chooser. But it is not as simple as that. Alice is not the only customer. Our success or failure hinges not only on her, but also on many other customers, each of whom has different desires and different beliefs.

To illustrate the complexity this gives rise to, we shall examine a tiny market consisting of only three respondents, Alice, Jane, and Mary. Even for such a trivial case, the solution is no longer self-evident. Table 16–2 shows the data for Alice, Jane, and Mary. The table has a lot of numbers, and it may seem tedious to examine them all, but it is worth the trouble because this table fully illustrates the conceptual features of SUMM.

First, the table shows the attribute desirability and the desirability contributions credited to the three brands, A, B, and C, for each of the three respondents, Alice, Jane, and Mary. At the bottom of the page we see the SUMM scores and the choices implied by these SUMM scores. Alice is a chooser of Brand C; Jane is a chooser of Brand B; Mary is a chooser of Brand A. Therefore, each of the three brands has a 33% share of the three-customer market.

Table 16–2
The Three-Person Widgies Market

	Alice Desirability of Attribute	Contribution to Brand A	B	C	Jane Desirability of Attribute	Contribution to Brand A	B	C	Mary Desirability of Attribute	Contribution to Brand A	B	C	Average Desirability
2 feet	60				0				0				20
3 feet	25		25	25	15		15	15	14		14	14	18
4 feet	21				15				36				(24)
5 feet	0	0			9	9			30	30			13
Square	20		20	20	29		29	29	26		26	26	(25)
Oval	5				55				0				20
Round	0	0			0	0			30	30			10
Beautiful	5			5	15			15	10			10	(10)
Attractive	3	3	3		15	15	15		0	0	0		6
Ordinary	0				0				0				0
Upper class	0		0		15		15		0		0		5
Middle class	15			15	0			0	24			24	(13)
Lower class	12	12			0	0			24	24			12
SUMM score		15	48	(65)		24	(74)	59		(84)	40	74	
Chooser of				**C**			**B**			**A**			

The SUMM What-If Game

To understand what the data tell us about the market, more particularly what they tell us about which strategy will improve Brand A's market share, we must summarize the data somehow. Traditionally, this has meant calculating the average desirabilities of the attributes. These are shown in the far right column of the table. But we will now go about the job in an entirely different way.

Instead of focusing on averages, instead of poring over telephone books of output, we will interrogate the data dynamically, asking questions and generating answers. Each of these questions is called a *SUMM What-If Game,* ("game," for short) and is designed to evaluate the impact of some potential course of action. For example, Brand A is currently believed to be 5 feet high. All three respondents characterize it that way, perhaps because it is objectively so, perhaps because Brand A was 5 feet high until last year and none of the customers have yet learned that its height has been changed. In either case, we can ask whether the brand would benefit from a change in this belief. What would happen if we could persuade all respondents that Brand A is 4 feet high? Would this increase Brand A's market share, leave it unchanged, or conceivably decrease it, making matters worse than they are right now?

In posing this or any other what-if question, the focus is on the relationship between beliefs and choice. The question is always whether some belief change would be good or bad for a brand, without prejudice as to whether such a change would be easy or difficult to accomplish or what specific steps would be required to accomplish it. For example, if Brand A were actually 5 feet high, persuading customers that it is 4 feet high might require a redesign of the physical product. On the other hand, if Brand A is actually 4 feet high, persuading them that this is the case might require only an advertising campaign to demonstrate the facts.

Exploring strategic options in SUMM always involves changing one or more beliefs about one or more brands and assessing the potential impact on market share, as measured by chooser share. Speaking loosely, we may ask whether we should change the "shape" of a brand. However, this is only a convenient shorthand. We really mean *beliefs* about the shape. The question should always be understood to be of the form:

THE SUMM-GAME QUESTION

What would be the impact on chooser share if beliefs about one or more brands could be changed from $X_1, X_2, X_3, \ldots$ to Y_1, Y_2, Y_3?

By the same token, every answer is of the form:

THE SUMM-GAME ANSWER

If beliefs about one or more brands could be changed from X_1, X_2, X_3, . . . to Y_1, Y_2, Y_3, the chooser shares of Brands A, B, and C would change by Z_a, Z_b, Z_c, . . . share points.

Each game simulates a possible marketing action and functions as a stand-in for a STEP group in which the impact of that action could have been investigated experimentally.

Let us now return to the question: Would it be a good strategy to change the height of Brand A to 4 feet? We are considering this possibility because we noticed that 4 feet has the highest average desirability score for this topic. To answer this question, we examine the respondents one at a time, beginning with Alice. If her belief about Brand A were to change to 4 feet, the desirability of Brand A would go up by 21 points, from 15 to 36. This would not be enough to beat Brand C's 65, and she would remain a Brand C chooser. For Jane, Brand A's desirability would go up by 6 points, from 24 to 30, which would not be enough to beat Brand B's 74. She would remain a Brand B chooser. For Mary, Brand A's desirability would go up by 6 points, from 84 to 90. She is a Brand A chooser and would remain a Brand A chooser. The net result would be that the chooser shares of all three brands would remain unchanged at 33% each.

Perhaps some other strategy would do better. Again, we look for something the customers want, a characteristic that has a high average desirability score. We note that Brand A is uniformly perceived to be round, which has an average desirability of only 10. But the average desirability score for a square widgie is 25, a full 15 points higher. Wouldn't this be a good strategy for Brand A? Once again the average desirability is misleading. When we examine the consequences of making Brand A square, the 20-point gain for Alice is not enough to win her over, the 29-point gain for Jane is not enough to win her, and the 4-point loss for Mary is not enough to lose her. Once again, the net result is no change in choosers. The shares remain 33% for each of the brands. How about making Brand A beautiful rather than just attractive? Or middle class rather than lower class? These strategies don't work either.

Suppose we adopted a compound strategy? In particular, suppose we made all four changes simultaneously, giving Brand A the height that has the highest average desirability (4 feet), the shape that has the highest average desirability (square), the appearance that has the highest average desirability (beautiful), and the social class that has the highest average desirability (middle class)? These changes are illustrated in Table 16–3. For

Table 16–3
A Four-Shift Game in the Three-Person Widgies Market

	Alice Desirability of Attribute	Contribution to Brand A	B	C	Jane Desirability of Attribute	Contribution to Brand A	B	C	Mary Desirability of Attribute	Contribution to Brand A	B	C	Average Desirability
2 feet	60				0				0				20
3 feet	25		25	25	15		15	15	14		14	14	18
4 feet	21				15				36				(24)
5 feet	0	(0)			9	(9)			30	(30)			13
Square	20		20	20	29		29	29	26		26	26	(25)
Oval	5				55				0				20
Round	0	(0)			0	(0)			30	(30)			10
Beautiful	5			5	15			15	10			10	(10)
Attractive	3	(3)	3		15	(15)	15		0	(0)	0		6
Ordinary	0				0				0				0
Upper class	0		0		15		15		0		0		5
Middle class	15			15	0			0	24			24	(13)
Lower class	12	(12)			0	(0)			24	(24)			12
Before SUMM score		15	48	(65)		24	(74)	59		(84)	40	74	
Chooser of				C			B			A			
After SUMM score		61	48	(65)		59	(74)	59		(96)	40	74	
Chooser of				C			B			A			

Alice, Brand A gains 46 points (21 + 20 + 2 + 3 = 46), which is not enough
to beat brand C. For Jane, Brand A gains 35 points (6 + 29 + 0 + 0 = 35),
which is not enough to beat Brand B. And for Mary, Brand A gains 12 points
(6 - 4 + 10 + 0 = 12), which is fine, except that Mary was a Brand A chooser
to begin with. So the compound strategy too has come to naught.

Does this mean that there are no strategies that make a difference? Not
necessarily. It does mean that it is high time to abandon the pursuit of
averages and to attack the problem on the merits. This requires one of two
approaches: exploring a large number of potential strategies systematically
by brute force, or thinking about the marketing problem, formulating
major hypotheses, and testing these by means of games. Doing the latter,
we note that there is no 2-foot brand and no oval brand on the market. We
also decide to explore the potential of shifting to an upper-class positioning. Characteristically, we investigate the potential of these strategies by
examining each of these changes separately (three games), all pairs (three
games), and the combination of all three (one game)—altogether seven
games. The outcome is summarized in Table 16–4. When we make Brand
A 2 feet high, we do indeed capture a new customer. Alice wants the 2-
foot height so much that this alone is sufficient to make her switch away
from Brand C. Jane sticks with Brand B. But now we encounter an inex-
orable fact of life: The very change that was instrumental in winning over
one customer, Alice, *loses* another customer, Mary, to whom the 2-foot
height is sufficiently undesirable to induce her to switch away from Brand

Table 16–4
Investigating Potential Strategy for Brand A
by Means of Seven Games

Game Number	Changing Belief of Brand A to			Results in Choice of Brand			Brand A Chooser Share
	2 ft.	Oval	Upper Class	Alice	Jane	Mary	
1	x			A	B	C	33
2		x		C	A	C	33
3			x	C	B	C	0
4	x	x		A	B	C	33
5	x		x	C	B	C	0
6		x	x	C	A	C	33
7	x	x	x	A	A	C	67

A to Brand C. Thus, this strategy would result in churning but no net gain. The oval strategy results in even more churning. We don't capture Alice, who stays with Brand C. We do capture Jane from Brand B. But we lose Mary to Brand C. Again we have traded one customer for another. In the process, we have weakened one competitor, strengthened another, and achieved no gain for ourselves. By the same token, none of the pair strategies yields a gain. But when we examine the compound strategy of offering a widgie that is 2 feet high, oval, and upper class, we find that whereas this repositioning is totally unacceptable to Mary and we lose her to Brand C, the 2-foot feature is sufficiently desirable to Alice to induce her to switch to Brand A, and the oval-plus-upper-class combination is sufficiently desirable to Jane to induce her to switch to Brand A. The net result is the loss of an existing customer and the gain of two new customers, giving us a market share of 67%.

Insofar as the data are concerned, the answer is clear. We have identified a strategy that will increase our share of the three-person market from 33% to 67%. Whether we would be well advised to pursue this strategy is another question. In particular, it might be necessary to evaluate gains and losses differently, depending on how widgies are sold. If widgies are bought frequently, we might expect to lose current customers quickly, since they would realize at once that the product has changed. On the other hand it might take some time, and might require an uphill struggle, before we could succeed in arousing sufficient curiosity among noncustomers to overcome their inertia and try our brand. In general, no actual change in an established brand should be undertaken without careful scrutiny of whether the potential gains are large enough to offset probable losses. This point, of course, becomes moot if the proposed strategy does not involve losses or if the losses are negligibly small.

The alternative is to consider introducing a new brand or a line extension. This option can also be investigated by means of the appropriate SUMM game. Suppose we left Brand A unchanged but introduced a new brand, AA, which is 2 feet high, oval, beautiful, and upper class. For Alice, this brand would have a desirability of 70 ($60 + 5 + 5 + 0 = 70$), thus capturing her from Brand C. For Jane, it would achieve a desirability of 85 ($0 + 55 + 15 + 15 = 85$), capturing her from Brand B. But for Mary, it would achieve a desirability of only 10 ($0 + 0 + 10 + 0 = 10$), leaving her a chooser of Brand A. The net result would be that we could potentially hold on to our Brand A share of 33%, while pursuing the development of the new Brand AA, which, if marketed successfully, could capture a 67% share of market in its own right, all from competitive Brands B and C and none from our existing Brand A, so we would end up with a 100% share of the market.

This is all well and good for the illustrative three-person market. As we progress to a real market consisting of millions of customers, or merely to a real sample consisting of 1,000 respondents, more or less, the answers are not as pat. The complexity becomes greater, and no variation of any existing brand, or even combination of two or three existing brands, may achieve a majority share of an established product category. Concurrently, the marketing costs associated with multiple brand strategies and the difficulties of implementing them successfully become commensurately larger, so there are real limitations on how effectively some theoretically viable options can be exploited in practice. No matter how large the market, however, or the number of brands in it, or the difficulties of manufacturing, distributing, and promoting entries, the basic problems and the basic principles that must be kept in mind remain essentially the same as those encountered in the three-person widgies market.

This market illustrates the ultimate dilemma of marketing. As long as we can custom-produce a different product for each customer, we need only "sell." This means that we must find out what each customer wants and make it for her. We may not be able to do that because our product design effort is not good enough or our manufacturing process is not efficient enough, but there is no puzzle to solve. The moment we need to sell the *same* product to many people, however, we face an entirely new problem. In satisfying one customer, we run the risk of losing another. In that circumstance, it is no longer meaningful to ask, "What do customers want?" Instead, we must focus on what we can do to improve our position. This is the most relevant, if not the only, way of learning what the data can teach us about the product category.

Marketers and researchers, who have been brought up to look at data in the aggregate, are often frustrated and disappointed by this approach. They are willing to accept the idea that recommendations for action may flow from SUMM games, but they want to look at "actual data" first, by which they usually mean average scores. It is certainly easy enough to furnish these. But we have seen that averages can obscure as much as they reveal. If we had used them as the basis for constructing a marketing strategy for Brand A, we would have been wrong. What is often overlooked is that conventional summaries don't necessarily provide better descriptions of data than do SUMM games. The raw responses of the respondents contain information of great complexity. The average desirability of the attributes is one possible reduction of these data. It gives a lot of information, and leaves out a lot of information. The output of a SUMM game is another reduction of the data. It gives a lot of information and leaves out a lot of information. Which is right? Again, it is not a matter of right or wrong but of relevance. Although conventional data aggregation is universally familiar, it just doesn't happen to be appropriate for dealing with the marketer's problem. SUMM, on the other hand, was specifically designed to do just that.

We can now formulate the marketer's problem rigorously, as follows:

> THE UNIVERSAL MARKETING PRINCIPLE
>
> In a market in which a small number of brands are competing for a large number of customers, most of whom have different desires, the universal marketing question is: Which promises will induce the largest possible number of customers to choose my brand?

This is the universal question. Every marketer confronts it and must answer it, explicitly or implicitly, with data or without, with data that have been specifically designed to contribute to its answer or with data that have been collected for other purposes. Our desire to help the marketer answer this question has brought us to where we are.

Almost by inadvertence, we have disposed of the diagnostic problem as well. The effort to aid strategy planning led to the creation of the map, the assessment of the relative desirability of the various attributes comprising the map, and the partitioning of the desirability of brands into components contributed by the various attributes. But I previously identified just such a partitioning as the sine qua non of diagnosis. I said that to qualify as a diagnostic method, a method would have to offer a prediction of what would happen to a brand's share if new messages were created and tested. This is precisely what we have done. Thus it is obvious, though I did not grasp it for a long time, that the strategy planning problem and the diagnostic problem are one and the same. Each requires estimates of the probable effects of future actions.

By the same token, STEP and SUMM are interchangeable methods. In STEP, we give the respondents a booklet. They answer *one* question, making choices among brands by dividing stickers among them. The result is a share for each brand in the competitive frame. In SUMM, we give the respondents a booklet. They answer *many* questions. We combine the answers to these questions. Again, the result is a share for each brand in the competitive frame. If we have done the job properly, the shares so obtained will be approximately equal. Thus, it might seem that all we have done in constructing SUMM is to create a long interview to generate a share that could have been generated with a short interview. That is true, but something important has been gained in the process. Because

the long interview generates the share not from a single behavioral measure but from many contributing components, we can rearrange these
components at will and evaluate not only a single message but an almost
unlimited number of messages. This allows us to evaluate prospective
strategies on the one hand, and to answer requests for diagnostics on the
other hand, in each case by predicting the probable consequences of
potential future actions.

CHAPTER 17

Constructing the Map

A SUMM map consists of attributes. For simplicity's sake, we have so far referred only to attributes that are verbal descriptions, but this is not an intrinsic requirement. Attributes can be pictures, for example: "It has a shape like that shown in [Illustration A, Illustration B, etc.]," or physical prototypes, for example: "Its softness is like the softness of [Prototype A, Prototype B, etc.]." The only requirement is that attributes must characterize brands, in words, pictures, or otherwise.

Attributes are organized into topics. The general rule is that the attributes of a topic must be mutually exclusive and that the attributes of different topics are not allowed to be mutually exclusive. In practice, the implications of these rules are not always self-evident. For example, the attributes

- It is a two-wheel-drive vehicle.
- It is a four-wheel-drive vehicle.

may not form a properly structured topic. Respondents who take the words literally might feel obliged to check both of these attributes when referring to a four-wheel-drive vehicle. A more conservative structure would be:

- It is a two-wheel-drive vehicle.
- It is a vehicle that usually operates in two-wheel drive but can be shifted into four-wheel drive.
- It is a vehicle that operates in four-wheel drive all the time.

Given this topic, it is not appropriate to construct another topic composed of the attributes:

- It has a manual transmission.
- It has an automatic transmission.
- It has an automatic transmission, including an automatic shift from two-wheel drive to four-wheel drive.

The reference to the automatic shift from two-wheel to four-wheel drive should have been broken out and included as an attribute of the four-wheel-drive topic, where it could have been mutually exclusive with the other attributes of that topic, for example:

- It is a vehicle that automatically shifts from two-wheel drive to four-wheel drive as needed.

Levels of Generality

A SUMM map is a representation of a psychological terrain. Like all maps, it involves stylization and simplification, omission of irrelevant detail, and focus on elements that are deemed essential. A topographical map may show elevations but not political boundaries. A map of bus routes may show bus stops, arranged in rectangular patterns, ignoring the shapes of the roads and the distances between the stops. By the same token, the topics and attributes of a SUMM map may include some details and omit others, depending on the purpose for which the map is designed. As in the case of a geographical map, the first step in the construction of the map is to select a scale. In the case of SUMM, this amounts to selecting a level of generality, which is determined by the breadth of the competitive frame. If the scale is small, the topics and attributes can be detailed. If the scale is large, the topics and attributes must be commensurately general.

Suppose we undertake a study of powdered orange drinks. Such a study might cover aspects of powdered orange drinks in considerable detail. For example:

- It is a fine powder.
- It is a coarse powder.
- It is a powder consisting of large crystals.
- etc.

- The powder dissolves instantly upon contact with water without stirring.
- The powder dissolves within thirty seconds of contact with water without stirring.
- etc.

- Once dissolved, the powder remains in solution indefinitely.
- The powder settles out after several hours and must be re-stirred before use.
- etc.

If it is desired to enlarge the competitive frame to include all fruit-flavored beverages, such as juice drinks and juices, the detailed topics listed above, and others similarly focused on powdered beverages, are no longer appropriate. In judging which topics and attributes are appropriate, we must remember that the system calls for two kinds of judgments from the respondent: how much she desires each attribute and which of the attributes of each topic best describes each brand. Clearly, it does not make sense to ask the respondent which powder coarseness best describes a cranberry juice cocktail that is sold as a liquid in a bottle. Instead, the scale of the map must be enlarged, using topics and attributes that span the broader competitive frame and are applicable to all brands of the broader frame:

- It comes as a ready-to-drink liquid.
- It comes as a frozen concentrate you mix with water.
- It comes as a powder you dissolve in water.
- etc.

- It is a fruit juice.
- It is a blend of fruit juices.
- It is a blend of water and fruit juices.
- It is a blend of water, sweeteners, and flavor ingredients.

If the scope of the study is expanded again to cover all cold beverages, including beer, carbonated beverages, and mineral waters, the level of generality of the topics may be expanded again to accommodate the broader span. The map might now include such topics as:

- It contains alcohol.
- It does not contain alcohol.

- It is a carbonated beverage.
- It is not carbonated.

- It contains around 150 calories per glass.
- It contains around 100 calories per glass.
- etc.

Which of these levels of generality is right? All are right. Some may be more useful than others for a particular purpose. The more general the level, the wider is the range of the recommendations it can yield. Such recommendations may, however, become so general that they will frustrate the marketer. Conversely, as the level of generality is reduced, finer detail can be included, but the range of the subject matter covered shrinks. In principle, we can conceive concurrent studies covering different levels of generality simultaneously. In practice, a single level of generality is usually selected, derived from the specific concerns that prompt the marketer to undertake the study.

Sequence Analysis

Where do the topics and attributes of a typical SUMM map come from? Technically, they are constructed by judgment. This, however, takes an unduly harsh view of the process. It is certainly true that topics and attributes can be added and deleted by quasi-arbitrary judgments. But the process of map construction can be approached in a systematic way that is likely to yield considerable overlap when pursued independently by different researchers. This is called a *sequence analysis*.

The basic idea behind a sequence analysis is to trace the probable sequence of a customer's experience in shopping for, buying, and using the product. The method is illustrated by constructing a map for bathroom tissue. The customer first encounters a brand of bathroom tissue on the supermarket shelf. There she obtains some basic information about the brand. Even from a distance she can see how the brand is packaged. Thus, rolls per pack becomes the first topic, with such attributes as:

- It is sold in one roll per package.
- It is sold in two rolls per package.
- etc.

As we fill in the attributes for this topic, we make certain to include all the major variants currently on the market, such as four rolls per package, six rolls per package, etc. But we need not limit ourselves to what is available or even to what is logistically or technologically possible, and may push out beyond the boundaries of today, allowing for the possibility that even "nonfeasible" options might come to be viewed in a different light if they proved to have customer appeal.

Still looking at the shelf from a few feet away, we notice the size of the individual rolls. This generates the topic:

- It is a large-size roll.
- It is a medium-size roll.
- etc.

Judgment dictates what level of detail will be useful. For some variables, we may make fine distinctions. For others, like roll size, a coarse distinction between large, medium, and small may be sufficient.

We next observe how the product is packaged:

- The rolls are wrapped in paper.
- The rolls are wrapped in plastic.
- etc.

Coming closer, we read some relevant information on the package. We ignore vague, subjective promises for the moment, and limit ourselves to objective statements, which we accept as factually true:

- It has 1,000 sheets per roll.
- It has 800 sheets per roll.
- etc.

The topic may be extended all the way to 100 sheets per roll even if this size might appear to be utterly lacking in customer appeal, and, in the other direction, all the way to 2,000 sheets per roll even if this might be impossible to produce.

There is more:

- It is a one-ply tissue.
- It is a two-ply tissue.
- etc.

Finally, we note the most crucial piece of information available at the shelf: the brand's price. There is no right way of handling price. A great deal depends on the objectives at hand and on prevailing marketing practices for brands in the category. For that reason, we have handled price differently in different studies over the course of time. The most direct approach is to list literal prices, for example:

- It is sold at 59¢ per roll.
- It is sold at 64¢ per roll.
- etc.

This has the advantage of being directly applicable but yields data that are time- and place-specific. A year or two later, the data may no longer be relevant. Conversely, we may take a cruder approach, defining price in terms of broad categories:

- It is a high-priced bathroom tissue.
- It is a medium-priced bathroom tissue.
- It is a low-priced bathroom tissue.

This approach may not allow us to make a direct comparison of 59¢ and 64¢, but is neither time-specific nor place-specific. The general desire for high, medium, or low prices by different customers is likely to remain relatively constant. The objection may be raised that broad categories like high, medium, and low are too vague to be of practical value. But if we know the prices at which different brands are actually sold, we can calibrate the price beliefs about the various brands and can construct SUMM games like: "What would happen to the share of my brand (currently sold at price X) if beliefs about its price were increased to parity with beliefs about a competing brand (currently sold at price Y)?" Such a game can be implemented by changing the price beliefs of the test brand to conform to the price beliefs of the competing brand.

Continuing the experience sequence, we have bought a brand, carried it home, and installed it on the bathroom holder. We could have included a topic that has to do with the ease of carrying the product home, but judge that this has been adequately covered in the rolls-per-package topic. We could have included a topic about the ease of removing the roll from the package, but judge that this is trivial and elect to omit it.

There is no guarantee that these judgments are correct. To the extent they are incorrect, they will be one more source of error, a risk we are willing to accept in the spirit of constructing a "reasonable" map of the category.

We now start the new roll, which gives rise to:

- A new roll is easy to start without wasting sheets.
- etc.

Sheets need to be torn from the roll. This generates the topics:

- It never leaves a ragged edge at the perforations when tearing.
- etc.

- You usually get too many sheets when you tear it.
- etc.

Once the paper has been torn from the roll, we note some of the characteristics that are apparent just from handling the paper:

- The individual sheets are very thick.
- etc.

- It has an embossed surface.
- etc.

These are followed by the experience of using the product:

- It feels extremely soft when using.
- etc.

- It holds together very well in use.
- etc.

- It is extremely absorbent when using.
- etc.

After use, the paper is flushed, which generates the topic:

- It is completely biodegradable and will not clog a septic system.
- etc.

And finally, there is the utility of the brand over time:

- One roll lasts a long time.
- etc.

This sequence, which traces the product from point of purchase through observation, storage, maintenance, use experience, and residual effects, should enable us within reason to cover the essential factors involved in the customer's choice of a brand. There are exceptions, however. In some cases, we may have only a cursory familiarity with the category and may not want to rely on logic and on the marketer's and researcher's insight alone in defining the sequence. Alternatively, we may feel confident that we can perform the task but may want additional assurance that nothing of importance has been left out. This assurance can be obtained from an *attribute-definition pretest.*

The Attribute-Definition Pretest

This test is qualitative in the true sense of the term. Its purpose is neither to draw conclusions nor to distinguish among attributes, but to generate a list of attributes, expressed in the customer's own language. It serves as an additional input to the construction of the map.

The respondent is asked to name a brand she particularly likes (Brand

A) and to name a brand she particularly dislikes (Brand B). She is then asked to tell us all the ways in which Brands A and B differ. General answers are not accepted. They are followed up with requests for details. For example, if the respondent says that the two brands differ in taste, she is asked: "In what ways do Brands A and B taste different? Be specific. Describe the taste of Brand A. Describe the taste of Brand B." In this interview, it is not essential to obtain comprehensive information from any particular respondent. The responses are not counted. No note is taken of whether a given characteristic is mentioned by most of the respondents or by only a single one. The purpose of the test is to create a list, and the results converge rapidly. After 25 to 50 interviews, 100 at the outside, it is unlikely that anything that is not already on the list will turn up.

Both the sequence analysis and the attribute-definition pretest are intended to help ensure completeness. But enumeration can never accomplish this fully. No matter how carefully it is done, the selection of topics retains an element of judgment on which reasonable people can disagree. It is possible, however, to approach the task from the other end of the telescope: Instead of enumerating a large number of specific topics, we can go back to first principles and use the primary topics.

The Primary Topics

In Chapter 1, I identified four primary topics: product, branding, price, and familiarity. This universal classification hopefully subsumes everything. I did not, however, specify the fourth primary topic properly in the early years. At the outset, my focus was on distinguishing between what the customer gets, which I identified as product and branding, and what the customer gives, which I identified as money and effort. By "effort" I then meant the work expended in buying the brand. Accordingly, the early studies used product, branding, price, and effort. It was some time before I realized that effort does not belong in this quartet. Accessibility is an external barrier to be overcome, not a component of desirability. If a brand is on the shelf one day but not the next, on the shelf in one store but not in the next, the customer's buying behavior will certainly be critically affected by these differences in accessibility, but the desirability of the brand will not change. Once I realized this, I dropped effort and reduced the number of primary topics to three.

SUMM studies that use only the primary topics are called *primary SUMM* studies. They usually employ specific attributes for each of the primary topics. There are two variants of SUMM, however, specifically hierarchical SUMM and Topic-SUMM (see Appendix F), that use only a single phrase to represent each of the primary topics. This is also true in enhanced STEP (see Appendix G). The actual phrases used in these techniques have evolved gradually. In the beginning, I was confused about the distinction between branding and familiarity. I considered familiarity to be just a special aspect of branding. This fuzzy thinking led to a succession of verbal representations of branding. Branding is supposed to deal with the emotional biases that have been extraneously associated with the brand by the label, the advertising, and other symbol manipulations. But when these biases are effective, they are largely unconscious, and respondents are not likely to admit that imagery is important to them. Accordingly, I groped for socially acceptable stand-ins for branding, language that identifies benefits distinct from the product itself, that respondents would be prepared to admit are important to them. First I focused on the brand name, the package graphics, the label, and the emotional security derived from familiarity with these. This led to the phrase,

- It has a brand name and package design I feel comfortable with.

Although I adopted this language, I was not happy with it. The term "package design" could refer to the way the product was packaged, which was not what I had in mind at all. But the substitutes were not satisfactory either. Accordingly, the language underwent several transformations in an ongoing effort to capture the elusive branding component. At one time it became:

- It has a label and brand name I know well and feel comfortable with,

but it continued to change as time passed, until I finally grasped the conceptual difference between branding and familiarity and broke them apart into two separate topics.

Nowadays, when it is appropriate to represent the primary topics by single phrases, I use the following four phrases for product, branding, price, and familiarity, respectively.

- The characteristics and features of the actual product.
- The reputation of the brand and what it stands for.
- The price of the brand.
- Your familiarity with the brand.

These phrases are used only in the special techniques mentioned above. In standard primary SUMM studies, each primary topic is represented by specific attributes for different levels of the topic (for example, actual prices).

By definition, a primary SUMM study is about as general as a SUMM study is likely to get, and it has both the virtues and the limitations of that generality. On the one hand, it can be applied to any product category, and it is unlikely that anything of relevance will have been left out. On the other hand, such a study can yield only very broad conclusions capable of providing only the most general guidance. One might suppose at first glance that anything this broad could hardly have practical value at all. But this is not so. A primary SUMM study can be used to study the interplay among the primary topics. For example, it can address such questions as: "How much share would my brand gain or lose if its physical characteristics became as acceptable as those of Competitor C, while its price was changed from P_1 to P_2?" Thus studies that focus entirely on price, a perennial subject, can usually be accomplished by a primary SUMM in which the price topic is covered in substantial detail.

CHAPTER 18

Twists and Turns in Measuring the Desirability of Attributes

The principal measurement challenge in SUMM is to measure the relative desirability of the attributes. The numbers generated for that purpose must have two properties: They must have a viable metric—that is, they must be additive across topics, since that is what the SUMM system will do with them—and they must allow comparisons of a large number of attributes, in some cases as many as 150 or more. This means that any technique under consideration must not only meet conceptual requirements, but must also meet practical tests, must give the respondent tasks that are comprehensible and doable.

Given my long commitment to experiment, my first impulse was to employ some analogue of STEP; call it a quasi-experiment. Toward that end, I started in 1968 by giving respondents a series of attribute collections and asking them to rate these collections. A collection might be: "a widgie that is 3 feet high *and* square *and* attractive *and* middle class." Another might be: "a widgie that is 2 feet high *and* oval *and* beautiful *and* upper class." And so on. If the respondent rates a sufficient number of such collections, it is possible to use these data to infer the relative desirability of the attributes analytically. Conceptually, each of the collections was supposed to represent a hypothetical "brand" and the respondents were supposed to evaluate these brands in their entirety. That is what I thought, or hoped, they would do. But that is not what they actually did.

The "brands" were disembodied combinations of abstract phrases that did not readily coalesce into coherent, integrated images. To make matters worse, the same phrases appeared and reappeared in different brands. In those circumstances, the respondents sought and quickly found the easiest way out. Far from responding to each look-alike jumble of words as a whole, they searched for differences among the various collections of attributes and based their ratings entirely on those differences.

I conducted a series of pretests in futile efforts to induce the respondents to treat each hypothetical brand as a whole, but I was just fooling
myself. Once again, I was up against the principle of organic response. No
matter how I coaxed them, the respondents drifted into looking for the
one or two attributes that differed from collection to collection, thereby
subverting the intent of the measurement. This was compounded by the
problem of scope. As the number of topics increased, both the size of
each attribute collection and the number of collections the respondents
needed to evaluate became increasingly cumbersome, and finally
mechanically impossible. In the end, I concluded that it was pointless to
fight the respondents' inclination to rate, insofar as they could, one topic
at a time. The best course of action was to eliminate the complications
and ask them explicitly to do that which they were going to do in any
case. This led to the straightforward measurement system employed in
SUMM.

During the past twenty years, variations of the approach I rejected in
1968 have become widely fashionable under the broad umbrella of "conjoint analysis." One reason for this popularity is doubtless the fact that
conjoint has been supported by a large body of academic literature. By
contrast, SUMM has been promulgated in private, in presentations and
reports to clients, with almost no publications. I did present the SUMM
system at a meeting of the Advertising Research Foundation in October
1968, and again at a meeting of the American Marketing Association
(Attitude Research Bridges the Atlantic) in Madrid in 1973. In addition,
the Ford Foundation published a SUMM study in 1974 under the title
The Finances of the Performing Arts, Vol. 2, in which I described in detail
SUMM and the measurement method I then used. But as far as I know
none of these have been noted in the literature.

People who have some familiarity with both SUMM and conjoint have
sometimes sought to compare the two. Such comparisons seem to me to
miss the point. As long as the total number of attributes comprising the
map is relatively small, neither SUMM nor conjoint is appropriate,
because STEP, a controlled experiment in which each respondent is
exposed to a single test stimulus, is preferable to any model, no matter
how good. Once the scope of the problem grows to where the number of
necessary test cells makes STEP impractical, the same practical con-
straints overburden conjoint as well. At that point SUMM is available to
fill the gap. In my view, the perennial trade-off between rigor and flexibility leads to the choice of STEP when small scale allows emphasis on
rigor, and to the choice of SUMM when rigor must be sacrificed for a substantial increase in flexibility. Assuming the approximate independence of
the topics (an assumption that may not hold fully in all cases but holds

approximately in most cases), we can decompose the measurement process into manageable parts.

The instruments used in SUMM have undergone major changes since the first SUMM study was completed in 1970. Examining these changes will help clarify the rationale behind today's measurement system. This system has evolved along a path that twists and turns from the complicated to the simple. Here are the major stations along the way.

The Top-Attribute Method

The original SUMM studies employed a three-stage process called the *Top-Attribute* method. The respondent was shown a card containing all the attributes of one topic, each printed on a removable plastic strip, and selected the one attribute she liked best or wanted most. This attribute, which was called the *top-attribute* of the topic, was given a 10. The respondent then used a scale from +10 to -10 to indicate how she felt about each of the remaining attributes, relative to the top-attribute, which had been anchored at +10. "If you gave a 2-foot widgie 10 points, how many points will you give a 3-foot widgie?" and so on. The resulting numbers were called the *attribute scores*. Thus, the respondent expressed her judgment of the desirability of each of the attributes relative to a single reference attribute, the top-attribute, the one she liked best, which accounts for the name of the method.

The strip containing the top-attribute was removed and placed on a separate board. The process was repeated for each of the topics. At this point, the display board held all of the chosen strips, permitting a simultaneous overview. The respondent next distributed fifty stickers among the top-attributes by pasting the stickers on a sheet next to the top-attribute display. In this measurement, the respondent indicated how valuable or important the various topics were relative to each other, each topic being represented by its top-attribute. The share of stickers given to a topic was called the *topic weight*.

The topic weights provide a direct head-on comparison of the top-attributes of the different topics, yielding scores that are clearly additive, since they have been obtained by distributing a fixed number of stickers among the top-attributes. If we make a widgie that gives the respondent everything she wants—the top-attribute of each topic—its SUMM score will be 100. Conversely, all the other attributes of each topic have been rated relative to that topic's top-attribute. Thus, all the attributes in the system are linked through the top-attributes, which constitute the bridge for crossing from one topic to the next. The computation consists of multiplying the attribute scores by their topic weights.

The Meaning of Topic Weights

The measurement system just described has some subtle psychological implications. Marketers and researchers alike often want to identify the topics that
play the major role in the purchase decision in a product category. We can
satisfy this request easily enough by asking respondents to rate or rank the
relative "importance" of, say, horsepower and windshield wipers in choosing
a car. Respondents have no difficulty in answering this question. They are
likely to tell us, individually and collectively, that horsepower is "more important" to them than windshield wipers. But what does that mean?

A little reflection reveals that this apparently simple, self-evident statement is neither simple nor self-evident, and that its meaning, assuming
that it has a meaning at all, requires a fairly involuted theory about what
goes on in the respondent's mind. To begin with, it does not really make
sense to assign importance to the *topic* horsepower. The topic represents
all possible levels of horsepower, both acceptable and unacceptable. But
the respondent can want only some particular level of horsepower; for
example, 250 hp, or 200 hp, or some other hp. For this reason, the Top-
Attribute method did not ask the respondents to distribute stickers
among the topics, but among the top-attributes of the topics. For example, the respondents might have been asked what was more important to
them, 250 hp or variable-speed windshield wipers.

But that is not all there is to it. Since we are calling on the respondent
to make a choice between some aspect of horsepower and some aspect of
windshield wipers, this choice is not really defined until the alternatives
have been fully specified. For example, suppose the alternatives (the
attributes) for the windshield wipers topic were:

- Variable-speed windshield wipers
- Single-speed windshield wipers

and suppose the alternatives for the horsepower topic were:

- 250 hp
- 249 hp

Given those options, respondents could easily conclude that windshield
wipers were "more important" than horsepower.

Thus, it is not really meaningful to say that one *topic* is more important
than another. It is not even meaningful to say that the top-attribute of one
topic is "more important" than the top-attribute of another topic. To be
meaningful, a statement would have to compare the importance of a *dif-*

ference between two attributes of one topic with the importance of the *difference* between two attributes of another topic. Formally, the question would have to be posed as follows:

Is it more important to you to get a variable-speed windshield wiper instead of a single-speed windshield wiper *or* to get 250 hp instead of 249 hp?

This simplest, two-topic comparison requires the simultaneous assessment of at least four attributes, two from each of the topics.

We know that people do not ordinarily think in such involuted terms. The opposite is the case. If we make a serious effort to structure the measurement task in a way that is logically sensible, the respondents find it difficult to understand and do not carry it out as instructed. On the other hand, they usually experience no difficulty in performing a task that is logically meaningless and ought to be difficult, if not impossible, for them. We can deal with this fact sensibly only if we remember that there is no such thing as a stupid respondent, only a stupid researcher. All of this can be summarized in the following principle.

THE LOGIC PRINCIPLE
That which is logical is not necessarily psychological.

The fact is that the respondents' psychological inclinations follow laws of their own. I received a powerful object lesson in the operation of this principle early in the development of the SUMM measurement system. Having understood that the only logical task was to ask the respondent to compare differences of attributes for one topic with differences of attributes for other topics, I structured the task explicitly in this form and watched respondents performing it. I went to great pains to explain to them that it was important to rate how they felt about the *differences* between attributes. Nevertheless, the respondents departed from this assignment almost immediately, concentrating on the top-attributes and ignoring the others. When this lapse was called to their attention, they smiled sheepishly, said, "Oh yes," made a valiant effort, and promptly relapsed. The task was simply not organic, not in harmony with their natural inclinations. Asking them to divide stickers among the top attributes, on the other hand, something they should have experienced as unreasonable and illogical, felt right to them. They did it easily, without hesitation or qualms.

What implications does this have for the way we approach the measurement problem? At the time of constructing the original SUMM measurement system, I concluded that the respondents were in effect supplying "zero points" of their own. When confronted with the task of dividing stickers between 250 hp and variable-speed windshield wipers, they were indeed rating a difference against a difference. But they were filling in some hypothetical level of horsepower, an affectively neutral horsepower, one that was neither desirable nor undesirable, and they were telling us that on balance 250 hp would have some positive value to them compared to that hypothetical neutral horsepower, and that "variable-speed windshield wipers" would have some positive value to them compared to some hypothetical neutral windshield wipers. In giving six stickers to 250 hp and only two stickers to variable-speed windshield wipers, they were telling us that getting the most desirable horsepower was three times as valuable to them as getting the most desirable windshield wiper.

Based on this conviction, derived from observation during pretests, I chose to sacrifice the logical for the psychological and constructed the Top-Attribute method, evaluating the relative "importance of the topics" by asking the respondents to divide stickers among the top-attributes. When asked why I had adopted this procedure, I explained that the top-attributes were "stand-ins" for the entire topic, an explanation that was generally accepted. Although I received all kinds of critiques of various aspects of the measurement system, neither my colleagues nor my clients raised the objection that the task, as specified, was inherently illogical.

The Multiple-Attribute Method

Having adopted the Top-Attribute method in the form described, the early SUMM studies were conducted by personal interviews. This troubled me. Although I used all forms of interviewing—personal, telephone, and mail—my bias always favored self-administered questionnaires. Data collected by interviewers, no matter how well trained or reputable, left me with an uneasy feeling that in the end the conclusions were based on trust and hearsay. One could never be certain about what had happened in the interview, what explanations had been supplied by the interviewer, what portion of the final data had been influenced, if not generated, by the interviewer. Certainly the self-administered interview had problems of its own and imposed special challenges and disciplines on the crafter of the instrument. Lack of clarity, ambiguity, and excessive difficulty were punished promptly. They led respondents to ignore the instructions, to carry them out incorrectly, or to abandon the task altogether. But it was precisely this discipline that always attracted me. All respondents received the same instructions and explanations. They participated voluntarily. They took the trouble to fill in the questionnaire, place it in the envelope, and drop it into a mailbox, all evidence of respondent motivation. If the instrument had been poorly crafted, the results would be flawed. But no matter how flawed, they would be "true" in the sense that they would be real answers from real people.

STEP tests have been self-administered most of the time. This did not initially seem feasible for SUMM, which required props that made the participation of the interviewer mandatory. But my conviction that self-administered data are better prompted me early to attempt to construct a self-administered SUMM. I was also eager to reconsider representing topics by their top-attributes. That had been a conscious trade-off between the logical and the psychological, but I was not happy with the solution. I conceded that the psychological governed and could not be ignored except at one's peril, but I was searching for some way, however elusive, of eating my cake and having it too, of coming up with a measurement system that would be both logical and psychological. In attempting to do so, I experimented with many forms, conducted many pretests, and finally settled on a patchwork measurement system that had little to commend it except that it worked.

The respondents first checked how much they liked or disliked each of the attributes and then distributed fifty stickers among those attributes they had checked either "Like a lot" or "Dislike a lot." This method was called the *Multiple-Attribute* method because the respondent could, under some circumstances, assign stickers to several or even all attributes of a topic. The supplemental scoring was arbitrary. The attribute ratings were scored as follows:

Like a lot	+2
Like a little	+1
Indifferent	0
Dislike a little	-1
Dislike a lot	-2

The stickers given to the attributes were added to these scores with appropriate sign. Thus, an attribute that had been checked "Like a lot" and had received three stickers received a total attribute desirability of +5.

There was some method to the madness. In effect, the respondents were being asked to divide stickers among all of the attributes in the system—the attributes they liked and those they disliked—presumably indicating how much they wanted to get or avoid each attribute. But in order to make the task simpler and to avoid the need for using an excessive number of stickers, the initial attribute rating was used to reduce the set of attributes that would participate in the sticker allocation. The Multiple-Attribute method was evaluated in a methodological study. That study provided support for the SUMM system in general and for the Multiple-Attribute method in particular.

The Integrated Method

Although the Multiple-Attribute method worked well enough, I did not like it. I thought of it as a compromise that had the very features that offended me most: conceptual sloppiness, and capricious scoring in which numerical values flowed not from the respondents but from arbitrary assignments by the analyst. I had constructed this method as just one more version to put into a pretest, and the pretest had rendered a favorable verdict on it. The throw-away candidate had won. The original impetus had come from my desire to render the topic rating not only psychologically but also logically meaningful. But attributes within topics and attributes between topics are bound by different rules. The attributes within topics are mutually exclusive; the attributes between topics are coexistent. Accordingly, to be logical, the allocations should have compared only *differences* within one topic with *differences* within other topics, and the Multiple-Attribute method did not do that.

In an effort to reconcile the logical and the psychological, I had oscillated between them. In the Top-Attribute method, I had knowingly adopted an illogical position in deference to my then understanding of the psychological reality. In the Multiple-Attribute method I had unsuccessfully attempted to close the gap between the psychological and the logical. Now I was circling back in still another effort to construct a stable compromise between the logical and the psychological. The result was the *Integrated* method.

In the Integrated method, the stickers are no longer associated with particular attributes but are placed in a separate box at the bottom of the page. The respondent is asked to paste stickers on the various pages to indicate how important it is to her to get the things she likes on the page *or* to avoid the things she dislikes on the page. The procedure does not prejudge the respondent's way of thinking. It defines the topic by the collection of attributes, calls attention to the fact that it may be important to her to avoid the negatives as well as to obtain the positives, but otherwise leaves her to perform the task in any way that makes sense to her.

In the interim, I had also developed the unbounded write-in scale, which I believed to be a more effective instrument for measuring desirability than any of the absolute scales I had previously used for that purpose. Accordingly, I replaced the absolute eleven-point scale with the unbounded write-in scale. Quite apart from conceptual considerations, these changes had the advantage of materially simplifying the physical layout of the page. The Integrated format is illustrated in Figure 18–1. I was under no illusion

Figure 18–1
Sample SUMM Page for Integrated Method

Write one or more letters
into each box.

Like = L, LL, LLL,
or as many L's as you want

Dislike = D, DD, DDD,
or as many D's as you want

Neutral = N

It is slightly sweet.

It is moderately sweet.

It is very sweet.

It is extremely sweet.

STEP 2: Importance to you of the characteristics on this page.

that the new instructions would make the difference. I held firm to my belief that no matter what instructions were used, the respondents would deal with the task in their own way. The question was not whether the instructions would change the task, but whether the new task itself conformed more closely to what we hoped the respondents would do.

In the Integrated method, the attribute ratings are converted into constant intervals. If a respondent assigns the following ratings to five attributes of a topic, LLLL, LLLL, L, N, D, these ratings are numerically equivalent to +4, +4, +1, 0, -1. The range is 5 (+4 - [-1] = 5). Transforming all scores into shares of the range on a topic-by-topic basis gives identical intervals for each topic. Multiplying the scores by their topic weight (the topic share of stickers) results in crediting each attribute with the appropriate proportion of the sticker share given to that topic. This scoring system has the property that a brand characterized by the top-attribute of each topic receives a SUMM score of 100, a brand characterized by the bottom-attribute of each topic receives a SUMM score of 0, and other brands receive appropriate intermediate SUMM scores.*

The Absolute Method

Soon after the Integrated method was in place and had become the new standard for SUMM studies, the question arose whether it might be possible to simplify the method still further and to dispense with the topic weights altogether. As long as we had been using a bounded scale such as +10 to -10, +5 to -5, or +2 to -2 to generate the attribute scores, as in the Top-Attribute and Multiple-Attribute methods, there had been little temptation to do away with the topic weights. This would have been tantamount to assuming that all topics were equally important. The introduction of the unbounded write-in scale, however, changed all this.

Conceivably, I reasoned, the unbounded write-in scale measured not only the respondent's relative feelings about the attributes within a topic but also her relative feelings about the attributes across topic boundaries, giving the various attributes of an "unimportant" topic more similar

---

*In particular, if the share of stickers given to topic i is W_i and if the attribute scores given to various attributes of that topic are a_H for the top-attribute (the highest score), a_L for the-bottom attribute (the lowest score), and in general a_j for any attribute j, then the desirability score (d_{ij}) for attribute j of topic i is

$$d_{ij} = W_i \frac{a_j - a_L}{a_H - a_L} \quad \text{(If } a_H = a_L \text{, the topic is eliminated).}$$

scores than those given to the various attributes of an "important" topic. In that case, the unbounded write-in scale might be able to stand alone and accomplish the total measurement task in a single operation. The method that does this is called the *Absolute-Desirability* method, or just the *Absolute* method for short. The Absolute method is identical to the Integrated method, except that the topic weights are eliminated and the desirability of each attribute is defined as the raw score assigned to the attribute by the unbounded write-in scale. The SUMM score is defined as the average of these desirabilities.

I was not properly objective when it came to evaluating the Absolute method. The fact is, I had spent so much time thinking about the topic weights, about what they meant, how to collect them, and how to use them, that I was reluctant to let them go. Starting from the premise that the topic weights were necessary, the first test I conducted was "disappointing." The topic weights did not make much of a difference. When the data collected with the Integrated method were reanalyzed with the Absolute method, that is, by throwing away the topic weights, the correlation with first-choice share was only marginally lower.

The responsible reaction would have been to place the topic weights on probation immediately and to embark on a vigorous investigation of whether they were in fact necessary. But this is not what I did. Unwilling to let go, I took the position that though the topic weights might not be contributing much, they were certainly doing no harm, and that it was most conservative to retain them. If retained, they could always be thrown out later, but if they were eliminated prematurely, we might do irreparable harm and would never know. On the basis of this reasoning, the topic weights stayed, and the Integrated method remained EMA's standard for years. Under the sway of a strong bias, I thus applied an unreasonably stringent standard of proof.

Let us now examine the Integrated and Absolute methods on their merits and hopefully draw an objective conclusion about them once and for all. Since SUMM computations typically culminate in SUMM scores, which define the chosen brand, the most appropriate criterion for evaluating a SUMM method is the respondents' first-choice, that is, their responses when asked which brand they like best or would be most likely to buy, all things considered. This criterion is most closely analogous to what SUMM is supposed to measure. Its disadvantage is that, being a fleeting response to a single question, it can be volatile, with the attendant risk that the criterion variable may in the end contain more noise than what it is supposed to assess.

The following comparison is based on ten SUMM studies for which cri-

Table 18–1
Criterion versus SUMM Share for Basic SUMM Studies
Integrated and Absolute Methods

Category	Criterion	Correlation Integrated Method	Absolute Method
Airlines	First-choice	.944	.941
Bathroom tissue	Use share	.980	.984
Business computers	First-choice	.981	.983
Frozen entrees	Use share	.963	.959
Luxury cars	First-choice	.667	.728
Panty liners	Use share	.968	.977
Peanut butter	Use share	.911	.914
Puddings	Use share	.997	.994
Retail stores	Sim-SUMM	.944	.943
Telephones	First-choice	.997	.992
Average		.935	.942

terion variables are available. These will be called the *Basic* SUMM studies, covering airlines, automobiles, bathroom tissue, business computers, frozen entrees, panty liners, peanut butter, puddings, retail stores, and telephones. For those of the Basic studies for which first-choice is available, it was used as the criterion variable. For those studies for which it is not available, brand use share was used. In one case, share of highest overall desirability (Sim-SUMM share) was used.

Table 18–1 lists the individual studies and their respective correlations. These range from a low of .67 to a high of .997. Consolidating the data, the upper panel of Figure 18–2 shows a plot of criterion-variable share versus SUMM share for all the brands of all the Basic SUMM studies, computed by the Integrated method. The lower panel of Figure 18–2 shows the same plot for the Absolute method. The most important conclusion that emerges from these charts has to do with the SUMM system itself. Regardless of which method is used, the model is effective in predicting the criterion variable. The average correlation between SUMM share and the criterion variable is .94 for each of the methods. In addition, each method produces a marginally higher correlation than the other method in half the cases. We can therefore say that, for the static case at least, there is no difference between the two methods. The Absolute method is just as good as the Integrated method.

Figure 18–2
Criterion versus SUMM Share for Basic SUMM Studies
Integrated and Absolute Methods
(N = 10,027)

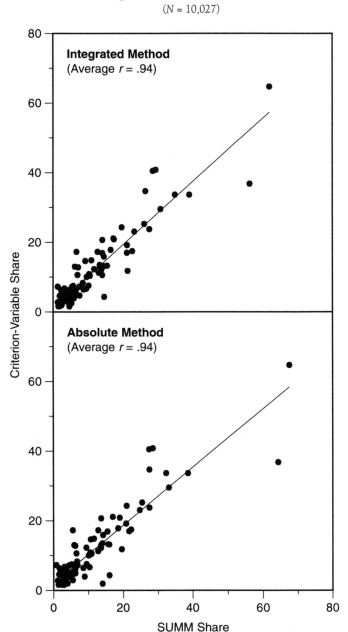

CHAPTER 19

Dynamic Assessments

The comparisons provided in Chapter 18 were based on static correlations between first-choice or use share and SUMM share. Such correlations are certainly necessary but may not be sufficient. Suppose SUMM share correlated with first-choice but failed to predict dynamic changes. This would not only dampen our enthusiasm for the model but would lead us to reject it outright. Accordingly, the definitive assessment of SUMM requires an evaluation of how well the system predicts *changes*. To do this, we need a SUMM study in which offers can be modeled by SUMM games, and a concurrent STEP study that measures the empirical choice shares generated by these same offers.

Such data are not come by easily. EMA did not usually conduct both STEP and SUMM studies for the same problem at the same time. When the number of options to be investigated was relatively small, these options were usually evaluated by STEP. When the number of options was large, they were usually evaluated by SUMM. But we do have two substantial studies that used both STEP and SUMM. One of these will be called the *Pricing* study; the other is the *Spectrum* study. Although these studies were done at different times, the first in 1982 and the second in 1993, and the design of the Spectrum study differs somewhat from that of the Pricing study, the practical impetus for the concurrent collection of STEP and SUMM data was the same in both. STEP was viewed as the definitive method for measuring the deserved share of various prices or product variants, and SUMM was added as a device to reduce the number of STEP groups required, a device for interpolating between STEP data and enlarging their scope.

The Pricing Study

The Pricing study covered four product categories. These were studied simultaneously and will be examined simultaneously, but each is a separate study. As the name indicates, the purpose of the study was to guide pricing decisions. For each of the four product categories, four STEP cells were used, identical in all respects, except that the respondents in each cell saw the test brand, an existing brand in the category, at a different price. In addition, we wanted the ability to model various pricing scenarios, not only intermediate price levels but also price changes by competitive brands. To create this capability, concurrent SUMM studies were conducted among different samples of respondents. Since we were interested only in the ability to run games relating to price, the SUMM studies used only the primary topics: product, image, price, and effort. (At that time, I still thought of "effort" as the fourth primary topic.) The price topic enabled us to run four SUMM games, estimating what share the test brand would command at each of four price levels. These shares could then be compared to the shares the test brand actually obtained in the corresponding STEP groups.

The panels in Figure 19–1 show this comparison separately for each of the four STEP-SUMM pairs that comprise the Pricing study, using the Integrated method. The absolute STEP and SUMM shares were not the same, but the relationship between STEP and SUMM was almost perfectly linear. The correlations are between .92 and .99. The slope of the line is highest for the test brand with the lowest share in its product category, and decreases for test brands with progressively higher shares in their respective product categories. These data offer dramatic support for the conclusion that SUMM not only produces high static correlations but also predicts dynamic changes. Important though this conclusion is, it must be qualified. The Pricing study employed only four primary topics. Do comparable relationships hold for full SUMM studies using twenty to thirty topics? The changes studied in the Pricing study involved only price. Does SUMM properly predict the effects of changes in characteristics of physical products?

In addition to these unresolved questions, we note an important limitation. We can have confidence in the relative share changes produced by SUMM, but cannot expect that these will be the same as the changes produced by STEP. The data demonstrate that they will not. This means that, if absolute estimates of what would have been produced by a STEP experiment are desired, we need to calibrate the data with a minimum of two concurrent STEP cells, which should then allow us to employ SUMM to estimate the value of other scenarios for which no specific experimental STEP cells are available.

The Spectrum Study

The Spectrum study is the most comprehensive source of data we have for answering many of the outstanding methodological questions con-

Figure 19–1
STEP Share versus SUMM Share
Pricing Study, Integrated Method

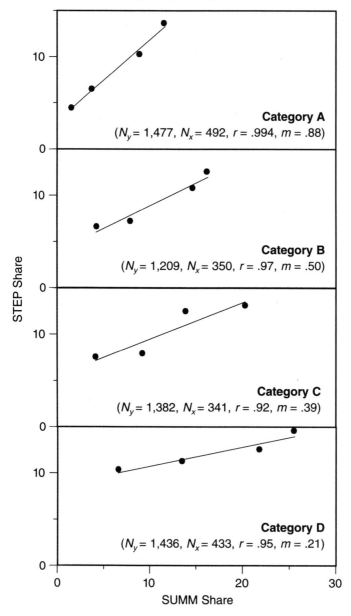

cerning SUMM. It covers only a single product category, but it is a major study. It was conducted at a time when I had arrived at a deeper understanding of the structure of SUMM, including, among other things, SUMM's conceptual relation to STEP, a subject covered in greater detail in the next chapter, and was therefore able to design the study with an eye to addressing, and hopefully resolving, some of the outstanding questions. In this I was especially aided by a fortuitous convergence between those questions and the client's practical needs.

The marketer had two established brands in the same product category, one at a low price and one at a high price, and was embarking on a major effort to improve these brands' positions, by adding line extensions to them or by replacing the physical product in one or both. Sixteen physical product variants were available as candidates to be evaluated. This clearly pointed to using sixteen groups of Product-STEP, each receiving one of the variants. Each of the variants, however, was at least in principle eligible for use either as a replacement or as a line extension for either existing Brand A or existing Brand B. Taken at face value, this would have required multiplying the number of cells by four to obtain sixty-four. Finally, there was a strong feeling among at least some members of the marketing group that none of the sixteen then available variants was necessarily optimal and that the study should have the capability to estimate through modeling the potential of product variants that had not been made yet. This pointed to the concurrent utilization of SUMM.

The SUMM study could of course have been set up as a completely separate study, but it was also deemed desirable that any potential modeling of new variants should use specific product experience as a jumping-off point. The convergence of these requirements led to testing the sixteen variants under a decoy label and adding two groups that received Brands A and B fully identified. For the present purpose, the data from the identified cells are irrelevant, and I will confine the analysis to the sixteen randomly equivalent groups that received the sixteen different product variants in the decoy label.

Three weeks after the product was delivered, the respondents received a questionnaire. The first part was a standard STEP questionnaire covering nine brands, the decoy brand and eight established brands. The second part was a Bipolar-SUMM questionnaire covering desirability for twenty-five topics and beliefs on these topics for the nine brands covered in the STEP section. (The Bipolar method is described in Appendix F.) All questionnaires were identical, except that each of the sixteen groups was split further. In the STEP portion, half of the respondents saw the decoy brand at the high price (the price of Brand A); the other half saw the decoy brand at the low price (the price of Brand B). The relevant portion of the study therefore had thirty-two experimental treatment groups, with a total sample of 6,633 interviews, an average of around 207 interviews per group.

Because the design provided for measuring the share potential of many offers by means of both STEP and SUMM, it enables us to make some crucial comparisons. The respondents received the test product under the decoy label. They experienced it as a "new" brand, certainly one they had not previously used, seen, or heard of. Before exposure, that unknown brand's STEP and SUMM shares should have been zero, or close to zero, except for the share attributable to the decoy brand's name and package graphics. We know that this share was in fact minimal, .4% and 1.5% in STEP and SUMM, respectively, as measured in the groups that did not receive any product in the decoy label but were asked to rate the decoy brand anyhow, knowing nothing about that brand beyond its name and label as presented in the STEP questionnaire. We may therefore think of the product in the decoy label as a stimulus that produced a change in the respondents' beliefs about the decoy brand. We also know that the different products produced different changes in beliefs. Accordingly, each product variant was in effect equivalent to a different SUMM game.

Instead of postulating a change and asking "What would happen if we could get respondents to believe A, B, C . . . about the test brand?" we had given the respondents product experience and had actually induced them to believe A, B, C . . . about the test brand. In this way, we had produced different beliefs in the different groups, which in turn had resulted in SUMM shares that ranged from 5% to 35%. But since we had also obtained STEP shares generated by these same product offers, we can assess the dynamic relationship between STEP and SUMM.

The most obvious first step is to compare the SUMM shares for the test brand with the STEP shares obtained from the same respondents. This comparison will be called the *measured SUMM* comparison. It is shown in the upper panel of Figure 19–2, which demonstrates several important points. First, there is a high correlation between STEP and SUMM ($r = .86$). Thus we have confirmed the relationship between STEP and SUMM for a dynamic case in which both price and product vary. Once again, we see that though the correlation between STEP and SUMM is high, the regression line has a slope substantially smaller than 1. This means that the SUMM shares generated for the decoy brand predict the STEP shares but are consistently higher than the STEP shares, allowing us to draw relative but not absolute conclusions about the performance of the different products and requiring a calibration of some kind if absolute estimates are desired. (The implications of the STEP-SUMM slope are explored further in Appendix D.)

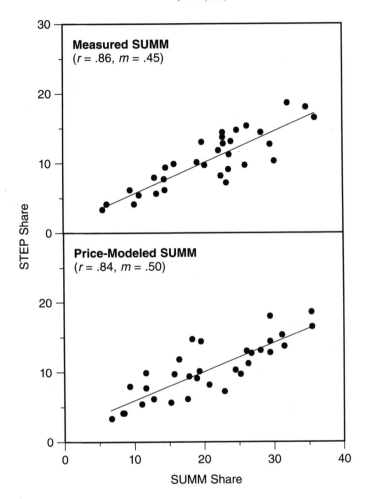

Figure 19–2
STEP versus SUMM, Integrated Method
Thirty-two Variants of Decoy Brand in Spectrum Study
(N = 6,633)

The objection could be raised that the STEP versus measured SUMM comparison may be at least partly artifactual if the STEP and SUMM measurements contaminated each other somehow. Given the fundamental differences in the data collection procedures, I consider the possibility far-fetched, but the design allows us to address this objection by making another comparison. Starting with groups that received the test product at the low price, we can run SUMM games changing the low price to the high price, and we can compare the resulting SUMM shares to the STEP shares in the groups in which the test product was presented at the high price. Similarly, we can change the high price to the low price and compare those SUMM shares to the STEP shares obtained in the groups in which the test product was presented at the low price. This yields thirty-two data points, which will be called the *price-modeled* comparison.

The price-modeled comparison compares SUMM results modeled for one group of respondents with STEP results obtained experimentally from a different group of respondents. It is therefore very conservative. Its disadvantage is that the jump across groups introduces additional sampling error. Even if both groups had received the identical treatment and had been measured by the same method—either STEP or SUMM—the resulting shares, given samples of 200 per group, would not have been identical. Nevertheless, the correlation of .86 in the STEP versus measured SUMM comparison holds up in the more conservative STEP versus price-modeled SUMM comparison ($r = .84$) as shown in the lower panel of Figure 19–2. The two charts look almost identical and produce the same regression line, confirming the earlier conclusion.

The Fully-Modeled Comparison

We now extend our examination of SUMM's dynamic capability of predicting experimental outcomes. The most stringent test is to ask what would have happened if we had not been dealing with an experiment in which different product variants were measured individually but had relied on SUMM exclusively to model all product variants. Such modeling represents the most frequent practical application of SUMM. In particular, the usual question is, "What would happen if the beliefs about some brand were changed this way or that?" By extension, the more general question is, "What would happen if we constructed an entirely new brand that would have some specified distribution of beliefs?"

In posing questions of this kind, we are usually aided by an examination of the belief distributions of existing brands. We may make the new brand's beliefs the same as or similar to one or another brand on some topics and may judiciously vary other topics to explore configurations of beliefs we judge to be potentially achievable. But we do not ordinarily have any basis for assuming any particular way in which the various topics are related to each other on a respondent-by-respondent basis. For that reason, we usually model the topics independently of each other. We know that such independence is never literally true, but we postulate it as an acceptable approximation that facilitates the construction of hypothetical nonexisting brands and the assessment of the shares they might capture if they could be constructed. The Spectrum study enables us to test this hypothesis dynamically and, incidentally, to subject the SUMM system to the most stringent of tests by asking how well we would have done in predicting the experimental outcomes if we had hypothesized belief distributions for each topic and had attempted to predict the potential shares of the resulting offers.

To investigate this question, we first eliminate the decoy brand from all of the thirty-two test cells. Since all the other brands are identical in all the test groups of the study, this yields a single SUMM study of 6,633 respondents. We next model each product variant, one at a time, constructing thirty-two "new" brands in SUMM. For each of these "brands," we have beliefs from 200 respondents who rated it based on actual product experience. Topic by topic, we randomly assign these beliefs to all 6,633 respondents. This simulates what we would have done in modeling an entirely new brand for which no empirical beliefs data were available. We call a brand modeled this way—that is, a brand for which all topics are modeled—a *fully-modeled* brand.

In this case, we obtained fully-modeled shares for each of the thirty-two test products, taken one at a time. We can now compare the fully-modeled SUMM shares with the actual STEP shares obtained experimentally by each of the test products. Figure 19–3 shows this comparison. The fully-modeled SUMM shares predict the experimentally observed STEP shares with a correlation comparable to that obtained for the measured SUMM shares. Thus we can say that, if we had employed SUMM to hypothesize thirty-two different product variants defined by thirty-two different belief distributions, we would have been able to predict the STEP shares generated by these hypothesized products with a correlation of .87.

Conclusions about the Integrated and Absolute Methods

We saw in Chapter 18 that, based on static comparisons, the Integrated and Absolute methods were equivalent. Does the same hold true for dynamic comparisons? Table 19–1 contrasts the dynamic STEP-SUMM correlations obtained when the Integrated method was used with the corresponding correlations we would have obtained if the Absolute method had been used. For the four product categories of the Pricing study, the average correlations between STEP and SUMM are .96 and .97 for the Integrated and Absolute methods, respectively. Thus, the Absolute method is as good as the Integrated method—if anything, a hairsbreadth better. The differences are certainly insignificant in their own right. But the four cases constitute independent replications. The least we can say is that, for these four data sets at any rate, nothing is lost by using the Absolute method, that is, by dispensing with the topic weights. For the Spectrum study, the correlations

Figure 19–3
STEP versus SUMM, Fully-Modeled
Thirty-two Variants of Decoy Brand in Spectrum Study
($N = 6{,}633$, $r = .87$, $m = .69$)

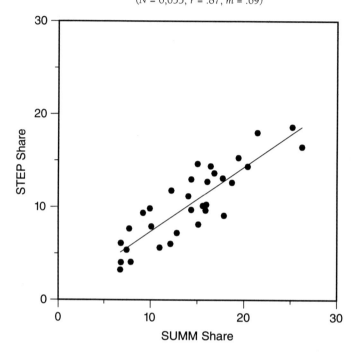

between STEP and SUMM for each of the three analyses we have examined (measured, price-modeled, and fully-modeled) are marginally higher for the Absolute (average $r = .88$) than for the Integrated method (average $r = .86$). Once again the Absolute method is at least as good as the Integrated method. This is further confirmed by comparing the sensitivities of the two methods (see Appendix E). Since the Absolute method is simpler than the Integrated method, parsimony demands its adoption.

After years of fretting about what the topic weights really mean and how they should be measured, it turns out that they can be done away with altogether, because when the unbounded write-in scale is used to measure the desirability of the attributes, it furnishes all the information we need. Justice prevails. In the contest between the logical and the psychological, a method that synthesizes the two has won out in the end, for the Absolute method satisfies both the psychological and the logical requirements.

If we had taken a purely logical approach to the measurement task, we

Table 19–1
Dynamic STEP versus SUMM Correlations

| | | Pricing Study | |
		Integrated Method	Absolute Method
Product category	A	.99	1.00
	B	.98	.97
	C	.95	.96
	D	.92	.94
Average		**.96**	**.97**

| | Spectrum Study | |
	Integrated Method	Absolute Method
Measured	.86	.92
Price-modeled	.84	.84
Fully-modeled	.87	.88
Average	**.86**	**.88**

would have set up a large number of attribute differences, for example, 350 hp versus 349 hp, three-speed windshield wipers versus two-speed windshield wipers, and so on, and we would have invited the respondents to rate all of these differences. That would have been difficult to do mechanically, but the Absolute method in fact accomplishes just that. When the respondents are presented with all the attributes of a topic on a page and assign a desirability to each attribute, they are implicitly assessing the relative desirability of the various differences. The principal issue remaining is whether it is reasonable to expect any absolute scale to carry over from one topic to the next without losing the integrity of the metric. In other words, does the way the respondents assign I's and D's to

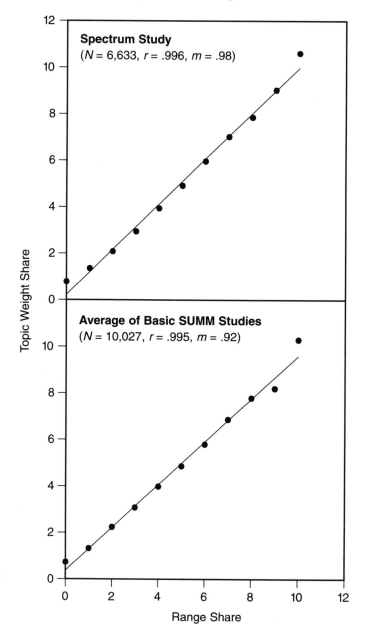

Figure 19–4
Topic Weight Share versus Range Share
for Spectrum Study and for Average of Basic SUMM Studies

the attributes of the different topics implicitly capture the information contained in the topic weights?* To explore to what extent it does this, we begin by defining the *range share* of a topic as that topic's range divided by the sum of all of the topic ranges. The upper panel of Figure 19–4 shows topic-weight share versus range share for the Spectrum study. The correlation is .996 and the slope is .98. The lower panel of Figure 19–4 shows the same relationship for a composite of the ten Basic SUMM studies (airlines, automobiles, bathroom tissue, business computers, frozen entrees, panty liners, peanut butter, puddings, retail stores, and telephones). The correlation is .995 and the slope is .92. Thus, the hypothesis is strikingly confirmed. The ranges of the attribute ratings generated by the unbounded write-in scale do indeed reflect information about the relative importance of the topics, closely mirroring the information obtained by asking the respondents to distribute stickers among the topics. Accordingly, the conclusion we have drawn about the Absolute method is not only sustained by the bottom line, but is also confirmed by the internal structure of the data.

Variants of SUMM

While the Absolute method is the standard SUMM method, several important variants of that method address specific problems. To introduce deliberate imbalances in the construction of the map, hierarchical SUMM is used. For vague competitive frames or competitive frames that are inordinately large, Sim-SUMM (simulated SUMM) is used. For simplifications, usually, though not always, driven by financial requirements, Topic-SUMM or Bipolar-SUMM is used. And to screen a very large number of games in search of optimization, the game-simulator is used. All of these techniques are described in Appendix F.

---

*Since the desirability of attribute j of topic i in the Integrated method has been defined (in Chapter 18) as

$$d_{ij} = W_i \frac{a_j - a_L}{a_H - a_L}$$

it follows that if the range $r_i = a_H - a_L$ is highly correlated with the topic weight W_i, the two measures cancel, leaving behind only a constant. In that case, d_{ij} can be defined as $a_j - a_L$, which is equivalent to defining it as a_j for all dynamic purposes, since the dynamic use always deals with a difference, so that $(a_j - a_L) - (a_z - a_L) = a_j - a_z$. This indeed is a formal statement of the basic hypothesis on which the Absolute method is predicated.

CHAPTER 20

The Synthesis of STEP and SUMM

STEP and SUMM are related techniques. Fundamentally they address the same problem. Both measure the share of a test brand in a competitive frame, but for good and sufficient reasons they attack the problem differently. The principal strength of STEP is that it provides a behavioral measure of choice. Its principal limitation is that each measurement is specific to the unique message and competitive frame studied. SUMM approaches the problem from the other end. Its conclusions are based on inference, on combining data elements by computation. But it allows us to change the composition of competitive frames and to change beliefs about brands. This leads to the obvious question whether it is possible to combine the two techniques, garnering the benefits of each without the limitations of either.

Tie-SUMM

Tie-SUMM is a SUMM study to which a STEP measurement of the principal brands has been appended. Since the scope of a typical SUMM questionnaire is large compared to what is minimally required for a STEP measurement, we may think of Tie-SUMM as an enhanced SUMM study. On a trivial operational level, one could collect the SUMM and STEP measurements simultaneously and analyze them separately. This, however, would beg the question. It would deal with mechanics rather than with conceptual fundamentals, and would result in multiple criteria to boot. For what would we do when STEP and SUMM generated different shares, as undoubtedly they would, even if only by virtue of ordinary measurement error? The real challenge does not lie in allowing the two measures to coexist, ever watchful for embarrassing inconsistencies, but in integrating them in a genuine synthesis of what is best in each, thereby generating more relevant information than either would have generated alone. The key to accomplishing this lies in the Second Law and in the implications of that law, as discussed in Chapter 14.

Table 20–1
Standard Scoring and Tie Scoring for
One Hypothetical Respondent

STEP score	2	4	3	0	1	0
SUMM score	65	63	59	56	48	42
SUMM score rank	1	2	3	4	5	6
Standard scoring	100%	0	0	0	0	0
Tie scoring	33%	33%	33%	0	0	0

Suppose we have collected both STEP and SUMM data from a respondent, have calculated her SUMM score for six brands, and have arranged these scores in rank order of the SUMM scores as illustrated in Table 20–1. SUMM typically accepts these scores at face value and applies the Second Law to them directly. According to the Second Law, the customer chooses the brand she likes most, the brand with the highest SUMM score, namely, Brand 1. Accordingly, SUMM designates this particular respondent a "chooser" of Brand 1 and assigns 100% of that respondent's choice to Brand 1 and 0% to the other brands. This is fine as far as it goes. It does not mean that we believe the respondent will necessarily always buy Brand 1. But because she must buy some particular brand on any single occasion, we interpret the data to mean that she would have bought Brand 1 at the moment of her interview, which will be appropriately offset by other respondents, who would have bought various other brands at the moment of their interview.

Thus the standard SUMM analysis is consistent with the Second Law and, as we have seen, works well empirically. But we can extend the application of the Second Law. The Second Law does not only provide that the customer chooses the brand of highest desirability, but also that if n brands are tied for first place, she chooses each of these brands with probability $1/n$. It is precisely this provision that is embodied in the tie matrix and its attendant implications. The crux of the issue lies in what it means for n brands to be "tied" for first place. If several brands have identical numerical scores, say 60, 60, 60, they are certainly tied. This, however, depends on the measurement instrument used and on the way each respondent understands the categories of that instrument. It is therefore possible that even when SUMM scores of several brands are literally different, they may nevertheless be de facto "tied," in that the respondent does not really discriminate among them, so that the differences reflect no more than chance vagaries of the measurement instrument.

I dealt with this issue in Chapter 14 by demonstrating that when we arrange a respondent's STEP scores in rank order of desirability and compute tie scores for the respondent, these scores fit the actual STEP data almost perfectly and can be used in their place. We now perform the same analysis from the other end, not to dissect the STEP data, but to refine the scoring of SUMM.

The Tie Interval

Having arranged the brands in rank order of their SUMM score, we ask which tie-type "fits" the STEP scores best. In the example, this is clearly Tie-Type 3.* But saying that the respondent is a Tie-Type 3 is tantamount to saying that, taking into account both the STEP data and the SUMM data and abiding by the Second Law, these three brands are de facto "tied" for first place even though their literal scores were 65, 63, and 59. This defines the interval 65 - 59 = 6 as the *tie interval,* namely the interval over which the respondent's apparent discrimination among the brands can be assumed to be illusory. The term *standard scoring* refers to the procedure in which the brand with the largest SUMM score becomes the chosen brand and receives all the credit. The term *tie scoring* refers to the procedure in which the SUMM and STEP scores are used to generate tie intervals and the total credit is divided equally among all brands inside the tie interval. The shares generated this way are the tie-score shares.

Tie scoring is not arbitrary but flows directly from a reconciliation, within the framework of the Second Law, of STEP and SUMM, which would otherwise have appeared to be inconsistent. The distinction between standard and tie scoring is illuminated by rows 4 and 5 of Table 20–1. In the absence of the STEP scores, we would have assigned a SUMM share of 100 to Brand 1 and a SUMM share of 0 to all the other brands. That would have been sufficient, indeed quite good, as we have seen. But we have refined the measurement, in particular the transformation of SUMM scores into SUMM shares, by making use of the information provided by the STEP scores. These tell us that, from STEP's perspective, Brands 2 and 3 have at least as much claim to being considered "chosen" brands as Brand 1. The tie score reconciles these discrepancies. It extracts information from both sources and integrates them. It says that we come closest to a true representation of this respondent's

---

*Tie-Type 2 would yield a sum of squares of $(2 - 5)^2 + (4 - 5)^2 + (3 - 0)^2 + (0 - 0)^2 + (1 - 0)^2 + (0 - 0)^2 = 20$, Tie-Type 4 would yield a sum of squares of $(2 - 2.5)^2 + (4 - 2.5)^2 + (3 - 2.5)^2 + (0 - 2.5)^2 + (1 - 0)^2 + (0 - 0)^2 = 10$, while the sum of squares for Tie-Type 3 is $(2 - 3.3)^2 + (4 - 3.3)^2 + (3 - 3.3)^2 + (0 - 0)^2 + (1 - 0)^2 + (0 - 0)^2 = 3.3$.

choosing behavior by crediting Brands 1, 2, and 3 with shares of 33% each, and all other brands with shares of 0%.

Empirical Consequences of Tie Scoring

Because the Spectrum study included a STEP measurement, we can apply tie scoring to its data. The upper panel of Figure 20–1 shows the relationship between STEP and SUMM for the same respondents (measured SUMM) for the thirty-two variants of that study. The STEP and SUMM shares are almost totally aligned. The correlation is .98 and the slope 1.0. The objection may be raised that this chart has artifactual aspects. The SUMM scoring is based on both SUMM and STEP data, the very same STEP data that are serving as the criterion. No wonder, therefore, that tie scoring, which draws on STEP data, has brought the resulting SUMM shares in line with the STEP shares. This objection is valid as far as it goes. It underscores the fact that the observed relationship is a necessary but not sufficient condition for establishing the empirical virtue of tie scoring. Without detracting from the need for further supporting evidence, the observed relationship nevertheless has significance in its own right. First, it depends on a good relationship between the STEP and SUMM ranks of individual respondents. For if the respondents' SUMM and STEP ranks were uncorrelated or negatively correlated, all discrimination among the brands would vanish. Second, the relationship demonstrates that tie scoring can serve as an effective calibrating device, ensuring that SUMM shares conform to STEP shares not only predictively but also quite literally.

We are not limited to this minimal conclusion, however. If we recompute the fully-modeled SUMM shares based on tie scoring, the objection of artifact falls by the way. In this analysis, we first employ the STEP and SUMM data of all 6,633 respondents to model the share each product should command if constructed from scratch, and then compare these modeled shares to the STEP shares obtained experimentally from the particular 200 respondents who actually experienced those offers in the form of physical products sent to them. The lower panel of Figure 20–1 shows this relationship. It closely resembles the relationship for the standard scoring case reported in Figure 19–3, except that the slope is higher, indicating that the SUMM shares have been brought into closer literal correspondence with the STEP shares.

Table 20–2 summarizes the STEP-SUMM correlations and slopes for standard scoring and tie scoring. We conclude that the STEP-SUMM correlations are about the same, whether standard scoring or tie scoring is employed. Tie scoring does, however, serve to bring the SUMM shares closer to the STEP shares. In particular, the slopes for tie scoring are

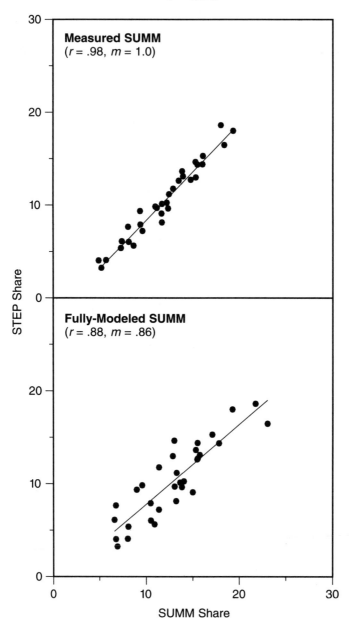

Figure 20–1
STEP versus SUMM, Absolute Method, Tie Scoring
Thirty-two Variants of Decoy Brand in Spectrum Study
(N = 6,633)

Table 20–2
STEP versus SUMM in Spectrum Study
Standard Scoring and Tie Scoring

	Correlation		Slope	
	Standard Scoring	*Tie Scoring*	*Standard Scoring*	*Tie Scoring*
Measured	.92	.98	.46	1.00
Fully-modeled	.88	.88	.68	.86
Average	**.90**	**.93**	**.57**	**.93**

higher than for standard scoring (.93 versus .57). This, of course, should be intuitively obvious. The principal measurement difference between standard-scored SUMM and STEP is that standard-scored SUMM assigns choice to a single brand, while STEP distributes choice among a number of brands. Like STEP, tie-scored SUMM distributes choice among a number of brands, thereby coming closer to STEP conceptually. Appropriately, it also generates shares that are empirically closer to STEP.

This leads to a rethinking of the boundaries of STEP. Situations arise when it is desirable after the fact to eliminate one or more brands from the competitive frame. Such a restructuring of the competitive frame is ordinarily incompatible with STEP but is an elementary feature of SUMM. The synthesis of STEP and SUMM opens the door to using SUMM concepts to expand the power of STEP (see Appendix G, Competitive Frame Reduction).

CHAPTER 21

Brand Positioning

Everything we have dealt with so far has focused on the marketing strategy problem in terms of change and on SUMM as the principal tool for answering questions related to change, epitomized in the SUMM what-if question which asks: "What would happen to my share of market if I could change what customers believe about my brand?" There is one strategic problem, however, that requires looking at the process from a different, in fact diametrically opposite, perspective: the "positioning" problem.

As a preliminary step toward dealing with this problem, we construct an analytic technique for partitioning a brand's SUMM share into components contributed by the various attributes. This technique is called *Share Partition*. Its mirror image, the technique for partitioning the share of the brand's *competitors* into components, is called *Countershare Partition*. Generically, both techniques are referred to as *Partitions*. (The logic and the computations employed in Partitions are detailed in Appendix H.) Superficially, Partitions appear to provide a forthcoming response to the perennial question most marketers and many researchers ask, "Help me to understand my product category and my brand's role in it. Why are the buyers buying it? Why are the nonbuyers not buying it?" The marketer believes that answers to these questions are the starting point for the development of marketing strategy and, by long habit of thought, is pleased when she receives answers in this form and dismayed or at least discomfited when she does not.

In the circumstances, there is a real temptation to satisfy the clamor for "explanations" by generating the Partitions and issuing them, but this is not the responsible thing to do. If I tell the marketer that her brand is bought by some because it is tart and is rejected by others because it has fruit particles in it, I still haven't told her what to do, even if the information is correct. Should she remove the fruit particles? She may lose customers if she does. And what should she say about the brand? These questions cannot be answered by Partitions. If they are to be addressed seriously, they require experiments like STEP or simulated experiments like SUMM games. Thus the Partitions only *appear* to be responsive to the marketer's desire to "understand" the product category. Actually, the game-simulator serves this purpose better (see Appendix F). But we do need the Partitions because there is one problem they are uniquely equipped to address: the problem of brand positioning.

Positioning a New Brand

The positioning problem arises when, for one reason or another, we are required to accept a product as a given and are trying to decide what to say about it. In the case of a new product, the marketer may pose the problem this way: "My labs have created a product at great cost. I think it has potential—in fact, I have done a STEP test that has convinced me that it has—and I am prepared to market it. I thought I knew my product's principal strengths, but I am no longer sure. Some people seem to be interested in it but apparently not for the reasons I thought they would be. Can you tell me how I should name this product, label it, advertise it, in brief, *position* it to maximize my chances of selling it?" Thus, the marketer has turned the question around. Instead of asking, "How should I change?" she is asking, "How do I make the best of what I am?" PLOT (*Positioning Locator test*) is an analytic expansion of SUMM designed to answer this question. I call it an analytic expansion, because PLOT is structurally a SUMM study. The essential view of the choice process is the same. The measurement system is the same. The physical questionnaire is the same. The difference lies only in how we think about the data, how we analyze, report, and use them.

Typically, the respondents first receive a sample of the test product in a decoy label (the target brand), free of any claims or promises about the product. Several weeks later, they receive a SUMM questionnaire covering the brands in the competitive frame and, of course, the target brand. PLOT consists of a Share Partition of the target brand under those conditions, that is, when respondents "choose" the brand based solely on what they have learned from direct experience with it.

Suppose we believe that the target brand is sweet, but the Partition reveals that those who chose it did so not because it is sweet but because it is tart. If we advertised the brand as sweet, we would attract customers looking for a sweet brand. These customers would try the brand and find it unsatisfactory. If we advertised it as tart, we would attract different customers. Upon trying the brand, these customers would conclude that it is indeed tart and would continue to buy it for that reason. Thus, PLOT looks for people who become choosers of the target brand after unbiased product experience. It ascertains what aspect of their experience led them to choose the brand, and it recommends feedback of these reasons into the market, to position the product in harmony with its performance.

Why does PLOT ignore reasons for *not* choosing the target brand? Aren't those reasons equally relevant? And inasmuch as we are dealing with a SUMM study, couldn't we have obtained the same conclusions by means of SUMM games? And if not, just what is the difference between the conclusions that can be drawn from PLOT and those that can be drawn from SUMM games? By definition, PLOT is concerned only with cases in which the product is a given. If we cannot change the tartness of the product, there is no point in worrying about the fact that some people don't like tart products. We must accept this fact and go on from there. Accordingly, PLOT focuses on why potential buyers will buy the brand and ignores why potential nonbuyers won't buy it.

The distinction between what we can learn from PLOT and what we can learn from SUMM games involves similar considerations. SUMM is concerned with *changing* beliefs, whether that requires product changes or not. A SUMM game might show that if we changed people's beliefs about the target brand from tart to sweet, we would increase its market share by 6 share points. This finding sidesteps what it would take to accomplish this. We might be able to achieve such a gain by changing the product, but an attempt to do so by advertising alone could lead to disaster. In trumpeting to the whole world that our brand is sweet, we might alienate the minority of customers who want it tart and fail to win the majority who want it sweet. This does not mean that the SUMM game would have been wrong. The fault would not have been in the recommendation generated by the game but in the improper judgment that this recommendation could have been implemented by brand positioning alone.

A PLOT analysis, on the other hand, might indicate that the new brand potentially commands a share of 12%, and that this share is largely attributable to the belief that the brand is tart. Accordingly, PLOT would recommend focusing on this characteristic (which the brand can in fact deliver), to create a real franchise and a basis for a stable business. Thus SUMM is the tool of strategy planning when no holds are barred, when everything is on the table, and when the only issue is to identify a successful niche in the market. PLOT is the tool of positioning when the product itself is a given, and the assignment is to accept this reality and to figure out how to make the best of it.

Repositioning an Established Brand

Suppose we are asked to help "reposition" an established brand. Does the technique for brand positioning described above apply to that situation? Speaking generally, it does, but with some important changes in the logic and in the strategy of interpreting the results. The decision to reposition an established brand is made for two reasons. There are times when marketing is dissatisfied with the way the brand is currently thought of, perhaps because new competitors have changed the dynamics of the market or because a new marketing director has decided that the brand could command a higher share if only it were sold "right." And there are times when a new variant of a product has been created, slated to replace the current product, either gradually or all at once, and the question arises how this change is to be presented to the public. What should be said?

Both of these cases differ from genuine new product introductions in one important respect. The established brand has an image which tends to have inertia. For better or worse, the beliefs of potential customers will be shaped by their past impressions, and we cannot afford to ignore this fact. Accordingly, the product experience given to the respondents needs to be based on the fully identified product. The Partition of the sampled brand will then indicate which characteristics of the product would induce respondents to choose the brand in full awareness of its identity, which is of course how it will be in the marketplace.

This, however, is no longer enough. Once we are dealing with an established brand, we need to find out not only which characteristics of the product will induce people to buy, but also which characteristics of the image will deter them from even considering the brand. If prospective customers have negative beliefs about a brand, these beliefs must be addressed explicitly. This means that we must distinguish between those reasons for *not* buying the brand that are based on real, unavoidable differences between what customers want and what the brand delivers, and those other reasons for not buying the brand that are based on incomplete or downright false conceptions about it.

Thus repositioning has two separate strategic objectives:

1. Offensively, to determine what promises will induce customers to choose the brand.
2. Defensively, to determine what promises will correct misconceptions that deter customers from giving the brand a fair trial.

To accomplish these objectives requires a SUMM study with two groups of respondents: a group that receives a free sample of the target brand in its regular package and a group that does not. The analysis consists of

1. A Share Partition of the sampled brand, to identify promises to be made.
2. A Countershare Partition* of the current brand minus a Countershare Partition of the sampled brand, to identify misconceptions to be corrected. When a reason for *not* choosing the current brand is reduced by actual experience with the brand, this indicates that experience can convert a deterrent into a lesser deterrent or, conceivably, into an asset.

Consolidating the two yields a repositioning strategy insofar as such a strategy is warranted by the data.

Customer Satisfaction

Customer satisfaction is the buzzword of the 1990s and has become a veritable industry. Elaborate measurement systems vie with each other, pursuing large corporations, which in turn are pursuing Baldrige awards. But just what is customer satisfaction anyhow? From the perspective of Choice Research, customer satisfaction is the simplest thing in the world.

Apart from the public relations value of awards, the real business purpose of customer satisfaction studies corresponds to the classic question in an employee reference check: "Would you hire him again?" Analogously, customer satisfaction comes down to whether the customer would buy the brand again. In the context of STEP and SUMM, this amounts to measuring the STEP or SUMM share of each brand among the brand's own customers. When a user of a brand gives the brand seven stickers, a high number, it leaves three stickers that have gone to one or more other brands. In effect, the customer is still flirting with defection. Under some circumstances, she is saying, she might vote for one of the competitors. Speaking as a marketer, this is not good enough for me. I want more of her stickers, more of her commitment. All ten of her stickers would do just fine. But if I can't get all ten, I'll take as many as I can get. And the more I get, the safer I feel.

This is the real substance that can justify the demand for customer satisfaction data. It leads to a simple, unambiguous definition of customer

---

*A Countershare Partition provides "reasons" for *not* choosing a brand (see Appendix H).

satisfaction. It requires no new method, not even the adaptation of a questionnaire. Any study that measures the deserved share of a brand will do. Such studies are automatically "customer satisfaction" studies. All that is necessary to present them in this chic new dress is to tabulate each brand's share among its own customers. In the case of STEP, this generates a single *customer satisfaction score,* defined as the STEP share among the brand's customers. In the case of SUMM, it generates many scores: the SUMM share among the brand's customers, as well as the beliefs profile among these customers, both supplemented by the opportunity to run SUMM games to determine how to improve the brand's position among its customers. All of this is summarized in the following principle.

> THE CUSTOMER SATISFACTION PRINCIPLE
> Customer satisfaction is nothing but a brand's deserved share among its own customers.

The upper panel of Figure 21–1 shows the STEP shares of the eight established brands of the Spectrum study, arranged in order from the highest STEP share to the lowest STEP share. The lower panel shows the customer satisfaction scores of these same brands. We see a correlation between STEP share and customer satisfaction. By and large, the brands that have relatively high STEP shares also have relatively high customer satisfaction. But this correlation holds only in a general way. Specific brands deviate from the pattern, sometimes considerably. Brands C and D, which have almost identical STEP shares (10.4 and 10.3) have very different customer satisfaction scores (37 and 54, respectively). Brands F and G have equal STEP shares of 7.5, but customer satisfaction scores of 28 and 41, respectively. In addition, Brand G, with less than half the STEP share of Brand B (7.5 versus 16.7), actually has higher customer satisfaction than Brand B (41 versus 39).

Another way of examining these data is to plot customer satisfaction versus STEP share, as shown in the upper panel of Figure 21–2. The correlation is .48. The corresponding plot for the SUMM data of the Spectrum study is shown in the lower panel of Figure 21–2. That correlation is .70.

The pattern of moderate correlations between customer satisfaction and STEP-SUMM share, coupled with substantial deviations by specific brands, holds more generally. Figure 21–3 shows customer satisfaction versus STEP share for three product categories (peanut butter, facial tissue, and sinus tablets). Figure 21–4 shows customer satisfaction versus SUMM share for three different product categories (puddings, panty liners, and telephones).

Figure 21–1
STEP Share and Customer Satisfaction for Eight Brands
Spectrum Study
(N = 6,633)

STEP Share

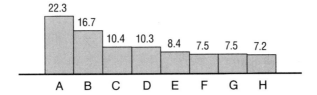

Customer Satisfaction

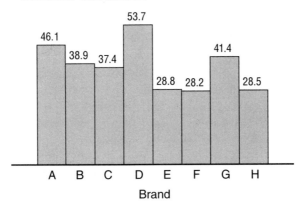

Brand

We can attribute specific marketing meaning to the place a brand occupies on such a chart. Brands that are below the line enjoy relatively high STEP or SUMM shares but have low customer satisfaction compared to other brands in the category. These brands are at risk of losing share. Their customers are less loyal, more prone to defect. Brands that fall above the line are less vulnerable. Since they may be recipients of defections from other brands, they have potential for growth.

Figure 21–2
Customer Satisfaction versus STEP and SUMM Share
Spectrum Study
(*N* = 6,633)

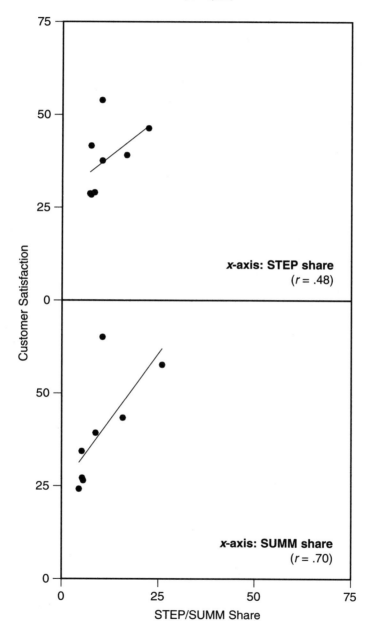

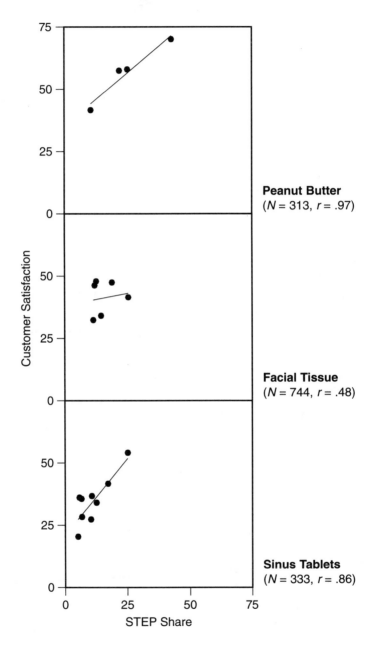

Figure 21–3
Customer Satisfaction versus STEP Share

Peanut Butter
($N = 313$, $r = .97$)

Facial Tissue
($N = 744$, $r = .48$)

Sinus Tablets
($N = 333$, $r = .86$)

Figure 21–4
Customer Satisfaction versus SUMM Share

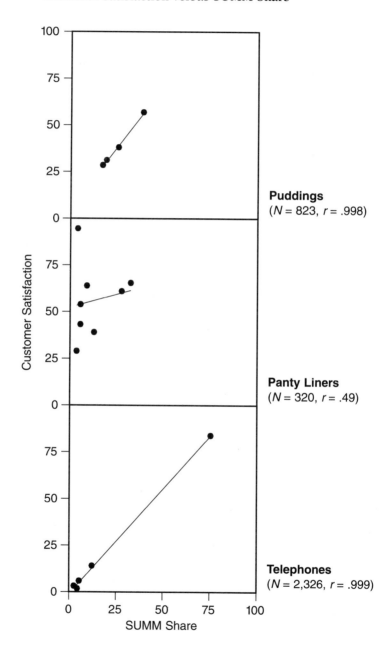

Puddings
(*N* = 823, *r* = .998)

Panty Liners
(*N* = 320, *r* = .49)

Telephones
(*N* = 2,326, *r* = .999)

PART V

MESSAGE DELIVERY

This part of the book deals with advertising.

Chapter 22 (Measuring Advertising) covers the objectives of advertising.

Chapter 23 (Measuring Print Ads) discusses the institutional aspects of advertising. It summarizes substantive findings from four years of measuring the effects produced by single print ads under real-life conditions of exposure, and addresses the question whether ads can produce negative effects.

Chapter 24 (Measuring Television Commercials) examines the problems of measuring the effects of single TV commercials, and methods for doing so.

Chapter 25 (Measuring Television Campaigns) deals with the ultimate problem of advertising research: how to measure the effects produced by different advertising weights over the course of time. It presents Ad-Weight, a method for accomplishing this, summarizes a large body of substantive findings, compares the effects produced by television, coupons, and free samples, and identifies the generic relationship between advertising weight and effectiveness.

Chapter 26 (The Third Law: The Law of Persistence) presents substantive findings about the decay and persistence of the effects of messages. This culminates in the Third Law, which has practical implications for business readers and theoretical implications for social scientists.

Chapter 27 (Budget Allocation Across Brands) presents a strategic method for deciding which of a company's brands should be supported, and how.

CHAPTER 22

Measuring Advertising

In 1955, I went to work for Kenyon & Eckhardt, a major advertising agency at the time, and began to think about measuring the effectiveness of advertising. Approaching the problem from scratch, I felt that, before we could do any sensible measuring, we had to specify the objectives of advertising. There was a great deal of confusion on this subject. On the one hand, there was the commonsense business perspective. Presumably the advertiser runs ads in the hope of selling products. His objective is therefore self-evident: to sell. If the advertising succeeds in doing so, it is effective. If it does not, it is not. Further thought, however, suggested that it was not that simple. Suppose we succeeded in constructing an ad that sells and the retailer subsequently removed the product from the shelf so no sales could take place. Were we really to believe that this extrinsic act had suddenly rendered the previously effective ad ineffective? This could not be right. The ad itself was only one ingredient in the total mix.

Some people, particularly those engaged in the production and selling of advertising, took the position that there were as many different objectives as there were potential campaigns and that it was the responsibility of individual advertisers to specify objectives against which their efforts should be judged. In my view this was a grand confusion between means and ends, between fundamental objectives and transitory tactics.

From the other end of the continuum, there was confusion of a different kind. A great deal of advertising measurement was undertaken without any explicit theory about how advertising works. The cart was before the horse. Approaching the problem from the perspective of their craft, survey researchers typically asked respondents every possible question they could think of: Did you see the ad? Did you like the ad? What did the ad say? How did the ad make you feel? And so on. Surveys of this type were in vogue, some practiced on an ad hoc basis, others in the form of syndicated services, none of which, it seemed to me, confronted the basic issue.

As I saw it, the very decision to advertise indicated that the marketer had already made one fundamental assumption, namely that if she could appropriately change the state of mind of the customer, that change would manifest itself subsequently in a changed probability of buying the brand. The purchase itself, of course, would be consummated only if other conditions were also satisfied at that future time. In particular, the brand would have to be available, preferably visibly available, at an acceptable price. These supplementary requirements, however, were clearly beyond the responsibility of the advertising. The advertising's task was to enter the customer's eyes and ears, do its job, and be done with it. But what was that job? People were prone to include as many aspects of it as possible. As a would-be theory builder, however, my inclination went in precisely the opposite direction.

The question I posed was not how many relevant things we might be able to measure but how few. In particular, I asked: "What is the smallest number of variables that is both necessary and sufficient to characterize the state of mind of a customer with respect to a brand, insofar as that state of mind has any bearing on what the customer may buy subsequently?" My answer was that this number was two: (1) how much the respondent liked or disliked the brand, all things considered, and (2) how likely the respondent was to evoke the brand. I called these variables *attitude* and *awareness*, respectively.

Attitude was defined as the score obtained in response to the question:

Please use a scale from +5 to -5 to tell me how you feel about each of the following brands. The more you like the brand I mention, the bigger the plus number you should give it. The more you dislike the brand I mention, the bigger the minus number you should give it. If you neither like nor dislike the brand, you may give it a 0.

Awareness was defined as the percentage naming a brand in response to the question:

Please name a brand of _____. Just tell me the first one that comes to your mind.

Thus awareness reflected the old politician's rule: Never mind what you say about me, just so long as you spell my name right.

With this formulation, I had embarked on the first step in the construction of a theory of choice. I postulated that both variables were necessary. I held that the two variables were fundamentally different, even if they should turn out to be highly correlated, as indeed they usually were. Correlations between them were empirical rather than conceptual. Attitude had polarity. It could be either positive or negative. Awareness did not have polarity. It was possible to increase awareness without increasing attitude. It was possible to increase attitude without increasing awareness. And it was up to advertising to do both: to make people like the brand better *and* to make enough of an impression on them to embed the brand more deeply in their consciousness. Those were the criteria by which the effort had to be measured. All else was foolishness—irrelevant at best, downright wrong at worst.

When told that the purpose of advertising was to produce sales, I countered that one ran advertising to produce awareness and attitude and that, if market conditions, price, availability, etc., were right, the higher awareness and attitude would eventually translate itself into sales. If an ad for a motor oil succeeded in increasing awareness and attitude for the advertised brand but sales did not improve, perhaps because the customer routinely relied on the gas station attendant to supply any brand that happened to be in stock, the proper conclusion was not that the ad had been ineffective but that the idea of advertising a motor oil to the general public rather than to gas station operators had been foolish to begin with.

When told that the purpose of a campaign was to convince people that the brand was made "for successful young people," I replied that this was an obfuscation. "Tell them anything you want in your ads," I would say. "By all means tell them that your brand is made for successful young people. If this is an effective way of selling the brand, the ad will produce gains in awareness and attitude for the brand. If it fails to do so, the ad is worthless, no matter what else it may do." This was the gospel of awareness and attitude I preached during the mid-1950s and early 1960s inside the advertising agency, among the agency's clients, and outside.

What I then called attitude drifted dangerously between the two variables I have identified as desirability and choice. In some contexts, attitude was pure desirability, in others pure choice. I changed nomenclature and stopped using the term "attitude" when the distinction between the two variables finally became clear to me. At that time, I decided that "desirability" would be a better term, more neutral, less burdened by a long history of prior use, a term I could define explicitly and unambiguously. Nevertheless, I have not dropped the term "attitude" altogether from this account, because I do not want to rewrite history. I am continuing to use it when speaking of work that was done in the 1950s and in the early 1960s, and am using the more precise terms "desirability" and "choice" when referring to more recent work.

In the beginning, I did not think in terms of choice. Desirability, alias attitude, the extent to which people like or dislike different brands or objects, was the central variable. Measuring it effectively was the central problem. I believed that a truly effective measuring instrument would open all doors. My energy was therefore focused on problems of measurement. Nevertheless, rudimentary elements of what subsequently evolved into measurements of choice crept into the work from the start. In particular, it was intuitively obvious that if we wanted to measure the effectiveness of ads in changing attitude toward the advertised brand, we would have to consider what happened to attitude toward competitive brands as well. So I incorporated measurements of attitude toward competitive brands into the tests. These were initially conceived as controls rather than as intrinsic aspects of the measurement. Awareness, on the other hand, was, by its very nature, a measure of choice from the outset, automatically generating shares for the test brand relative to all brands in the category.

The technique I constructed for measuring the effectiveness of an ad was an artificial before-after experiment. The interview started by administering awareness and attitude questions to the respondents for a number of product categories. The respondents were then given a portfolio of print ads and were asked to leaf through the portfolio, taking as much or as little time as they pleased to look at the ads. The portfolio contained twelve ads for twelve unrelated brands. Nine of these were buffer ads; the remaining three were test ads. After examination of the portfolio, the awareness and attitude measurements were repeated. Randomly equivalent groups of respondents saw different test ads. The criterion was before-after change in awareness and attitude for the test brand, though I soon began to subtract the attitude change for the competitive brands. This turned into an allocation of poker chips among brands and eventually into the allocation of stickers among all brands of the competitive frame. These shifts began to take place during the last few months of my tenure at Kenyon & Eckhardt, but it was only several years later that I began to think of choice as the central variable to be studied.

As I moved from the advertising agency to my own firm, my outlook changed in some fundamental respects. This was a source of major surprise to me when I thought about it years later. At the time, I believed strongly, indeed took pride in the belief, that I was impervious to the influences of my environment. The researcher was obligated to pursue the "truth," such as it was, no matter where it led. Data were sacrosanct. Reports had to be rigorous. One's point of view was not negotiable. To be sure, I encountered pressures from time to time, but I resisted them, always successfully, and I was young enough, naive enough, and vain enough to believe that my perspective was objective. Every now and again, I confronted the indignant cry from some account executive: "Whose side are you on anyway, ours or theirs?" ("they" being the client). I always replied smugly that it was in the best long-term interest of the agency to be on "their" side, and that was where I was. So I felt good about my job at the agency and took pride in my ability to do honest work there. If anyone had suggested that my work was distorted by the environment, I would have denied this indignantly. Yet I concluded later, quite a bit later, that I had been subject to bias after all, a very subtle bias, but a bias just the same. The bias had not been in what I did, not in the theory I had adopted, not in the methods I had used, not in the answers I had generated, but in the questions I had chosen to ask in the first place.

After having worked hard to develop the before-after portfolio method for testing print ads, one might have supposed that, upon forming my own company, I would have drawn on that experience and attempted to continue this work. But that is not what I did. The before-after portfolio test measured ads under artificial exposure conditions. It measured the relative effectiveness of ads and did not, indeed was not designed to, throw light on their absolute effectiveness. When I began to think about the same problem in my own company, I noted that the previous work had dealt with only half of the problem. I should have been trying to measure the absolute effectiveness of ads and, what is more, measure that effectiveness under real-life conditions of exposure. Why had this thought, certainly the most obvious and natural thought, not occurred to me while I was with the agency? Was that an accident, or had it been an unconscious evasion of an issue that would have created problems if I had attempted to tackle it before? I do not know. The fact is that I started to think in those terms in an intense way as soon as I was on my own.

An advertising test, I reasoned, can be characterized by two things: by the type of exposure and by the type of criteria it uses, as illustrated in Figure 22–1. The exposure can be either artificial or real-life. Showing respondents

Figure 22–1
Classification of Advertising Measurement Methods

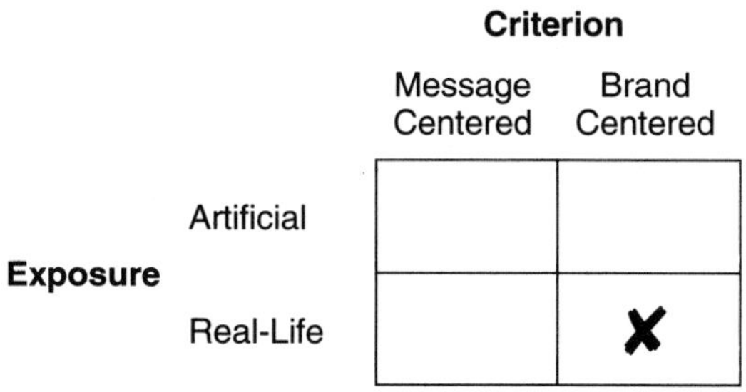

Criterion

	Message Centered	Brand Centered
Artificial		
Real-Life		**✗**

Exposure

an ad in a portfolio, in a magazine, or in a newspaper, and asking them to look at it or read it are instances of artificial exposure. Allowing respondents to experience the ad on their own is real-life exposure. I defined a *real-life* test as one in which the respondent does not know at the time of the exposure that the exposure is part of a test and does not know at the time of the measurement that the measurement has anything to do with the prior exposure.

The criteria used in a test can be either message-centered or brand-centered. *Message-centered* criteria encompass such things as: Do you remember the ad? What did it say or show? Did you like the ad? These questions generate reports of how the respondent reacted to the ad itself. By contrast, *brand-centered* criteria focus on how the respondent reacted to the advertised brand. Did she buy it? What was her awareness of it? What was her attitude toward it?

Ideally, I wanted to design a test that would employ real-life conditions of exposure and brand-centered criteria of effectiveness. As far as the latter were concerned, I did not, of course, believe in a wide range of options. I felt that I knew which particular brand-centered criteria should be used, namely, awareness and attitude. The trick was to design a test that would measure the ability of a real ad to produce changes in awareness and attitude under real-life conditions of exposure. The result was the POST program.

CHAPTER 23

Measuring Print Ads

I began my effort to construct a real-life test of advertising by approaching people at various publications in the hope of finding someone to work with. My request involved considerable headaches for the publication. I wanted them to bind test ads into subscription copies on a regular basis. Several publications turned me down outright, but the *Saturday Evening Post* had a research director, Charles Swanson, who had some influence in his organization and who liked the idea. He was instrumental in persuading his management to go along and in maintaining the necessary liaison to lick the logistics problems. It could never have been done without him. The formal name of the program was The Marder Ad-Testing Program. I refer to it as the "POST program" throughout this book.

The POST Program

Once every other month, the operations people at the *Post* drew a random sample of households from their subscription lists. The chosen households were coded to avoid repeat use of the same household. The sample was divided into three randomly equivalent subsamples of households, Samples I, II, and III, and the lists were delivered to us. At the same time, we furnished twelve ads to the *Post*: two ads for each of six different brands (A, B, C, D, E, F) in unrelated product categories. These ads were arranged in three four-page units, as shown in Figure 23–1, and bound into the relevant issue of the *Saturday Evening Post* as inserts through the magazine, one sheet appearing in the first half of the book, the other sheet in the second half. The test copies were indistinguishable from regular copies of the *Saturday Evening Post* and were sent to the subscribers in the course of the regular subscription mailing. Thus, we had three randomly equivalent samples of households of *Saturday Evening Post* subscribers, who differed only in that each sample received different test ads. Sample I, for example, received an issue of the *Post* containing Ad A1, Sample II

Figure 23–1
Design of POST Program Tests

	Sample I	Sample II	Sample III
Front	A1	A2	B1
Position in magazine	B2	C1	C2
	D1	E1	D2
Back	E2	F1	F2

received an issue containing Ad A2, and Sample III received an issue containing no ad for Brand A.

Two weeks after arrival of the subscription issue, all respondents were contacted and interviewed over the telephone. The interview made no mention of the *Saturday Evening Post* or of advertising. Neither the respondents nor the interviewers knew that they were participating in an ad test. They certainly did not know that different test groups had received different treatments. As far as the respondents and the interviewers were concerned, we were conducting a survey to gather opinions about brands.

Since I had defined the objectives of advertising as building awareness and attitude, the program measured those two variables. The difference in awareness between a group exposed to an ad for a brand and the control group not exposed to an ad for the brand was defined as the *awareness effect* (or the *awareness score*) of the ad. The difference in attitude between the groups was defined as the *attitude effect* (or the *attitude score*). By the time I instituted the program, I had already switched from measuring desirability to measuring choice, though the distinction between these variables was still blurred in my mind. I had merely come to believe that inducing the respondents to divide points among competitors was a better way of measuring what I wanted to measure and was not yet explicitly aware that in making this shift I had done more than just change the tool: I had in fact changed the variable itself. In that sense, intuitive understanding preceded a fully articulated rational position.

I did, however, face an implementation problem. All the original studies in which the respondents had been asked to divide points among brands had been done by personal interviews. The respondents had placed poker chips on exhibit boards. The POST program required large sample sizes, widely dispersed across the country, and could not realistically be done by personal interviews. The idea of using self-administered questionnaires through the mail did not even occur to me. Like most practitioners at the time, I believed that mail questionnaires were the last resort of budget cutters, that the return rates they produced were unconscionably low, and that no self-respecting researcher would use them for a serious purpose. These judgments were certainly completely wrong, but they led to the conclusion that the data for the program would have to be collected by telephone interviews. This in turn gave rise to the question of how to get respondents to divide points among competing brands over the telephone.

I adopted a two-step procedure. A list of five competing brands was read to the respondent, and she was asked for her first choice. If she named the test brand, she was asked for her second choice. This generated a *principal competitor* for the test brand: her first-choice brand, or, if her first-choice brand happened to be the test brand, her second-choice brand. The respondent was then asked to divide ten points between the test brand and the principal competitor. This was intended to approximate the allocation of ten points among all five brands, the test brand and the principal competitor receiving the allocated points, all other brands receiving zero points. The average share of points given to the test brand was defined as the test brand's *attitude score*, which is structurally a share.

One overriding principle was scrupulously observed. The measurements did not deal with advertising. They dealt with how the respondents felt about brands. Chance variations aside, we were measuring the effects of advertising. This perspective was quintessentially conservative. Yes, some respondents might not have read the issue of the *Post*. Yes, some respondents might have read the issue but might not have gotten to the page on which the test ad was located. Yes, these factors might have diluted the effects. But this dilution was real. We were measuring the effect of a single ad in a real publication, read under real-life conditions, in changing awareness and attitude for the advertised brand.

EMA paid the *Saturday Evening Post* for the production costs and required clients to subscribe to testing a minimum of twelve ads per year (two ads, six times per year). The sample sizes were approximately 4,800 completed interviews per test, 800 men and 800 women in each of the three test groups. The program started with the November 3, 1962 issue and terminated with the September 24, 1966 issue, around the time when the *Saturday Evening Post* suspended publication.

The Environment

From the beginning, the POST program was a labor of love. It had its ups and downs, but it always involved struggle. The effort to measure the effectiveness of advertising was a thankless job. People talked a good game and claimed they wanted to know, but that was not my experience in practice.

The advertising agencies were resisting with all the power at their command, which was considerable. Presumably they were the agency of record because the client had been prepared to assume that running their advertising would advance his business. Accordingly, measurement could not help the agency. If it proved the advertising to be effective, it would merely confirm an assumption the client had already made. "Of course it is working," would be the client's implicit comment. "I wouldn't be running it if I didn't believe it was working." If the measurement showed that the advertising was not working, it would produce chagrin, disappointment, and trouble for the agency. Reasonably enough, the agency responded with a cry to battle. The method was no good. Advertising is intangible. You can't expect a single ad to produce results. You have to advertise for a long time. You must have faith, the strength of your convictions, the manly courage to rely on your judgment without succumbing to ephemeral numbers that are bound to lead you astray.

I did not really blame the agencies for this stand. The fault was not theirs. They had much to lose and little to gain. They had managed very well for many years without measurement, thank you. If the client could be kept happy that way, why look for trouble? This position was inherent in their business. But their business depended entirely on the client and could prevail only if the client bought and embraced it. I therefore held the client responsible. If he accepted the agency's argument and continued to run ineffective advertising, he got exactly what he deserved.

But why should the client have been so diffident about measuring the advertising? The client ran advertising to sell his product, to make a profit, didn't he? Not necessarily. Institutionally, the role of advertising is more complex than that, and most of the time the agency's resistance played to a subtle counterpoint in the client organization. First, there is the matter of the budget. Advertising budgets are made, not born. Someone has to conceive them, champion them, win approval for them, and become their steward. Whether that is a brand manager, an advertising manager, a marketing vice president, or an even more highly placed member of management, that person usually has an emotional stake in the process before a single ad has been run. The chances are he has fought for the budget and has convinced someone to allocate it. The larger that budget, the higher his personal stock is likely to be, as manifested in title, salary, influence, and promotability. Thus, the very people charged with administering the advertising budget usually have a subtle, and often not-so-subtle, stake in the outcome of advertising measurements.

Even more pervasive is the art syndrome. An advertisement has two aspects. It is a selling tool, a persuasive message designed to influence the choices of prospective customers. It is also a photograph, a poem, an essay, a collage, a thirty-second film, and as such a "work of art." This dual aspect manifests itself in every aspect of advertising production and management. But the two faces of advertising reflect different objectives and different value structures.

A selling tool is an instrument constructed for a single purpose: to sell. Accordingly, it must be judged by whether it succeeds in influencing prospective customers to choose the advertised brand. If it does so, fine. If it does not, it is useless. A work of art, on the other hand, has no purpose outside itself. It is usually judged by critical acclaim. Does the public like it? Do the critics like it? Do a few like-minded artists like it? The artist may even decide that the only thing that matters is whether he himself likes it. There are no hard rules. Who would dare denigrate James Joyce for having written *Finnegans Wake,* a work hardly anyone can read? It should not come as a surprise, then, that the demands of selling and the demands of art pull in different directions.

The casual observer, unfamiliar with the nuances, is likely to assume that businesses run advertising for the purpose of making money, that the demands of the selling tool must be paramount, and that the ethos of art is irrelevant or at most incidental. Nothing could be further from the truth. The fact is that advertising is dominated by "art." This is said without prejudice concerning the caliber of that art. It merely notes that the value structure, the ethos that drives advertising, is not the ethos of selling but the ethos of art. This starts from the ground up, with the people engaged in making the advertising, and bubbles up from them throughout the entire system.

When a business needs salespeople, it seeks people who are aggressive, persistent, persuasive, and eager to influence others. But when the selling is to be accomplished on the printed page or on film, it seeks people with competence in those media: would-be poets, novelists, essayists, painters, and filmmakers who happen to want to eat. These people join the advertising agency but continue to pursue their calling. Characteristically, they refer to themselves as the "creative" people and the departments in which they work as the "creative" departments. Why creative? Why not the selling departments? Isn't their purpose to sell? Certainly lip-service is paid to selling, which after all pays the bills, but fundamentally the creative people are in the business of "creating." They are in pursuit of the rewards of artistic excellence: critical acclaim from clients, from colleagues, and from the critics of their craft, as manifested in art director awards, awards for the "best" commercial, etc.

In an effort to explore the implicit conflict between advertising as a selling tool and as art, I once posed the following question to the senior vice president in charge of creative services of an advertising agency.

"Suppose you had to choose between two ads. Ad A is original, tasteful, beautifully crafted, but does not sell. Ad B is ordinary, vulgar, badly done, but does sell. Which one would you run?"

He replied, "I would try to make an ad that does both."

"But suppose you couldn't? After all, you would hardly be surprised to learn that more people read comic books than read Shakespeare. Suppose it turned out that no matter how hard you tried, the ordinary, vulgar ad always sold more than the original, tasteful ad?"

We danced around this question for half an hour, but he refused to be drawn into the net and continued to insist that he would try to do both. Thus, he attempted to reconcile, somehow, the need to sell with the demands of "art." As a member of the top management of an advertising agency, he could not say blatantly that he would run an ad he knew did not sell; but as the head of creative services, he could not bring himself to say that he would run an ad "only" because it sells.

This tendency to view advertising as art is not confined to those engaged in producing it. Up and down the ladder, no matter how low or lofty one's position, knowledgeable or not, we are all consumers of art. We are all critics. ("I may not know much about art, but I know what I like.") And no matter how strong our resolve to maintain an objective frame of mind, our first impulse on seeing an ad or a commercial is to respond as art critics. "Did you see *Gone with the Wind?* What did you think of it?" "Did you see that ad for Volkswagen? What did you think of it?" "And how about that commercial for Federal Express? What did you think of it?" In that mode, everyone is entitled to an opinion. Everyone, of course, includes the client organization, the brand managers, the vice presidents, the CEOs, and all their uncles, cousins, and aunts.

Say to the CEO of a company, "Here are two machines. Which one do you think we should buy?" He is likely to answer: "Run tests. Figure out which is more cost-effective." But say to him, "Here are two ads. Which one do you think we should run?" and he is likely to examine the ads and to reply, "I like this one better." The very inquiry seduces him into abandoning his role as a businessman and causes him to lapse into the role of art critic. In that capacity, he can do no wrong. He can respond with certainty. Ad A appeals to him more than Ad B, and he loses sight of the fact that this is irrelevant.

In direct extension of this mechanism, executives at various levels of the organization, sometimes at the very top, become emotionally attached to particular advertising. Question the effectiveness of such advertising, and it amounts to a personal attack on them. And when the measurements happen to do that, there are only two options: scrap the advertising, or scrap the measurements. The latter decision is almost always shrouded in doubletalk. The company that has the budget to run millions of dollars' worth of potentially wasteful advertising can't "afford" to spend one or two percent to find out what, if anything, that advertising is producing. "We would be glad, indeed eager, to measure our advertising if we had more confidence in the instruments, if you could prove to us beyond a doubt that your measurements will always give the right answer." . . . "We would love to measure our advertising if you could only persuade our advertising agency, which is after all our indispensable partner, to embrace the measurement." And so on.

I remember only a single instance in which the real problem was articulated explicitly. The man's title was advertising manager. He served a multibillion dollar company. He subscribed to our service enthusiastically, but failed to renew the following year. When I went to see him, he did not put me off with the usual excuses. His words remain with me to the present day.

"Last year," he said, "I subscribed to your service. You demonstrated that our ads were not working, and I canceled them. I sincerely believe that I saved my company five to ten million dollars which went right to the bottom line." This, of course, was a lot more money in the early 60's than it is today.

"But," he continued, "my management was unhappy. They asked 'What's the matter with you? Other companies manage to produce good advertising. Why can't you?' Now we've come up with a new campaign. The agency loves it and my management loves it. Everyone is happy. I don't know whether the ads are any good. If I had my boss's job, maybe I would want to know. But as things stand, I don't want to know."

I thanked him and left. He was right. There was nothing I could or should have attempted to sell to him in good conscience.

The program survived for four years. Selling hard, arguing, cajoling, and persuading, we managed to sign up new subscribers only to see old ones drop out. The program consumed much psychic energy and wasn't making money. Nevertheless, I believed we were doing the right thing, and kept it going against odds. But when the *Saturday Evening Post* suspended publication, I made no effort to find a replacement. Four years were enough, and I folded quietly. Requiescat in pace.

Now I turn to the remains, which have not altogether escaped the passage of time. Although we had a library in which all materials were stored, old punch-cards were discarded. Reports were relegated to basement storage, where a fire destroyed some cartons and left gaps. I assume that the fire was statistically unbiased and that I am entitled to treat what is left as a representative sample of all the ads EMA tested, a collection which was hardly random to begin with, since it was by definition a haphazard collection of ads some advertisers had decided to test with EMA between 1962 and 1966. Out of a total of 264 tested ads, I am left with data for 219 ads, based on interviews with over 200,000 respondents. That is what I have. It may not be all I might have wished, but it is a major body of experimental evidence, and we can learn from it.

The Effect of a Single Ad

Figure 23–2 shows the distribution of awareness effects for all ads. For this purpose, every separate measurement is treated as an ad. For most brands, ads were tested among samples of either men or women. In some cases, the same ads were tested among both men and women. Those are treated as separate ads. Similarly, when ads were tested more than once, each measurement is treated as a separate ad.

The first thing that strikes us when we examine the distribution of the awareness effects is that these effects range from +7 all the way to -5 share points. The average awareness effect produced is .64%. Since this is the average of over 200 measurements, each derived from a comparison of two groups of approximately 800 respondents, this average effect is highly significant statistically. It represents over 4.5 standard errors. The probability of having obtained it by chance is less than 7 per million. But

Figure 23–2
Percent Distribution of Awareness Effects
Produced by 219 Ads
$(N = 143,928, \bar{x} = .64, SE = .14)$

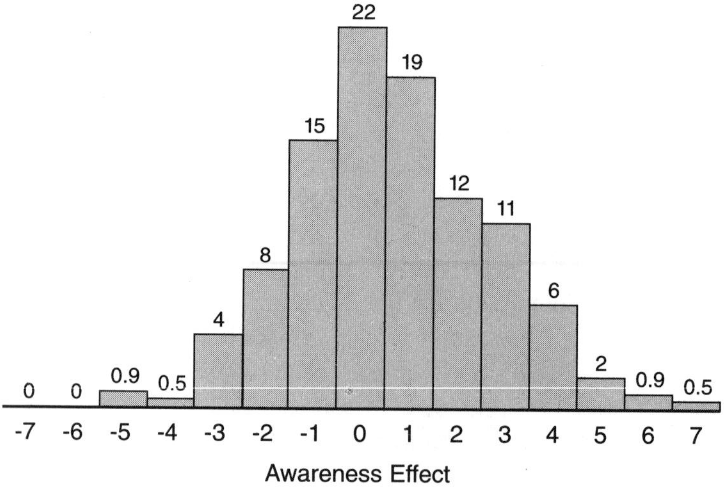

Awareness Effect

what does that mean? Minimally, we can be certain that the data are not just random numbers. Something real is being measured. On the other hand, the effect, at least the effect attributable to the "average" ad, is small, and certainly well below the order of magnitude that can be detected in single tests using samples of 800 respondents per cell.

This phenomenon is more pronounced in the attitude effects, shown in Figure 23–3. The average attitude effect is only .15%, almost negligible. The average, however, does not tell the full story. Something else is going on. The attitude effects show substantial dispersion, and the distribution appears to be bimodal. It looks as though we are dealing with two types of ads, some that produce positive effects and some that produce negative effects. In such a case, the average may be close to zero, even though the ads are producing real effects. One way of assessing whether this is the case is to test the shape of the distribution. Sure enough, this shape is not what one might expect to obtain by chance alone. Applying a chi-square test, the probability of obtaining a shape as different or more different from normal is less than 3 in 100.

Should we take the observed scores at face value? If so, they suggest that ads differ widely in effectiveness. Some produce major positive effects, some produce little or nothing, and some produce negative effects. On balance, the average effect appears to be small only because we have averaged some big positives with zeros and negatives. This will be called the *variable-effect hypothesis*. On the other hand, all or most of the ads may really produce only small effects below the threshold of detectability, and the wide distribution of scores may stem mainly from the operation of chance in the measurements. This will be called the *tiny-*

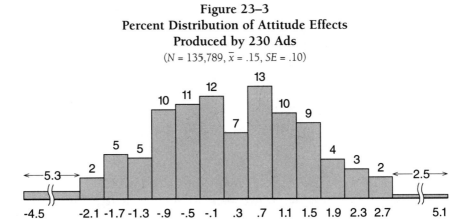

Figure 23–3
Percent Distribution of Attitude Effects
Produced by 230 Ads
($N = 135,789, \bar{x} = .15, SE = .10$)

Attitude Effect

effect hypothesis. This issue is more subtle than meets the eye. If we accept the variable-effect hypothesis for the moment and assume that the method is indeed capable of measuring real effects but that a large number of ads simply are not effective, then the distribution of scores will still look much like a distribution that could have been generated by chance, and this fact won't prove much, one way or the other. An advocate for the advertising will argue that the pattern proves the insensitivity of the system, that the effects produced by advertising are too small to be readily measurable, and certainly not measurable for a single ad. An advocate for the measurement system will argue that the system is measuring effects whenever such effects are produced, and that the data demonstrate that many of the ads tested were ineffective. All of which leads us to look for an independent way of evaluating these conflicting hypotheses.

The burden of proof for sustaining the variable-effect hypothesis is limited. We need only establish that an ad *can* produce a sizable effect and that the system *can* measure such an effect reliably. Once we know definitively that this is so, it does not matter whether this happens often or rarely. We don't need many cases to prove the point. Even a single case may be sufficient, provided the evidence is compelling and convinces us, truly beyond the shadow of a doubt, that the observed effects are real and of appropriate magnitude.

One way of obtaining such evidence is to select an ad that appears to produce a large effect and replicate the test to ascertain whether the effect survives. If it is just a chance vagary, the dice are likely to fall differently next time. If the effect is real, the scores won't necessarily come out the same, but are likely to confirm the finding. We are fortunate in having tested a few ads more than once. In some instances, the client or his agency found the result we produced strange or unbelievable and decided to retest for confirmation. In other instances, there were delays in the production of new ads, and the client decided to resubmit previously tested ads.

Altogether, eight different ads were tested more than once, one four times, one three times, and the remaining six twice each. But in order to decide whether high scores are real, we need ads that produce at least one high score. Accordingly, we shall focus attention on those of the retested ads that produced at least one high score, arbitrarily defined as an awareness or attitude score larger than 2 share points in either direction. There were four such ads. In addition, we shall also examine one low-scoring ad for comparison purposes.

We begin with two ads for Zerex Antifreeze (which were given the labels ESKIMO and GARAGE, respectively). ESKIMO was tested three times, GARAGE four times. The two ads were initially tested in the November 3, 1962 issue of the *Post* and produced awareness effects for Zerex of +3.7%

and -.3%, respectively, a major positive effect for ESKIMO and no effect for GARAGE. The retests therefore throw light not only on the question whether and to what extent the measurement system is capable of detecting real effects, but also on whether it can discriminate consistently between ads.

Figure 23–4 shows the awareness effects produced by ESKIMO and GARAGE in the course of the retests. The three-test average for ESKIMO was 3.5% (3.3 standard errors), a major effect. The four-test average for GARAGE was -.5%, no effect. All three ESKIMO scores were substantially positive; all four GARAGE scores were 0 or negative. Taken individually, two of the ESKIMO tests were statistically significant at the 95% confidence level, the third at the 90% confidence level. But the power of replication provides a multiplier. The odds of having obtained the combined result by chance alone are, conservatively, less than 1 in 1,000. Thus, the measurement system replicated an awareness effect of around 3 share points for one ad and replicated the absence of such an effect for another ad for the same brand.

The replication does not throw any light on the sensitivity of the attitude criterion, since neither ESKIMO nor GARAGE produced large

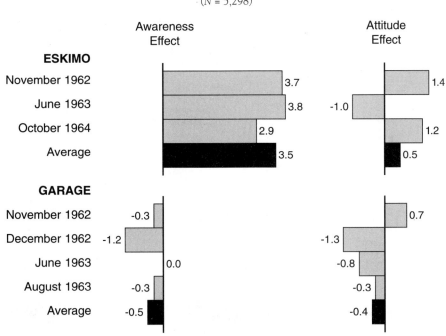

Figure 23–4
Awareness and Attitude Effects
Two Antifreeze Ads Retested
(N = 5,298)

enough attitude effects in either direction. Of the seven measurements, two scores (+1.4 and -1.3) were 1 standard error from 0, and all of the remaining five scores were closer than that. To be sure, ESKIMO's average effect of .5 is larger than the average effect of -.4 produced by GARAGE, but these changes are effectively zero, well within the bounds of chance.

Figure 23–5 shows the awareness and attitude effects produced by two ads for Dacron & Cotton (labeled DAY and FACT, respectively), each of which was tested twice. For these ads, the awareness effects did not replicate. Both ads produced small, nonsignificant, positive effects in the first test and large negative effects in the second test. Whereas it is conceivable that something real but unknown operated only in April to produce large negative awareness effects in both ads, it is also possible that we are dealing with a chance aberration in the April control group. If that group's awareness level happened to be unduly high by chance, it would have produced excessive negative effects in both ads tested that month. This, of course, is sheer speculation. If it is necessary to estimate the effect of these ads, the best estimates are the averages of their respective measurements, which are negative awareness effects of -2.0 and -2.3, respectively.

Although the awareness scores of these ads do not contribute evidence of replication, the attitude scores do. All four scores, two for each of the ads, are negative, consistent, as it happens, with the negative average awareness scores produced by these ads. The first -3.1 is followed by an

Figure 23–5
Awareness and Attitude Effects
Two Dacron-&-Cotton Ads Retested
(N = 2,821)

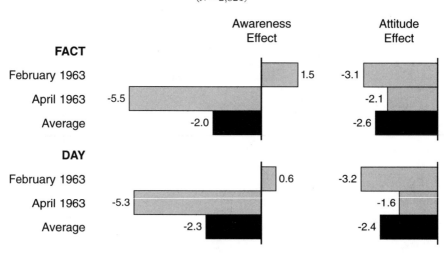

Figure 23–6
Awareness and Attitude Effects
One Firestone Ad Retested
(N = 1,361)

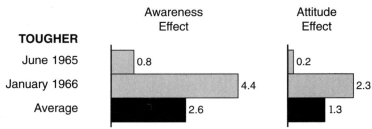

independent -2.1. The first -3.2 is followed by an independent -1.6. Averaging the data yields changes of -2.6 for DAY and -2.4 for FACT. These average scores represent -2.8 and -2.6 standard errors, respectively, each of which would have had less than a .02 probability of having come about by chance alone. Thus these data provide supporting evidence not only for the replication of attitude effects but also for the possible existence of negative effects, a subject which will be discussed in greater detail later in this chapter.

One more retested ad, for Firestone tires, produced awareness and attitude scores larger than 2. The data are shown in Figure 23–6. The Firestone ad produced an awareness score of only .8 the first time it was tested, and a 4.4 (1.8 standard errors) the second time. Its attitude score too was negligible in June 1965 and more substantial in January 1966. It is possible that the ad simply had different effects on the two occasions. It is also possible that the difference represents chance. Thus this test does not contribute to deciding between the variable-effect and the tiny-effect hypotheses. The real underlying effect is as likely to have been large as tiny, most likely, of course, in between.

Treating awareness and attitude scores separately, we have examined six "large" scores: four awareness and two attitude scores. Among these were three scores, one awareness score and two attitude scores, that produced replicated results of high credibility. Although this alone might be sufficient to conclude that it is *possible* for an ad to produce large awareness or attitude effects, we look for further evidence.

A Factorial Design

If we don't take the term *replication* too literally and remember the purpose of the exercise, which is to ascertain whether a single exposure to a single

Figure 23–7
Awareness Effect for a 3-Copy x 2-Picture Factorial
($N > 13{,}000$)

	Girl	Couple	Difference (Girl - Couple)
Men			
TELL	1.5	-2.5	4.0
BIRTHDAY	3.0	.7	2.3
THERE	2.1	-.6	2.7
Average	**2.2**	**-.8**	**3.0**
Women			
TELL	-1.5	4.5	-6.0
BIRTHDAY	-.5	3.2	-3.7
THERE	.7	1.4	-.7
Average	**-.4**	**3.0**	**-3.5**
Difference (Men - Women)			
TELL	3.0	-7.0	10.0
BIRTHDAY	3.5	-2.5	6.0
THERE	1.4	-2.0	3.4
Average	**2.6**	**-3.8**	**6.5**

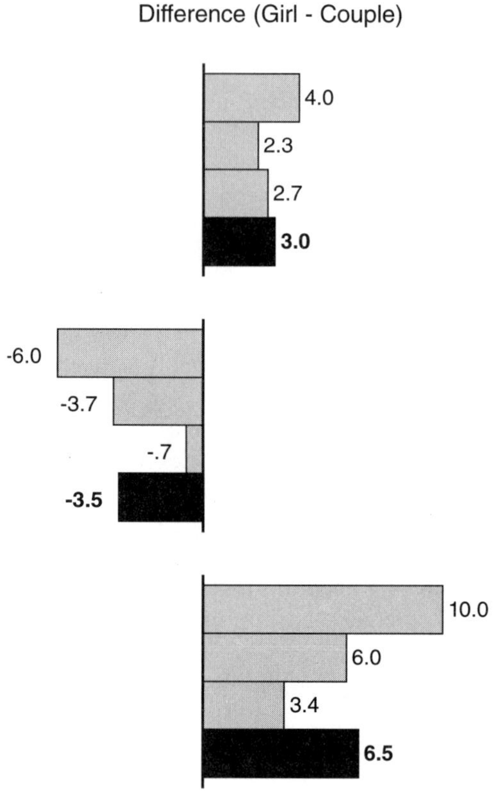

ad can produce large effects, we can turn to a major experiment. It was a test of six ads for long-distance calling, each tested among both men and women, utilizing an aggregate sample size of over 13,000 interviews. These ads used two pictures. The first ad, identified as COUPLE, showed a picture of a middle-aged couple, the woman speaking on the phone, the man sitting next to her. The second ad, identified as GIRL, showed a picture of a young woman speaking on the phone. Each of these pictures was used in conjunction with three different headlines. The first, identified as THERE, dealt with "being there." The second, identified as BIRTHDAY, referred to a birthday call. The third, identified as TELL, referred to how much there was to tell. Accordingly, we have a full 2 x 3 x 2 factorial design (2 pictures x 3 headlines x 2 genders), resulting in twelve awareness effects and twelve attitude effects, as summarized in Figures 23–7 and 23–8.

Figure 23–8
Attitude Effect for a 3-Copy x 2-Picture Factorial
(*N* > 13,000)

	Girl	Couple	Difference (Girl - Couple)
Men			
TELL	1.0	-1.9	2.9
BIRTHDAY	.4	-.4	.8
THERE	1.2	2.8	-1.6
Average	**.9**	**.2**	.7
Women			
TELL	-3.5	.8	-4.3
BIRTHDAY	-2.8	1.8	-4.6
THERE	1.0	-.4	1.4
Average	**-1.7**	**.7**	-2.5
Difference (Men - Women)			
TELL	4.5	-2.7	7.2
BIRTHDAY	3.2	-2.2	5.4
THERE	.2	3.2	-3.0
Average	**2.6**	**-1.7**	3.2

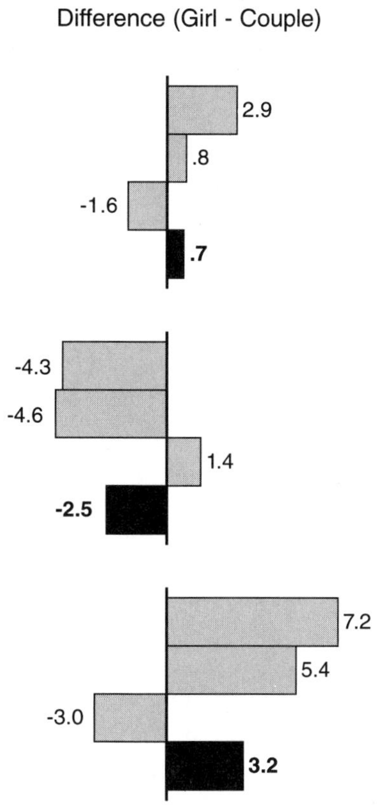

Among men, the average awareness effect produced by the three GIRL ads is +2.2; the average awareness effect produced by the three COUPLE ads is -.8. GIRL beats COUPLE in three out of three cases, with differences of 4.0, 2.3, and 2.7, respectively. The average difference (3.0) is substantial—2.1 standard errors. Among the women, the precise opposite happens. All three COUPLE ads produce larger awareness effects than the corresponding GIRL ads. The average of the COUPLE ads is +3.0. The average of the GIRL ads is -.4, for a commensurate difference of 3.4 in the opposite direction (2.4 standard errors).

The attitude results are more complicated. The changes are smaller and do not, at first blush, appear to be as consistent. Closer examination, however, reveals what must be a fascinating coincidence at least. Once again, GIRL does better among men, but this time in only two of the three cases. The third reverses. Once again, COUPLE does better among women, but also in only two of the three cases. The third reverses. And, as it happens, the reversals occur in the same ad (THERE).

What are we to make of these results? They tell a story of remarkable coherence and face validity, a story that fits so well into our prejudices that we may run the risk of giving it more credence than it deserves. We will examine that story on its merits but suspend final judgment until considering the statistical implications. It may not surprise us that a picture of a young woman is more likely to attract men's attention and build awareness for the advertised brand than a picture of a middle-aged couple, but it is reassuring to find that it happens three times out of three. We might have been less likely to guess that a picture of a middle-aged couple would be more apt to attract women's attention, and build awareness for the advertised brand, than a picture of a young woman. But this too happens three times out of three. These observations are completely independent. The three pairs of ads were tested at three different times, among different respondents, and the men and women are of course different groups and independent of each other. Thus the data say that, insofar as awareness is concerned, the two pictures affected men and women, differently. What worked better among men worked less well among women, and vice versa. The probability that this conclusion is due to chance is less than .002. We can be certain that we have observed a real difference in the relative effectiveness of these two ads among men and women. Insofar as awareness-building power is concerned we thus have a result that not only tells a story but also has overwhelming statistical support.

Whereas the attitude-building story is more mixed, in that one of the headlines constitutes an exception, the conclusion that the relative effectiveness of the two ads is opposite for men and women again holds in three out of three cases. Setting aside the attitude effects produced by the ads among the men as possibly due to chance, we note another crucial point. Among the women, two out of three of the GIRL ads produce negative attitude effects, not just small negatives but negatives of 2.3 and 1.9 standard errors, respectively. Could this result be due to chance, or is this really a demonstration of the fact that at least some ads produce genuine negative impacts at least some of the time? The probability of producing at least one negative effect of 2.3 standard errors and at least one negative effect of 1.9 standard errors in three trials by chance alone is around 1 in 1,000. The odds are that we are dealing with a genuine negative effect.

Thus we have examined six different but related ads and have observed the effects these ads produce among two populations, men and women. The three GIRL ads clearly produce positive awareness effects of around 2 share points among men. The three COUPLE ads produce positive awareness effects of around 3 share points among women. The ads generally work differently among men and women. Whenever one works better among men, it works more poorly among women, and vice versa. Finally, two of the three GIRL ads produce significant and, I believe, real negative attitude effects of around 3 share points among women. Putting it all together, the retests and the factorial experiment demonstrate that a single print ad tested under the conservative conditions of the POST program is capable of producing real effects of 2 to 3 share points in awareness and in attitude, and that the attitude effects may be negative.

Negative Effects

The finding that some advertising produces genuine negative effects is probably surprising. It seems definitive in this case. But isn't this a special case? Hasn't it been selected for special attention out of over 200 ads that were tested? And doesn't this very selection render the probability statements invalid by virtue of that selection? I believe not. The six ads were indeed selected, but they were not selected for their scores—either positive or negative—but for the replications they provide. Just as the previous section dealt with all ads that were tested more than once, regardless of whether they replicated or not, these six ads constitute a census, the only case, as it happens, of ads that were part of a factorial design. Nevertheless, the question arises whether there are any other ways in which we can check whether at least some of the negative scores reflect real negative effects.

We know, of course, that negative scores were observed. But we stipulated at the outset that, given the distribution of scores, the mere fact that negative scores were observed is not sufficient to prove the reality of negatives. So we loosen the criterion for what constitutes a replication once again. Suppose all ads tested were grouped by advertised brand. On the one hand, this might not contribute much to our understanding, for we know that ads for the same brand can differ widely in effectiveness. On the other hand, grouping ads by advertised brand is objective and extrinsic to the data and may provide a limited replication of sorts since ads for the same brand are more likely to have been produced by the same people, using a similar approach.

There are thirteen brands for which eight or more ads were tested, accounting for 168, or approximately three-quarters, of all the ads, plus a fourteenth group consisting of the remaining ads. If negatives are only chance aberrations, they should be distributed more or less randomly among these categories. Any unusually heavy concentration of negatives in any particular category can therefore throw more light on the question whether negative effects are real.

Table 23–1
Awareness and Attitude Effects for Thirteen Brands

	Awareness Effect			Attitude Effect		
	Number of Ads	*Mean*	*SE*	*Number of Ads*	*Mean*	*SE*
Firestone Tires	22	1.23	0.55	22	0.73	0.30
Extension Telephone	12	-0.18	0.43	12	0.71	0.52
Kotex	22	1.13	0.49	22	0.50	0.31
Ford Cars	8	-0.41	0.68	8	0.29	0.53
TWA	16	1.05	0.51	16	0.28	0.30
Zerex Antifreeze	9	1.17	0.63	9	0.28	0.44
Prophecy Perfume	10	0.23	0.16	10	0.10	0.37
Armstrong Flooring	8	0.29	0.88	13	0.08	0.55
Long Distance	12	1.00	0.72	12	0.00	0.43
RCA	8	0.28	0.65	8	-0.19	0.43
Purina Dog Chow	12	0.03	0.48	12	-0.51	0.64
Orlon	16	-0.12	0.58	16	-0.86	0.35
Dacron & Cotton	8	-0.10	0.81	8	-1.44	0.68
Residual	62	0.67		62	0.31	

Table 23–1 shows the average awareness and attitude effects produced by the ads for these thirteen brands. Whereas the overall average attitude effect of all ads tested was only +.15, the effects vary widely from brand to brand. At the positive end, we have Firestone Tires, with an average attitude effect of .73 for 22 ads (2.6 standard errors), an effect one would expect to observe by chance alone less than one time in a hundred. At the other end, we have two categories, Dacron & Cotton and Orlon, with negative average attitude effects of -.86 and -1.44 for eight and sixteen ads, respectively. In between are ten brands whose ads produced relatively small average attitude effects, one +.5, one -.5, and eight between +.3 and -.2.

For the present purpose, we cannot learn anything from the in-between categories. They are the result of the averaging of some positive and some negative scores, and their distributions are consistent with either of the hypotheses we are investigating. Accordingly, we shall focus attention on the two categories that display the largest concentration of negatives, being mindful that we are selecting these two categories for special analysis precisely because of their heavy concentration of negatives, and must, therefore, be prepared to make appropriate allowance for this fact in the end.

Keep in mind the purpose of examining the data from this particular vantage point. It is an empirical fact that a large number of the scores were negative. The critical question is what this means. Are these negatives merely measurement artifacts, the inevitable random variations one must expect in real experiments? Or are they evidence that negative effects are real, not only occasionally, but frequently when advertising is measured rigorously? To throw light on this question, the distribution of scores for these two categories will be examined in greater detail.

The upper panel of Figure 23–9 shows the distribution of the attitude effects for sixteen Orlon ads. It is obvious by inspection that the collective effect of these ads is negative. The average attitude effect is -.86, 2.5 standard errors below 0. The probability of obtaining a negative difference this large or larger by chance alone is .007. The lower panel of Figure 23–8 shows the distribution of attitude effects for eight Dacron-&-Cotton ads. This distribution is even more heavily skewed. Seven of the eight ads produce negative attitude effects, four of them negative effects larger than 1 standard error. The average of the eight ads is -1.44, 2.1 standard errors below 0, which would occur by chance alone with probability .017.

We have focused on these two categories precisely because they showed relatively heavy concentrations of negatives, which partially obviates some of the probability statements made above. If, for example, we had taken a thousand categories, it should hardly have surprised us if by chance alone these had included quite a few categories with heavy concentrations of negative scores. This is not what we have done, however. We are dealing with only fourteen categories (including the residual one) and have observed relatively unlikely negative concentrations in two of these fourteen categories. We can make conservative allowance for the fact that these categories were specially selected by asking: "What is the probability of obtaining by chance alone at least two categories out of fourteen that are at least -2.1 standard errors from the expected value, at least one of which is at least -2.5 standard errors from the expected value?" This probability is less than .02.*

All things considered, we can be confident that the negatives we have observed—first in the overall distribution of all the ads tested, then in the factorial design, and now in the concentration of negatives among the ads for two particular brands—are not merely chance aberrations. They are real in their own right, and must be accepted and dealt with as such.

---

*This probability (P) can be calculated from the expression $P = 1 - (1 - P_a)^k - kP_a P_c^{k-1}$ where k is the number of trials, P_a is the probability of obtaining a distribution more negative than A standard errors, and P_c is the probability of obtaining a distribution less negative than B standard errors. In this instance, $K = 14$, $P_a = .0069$, and $P_c = .983$. Substituting in the above expression, we find that the probability of having obtained the observed results by chance alone is .015.

Figure 23–9
Frequency Distribution of Attitude Effects Produced by
Sixteen Orlon and Eight Dacron-&-Cotton Ads

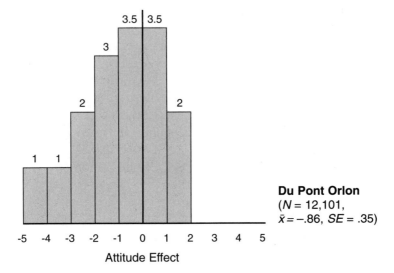

Du Pont Orlon
($N = 12,101$,
$\bar{x} = -.86$, $SE = .35$)

Attitude Effect

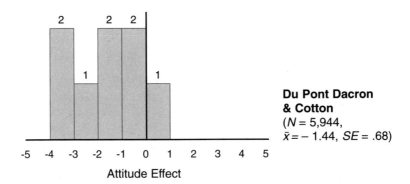

Du Pont Dacron
& Cotton
($N = 5,944$,
$\bar{x} = -1.44$, $SE = .68$)

Attitude Effect

Note: One Orlon ad had an effect of precisely zero and has been allocated equally to the bars on either side of zero.

This leads to the question whether it is plausible that advertising should produce negative effects, not only in a few exceptional cases, but so routinely that negative advertising must be thought of as a prominent feature of the advertising landscape. When I started, I would certainly not have expected this to be the case. Now the empirical evidence has shown that it is. But empirical evidence alone is not ordinarily sufficient to persuade people to accept otherwise implausible propositions. Before we can accept a fact, we need to integrate it, to understand how it could have come about. Let us try to do this.

If we believe that saying good things about a brand can increase the probability that customers will choose the brand, then saying bad things about the brand will certainly decrease that probability. In the extreme case, there is little doubt that telling people that a brand of toothpaste will give them mouth cancer would make them less likely to choose the brand. But who would tell them something like that in advertising? Actually, it happens more often than one might suppose, though obviously in more subtle form. Telling prospects for a small car that the advertised car is now "bigger and more spacious" may function as a negative message if these people don't want a car that is "bigger and more spacious." Telling people that a soft drink is for the "young" may not capture the young but may alienate their parents. All of which amounts to saying that mouth cancer comes in many forms, and that promises intended to be positive may be received negatively by some, and occasionally by many, members of the audience. But this is only the tip of the iceberg. I believe that most negatives are in fact attributable to another more subtle and more pervasive mechanism.

Suppose I ask you to divide 10 points between Pontiac and Mercedes. You consider both to be fine automobiles, so you give Pontiac 3, Mercedes 7. Now I show you an ad for Pontiac extolling luxury and prestige.

If you want unparalleled luxury, the ultimate in prestige—the automobile your neighbors covet, the world looks up to—buy Pontiac.

On the face of it, assuming for a moment that the audience craves prestige, there is nothing recognizably negative in this ad. Only good things are promised. But the ad focuses on a particular benefit, one that happens to have been preempted by another brand. Prestige brings to mind Mercedes, and the claim of unsurpassed prestige invites comparison. Implicitly, the ad says, "Think prestige, and choose a car." And when I next ask you to divide 10 points between Pontiac and Mercedes, you give Pontiac 2, Mercedes 8. Numerically and in fact, the ad has produced a negative result, not by making Pontiac less desirable but by making Mercedes more desirable. The particular illustration, of course, is a caricature of the psychological mechanism, but it illustrates the principle. If you invite a customer to compare your brand with your competitor's, you had better make sure that you come out ahead, because if you don't, you won't merely break even, you'll come out behind. All of which can be summed up in the following principle.

THE COMPARISON PRINCIPLE
Beware comparisons. If you don't win, you lose.

To some extent, this principle operates whenever advertising makes untrue, implausible, or excessive claims for the brand it advertises, a practice hardly limited to the esoteric world of theory from which this account flows, but one that has been known to happen in print and on the screen in the real world out there.

Sometimes advertising works in strange and unexpected ways. Let me tell you a personal anecdote. I can hardly lay claim to being an average consumer. I know something about how advertising is constructed and am more likely to read and consider advertising critically than many people, but in the end, I too am a consumer. And this is something that happened to me.

I am a serious runner and read running publications from time to time. One day, paging through one of these magazines, I encounter an ad—a four-color, double-page spread. The picture is a landscape with fields, meadows, and mountains in the background and a quiet country road. What runner would not love to run there. The headline, superimposed on the picture, stretches across both pages and arrests me instantly. It asks, "What would you do if you couldn't run anymore?" For an instant, I am seduced into believing that I will now be instructed in the deeper spiritual meaning of running. My eyes race to the copy, eager for the answer. But I am brought back to the real world quickly enough.

"This would be terrible, wouldn't it?" says the copy. "Don't let it happen to you. That is why we have made the ultimate shoes that will protect you from injury and keep you running indefinitely" (or words to that effect). I shake my head in grudging admiration as I introspect on how the message is affecting me.

"Son of a gun," I say to myself, "they have really done it." I can hear the story conference, the discussion that precedes the construction of the ad. Runners are compulsive and superstitious. Threaten them with being unable to run, and you arouse their worst anxieties. Then promise them relief, a talisman, an object that will protect them, not only by virtue of its magical properties, but also because, appealing to the rational side, it has been made with such care, with such ingenious construction that science and superstition have joined hands in your behalf. Who can resist? What do you have to lose anyhow? The chances are that most good shoes are more or less the same. On the other hand, perhaps this one is really special.

Approximately a week later, I am in a shoe store. The salesman shows me several brands. Finally, I ask, "By the way do you have that new Brooks shoe?" He brings it out. I try it on. Is it really better than the others? I don't know. Perhaps. In any event, it isn't worse, so I buy it. Still another week passes, and a friend who works in marketing visits our house. When the conversation touches advertising, I say, "You know, I can think of hardly any occasions when I bought something directly attributable to an ad. But I bought a pair of Brooks running shoes last week, and I can say categorically that I bought them on account of an ad. That ad hit just the right buttons. It manipulated me like a sheep. I knew exactly what they were doing, and it didn't make any difference. It worked just the same. Positively brilliant. Let me tell you about it. No, better yet, look for yourself. I still have the magazine."

I rummage among newspapers and magazines on our coffee table and find the magazine. I flip through the pages.

"Here it is. This is the ad that sold me my new Brooks."

I hand it to my friend, and my eyes travel to the lower right-hand corner of the ad. It has a small picture of the shoe and the brand name. It isn't a Brooks shoe at all. It is an ad for Etonic shoes, a competing brand.

At a measurement level, this episode would show up as a "negative," not because the ad did anything overtly negative to the advertised brand but because it failed to register the identity of the advertised brand and allowed the reader, for idiosyncratic reasons of his own, to fill in the blank—in this case, with a competing brand. Thus, it isn't necessary to tell people that the toothpaste will give them mouth cancer. It is sufficient to run an ad that will do more for a competitor than for the advertised brand, either because the claims and benefits attributed to the advertised brand induce the reader or viewer to make a comparison in which the competitive brand wins, or because the identity of the advertised brand is kept so carefully secret that the audience is compelled to fill in the blank, transforming an otherwise effective ad into an ad for a competing brand.

Most TV commercials are approximately thirty seconds long. A simple test that requires no more equipment than a stopwatch consists of measuring how many of these thirty seconds need to be cut before the identity of the advertised brand is obliterated altogether. Driven by the desire to produce interesting, mood-setting, award-winning little vignettes, the advertised brand is often given short shrift, so that cutting three or four seconds may be sufficient. This means that if the viewer's attention lapses for just a few moments, she may see almost the entire commercial without ever learning which brand she is supposed to buy. In that case, even an otherwise "effective" ad or commercial may produce strange results. All of this is summarized in the following principle.

THE IDENTIFICATION PRINCIPLE
Don't keep secret which brand you are advertising.

Color versus Black-and-White

Does color make a difference in print advertising? It is impossible to answer this question definitively from even a large body of data. In principle, the answer must depend on the particular ad, and it would be pointless to compare a group of color ads with a group of different black-and-white ads. We do, however, have fourteen rigorous experiments. On fourteen separate occasions, EMA tested an ad in the same issue of the *Post* in both color and black-and-white. Obviously these fourteen ads hardly constitute a sample

Figure 23–10
Black-and-White versus Color:
Awareness Effects for Fourteen Ads
(N>22,000)

	B&W	Color	Avg.	Color - B&W
Racing	6.6	4.2	5.4	-2.4
Map	2.2	5.4	3.8	3.2
Man	3.6	3.2	3.4	-.4
Breakfast	1.3	1.5	1.4	.2
Couple	1.5	1.3	1.4	-.2
Stretch	.4	1.7	1.0	1.3
Father	1.0	.1	.6	-.9
Speedway	.5	-.1	.2	-.6
Legs	-.1	.2	0	.3
Suburban Snow	-.2	.1	0	.3
Guarantee	.1	-.3	-.1	-.4
Models	-2.9	1.4	-.8	4.3
Water	-.6	-1.7	-1.2	-1.1
Brunette	-.6	-2.4	-1.5	-1.8
Grand average	**.9**	**1.0**		.1
Average of positive ads	**3.0**	**3.1**		.1

of any identifiable universe, certainly not of all possible ads, not even of all ads that were tested in the program. They are simply a collection of those cases in which a client submitted a single color ad to be tested, and EMA filled the second available slot with a black-and-white reproduction of that ad. The experiment is therefore limited, but it is major in scope, based on an aggregate sample size of over 20,000 respondents.

Figures 23–10 and 23–11 show the awareness and attitude effects of these ads, black-and-white in the first column, color in the second, the

Figure 23–11
Black-and-White versus Color:
Attitude Effects for Fourteen Ads
(N>22,000)

	B&W	Color	Avg.	Color - B&W
Legs	2.5	2.7	2.6	.2
Map	.3	3.3	1.8	3.0
Speedway	4.1	-.7	1.7	-4.8
Breakfast	1.6	1.2	1.4	-.4
Racing	1.8	.5	1.2	-1.3
Suburban Snow	.6	.8	.7	.2
Couple	.4	.5	.4	.1
Man	-.1	.7	.3	.8
Guarantee	-.3	-.1	-.2	.2
Models	.5	-1.2	-.4	-1.7
Water	-.5	-.7	-.6	-.2
Father	-.8	-1.3	-1.0	-.5
Stretch	-.2	-2.1	-1.2	-1.9
Brunette	-.6	-2.1	-1.4	-1.5
Grand average	.7	.1		-.6
Average of positive ads	2.1	1.4		-.7

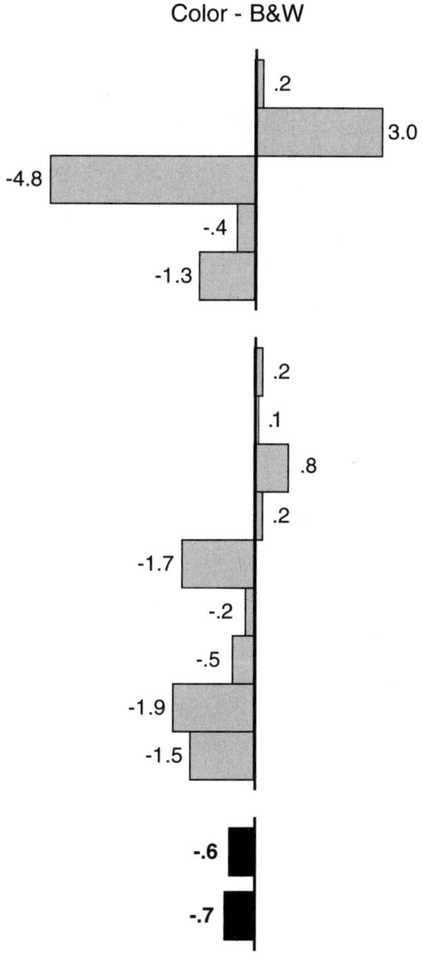

average of the two in the third. Altogether the average awareness effect of the ads was .95 (.9 in black-and-white, 1.0 in color), with a standard error of .57, clearly showing no discernible difference between the two. The average attitude effect of the ads was .39, (.67 in black-and-white, .11 in color), with a standard error of .36, pointing to the preliminary conclusion that the ads may have produced larger attitude effects in black-and-white than in color.

A straightforward reading of these averages could be misleading. At least half of the fourteen ads were ineffective. They produced negligible or zero effects. The inclusion of these ads necessarily dilutes the result, for if an ad is ineffective,it should make no difference whether it is presented in black-and-white or in color, and it should generate no more than random numbers around zero in either form. One way of dealing with this is to eliminate all ads that produced only negligible results, say changes of less than 1 share point in either direction. This results in dropping seven of the fourteen ads. The second consideration is more problematic: How should ads that produced negative effects be treated? On the one hand, one might expect color to ameliorate the negatives, rendering such ads less onerous. On the other hand, one might expect that if the ad alienates respondents, enhancing its effect should result in greater alienation. Since only two ads produced negative effects larger than 1 share point, the most conservative course is to eliminate these two ads as well, leaving five ads tested in both color and black-and-white that produced positive average awareness effects larger than 1 share point, and five ads that produced positive average attitude effects larger than 1 share point. Four ads are common to both groups, that is, produced both positive awareness and positive attitude effects.

Selecting five positive ads out of fourteen ads drastically increases the average scores, as indeed it must, but does not otherwise change the pattern of the results or the conclusion that can be drawn from them. The average awareness effect of the five qualifying ads is 3.04 for black-and-white and 3.12 for color, for a difference of less than .1%, neither substantively nor statistically significant, thus supporting the preliminary conclusion that there is no discernible difference between the awareness-building power of black-and-white and color ads. The average attitude effect of the five qualifying ads is 2.1 for black-and-white and 1.4 for color. Again, the five-ad analysis confirms the preliminary counterintuitive conclusion that the difference between black-and-white and color favors black-and-white over color. If the finding strains credulity and we ascribe the difference to chance, we can say at the very least that the data certainly lend no support to the proposition that color is worth a premium. All of this is summarized in the following principle.

THE GLITTER PRINCIPLE
Good looks aren't everything. They may not be anything. Just
because an ad looks better doesn't mean it will sell better.

Whenever I presented these findings to a client and its advertising agency,
someone in the audience invariably took a closer look at an ad and said:
"Come to think of it, in the case of this ad, color wasn't really necessary."

My reply was, "I agree, but you must have thought it was necessary
when you created it in color, and you must have thought it was necessary
when you decided to pay the extra cost of running it in color." If this had
not been so, the ad would not have existed in color, and the test could
not have been conducted in the first place.

Ad-STEP

I was well satisfied with the POST program. True, the service was cumbersome. It required the client to furnish print ads in finished form. It
tested only two ads against a control per wave. And it measured the
effects of ads in one particular arbitrary environment. But it occupied a
high rung on the measurement ladder. The measurements were rigorous,
ensuring that what was measured was real, obscured only by sampling
error, a demon subject to exorcism by replication. After I discontinued
the POST program, I replaced it with its logical sister service, Ad-STEP,
weaker than the POST program in some respects, stronger in others.

In Ad-STEP, the test ad is not inserted in a regular subscription copy
but is mailed to the respondents directly, ostensibly by the advertiser,
with a note saying: "We are sending you the enclosed ad, in case you
missed it." Approximately a week later, the respondents receive a STEP
booklet. Since it is likely that more respondents open the envelope than
get to a particular page in a magazine, the ad probably reaches more
respondents this way. In a magazine, the respondents have the option of
deciding how much of the ad to read and how much time to spend reading it. Presumably Ad-STEP respondents have a similar option. They can
discard the ad instantly, or read it, or save it if something in it captures
their interest. Since the ad is intended to run in more than one magazine,
there is some advantage in sending it to a general population sample from
which the different reader subgroups can be extracted analytically. The
sample size can be made as large as desired. And it is possible to test as
many ads simultaneously as necessary. All in all, the advantages and disadvantages about balance each other.

The STEP database contains tests of 196 print ads. Of these, 87 were tested
against the Universal Ad, a special control discussed below. Fifty-five were

Figure 23–12
Percent Distribution of Ad-STEP Share Increments
Produced by Seventy-two Print Ads
($N = 37,916, \bar{x} = 2.65, SE = .43$)

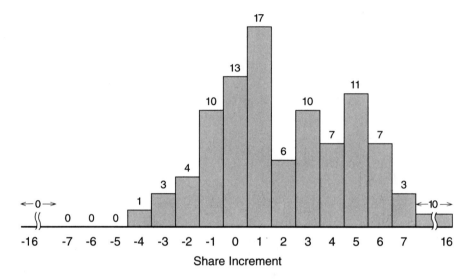

Share Increment

tested with no control because the client insisted on measuring only the relative performance of the ads. And 72 ads were tested against a no-ad control group. (This includes 18 ads that were tested against both the Universal Ad and the no-ad control.) The sample sizes averaged 379 per group. Figure 23–12 shows a distribution of the effects produced by these ads.

There are important differences between the POST tests and the Ad-STEP tests that militate against direct comparisons. The criterion variables are different: awareness and attitude for the POST tests, STEP share for Ad-STEP. The data sets represent different ads for different brands in different product categories, tested at different times. And the number of Ad-STEP cases is relatively small. Nevertheless, the average effect for these 72 ads (2.65) is larger—in fact more than six times as large—than the average of the awareness and attitude effects (.64 and .15, respectively) produced by all of the ads tested in the *Post*. There is no way to determine definitively why this is so. It is probably attributable at least in part to the higher level of exposure achieved through the direct-mail delivery of the ads. Thus the data suggest that direct mail may be a more effective medium than a magazine. In view of the large cost differential between the two, however, this does not necessarily make it also more cost-effective for practical marketing purposes.

The Universal Ad

Every now and again, a client expressed the desire to test not only her own ads but also the ads of competing brands to see "how well I am doing." Initially I avoided such comparisons because I believed that they were fundamentally flawed. Consider two assignments: to sell a 1-ounce nugget of 18-karat gold for $10 and to sell a 1-ounce beach stone for $10. An ad that induced 30% of its audience to buy the gold nugget might be a poor ad ("What, *only* 30%?"), while an ad that induced 10% of its audience to buy the beach stone might be a terrific ad ("*Wow,* 10%!"). Thus, the performance of the ad depends not only on the copy but also on the brand that is advertised. Some brands are intrinsically more desirable or have built up a larger reservoir of unconsummated goodwill and are therefore easier to advertise than others. On further thought, however, it struck me that we should be able to accommodate the request if we went about it the right way. If we want a pure measurement of the copy, we need a common yardstick for subtracting out the contribution of the advertisability of the brand and of the medium itself. The Universal Ad is such a yardstick.

The distinction between the contribution of the copy and the contributions of brand and medium is conceptual only, and is subtle and relatively imprecise at that. But it is useful. Saying that an effect is partially attributable to the medium means that some portion of the effect is attributable to the fact that the ad was there at all, quite apart from what the ad showed, said, or promised. The job of the copy should then have been to add value, to increase the effect beyond what it might be if the ad had, so to say, contained no copy at all. This, of course, is an inherent contradiction and is literally impossible, but can be approximated, provided we can craft an ad that says absolutely nothing.

From time to time, advertising agencies develop ads that say nothing, but they usually do so by inadvertence. The task in this case was to say nothing with a precise purpose in mind. If the ad truly says nothing, beyond the fact that it is an ad for a particular brand, then it should be equally appropriate for any brand of any product category. It would then be truly "universal." To judge whether this task has been accomplished, we need only check whether the Universal Ad can accommodate an unlikely range of products. The Universal Ad has been used for such diverse categories as business computers, paper towels, restaurant chains, and many others. It works as well for perfumes as for automobiles, as well for vacuum cleaners as for orange juice, and generally for any identifiable product category.

In print, the ad consists of a large photograph of the brand, covering three-quarters of the page. If the product is an intangible, the picture may be of the principal logo. Below the picture is a headline that reads

---

What do you look for in a _____? [Insert the prod-
uct category: perfume, desktop computer, motor oil, telephone, and
so on.]

Below that, in smaller letters, is the copy:

If you are like most people, you care about what you buy. Even if you
don't spend a lot of time thinking about it, you want a good product
. . . a product you can feel good about . . . a product just right for
you. [Insert the brand name.]

Eighty-seven ads were tested against a Universal Ad, and we can examine the effectiveness of these ads relative to their Universals. The distribution of these effects is shown in Figure 23–13. The average effect is .30. Once again, we encounter the precariousness of advertising efforts. Approximately half of the test ads were equal to or less effective than the Univer-

Figure 23–13
Percent Distribution of Ad-STEP Effects
Produced by Eighty-Seven Print Ads versus Universal Ad
$(N = 31{,}672, \bar{x} = .30, SE = .20)$

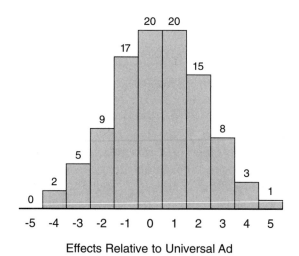

Effects Relative to Universal Ad

sal, and only around one-third were substantially more effective than the Universal, suggesting that the bulk of the 2.65 average effect observed in Ad-STEP is attributable to the brand and the "medium," that is, to the fact that the respondents received an ad for the brand at all. Only a relatively small portion of the observed effect is attributable to the value-added of the specific execution, which sometimes did more harm than good.

CHAPTER 24

Measuring Television Commercials

There are services galore that purport to test television commercials, mainly using artificial exposure methods of one kind or another. This is almost mandatory given the practical business demand for testing ads in "animatic" form, a preproduction version of a commercial in which the respondent is shown a sequence of stills designed to simulate the message that will presumably be delivered by the as-yet-unborn commercial.

In the early 1960s, I briefly experimented with an artificial exposure before-after design, modeled after the portfolio test I had used at Kenyon & Eckhardt. The respondents were recruited in central locations and were asked a brand-choice question before exposure to the commercial. They were then shown several commercials in unrelated product categories. Each of these was followed by two unstructured, content-free sensitizing questions. By "content-free" I mean that the questions contained nothing that could have reminded the respondents of any particular subject matter covered in the commercial. The questions were:

The BUY question: "Was there anything in this commercial that made you want to buy the advertised brand?" [Yes, No] "What was it?"

The NOT-BUY question: "Was there anything in this commercial that made you want *not* to buy the advertised brand?" [Yes, No] "What was it?"

At the end of the interview, the brand-choice question was repeated, yielding the after measurement. The commercial's effect was defined as the before-after difference in brand choice. These tests certainly produced scores that pleased clients, but I soon began to have doubts about what was being measured. Was it really a before-after "change" in brand choice? Or was the entire procedure a hoax we had unwittingly perpetrated—an elaborate, involuted way of asking the respondent: "Did this commercial sell you?"

In an effort to address this question, I defined the variable *conscious*

Table 24–1
Ad Effects in Artificial Before-After Design
and Conscious Persuasion

	Effect	Conscious Persuasion	Stand Alone
Brand A			
Ad 1	+4.5	46	84
Ad 2	+.6	32	
Ad 3	+.4	38	
Ad 4	-1.0	25	
Ad 5	-1.7	22	33
Brand B			
Ad 1	+3.7	36	42
Ad 2	+2.3	39	
Ad 3	+1.6	16	9
Brand C			
Ad 1	+2.3	49	59
Ad 2	+1.5	18	
Ad 3	+.5	24	50
Brand D			
Ad 1	+2.0	33	
Ad 2	+1.2	29	
Brand E			
Ad 1	+7.5	37	
Ad 2	+6.8	38	
Brand F			
Ad 1	+.2	36	
Ad 2	-2.6	32	

persuasion as the percent of respondents who replied affirmatively to the BUY question minus the percentage of respondents who replied affirmatively to the NOT-BUY question. We had tested 17 commercials for six different brands with the artificial before-after method: 5 commercials for Brand A, 3 each for Brands B and C, and 2 each for Brands D, E, and F. The results are summarized in Table 24–1.

Conscious Persuasion

Looking first only at the results for the five Brand A commercials, I concluded that the conscious-persuasion scores alone would have yielded the same recommendation as the effects obtained from the more elaborate artificial before-after design. Basically the five commercials fell into three groups. One commercial produced a large positive effect of 4.5; it also had the largest conscious-persuasion score (46). Two commercials produced negligible positive effects (.6 and .4); they had correspondingly lower conscious-persuasion scores (32 and 34). And two commercials produced negative effects (-1.0 and -1.7); they had the lowest conscious-persuasion scores (25 and 22).

Both the effects and the conscious-persuasion scores of the commercials are brand-specific and do not lend themselves to comparison across brand lines. But looking at each of the brands separately, we see that the two measures agree most of the time. For Category B, conscious persuasion would not have picked the winning commercial, but it would have eliminated the losing one. For Category C, it would have picked the winning one, though it would not have discriminated among the two losing ones. For Categories D and F, each consisting of only two commercials, it would have picked the winning one correctly, and for Category E, it would have failed to discriminate between the two commercials. While far from decisive, these data were sufficiently provocative to fuel my growing skepticism about just what the artificial before-after test was actually measuring.

In an effort to explore this question further, I set up a methodological study in which pairs of commercials, the winning and losing ones from product categories A, B, and C, were shown to the same respondents for the limited purpose of generating conscious-persuasion scores. The results from this test, which is identified as the "Stand-Alone" conscious-persuasion test, are in the last column of Table 24–1. The crude Stand-Alone test gave the same result, that is, picked the same commercial, as the artificial before-after design, in all three cases. Again, this is only marginal evidence. There is one chance in eight that this result could have come about by chance. But it confirmed what I had by then come to believe about the artificial before-after design, and was sufficient to push me over the line. Based partly on this evidence, and to a greater degree on conceptual grounds, I rejected the before-after design with the same people, without prejudice to conscious persuasion.

What I mean by "without prejudice" is that I did not rule out the possibility that conscious persuasion might prove to be a relevant variable for studying commercial effectiveness. If we assume that every commercial exerts some influences of which recipients are consciously aware and some influences of which they are not aware, then conscious persuasion could provide valid information about at least a portion of the total effect. And if that portion happened to be sufficiently large, it might serve as a reasonable estimate of the total effect. I was willing to allow this possibility, and even assign a reasonable probability to it. I did conclude, however, that if artificial before-after designs were useful at all, it was only because they were measuring conscious persuasion in a roundabout way and that if we were willing to use conscious persuasion as a measure of advertising effectiveness, we should do so explicitly and economically, and refrain from pretending that we were doing anything else, in particular that we were measuring "changes" in brand choice. This led to the more conservative TV-STEP.

TV-STEP

In TV-STEP, the respondents are recruited in central locations. They are shown several commercials for brands in unrelated product categories and are asked the conscious-persuasion questions after each commercial. These questions serve as sensitizers. A randomly equivalent control group is taken through the identical procedure but is shown no commercial for the test brand. At the end of the interview, the respondents are excused without being informed that they will be contacted again. Approximately one week later, they receive a STEP booklet through the mail. The commercial's effect is defined as the STEP share difference between the test group, which saw a commercial for the test brand, and the randomly equivalent control group, which was recruited and qualified in the same way but did not see a commercial for the test brand.

The STEP Database contains only a handful of TV-STEPs. Accordingly, I have gone back further and have located twenty-two studies that tested eighty-eight commercials altogether. Of these, forty-eight had no control, leaving forty commercials that were tested against a no-ad control. The distribution of effects of these commercials is shown in Figure 24–1. The average effect was 1.43. In addition, nineteen Universal Ads for television—not necessarily for the same brands—were also tested; they produced even larger effects on average (see Appendix I). Given a standard error of .29, the probability of having obtained either of these results by chance is essentially zero. To this extent, then, we can be confident that TV-STEP is measuring real effects. But effects of what? Is it measuring the effects produced by the commercial or the effects produced by the testing procedure?

The TV-STEP message consists of the artificial commercial exposure plus the circumstances attending that exposure. And therein lies the problem. We cannot determine with certainty how much of the observed difference between a test group and the control group is attributable to the commercial and how much is attributable to the fact that the respondent was asked to view the commercial and was artificially sensitized to it. One might ask whether the same objection does not apply to Ad-STEP

Figure 24–1
Frequency Distribution of TV-STEP Share Increments
Produced by Forty Test Commercials
($N = 16,778, \bar{x} = 1.43, SE = .29$)

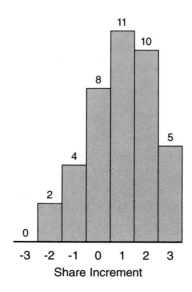

as well. It does not. Ad-STEP may also seem to be artificial in that the ad is delivered by direct mail rather than in a publication. But in the technical sense, Ad-STEP is a real-life test. The respondent is not a knowing participant in the exposure, and the medium of delivery is, at least in principle, an option the advertiser could, and in some instances actually does, employ. This is not true for TV-STEP. Here, the medium of delivery involves an interviewer, a third party between the advertiser and the respondent, which renders TV-STEP an artificial exposure design—a well-controlled artificial exposure design, as such designs go, but an artificial exposure design just the same—subject to the principal limitation of all artificial exposure designs, namely, that they may generate relative measurements but cannot measure absolute effects. For this reason, I adopted TV-STEP for pretesting purposes, but my doubts about the ultimate merits of even the best of artificial exposure methods led me to search for a real-life test of commercial effectiveness.

The Criss-Cross Design

Measuring the effectiveness of a television commercial under real-life conditions presents substantially greater challenges than measuring the effectiveness of print ads. My first inclination was to set up split samples, analogous to the POST program. This, however, posed major mechanical problems in the pre-cable era and would have been subject to progressive sample contamination, as it may still be today. Accordingly, I focused on trying to solve the problem some other way.

There is a major delivery difference between print and television. The print message is dispersed; different respondents are exposed to the ad at different times. The television message is synchronized; all respondents are exposed to the commercial at the same time. Accordingly, it is possible to consider a before-after design for television. I was, of course, acutely sensitive to the dangers of before-after designs, and concentrated on providing safeguards. We would interview respondents as closely before and after the telecast as possible. Where feasible, this meant that all interviews would be conducted on the same evening. Thus, if the commercial was aired early enough, say before 8:30 P.M., the before interviews would be conducted between 7:00 and 8:00 P.M. and the after interviews between 9:00 and 10:00 P.M. More frequently, practical considerations made it necessary to conduct the after interviews the following evening.

A critical question in constructing a before-after design is whether to conduct the before and after measurements among the same people or among different people. Each method has advantages and disadvantages. If the same people are interviewed both before and after the exposure, the comparability of the respondents for the two measurements is ensured; they are, in fact, identical. The repetition of the measurement, however, may create intolerable measurement artifacts. The respondents may remember how they answered the questions the first time. They may try to be consistent. They may try to answer differently. And there is no way of correcting for these effects. If different people are interviewed before and after, on the other hand, vexing sampling problems arise. The people who are at home and willing to be interviewed before and after may not be comparable. The challenge was to construct a design that would achieve the benefits of each of the two methods (before-after with the same people and before-after with different people) while avoiding the disadvantages of each. The solution was the Criss-Cross design.

In the Criss-Cross design, all respondents are interviewed twice, once before and once after the program. The total sample is split into two randomly equivalent groups, A and B. The respondents in Group A are initially interviewed on awareness and attitude for the test product. The respondents in Group B are initially interviewed on awareness and attitude for a dummy product (a brand not involved in the test). The interviews are identical except for the product. All respondents are called back after the commercial has aired. Now the respondents in Group A are interviewed on the dummy product, and the respondents in Group B on the test product. At the end of the second interview, all respondents are asked a viewing question to establish whether they viewed the program in which the commercial was aired.

Thus the Criss-Cross design achieves the best of both worlds. The respondents in Groups A and B are randomly equivalent. Both groups were at home and were willing to be interviewed both before and after the program. The only difference between them is the particular questionnaire form the interviewer used. Since each group is interviewed on the test product only once, there is no data contamination. Finally, all respondents can be classified as viewers or nonviewers based on the identical viewing question administered at the end of the second interview. This design generates scores among four groups:

1.   Viewers interviewed before the program.
2.   Viewers interviewed after the program.
3.   Nonviewers interviewed before the program.
4.   Nonviewers interviewed after the program.

The effect produced by the commercial is defined as the before-after change among viewers minus the comparable change among nonviewers. The change, if any, among the nonviewers is subtracted in an effort to control for changes that might have taken place in the interval between the before and after interviews due to global factors unrelated to the advertising. This does not leave a totally clean analysis. Some possibilities of confounding remain. These are inherent in before-after comparisons. No matter what adjustments are made, in the end there is the interval during which extraneous events could have influenced the criterion variable. If that interval is long, say a month or even a week, it is next to impossible to draw definitive conclusions about the cause of observed before-after differences. As the interval shrinks, the risk that some extraneous event may be distorting the data diminishes, but does not vanish altogether. The most blatant source of confounding, of course, would be commercials for one or more competing brands. If such commercials ran in the same time slot as the test commercial, they might have a selective impact on nonviewers and would militate against their serving as a control. Competitive commercials aired later that evening or on the following day would be progressively less confounding, since they would be more likely to affect both viewers and nonviewers of the test commercial.

Is it proper to treat the nonviewers as a control and to subtract their before-after differences from the before-after differences of the viewers? Assuming we find before-after effects among the viewers, we will be reas-

Figure 24–2
Awareness and Attitude Changes among Viewers and Nonviewers
in Twenty-four Criss-Cross Tests
(N = 10,525)

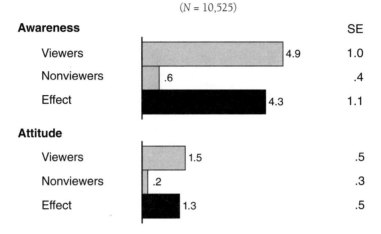

sured if, on the average, there are no comparable effects among the non-viewers. We certainly do expect to see before-after changes among the non-viewers in individual instances. They would not, in fact, function as a control if they did not pick up the impact of extraneous events. These changes, however, should be sometimes positive and sometimes negative, and should average out to approximately zero when tests are consolidated.*

Altogether, EMA conducted fifty Criss-Cross tests over a period of several years. For purposes of this count, every commercial or group of commercials measured for a single airing is treated as a separate test. One group of twenty-six tests, mainly conducted during the spring of 1971, turns out to have been contaminated in a sacrifice of rigor in the pursuit of economy, leaving twenty-four clean Criss-Cross tests. (The contaminated tests are of methodological interest and are presented in Appendix J.)

Figure 24–2 shows the average awareness and attitude changes produced by the twenty-four clean Criss-Cross tests. The ads produced an average awareness change of 4.9% among viewers, while the average change among nonviewers was only .6%. Thus, something is being measured that is showing up selectively among viewers. Subtracting out the nonviewers-effect increases the standard error of the final score by only a small amount, so the additional control seems useful, on balance, to pro-

---

*Provided we judge that the nonviewers have a conceptual contribution to make, we need not be concerned about increasing the variance of the final scores, because we usually have far more non-viewers than viewers, so the variance of the final score will depend mainly on the variance of the viewers.

Figure 24–3
Frequency Distributions of Net Effects
Twenty-four Criss-Cross Tests

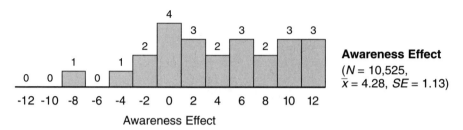

Awareness Effect

Awareness Effect
(N = 10,525,
$\bar{x}$ = 4.28, SE = 1.13)

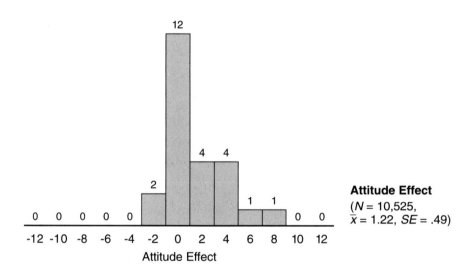

Attitude Effect

Attitude Effect
(N = 10,525,
$\bar{x}$ = 1.22, SE = .49)

tect against global events. Even after this correction, the net awareness change is 4.3%, approximately 4 standard errors above zero, a result we would expect to obtain by chance alone less often than 1 time in 10,000. The attitude changes show essentially the same pattern, though at lower levels. Once again the changes among viewers are substantial (1.5%, 3 standard errors) while the changes among nonviewers are negligible (.2%, .7 standard errors). Once again, we find that the overall average of the effects is positive (1.3%, 2.4 standard errors), a result one would expect to obtain by chance alone less often than 2 times in 100.

What do these data say about the effectiveness of television advertising, and what comparisons to print are appropriate? The net effects from the Criss-Cross design are much larger and more positive than those for print. For purposes of comparing print and television advertising, however, this is largely irrelevant. Quite apart from the fact that we are dealing with different brands and dates, the two methods cover different decay intervals. The POST tests measured the effect of ads a few weeks after the magazine had been delivered to the homes. Some of the respondents may have been exposed to the ad just a day or two before the interview, some as long as two weeks before, and some may not have gotten to the particular page of the magazine at all. The Criss-Cross design, on the other hand, measured effects less than a day after the respondents had been exposed to the program that carried the commercial. We don't know what these effects would have looked like if it had been possible to measure them one or two weeks later. But we may regard the Criss-Cross design as a microscope that allowed us to detect short-term effects before they had begun to decay. These short-term effects were strongly positive, absolutely and statistically.

Figure 24–3 shows the frequency distribution of the effects. Four of the awareness scores were negative, four were around zero, and sixteen were positive. What is more, six of the positives were at least 9 percentage points (more than 2 standard errors) above zero, a result that would be expected by chance with negligible probability. Fully half of the commercials tested produced no attitude effects, even under the microscope of the criss-cross design. Of the remaining twelve, however, ten produced positive attitude scores, two of which were 3.2 and 2.1 standard errors above 0, respectively, a result one would expect by chance less often than 5 times in 1,000.

There is no evidence of negative effects in either awareness or attitude. A few commercials did produce negative scores, but these scores are not significant when the data are examined in their entirety. The overall conclusion is that while there is substantial variation in the effects produced by different commercials, positive awareness effects are the rule in the short time frame of the Criss-Cross test. Even in that time frame, however, only ten out of twenty-four commercials produced positive attitude effects.

CHAPTER 25

Measuring Television Campaigns

From the beginning, I had mixed feelings about the Criss-Cross design. It was certainly the best I had been able to come up with. But was it good enough? Each individual study required large samples, two interviews per respondent, and a commensurately large budget. This would have been tolerable if the conclusions had been unequivocal, but this was not the case. Notwithstanding all the controls, the Criss-Cross design was and remained a before-after design, subject to the fatal flaws of all before-after designs. It measured not only the effects produced by the commercial but also the effects of any other events, known or unknown, that could have occurred during the test interval and could have influenced the criterion variable. This always left a lingering doubt. If we obtained a negative score or an unusual or otherwise implausible result, we had two concerns: the possibility that the observed data had been distorted or altogether generated by chance and the further possibility that the observed result, while real enough, had not been generated by the commercial, but by something else. This alone should have been sufficient ground for abandoning the Criss-Cross design. But I did not do so until a practical business-based demand from a client caused me to take notice and reevaluate whether the exercise made sense, quite apart from considerations of design cleanliness. My client asked the most obvious question: "Does my television campaign pay out? And what weight should I use to get the most for my money?" The instant I heard this question, I realized that my approach to measuring television advertising had been flawed, not so much in the solution I had proposed as in the question I had addressed.

Advertising inevitably involves two aspects: message and exposure. The word "message" is shorthand for the particular print page or the particular thirty-second video the respondent sees. The word "exposure" refers to where, when, and how often the respondent sees the message. There can be no message without an exposure. There can be no exposure without a message. The two are intertwined, separable only in conceptual abstraction. In some instances, the advertising may consist of a single insertion of a print ad in a particular publication or of the single airing of a TV commercial on a particular program. In the general case, the exposure consists of a *campaign,* which is fully defined as some combination of messages in some comprehensive insertion schedule.

This gives rise to two separate problems. We may want to do copy testing, that is, focus attention on the potential differences in the effects produced by different messages. In that case, we must hold the exposure constant, that is, select a standard exposure—probably the most manageable exposure, perhaps a single insertion of a print ad or a TV commercial—and test different messages under otherwise comparable conditions, as was done in the POST testing program. Or we may want to evaluate the incremental value of different weights. In that case, we must hold the message constant and vary the weights. In the most general case, we may want to assess the potential return of various message-weight combinations.

The Criss-Cross design fell squarely in between. It really was not suitable for comparing different messages. It could tell us, within the bounds of the before-after design, what effect a particular commercial had produced in a particular program on a particular date, but it was on weak ground in seeking to draw conclusions about the relative effectiveness of different messages, since differences between commercials were necessarily confounded by both program and date. On the other hand, it did not provide sufficient breadth to allow the evaluation of campaigns or the value of different advertising weights. One might say that it was too focused on testing advertising under real-life conditions to provide adequate comparisons of different messages, and not sufficiently focused on testing advertising under real-life conditions to provide the most important information of all, the incremental share produced by campaigns over time.

Realizing this at last, I abandoned the Criss-Cross design near the end of 1972 and turned to what I came to see as the real problem: measuring the effects produced by different advertising weights in order to calculate the dollar payout of television advertising. The result was a system that, unimaginatively enough, I called *Ad-Weight.*

Defining the Problem

Intent on measuring advertising weight, the first impulse is to propose an experiment: to schedule no advertising in some markets, advertising weight 1 in other markets, advertising weight 2 in still other markets, and so on. As soon as we think about this approach critically, however, we run into trouble. Quite apart from the fact that it is difficult to select comparable markets (which might be dealt with by split cable nowadays, but would have required many markets when I first tackled the problem in 1972), the definition of weight gives rise to a more crucial conceptual difficulty. Weight is usually thought of in terms of dollar expenditure, which in turn translates into advertising schedules. But what schedule should represent a given weight?

Advertising schedules are usually described in terms of the gross rating points (GRPs) they deliver. One rating point means that 1% of TV homes are tuned to the program that carries the commercial. But there are many different ways in which the same number of gross ratings points can be generated. Suppose the schedule calls for 100 gross rating points per week. At one extreme, one might buy a *reach schedule,* that is, a schedule designed to reach as many different households as possible. Such a schedule might reach 75% of households altogether, say 55% once a week, 15% twice a week, and 5% three times a week. This would yield 100 gross rating points ([55 x 1] + [15 x 2] + [5 x 3] = 100). At the other end of the spectrum, one might buy a *frequency schedule,* that is, one designed to reach a smaller number of households more often. Such a schedule—which may be unrealistic in practice, but is theoretically possible—might reach only 27% of households altogether, say 2% once, 3% twice, 4% three times, 10% four times, and 8% five times. This schedule too would yield 100 gross rating points ([2 x 1] + [3 x 2] + [4 x 3] + [10 x 4] + [8 x 5] = 100). Since the cost of advertising is roughly proportional to the total number of rating points bought, these two schedules, and of course many other schedules, would entail approximately the same dollar expenditure. But it is hardly plausible to assume that all of these schedules would produce the same, or even approximately the same, incremental effect for the advertised brand. Thus we cannot even begin to talk meaningfully about advertising weight before addressing the way that weight is to be bought.

One might be tempted to propose holding the schedule constant while varying the weight. This, however, is a contradiction in terms. As the total dollars and the total number of gross rating points change, the reach-frequency relationship changes too, automatically rendering the conclusions overly specific and severely circumscribed by both the dollar expenditure and the particular way these dollars were allocated between reach and frequency at different weights. Thus, the problem simply cannot be tackled this way. Another approach is called for altogether.

Thinking about this, it struck me that we were looking at the problem from the wrong end, from the perspective of the advertiser, who sends dollars and rating points into the world and is therefore prone to ask, "How many dollars should I spend?" rather than from the perspective of the customer, who encounters commercials in the stream of her television viewing. The problem had to be turned around—a simple thought, but one that was absolutely critical. Once again, the most important thing was not finding the right answer, but posing the right question. The moment this was done, everything fell in place. The complexities and ambiguities vanished. We had a problem that could be tackled and solved.

The principal insight was this: The customer never sees the advertising schedule, the weight used, or the dollars spent. She does not know whether she is in a high-weight or low-weight market. She only knows what she sees. She may be in a high-weight market, but if she does not see any of the commercials, she might as well have been in a no-advertising market. Conversely, she may be in a low-weight market, but if she sees many commercials, she is receiving a high weight. The weight sent into the market is an abstraction that begins and ends with the advertiser and his advertising agency. What matters is the weight received by the individual respondent. The real question is: "How much incremental share is generated when customers are reached once per week, twice per week, three times per week, and so on?" Each schedule can be characterized by a series of numbers such as: X% reached once per week, Y% reached twice per week, and so on. This series of numbers, which I call the *reach-frequency vector,* can usually be obtained from standard sources. It follows that if we can construct an *advertising-response* curve, a curve that shows how much incremental share or volume is generated by different exposure levels, we can determine the incremental value of any advertising schedule at any weight. We don't even need a computer to do this; a few hand calculations will be sufficient. Having thus recast the problem, we may turn to finding a solution to it, that is, to developing a design that will enable us to construct the advertising-response curve.

The Ad-Weight Design

The basic idea is to create a test schedule that will deliver different exposure levels to different respondents, ranging from zero exposure to very high exposure, under conditions sufficiently controlled to allow a comparison of the behavior of the different groups. We start by selecting a program that is on the air frequently and faces approximately comparable programs on competing channels in the same time slot. The early evening news qualifies. In many markets, early evening news programs run on each of the three major networks concurrently. We select three markets and purchase a schedule of one spot daily in each of these markets for some period of time, the *advertising period,* which may be any number of weeks, but make it thirteen weeks since advertising is often bought in that time unit. The schedule is purchased in accordance with the pattern in Figure 25–1, where the letter "E" represents thirteen weeks of daily spots

Figure 25–1
Single-Program Design

	ABC	CBS	NBC
1	E		
2		E	
3			E

(Markets, rows 1–3)

on the early evening news: on ABC in Market 1, on CBS in Market 2, and on NBC in Market 3.

Let us select a group of respondents who view the early evening news regularly, that is, five times per week, and divide these viewers into two groups. Group A, the "exposed" group, consists of viewers of ABC in Market 1, viewers of CBS in Market 2, and viewers of NBC in Market 3. Group B, the "unexposed" group, consists of viewers of CBS and NBC in Market 1, viewers of ABC and NBC in Market 2, and viewers of ABC and CBS in Market 3. After consolidation, these two groups are comparable in the following respects. All respondents in each of the two groups, A and B, are viewers of the time slot, more specifically of the early evening news. One-third of the respondents in Group A are from Market 1, one-third from Market 2, one-third from Market 3. The same is true for Group B. One-third of the respondents in Group A watch the early evening news on ABC, one-third on CBS, and one-third on NBC. The same is true for Group B. But though the two groups are comparable in these respects, Group A respondents will, by virtue of the way the schedule was bought, have been exposed to five commercials per week, or a total of 5 x 13 = 65 commercials in the course of their early evening news viewing, while respondents in Group B will have been exposed to no commercials over the course of their early evening news viewing during the same time.

Next, we expand the design, covering two additional time slots in analogous fashion, say the late evening news, designated by the letter "L", and a daytime soap opera, designated by the letter "D", again buying one spot daily for the same thirteen-week period, resulting in the total schedule illustrated in Figure 25–2. Those viewers in Market 1 who happen to view the early evening news regularly on ABC, the late news regularly on NBC, and the daytime program regularly on CBS will now receive an ultra-high frequency of fifteen exposures per week, or 13 x 15 = 195 exposures over the thirteen-week advertising period. Of course, this will apply to only a

Figure 25–2
Three-Program Design

	ABC	CBS	NBC
1	E	D	L
2	L	E	D
3	D	L	E

(Rows labeled "Markets")

small portion of the sample. The schedule will, however, generate a full distribution of intermediate viewing and exposure levels. For the sake of simplicity, I have described the design entirely in terms of regular viewers of a program, that is, respondents reporting viewing five times per week. The analysis, however, is readily expanded to the general case, in which we consider all respondents who report viewing any of the relevant programs on any of the relevant channels with any frequency.

The early Ad-Weight studies were conducted by telephone interviews. In later years they were conducted by mail. The criterion variable varied. When the advertised brand was a consumable with a relatively short purchase cycle, the criterion variable was the number of reported packages bought. To avoid the risk of systematic overreporting, this criterion was subsequently replaced by brand share of the number of reported packages bought. In the case of new product introductions in which the principal purpose of the advertising was to induce trial, the criterion was percent of respondents reporting having ever bought the brand. In the case of durables, or products with longer purchase cycles, the criterion was STEP share.

A typical Ad-Weight study provides for the selection of markets, time slots, and an advertising period. Daily spots are bought in accordance with the Ad-Weight schedule, and waves of interviews, usually weekly waves, are conducted throughout the advertising period. The interview covers one or more criterion variables for the test brand and competitors, and reports of the respondents' "usual" viewing for the relevant time slots. The result is an advertising-response curve that shows the number (or share) of packages bought by respondents exposed to different amounts of television advertising. Sometimes a post-advertising period is added. The inclusion of a post-advertising period is important if payouts are to be computed, since it must be assumed that the advertising will produce effects not only while it is actually running but also for some time after that. These effects must be added and credited to the advertising if accurate estimates of total effects are to be made. (More details about the design and analysis of Ad-Weight are in Appendix K.)

Ad-Weight can be integrated into wide-ranging experiments designed to assess the relative value and payout of advertising relative to various promotional programs. All we have to do is split the total Ad-Weight sample into randomly equivalent subgroups. One of these usually receives no special treatment and becomes the *advertising-only* group. One or more randomly equivalent subgroups receive some promotional mailing, such as a letter, a print ad, a coupon, or a free sample. By doing the Ad-Weight analysis separately for each of those groups, we can assess the value of various levels of TV advertising either alone or incrementally on top of a coupon or a sample, and compare these to the values of the coupon or sample.

Some Case Histories

By the nature of the design, Ad-Weight studies tend to be big. They require a special media buy, considerable time, and relatively large samples. Sample size is particularly critical because the analysis, consisting of the aggregation of increments, each based on the difference between two adjacent cells, weighted by $n_1 n_2/(n_1 + n_2)$, usually reduces the effective sample size by about half. When all the onerous conditions are met, however, Ad-Weight is powerful in its ability to yield incontrovertible results. Each Ad-Weight study has its own advertising-response curve and tells its own story. Accordingly, I will discuss a few of these studies individually before summarizing all of them. The individual cases provide perspective and illustrate some important principles.

One major Ad-Weight employed an advertising period of forty-eight weeks and a sample size of 32,727 interviews. (N' on Figure 25–3 gives the effective sample size after stratification.) The advertised brand was a durable product with a long purchase cycle. The criterion was STEP share. The size of the study was prompted by the need to examine advertising effects separately for different target groups. Setting aside this objective, which was of practical but not theoretical interest, leaves a single Ad-Weight with a sample size large enough to obviate concern about sampling error. Figure 25–3 shows the advertising-response curve, which is monotonically increasing. STEP share increases as the number of exposures increases. Specifically, it increases linearly up to 9 exposures per two weeks, leveling off somewhat at that point but continuing to increase further from 4.5 to 7.6 share points as exposures double from around 9 to around 21. In practice, exposures are usually consolidated into groups for the sake of stability of results. In this case, the groups were: 0, 1–3, 4–6, 7–10, and 11–30 exposures per two-

Figure 25–3
Ad-Weight: Impact of TV Advertising
on STEP Share
(N = 32,727, N′ = 16,569)

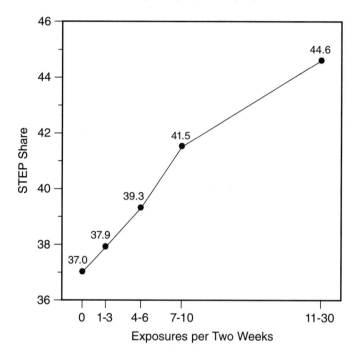

week period. On a one-week basis, these correspond to midpoints of 0, 1, 2.5, 4, and 10 exposures. The data clearly demonstrate the ability of advertising to produce large gains for an advertised brand.

Given the advertising-response curve, we can calculate the potential share increment for any proposed schedule and examine that increment in relation to what it would cost to produce it. This increment will be called the *effect* of the schedule. For example, suppose we were considering a schedule with the following hypothetical reach-frequency vector (percent of respondents reached 0, 1, 2 . . . times per week).

Exposures	0	1	2	3	4	5
Reach-frequency vector	26	10	20	30	10	4

This schedule would reach 100% - 26% = 74% of households at least once per week, generating (10 x 1) + (20 x 2) + (30 x 3) + (10 x 4) + (4 x 5) = 200 gross rating points per week. The effect of the schedule is

Table 25-1
Computation of Effect of Real Ad-Weight Data
for Hypothetical Schedule

Exposures	0	1	2	3	4	5
Advertising-response curve	0	.9	1.8	2.7	4.5	5.0
Reach-frequency vector %	26	10	20	30	10	4
Product	0	.09	.36	.81	.45	.2
Effect			$\sum f_i S_i = 1.9$			

obtained by multiplying the elements of the reach-frequency vector by the corresponding elements of the advertising-response curve, using interpolated values where appropriate. Table 25–1 shows the computation of the effect of this hypothetical schedule for the actual Ad-Weight data reported above. The advertising-response curve is represented by the observed plus interpolated values. The effect is 1.9.

In practice, we are usually interested in comparing the effects produced by different schedules for some particular Ad-Weight. These are easy enough to calculate. For purposes of this discussion, however, we have another objective: we want to summarize the effects obtained from different Ad-Weights in order to compare different advertising-response curves. For this purpose, and for this purpose only, we shall use the concept of a *reference schedule* and a *reference vector*. The reference schedule is arbitrarily defined as a schedule that reaches 100% of households with a rectangular reach-frequency distribution between one exposure per week and ten exposures per week, represented by the reference vector   0 10 10 10 10 10 10 10 10 10 10. This vector is not "real," in that it is not intended for practical use. In fact, it is usually impossible to construct any actual schedule with a reach-frequency vector equal to the reference vector. The reference vector can, however, serve as a constant yardstick that draws on all regions of the advertising-response curve and thereby generates an average of sorts, in effect summarizing the range of effects produced by the advertising with a single number. This number will be called the *effect of the Ad-Weight,* as distinguished from the effect of any particular schedule, and will be used to study the relative effectiveness of different Ad-Weights, or of the same Ad-Weight among different groups of respondents, or of the same Ad-Weight under different conditions. The effect of the Ad-Weight presented above is 5.8. Presumably, a realistic reach schedule of that same advertising would generate a substantially lower effect, while an ultra-high frequency schedule of the same advertising could conceivably generate an even higher effect.

We turn next to an Ad-Weight that provides conclusive evidence of the effectiveness of both television advertising and promotion. The advertised brand was a packaged-goods product studied early in its introduction. The total sample consisted of around 24,000 interviews, divided into four randomly equivalent groups. Group A (TV only) received no promotion. Group B received a 39¢ coupon. Group C received a coupon for a free sample of the product. Group D received an actual sample. Since the four groups are independent, we have, in effect, four separate Ad-Weights. These constitute replications in that they were all conducted at the same time, in the same markets, on randomly equivalent respondents, exposed to the same commercials, and differ only in the promotion received. The results can, therefore, throw light on how well Ad-Weight measures the effects of advertising and on the nature of the interactions, if any, between television advertising and basic promotions. Figure 25–4 shows the advertising-response curve for each of the four groups.

Looking first at the TV-only group, we see a monotonically increasing relationship between number of exposures and share of packages purchased.

Figure 25–4
Ad-Weight: Impact of TV Advertising on Share of Purchasing of a New Consumable Product
($N = 23,820$, $N' = 16,135$)

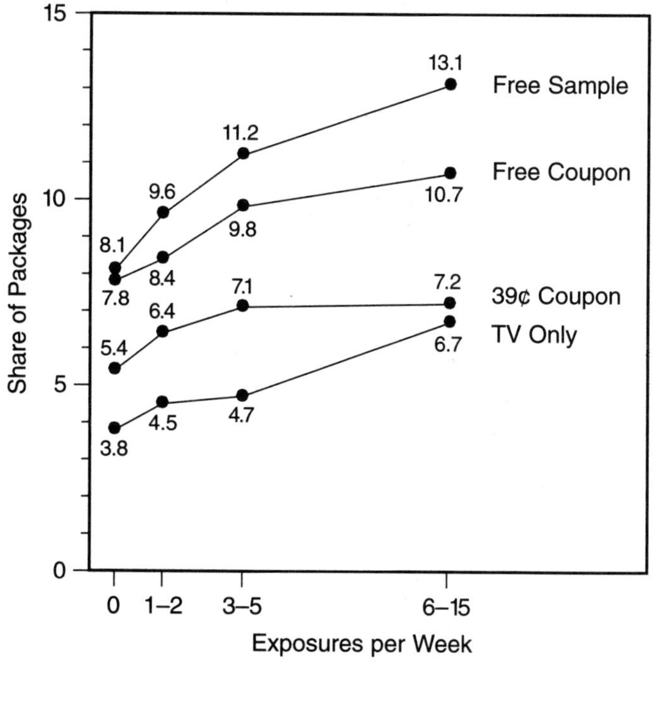

That share is 3.8% in the zero-exposure group and rises to 6.7% in the 6–15 exposures group. The 39¢ coupon raises the baseline share by 1.6% (from 3.8 to 5.4), the free-sample coupon raises it by 4.0%, and the sample raises it by 4.3%. Thus, each of those promotions has a substantial effect on purchasing. Nevertheless, the advertising adds further share increments to those produced by the promotions. The advertising-response curve is monotonically increasing in all of the groups. If anything, there appears to be some synergy between the sample and the advertising in that the effect of 6–15 exposures in the sample group is particularly large, a full 5%, which is an increase of more than 60% over the no-advertising base in that group.

From the point of view of measuring the effects produced by TV advertising, these data are powerfully consistent. They demonstrate that the advertising is working in approximately the same way in four different groups, even though the baseline shares in these groups are different. One conservative way of assessing the pattern is to ask whether the rank order of the brand-purchase shares in the different advertising-exposure groups could have come about by chance. The answer is, hardly. The probability of obtaining the same rank order four times by chance alone is approximately 7 in 100,000.

We next calculate the Ad-Weight effect for each of the four groups and

Figure 25–5
Relative Effect of Combinations
of Advertising and Promotion
($N = 23,820$, $N' = 16,135$)

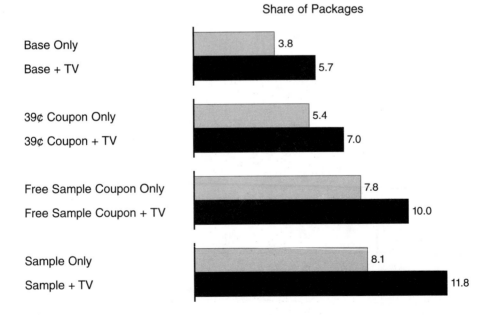

Share of Packages

Base Only	3.8
Base + TV	5.7
39¢ Coupon Only	5.4
39¢ Coupon + TV	7.0
Free Sample Coupon Only	7.8
Free Sample Coupon + TV	10.0
Sample Only	8.1
Sample + TV	11.8

add the respective effects to each group's base level (that is, purchase share in the respective zero exposure cells). This allows us to compare the relative contributions of TV advertising, each of the promotions, and relevant combinations. This comparison is summarized in Figure 25–5. In reading this chart, keep in mind that the TV effects are represented by the effects of the unrealistic reference schedule. In an actual practical cost analysis, these effects would be replaced by the effects of realistic schedules that could be bought for approximately the same dollars as the various promotional alternatives. The data do, however, offer some initial suggestion that the effects produced by advertising and promotion may be additive—certainly not precisely and certainly not in all instances, but approximately in some instances, a proposition that will be explored further.

A different type of Ad-Weight, for a different product, was concerned principally with assessing the extent to which the advertising succeeded in attracting new buyers. The advertising period was twelve weeks. The Ad-Weight was divided into two groups, a TV-only group and a group that received a free sample. The findings are summarized in Figure 25–6.

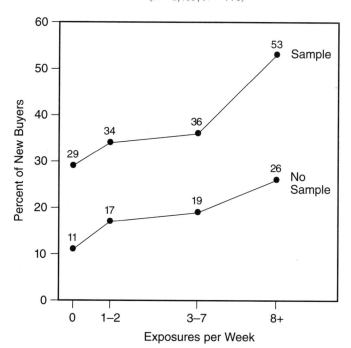

Figure 25–6
Ad-Weight: Impact of TV Advertising
on Percent of New Buyers
($N = 1,485$, $N' = 776$)

Once again the advertising-response curve, this time of new buyers, is monotonically increasing, from 11% buyers in the zero-exposure group to more than double that percentage, namely 26%, in the 8+ exposures group. The free sample boosted the percentage of new buyers to 29% in the absence of advertising. There is, of course, the possibility that some of the sampled respondents may have reported "buying" the brand by confusing what they had received with what they had bought. Even if we discount the role of the sample, however, the advertising as measured in Ad-Weight clearly generated additional new buyers, with the possibility of substantial synergy in the 8+ exposures group, in which the advertising raised the percent of new buyers by 24% (from 29% to 53%). The Ad-Weight effect, expressed in percentage of new buyers, is 9.4 for the TV-only group and 11.7 for the group that received the sample.

The effects of the advertising, even when positive, are not always monotonically increasing. One study stands out in this respect because it not only offers a strikingly replicated example of a nonmonotonic advertising-response curve but, by virtue of the special circumstances surrounding the advertising, also provides a methodological check on whether the nonmonotonic result deserves credence. The advertising in this case announced a manufacturer's offer of a special premium designed to induce people to buy one or more of three specified brands, A, B, and C. The advertising ran for four weeks. The criterion was reported number of packages bought of the three brands, quite apart from whether the respondents availed themselves of the offer in the advertising. The Ad-Weight sample was divided into two groups. One group received advertising only; the other group also received a letter describing the offer.

Figure 25–7 shows advertising-response curves for the number of reported packages bought of brands A, B, and C. Examining the results for Brand A, we find a surprising pattern. Both advertising-exposure groups buy more packages than the zero-exposure group, but the higher-exposure group (3+ exposures) buys less than the lower-exposure group (1–2 exposures). The letter has a major impact on reported buying, raising the number of reported packages by over 50%, from 98 to 148, but the pattern of the advertising effects on that higher base is about the same. It is important to remember that the letter group is an independent replication, an Ad-Weight among a different group of respondents who, by virtue of the letter, have higher buying rates, but nevertheless show the same advertising effects as the other group. Brand B shows the same pattern as Brand A, both for the advertising group and for the letter recipients. In each case, the advertising generates incremental buying, and in each case the number generated is smaller for the 3+ exposures group

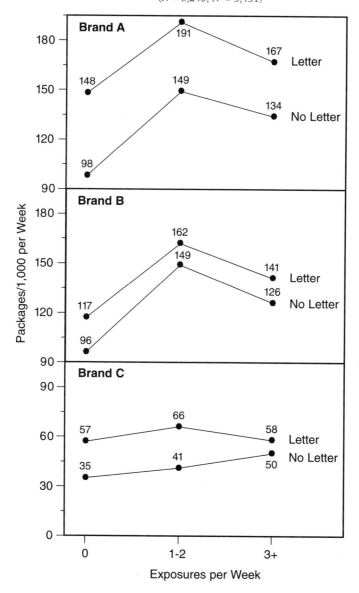

Figure 25–7
Ad-Weight: Impact of TV Advertising
on Purchasing of Three Brands
(N = 6,240, N' = 3,431)

than for the 1–2 exposures group. Brand C happens to be a minor brand. Its purchase levels are approximately one-third of either of the other two brands, and the effects on buying of this brand are relatively small. The advertising group does increase monotonically. The letter group shows the same pattern as Brands A and B.

Thus, the same effect shows up in five out of six comparisons. These are not fully independent replications because the effects for the three brands are observed among the same respondents. The two major brands A and B, however, for which the pattern is most pronounced, are brands with distinctly different brand names, in different product categories, and should be linked, if at all, only by the promotional advertising itself. There is little question that something real is going on. But is it something real produced by the advertising or something real caused by some artifact, perhaps some systematic distortion arising from Ad-Weight's stratification system? One way of checking this is to find out what happens when the Ad-Weight analysis is applied to a variable we are entitled to assume *must* be monotonically increasing. At the end of the interview, the respondents were asked whether they knew of any offer—and if so, to give details about that offer, details they could not have known without having seen either the advertising or the letter.

Regardless of what might have happened to purchasing among groups exposed to different amounts of advertising, proven knowledge of the offer should increase monotonically with exposure to the advertising. Figure 25–8 indicates that this is indeed the case. Proven knowledge does increase monotonically in the advertising-only group, from 2.5% at 0 exposures to 4.5% at 3+ exposures. The letter, moreover, increases proven knowledge in a major way, from 2.5% to 13.5%. And the advertising on top of the letter boosts proven knowledge even further, to 22.7%. Thus, proven knowledge is behaving exactly as it should. The more messages the respondents receive, the more they know. The letter boosts both proven knowledge of the offer and purchasing. A modest amount of advertising boosts both proven knowledge and purchasing. But as the amount of advertising increases, proven knowledge continues to increase even though purchasing is depressed. This serves as an important illustration of the principle that we cannot assume that the advertising-response curve will always be monotonically increasing, or that increased familiarity with copy points is equivalent to advertising effectiveness.

An important conclusion that emerged from the POST program was that print ads can be counterproductive, can produce negative effects for the advertised brand. Is this also true for television? Intuitively, it would be difficult to imagine that a fundamental finding like this would be true for print and not for television. On the other hand, there are important

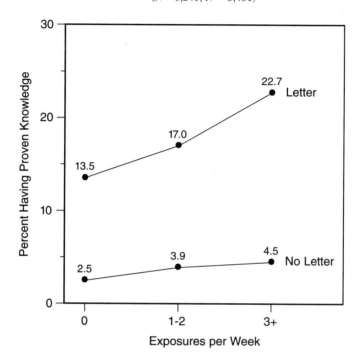

Figure 25–8
Ad-Weight: Impact of TV Advertising
on Proven Knowledge of Offer
(N = 6,240, N′ = 3,431)

differences between the two measurement systems. The POST program measured the effectiveness of a single ad. Ad-Weight measures the effectiveness of substantial amounts of television advertising over the course of time. If the negatives observed in the POST program were real enough but mainly attributable to flukes, to an occasional mishap or some misunderstanding on the part of respondents, such misunderstandings might correct themselves as the advertising is seen with greater frequency over the course of time. In that case, Ad-Weight would produce only positive effects, some of which might be disappointingly low, but not negative. This, however, is not how it is.

Counterproductive effects are not confined to single exposures of print ads; they show up in multiple exposures of television commercials as well. The upper panel of Figure 25–9 shows the advertising-response curve for a twelve-week Ad-Weight for an established packaged-goods brand, based on a total sample size of around 6,000 interviews. Once again, the advertising-response curve is monotonic, but this time it is

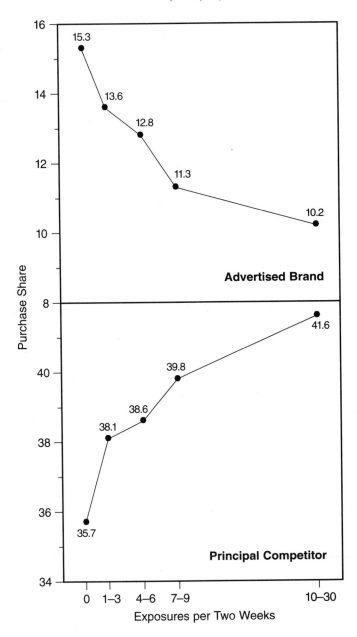

Figure 25–9
Ad-Weight: Effect of TV Advertising
on Advertised Brand and Principal Competitor
($N' = 3{,}554$)

monotonic in the wrong direction. It is a monotonically decreasing curve. The criterion variable is share of reported purchasing. Thus, the data indicate that respondents who receive 1–3 exposures per week buy less than those who are not exposed to the commercial, and that the more heavily the respondents are exposed, the less they buy. Could this be chance? I don't believe so. Even applying the crudest of tests, the probability of obtaining a complete negative rank order like the one observed is less than .01. We can, however, attempt to throw more light on how this negative, which was both puzzling and disconcerting to our client, could have come about. Toward that end, we examine which brands were the beneficiaries of the test brand's losses.

A negative commercial that simply alienated the respondents should have lost to the other brands in the category in approximate proportion to their shares. This is not what happened, as shown in the lower panel of Figure 25–9. The test brand had a principal competitor, a dominant brand in the category, which gained marginally *more* share than the test brand lost. This was true in every exposure category. Among respondents exposed 1–3 times per week, the competitor gained 2.4 share points, 1.7 at the expense of the test brand. In the 4–6 exposures group, the competitor gained 2.9 share points, 2.5 at the expense of the test brand. In the 7–9 exposures group, the gains and losses were almost identical, 4.1 and -4.0, respectively. And in the over 10 exposures group, the competitor gained 5.9 share points, 5.1 at the expense of the test brand.

A striking way of showing this is to put the increments from zero on the same chart, which is done in Figure 25–10. On balance, the effect of the Ad-Weight for the competitor was 3.4, and the effect of the Ad-Weight for the advertised brand was -3.0. Even assuming that the competitor's real gain is only equal to the test brand's loss, the data are clearly compatible with the conclusion that the client ran a highly effective campaign—highly effective, that is, for the competitor, and specifically so at the expense of the test brand! And though there is no way of determining precisely how this effect came about, it is my opinion that this finding illustrates on a large scale, for a sample of thousands of people and by inference for millions of people in the marketplace, the same psychological mechanism I described in the anecdote about the running shoes. One way or another, either by having failed to establish the test brand's identity or by having used claims associated with the competitive brand, the advertising became counterproductive, not necessarily by showing or saying anything that was negative in itself, but by successfully promoting the competitor.

I have chosen these cases because they are particularly dramatic examples. This is all right for illustrative purposes, but does warrant greater

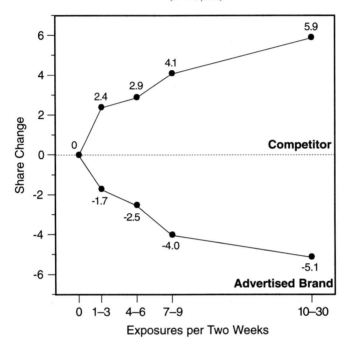

Figure 25–10
Ad-Weight: Incremental Effect of TV Advertising
on Advertised Brand and Principal Competitor
(N′ = 3,554)

scrutiny. Are these cases typical of what goes on in the world, or are they outliers that crop up in a large body of data? In addressing this question, it is important to keep in mind that each of the Ad-Weights reported above is a major study in its own right, based on a sample size of anywhere between 6,000 and 30,000 interviews, and certainly deserves to be examined in its own right. I do, however, want to provide an overview of the results obtained from the Ad-Weight studies in their entirety.

The Cumulative Results

EMA conducted sixty-five Ad-Weight studies, counting replications as separate studies. Each of these can be characterized by a single number, its *effect*, as defined in the previous section. Figure 25–11 shows the distribution of these effects. Obviously these studies do not constitute a "sample" of the advertising running on the air. They cannot be regarded as representative. Once again we are dealing with a haphazard collection of advertising—this time, advertising that a handful of advertisers chose

Figure 25–11
Frequency Distribution of Ad-Weight Effects
from Sixty-five Ad-Weight Studies
($N' = 222,295, \bar{x} = .85, SE = .29$)

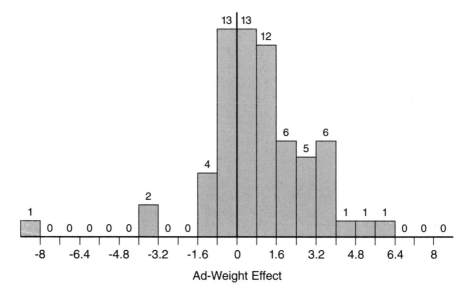

Ad-Weight Effect

to measure with Ad-Weight. Nevertheless, this collection deserves to be taken seriously. It must be apparent from the scope of these studies that the advertisers were major companies, prone to spend heavily on advertising, and likely to be served by prominent advertising agencies. All of the commercials were produced at considerable cost, in final form, and had to meet whatever standards their disseminators ordinarily imposed to qualify for running on the air. And they had to run for several months, something that would not have happened if the principals had not felt that the advertising represented their best efforts.

Given these considerations, the distribution of effects shown in Figure 25–11 tells a remarkable story, one we have already encountered in more limited form when examining the POST program data. The same story now turns up ten to twenty years later, in a different medium for different ads for different brands, with more dramatic implications because we are no longer examining the impact of single ads but the impact of substantial schedules of television advertising running for long periods of time.

Approximately 30% (20 out of 65) of the Ad-Weights produced large positive results, effects larger than 1.6. Approximately 20% (12 out of 65) of the Ad-Weights produced small positive effects, between .8 and 1.6. The remaining 50% (33 out of 65) of the Ad-Weights produced either negligible positive effects or negative effects. Stipulating that some of the negatives may have been minor, close to zero, and perhaps not really negative at all but merely zero, it is minimally true that at least some of the Ad-Weights produced large negative effects. The average effect of all sixty-five studies was .85 with a standard error of .29, a net positive in the aggregate, but composed of widely different effects.

How seriously should the negatives be taken? One way of throwing light on this question is to examine the effects of messages that should not produce negatives on a priori grounds. A coupon is such a message. Depending on its value and on the brand, we might expect it to produce a large or small effect, conceivably even no effect at all, but we certainly would not expect it to alienate respondents from the brand. Ten of the Ad-Weights EMA conducted were run with split groups, one group receiving no coupon, and a randomly equivalent group receiving a coupon. We can therefore use these studies to compare the Ad-Weight effects to the effects of coupons. This analysis is particularly germane since the coupons and the advertising were measured for the same brand, at the same time, among the same or randomly equivalent groups of respondents. For purposes of the advertising analysis, the coupons are ignored and constitute part of the background noise. For purposes of the coupon analysis, the advertising is ignored and constitutes part of the background noise. If there should happen to be synergy between them, it would be characteristic of what ordinarily happens in the marketplace, and would in any event accrue to the benefit of both the advertising and the coupon.

Figure 25–12 shows a study-by-study comparison of the advertising and coupon effects of the Ad-Weights that were conducted in conjunction with coupon tests. Keep in mind that the term "Ad-Weight effect" means the average effect we expect to produce as a result of eight to twelve weeks of continuous advertising with the theoretical reference schedule, a schedule that may never be achievable in practice. On the average, this schedule is equivalent to reaching 100% of the respondents five times every two weeks, or 250 gross rating points per week, a heavy schedule as schedules go. The coupon represents the mailing of a single coupon once at the beginning of the test period.

It happens that the ten Ad-Weights available for this analysis constitute an approximately representative subset of the total number. Like the larger group, they show a wide range of effects. Six are positive and four negative. Two of the positive effects and one of the negative effects are substantial. The remaining seven, four positives and three negatives, are less than .5 in either direction and may be taken as essentially equal to zero. On the other hand, all ten coupons produce positive effects over .5 share points. Six of these effects are over 1.5 share points. Moreover, these pos-

Figure 25–12
Ad-Weight and Coupon Effects
in Ten Ad-Weight Studies That Measured Coupons
(N' = 63,649)

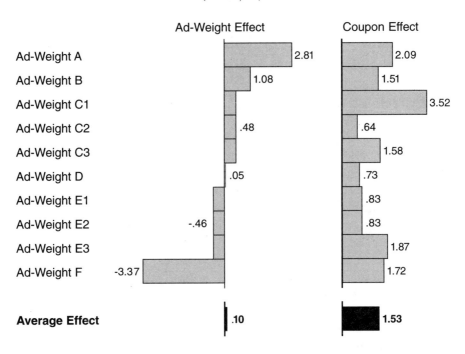

	Ad-Weight Effect	Coupon Effect
Ad-Weight A	2.81	2.09
Ad-Weight B	1.08	1.51
Ad-Weight C1		3.52
Ad-Weight C2	.48	.64
Ad-Weight C3		1.58
Ad-Weight D	.05	.73
Ad-Weight E1		.83
Ad-Weight E2	-.46	.83
Ad-Weight E3		1.87
Ad-Weight F	-3.37	1.72
Average Effect	.10	1.53

itive coupon effects are as much in evidence for studies in which the advertising produced negative effects as for studies in which it produced positive effects. The average Ad-Weight effect is .10. The average coupon effect is 1.53, many times as large. Without prejudice to the implications of this finding for cost effectiveness, which involves additional considerations, the data demonstrate conclusively that one kind of message, a coupon, is capable of producing substantial, uniformly positive results. In other words, when we use a message that works, we produce positive effects each time. When we use advertising, we do indeed produce large positive effects some of the time, but we also produce no effects and sometimes negative effects. All of this is summarized in the following principle.

THE ADVERTISING EFFECTIVENESS PRINCIPLE
Advertising is a game of chance. Even if you are a major marketer, served by a major advertising agency, you have around a 50% chance of running advertising that won't do anything for you and in some cases will actually hurt your brand.

This principle was anticipated long ago by John Wanamaker, who report-edly said, "I know that half my advertising is wasted, but I don't know which half." We have now documented empirically that Wanamaker was entirely right—but we don't have to stop at that.

Implications

Given this result, what is the appropriate course of action for the televi-sion advertiser? Having spent my entire career in measurement, it can hardly come as a surprise that I recommend measurement and more mea-surement. The elementary economic facts are that measurement, even on the grandest scale, can usually be accomplished for less than 5% of the intended advertising budget; and that if such a 5% expenditure can increase the effectiveness of the advertising even slightly, the leverage is so large that the measurement will pay for itself many times over.

My specific recommendation has been for the advertiser to adopt a two-track strategy, perpetually measuring both a current campaign and some alternative. If the current campaign outperforms the proposed alter-native, another alternative is selected for testing, and the current cam-paign remains on the air, possibly for years, until eventually some proposed alternative outperforms it. Only then does that alternative become the current campaign.

I have recommended this strategy for many years. Its intrinsic logic has often been admired, but I have never succeeded in inducing any marketer to implement it seriously. In the end, marketers have always found it eas-ier to use judgment to allocate still another thirty million dollars to still another campaign, always hoping for the best.

The Generic Advertising-Response Curve

The distribution of effects is important, but it is only a part of the story. The purpose of Ad-Weight is to determine the relative benefit of reaching respondents various times per week. Accordingly, we summarize the sixty-five Ad-Weights once again, this time by aggregating the sixty-five advertising-response curves. The result is shown in Figure 25–13. This chart provides a dramatic confirmation of everything we have seen. The curve is a smooth function well familiar as the growth function in many physical phenomena. In this case, it is

$$E_x = C(1 - e^{-Px})$$

where x is the number of exposures per week, E_x is the share increment

Figure 25–13
Advertising-Response Curve
for Sixty-five Ad-Weights
($N' = 222,295$)

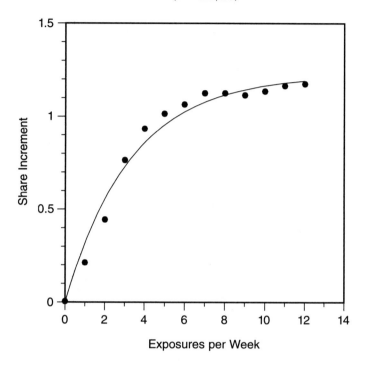

produced by these exposures, and C and P are two constants. Characteristically, this function starts at the origin (is zero at zero exposures), rises steeply at first so that an increase in exposures is associated with a substantial increase in effect, gradually flattens so that further increases in exposures are associated with progressively smaller additional effects, and eventually approaches an asymptote (C), implying that there is a maximum effect that can be approached but not exceeded as the number of exposures becomes very large.

The asymptote C is called the *ceiling* of the Ad-Weight. It is the maximum effect potentially achievable with the particular advertising. The constant P is called the *power* of the Ad-Weight. It is a measure of the efficiency of the advertising, indicating the rate at which exposures translate into effects. If the power of an Ad-Weight is large, it means that an additional exposure produces a relatively large increase in effect. If it is small, it means that an additional exposure produces a relatively small increase in effect. At the low end, a power of zero means that the advertising is not effective at all. The increment is $E_x = C(1 - e^{0x}) = C(1 - 1) = 0$. In other words, the effect is zero regardless of how many exposures the respondents receive.

Within the framework of this theory, we can describe any Ad-Weight, either some particular Ad-Weight or some aggregation of Ad-Weights, by means of two numbers, the power P and the ceiling C. These two numbers define an advertising-response curve—not the advertising-response curves we have dealt with so far, in which the points were values obtained by empirical measurement, but a theoretical advertising-response curve. To distinguish between the two, the curve consisting of the empirically measured points will be called the *literal* advertising-response curve; the curve obtained from the function $E_x = C(1 - e^{-Px})$, where P and C are the power and the ceiling of the Ad-Weight, respectively, will be called the *generic* advertising-response curve. The points in Figure 25–13 represent the literal advertising-response curve; the line represents the generic advertising-response curve. Deviations from this curve do not necessarily constitute error. In principle, all kinds of advertising-response curves are possible. When data deviate from the generic shape, it may be due either to error or to some real characteristics of the particular advertising studied. I do, however, call the curve generic, because it fits the aggregate data of the Ad-Weights so well that it provides a standard of how advertising response data behave when a large number of them are aggregated.

Analogous to the distinction between the literal and generic curves, we can make a distinction between the literal and generic effects of an Ad-Weight. If we believe that a particular Ad-Weight has a uniquely shaped advertising-response curve that does not closely resemble the generic curve, we may use the literal effect both to represent the Ad-Weight and to calculate the effect of various schedules utilizing that advertising. If, on the other hand, we are dealing with data that fit the generic curve sufficiently well that their deviations can be regarded as error, we may compute the generic curve that best fits the available data in the sense of least squares, and then use the generic curve to provide better estimates of the true underlying effects. For the sixty-five Ad-Weights, the literal effect is .89. The generic effect is also .89, indicating that the generic curve fits the literal data well.

The aggregation of the data in Figure 25–13 partially obscures what is happening. We have seen that some Ad-Weights produce net positive and some produce net negative effects. It seems hardly reasonable to consolidate these into a single curve. The positives and negatives must be partially canceling each other, understating the potential impact of the advertising for good or bad. Accordingly, we divide the Ad-Weights into two groups: forty-five with positive effects, and twenty with negative effects. Figure 25–14 shows the separate advertising-response curves of the positive and negative Ad-Weights.

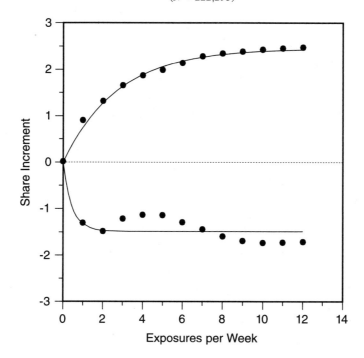

Figure 25–14
Advertising-Response Curves for Ad-Weights with
Positive and Negative Effects
(N′ = 222,295)

The generic advertising-response curve for the forty-five positive Ad-Weights has a ceiling of 2.45 and a power of .37. It fits the data almost perfectly. The curve for the twenty negative Ad-Weights has a ceiling of -1.7 and a power of .42. Its points are more erratic. This may be due in part to the fact that we are dealing with a smaller body of data, and in part to the presence of conflicting influences, a point that is explored more extensively below. Nevertheless, the curve of the negative Ad-Weights can be regarded as broadly similar to the positive curve in that the increments become negative rapidly at first and then tend to level off and approach an asymptote as the number of exposures increases. The literal effect of the curve is -1.42; its generic effect is -1.47.

Advertising-Response Curves with Dips

One might be tempted to view the deviations from the generic shape in the mid-region of the negative curve as aberrations, but there is more to

Figure 25–15
Advertising-Response Curve for
Seven Ad-Weights with a Dip
($N' = 18,057$)

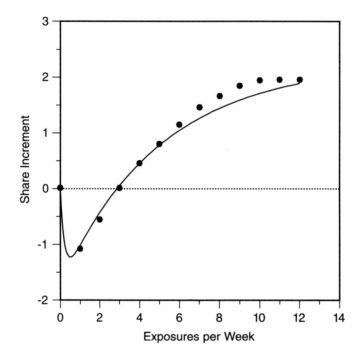

it. Every now and then in the course of testing, I encountered an Ad-Weight with what I originally thought was an abnormal advertising-response curve, a curve I characterized as having a "dip." At low exposures the increment was negative, but as the exposures increased the increment turned positive, and became increasingly so at still higher exposures. The first time I saw this pattern, I dismissed it as probably due to chance. But when it showed up again, I began to take it more seriously. Figure 25–15 shows an aggregation of seven Ad-Weights, each of which has an advertising-response curve with just such a dip.

After seeing several Ad-Weights with the same strange pattern, I concluded that these curves were telling a story. If we believe that some advertising produces positive effects and some produces negative effects, we should hardly be surprised if some advertising produces positive effects among some people and negative effects among others. For such advertising, the net impact of the advertising is the weighted sum of the positive and negative advertising-response curves or, in the general case, of many advertising-response curves, which can give rise to a curve with just the kind of dip shown in Figure 25–15. If, for example, we had an Ad-Weight that affected 50% of the respondents positively, with an advertising-response curve of power .2 and ceiling 8, and affected 50% of the respondents negatively, with an advertising-response curve of power 5 and ceiling -3.5, the net result would be the advertising-response curve with a dip illustrated in Figure 25–15. In that figure, the points represent the empirical data and the line represents the average of the two hypothesized curves. The two hypothesized curves and the resulting average curve are illustrated in Figure 25–16. From this perspective, a curve with a dip, far from being abnormal, actually represents the general case: advertising that influences some respondents positively and some negatively. And the curves we previously designated as "generic" represent the special case in which either the positive or the negative effect is large enough to drown out its opposite, yielding what appears to be a pure curve.

Without attempting to pinpoint this phenomenon in rigorous detail, it

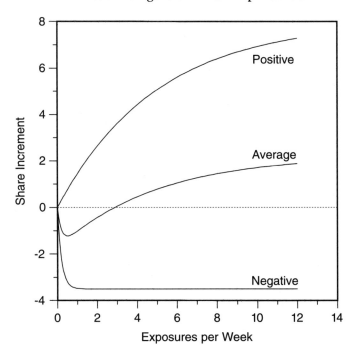

Figure 25–16
Hypothetical Positive and Negative Curves
Whose Average Is the Real Empirical Curve

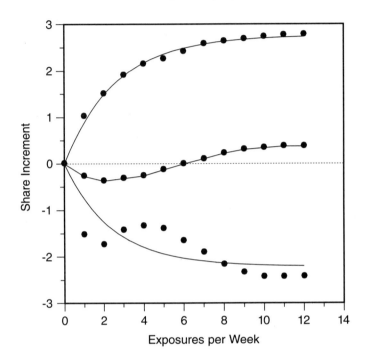

Figure 25–17
Advertising-Response Curves with
Positive, Zero, and Negative Effects
($N' = 222,295$)

suggests that, other things being equal, Ad-Weights with effects close to zero may consist of either advertising that produced no effects or advertising that produced mixed effects. And though mixed effects may be the rule all along the effectiveness spectrum, they should be more prevalent among Ad-Weights that produce intermediate rather than large positive or large negative effects. If this is the case, such an intermediate category of Ad-Weights should contain many, if not most, of the mixed-result Ad-Weights and should itself show the typical mixed advertising-response curve. If we define the *intermediate* group as Ad-Weights that produced effects between +.3 and -.3, we are left with three categories of thirty-nine positive, eleven intermediate, and fifteen negative Ad-Weights. Their advertising-response curves are shown in Figure 25–17. Of the seven Ad-Weights with dips, four are in the intermediate group. And the intermediate group in its entirety displays precisely the mixed pattern hypothesized above.

Flighting

Some advertisers believe in scheduling their advertising in flights, typi-cally several weeks on and several off. Ad-Weight is readily adapted to such a strategy. If the full Ad-Weight schedule is bought on a flighted basis, the flighting runs uniformly through all the exposure groups and allows the estimation of the effects of various schedules on a flighted basis. Such measurements, however, are strictly confined to the particu-lar flighting pattern studied. In other words, if we obtain an advertising-response curve for some advertising based on a two-weeks-on, two-weeks-off flighting pattern, the curve, the effects of schedules using the advertising, and the conclusions drawn are all predicated on the two-weeks-on, two-weeks-off flighting pattern, and cannot be extended to advertising using other flighting patterns or to unflighted advertising.

Of the forty-five Ad-Weights that produced positive effects, sixteen were flighted and twenty-nine unflighted. Strictly speaking, there is no justification for comparing the effects of the unflighted and flighted stud-ies. They are just arbitrary collections of studies our clients elected to test in unflighted or flighted form. There is no reason to believe that they are comparable with respect to either the advertised brands or the commer-cials employed. Furthermore, the total number of studies in the compar-ison is relatively small, and we cannot rely on chance to average out extraneous differences between the two. Nevertheless, it is difficult to resist the temptation to examine the data separately for the two groups. I present them, keeping my fingers crossed and adding a warning: "These comparisons may be dangerous. Avoid overdose. Keep out of reach of children." With that qualification, here they are.

The average effect of the unflighted positive Ad-Weights was 1.96. The average effect of the flighted positive Ad-Weights was 1.60. Of the twenty Ad-Weights that produced negative effects, seventeen were unflighted and three were flighted. The average effect of the negative unflighted studies was -1.38; the average effect of the negative flighted studies was -.65. Happenstance or not, the data are coherent. The flighted positives produce smaller positive effects than the unflighted ones. And for what it is worth, given that there are only three negative flighted Ad-Weights, these three do happen to produce smaller negatives than the seventeen unflighted ones. Keeping the caveats strictly in mind, the data suggest that flighting may be a reasonable strategy, since the flighted studies used on the average only around half of the advertising insertions to produce 82% of the effect. In practice, the wisdom of flighting needs to be assessed on a case-by-case basis.

CHAPTER 26

The Third Law:
The Law of Persistence

Much of this book has dealt with the effects of messages of one kind or another. We have examined the effects of products, ads, and coupons, measured at points in time that were deemed reasonable in the light of practical considerations. Product-STEP measurements usually took place two to four weeks after delivery of the product, long enough to give the respondents an opportunity to use the product, but hopefully not longer. The various advertising measurements were governed by similar considerations. Implicit in all of this was a tacit assumption about the nature of effects and what happens to them over time; an assumption that seems intuitively self-evident, namely that nothing lasts forever, and that if we intend to measure anything, we had better hurry up and measure it quickly before it vanishes. In technical terms, this is equivalent to saying that the effects produced by messages decay over time, which is certainly consistent with what we know about remembering and forgetting. But making the assumption is one thing, demonstrating it empirically is another, and properly quantifying it is yet another. Let us attempt to do so.

Nonadvertising Periods

Chapter 25 dealt with the effects of sixty-five Ad-Weight studies. These effects were measured while the advertising was running. But it is obvious that at least some effects extend beyond the time when the advertising is running and that it is therefore necessary to extend the measurements some indeterminate period beyond that time—in theory forever, in practice at least long enough to ensure that no measurable residual effect remains. Measuring such additional time periods is essential if some quasi-realistic estimate of the total effect of the advertising is to be made. Suppose a single ad generated an incremental share of 1% for the advertised brand during the week after it ran. This gain might not warrant its cost. If that increment were still in evidence one month later, its value would be higher, and if the increment persisted for a long time, say for a year or longer, its total value could be very large.

In practice, it is expensive to measure residual effects, and clients often feel that they are making better use of their research dollars by measuring what the advertising produces while it is running than by measuring what, if anything, it continues to produce after it has stopped running. In my view, it is the other way around. I believe that the measurement of what the advertising produces after it has stopped running is usually more important than the measurement of what it produces while it is running. Accordingly, my routine recommendation was to measure both the advertising period and a post-advertising period. But most clients declined to do so.

Of sixty-five Ad-Weights, forty-eight used advertising periods only; seventeen used both advertising and post-advertising periods. I don't know whether this reflects a built-in bias in favor of tests that have the potential of producing big numbers, whether it is evidence of poor sales-manship on my part, or whether it can perhaps be taken as a testimonial to excellent salesmanship, in having managed to include post-advertising periods in as many as seventeen of sixty-five Ad-Weights. In any event, that is what we have. I am not aware of any systematic differences between the Ad-Weights that did and those that did not include post-advertising periods. Of the seventeen Ad-Weights that included post-advertising measurements, fourteen produced positive effects. Figure 26–1 shows the advertising-response curves for these fourteen studies, separately aggregated for the advertising and post-advertising periods. The average effect was 2.33 for the advertising period and 1.52 for the post-advertising period. The ceiling and power for the advertising period are 3.30 and .32. The ceiling and power for the post-advertising period are 2.40 and .25.

These data are important both from a methodological and from a sub-stantive point of view. First, the post-advertising periods can be thought of as replications. They measure the same advertising with the same method at later points of time and on different samples of respondents. Finding similar advertising-response curves therefore amounts to inde-pendent replications of many studies, lending support to the method and to the observations made with it. Second, there is an a priori expectation that the post-advertising-period effect should be smaller than the adver-tising-period effect. And this is indeed the case. In particular, the former is approximately 65% of the latter, and the increments are lower over the entire range of the two curves. Thus, we can be confident that the decay

Figure 26–1
Advertising- and Post–Advertising-Response Curve
for Fourteen Positive Ad-Weights
($N' = 83{,}369$)

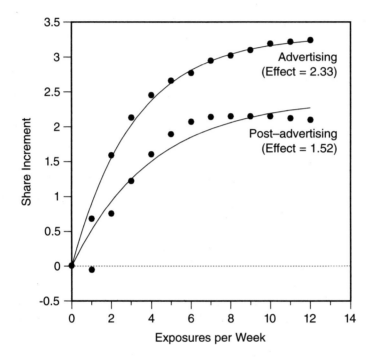

is real, not only because that seems to be a conceptual truism but also because we have confirmed it empirically in the aggregate effect of fourteen Ad-Weights. This leaves the question: What is the scope of the decay? How rapid is it? Do the observed effects go to zero, or do they leave measurable residuals in their wake?

One way of engaging this issue is to begin by postulating that every effect produced by a message decays exponentially. By effect I mean an effect on choice. The assumption that the decay is exponential is natural. Exponential decay manifests itself in many physical phenomena. It implies that, from time interval to time interval, there is a proportionate reduction of the remaining portion of the effect. This assumption is captured mathematically by saying that the effect E_t at time t after message delivery is

$$E_t = E_i + E_0 e^{-rt}$$

where E_0 is the *transient effect* produced by the message, r is the rate at which this transient effect decays, and E_i is the asymptote that is approached. Let me call this asymptote the *intrinsic effect*. This function is very general and can be used to describe different outcomes by allowing the constants to take on different values. For example, if the effect lasts only as long as the advertising is running (time 0) and vanishes when the advertising stops, the function can fit the data with $E_i = 0$ and a very large r. With these constants, $E_t = E_0$ at time 0 and drops to 0 for all later points in time, that is, as soon as t takes on a positive value. At the other extreme, if there is no decay, the second term will be 0 and $E_t = E_i$. This means that it will remain unchanged and equal to E_i for all values of t, that is, for all points of time. Thus, very different empirical patterns can be described by the same function by allowing the parameters to take on different values.

Decay and Persistence

Two hypotheses are of special interest: the *decay hypothesis* and the *persistence hypothesis*. The decay hypothesis holds that the effect of every message decays over time, presumably as a function of forgetting or of the intrinsic consequences of the passage of time, until it disappears altogether. In accordance with this hypothesis, we would expect all effects to go to zero, or at any rate to head toward zero in some reasonable period of time. The persistence hypothesis holds that though there may be forgetting of cognitive information, there is no comparable "forgetting" of choice behavior. If I induce you to choose one brand over other brands, you will continue to choose it until some other message influences you and shifts your choice to some other brand. In accordance with this hypothesis, we would expect intrinsic effects to persist forever, or at any rate for long periods of time.

At first glance, the persistence hypothesis may seem preposterous. Common sense and everyday experience indicate that the effects of messages don't just accumulate. The marketer can't just take some single action, say drop a sample or run an ad, and expect to reap profits from it forever. If she does not continue to support her brand, the brand will decline. At any rate, we believe that it will. But even if it does, and even if it does so invariably, this does not refute the persistence hypothesis, for it is conceivable that though competitive activity is gradually eroding the brand's position, the incremental effect of the one successful action persists. If that is the case, this effect should remain detectable for a long time in the form of differences between respondents who received the message and respondents who did not.

Determining which of the two hypotheses is true, or which is more nearly true in particular situations, is not merely an abstract intellectual exercise. It goes to the very heart of the marketer's principal concern, namely, to decide whether some particular marketing tool, say a sampling program or an advertising campaign, pays out or does not, or, in the event that a small intrinsic effect remains, how long it will take for the program to pay out. In terms of the decay function, the difference between the decay hypothesis and the persistence hypothesis boils down to determining whether the asymptote E_i, that is, the intrinsic effect, is zero or positive.

In principle, the post-advertising periods of Ad-Weights would provide an ideal opportunity to address this question empirically. The difficulty is that, for the most part, the post-advertising periods were not long enough and did not employ sufficiently large sample sizes to yield definitive decay curves. Strictly speaking, the tests should have been extended beyond the point at which the increments had effectively stabilized, either at 0, implying that they had worn off completely, or at some other level, implying that some portion of the increments could be expected to persist indefinitely. Instead, five of the fourteen Ad-Weights had post-advertising periods that were only eight or twelve weeks long,

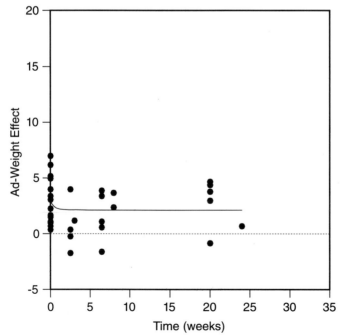

Figure 26–2
Effect of Advertising in Post-Advertising Period
Fourteen Ad-Weight Studies
$(N' = 22{,}564, \; E_t = 2.1 + .78e^{-1.8t})$

with small effective sample sizes even after the data were consolidated into four-week units. The other nine studies did have post-advertising periods up to twenty, and in one case twenty-four, weeks, but provided for only one or two post-advertising waves of interviews. In the circumstances, it is not feasible to construct separate decay curves for the individual studies. But when all of them are consolidated in a single chart, as is done in Figure 26–2, the data offer strong suggestive support for the persistence hypothesis. The best-fitting exponential curve is $E_t = 2.1 + .8 e^{-1.8t}$. This curve has a nonzero asymptote, a persisting intrinsic effect, of around 2 share points.

The question of decay versus persistence is not limited to advertising. It applies equally to any message, be it advertising, a coupon, or a free sample. A number of the Ad-Weight studies were split. Half of the respondents received a coupon while the other half received no promotion. The primary purpose of these studies was to assess the effectiveness of advertising, but we can ignore the advertising as just another aspect of the background noise and focus on the coupon. These studies, then, constitute controlled experiments in which the effect of a coupon was assessed relative to a control group. And since the data were, in most instances, collected for eight to twenty weeks, and in a few instances for longer, we can use these data to estimate the decay of coupon effects.

Figure 26–3 shows the coupon-minus-control differences for ten such studies, measured various numbers of weeks after receipt of the coupon. The best-fitting exponential is $E_t = 1.2 + 3.3e^{-.35t}$. Thus, we find a positive intrinsic effect that persists many weeks after the coupon was sent. The data have variability, and the parameters of the fitted curve may be unstable. Fluctuations in a few points could change them. However, if we set aside the issue of precise quantification of the intrinsic effect and concentrate on the more fundamental question whether the data support the decay hypothesis or the persistence hypothesis, there is no doubt that they support the latter. Of thirty-four data points obtained ten or more weeks after the coupon was sent, thirty-two are positive, still showing an incremental effect attributable to the coupon. The probability of having obtained this result by chance alone is essentially zero. Furthermore, five of the six points collected in Weeks 30–35 are positive. This means that the effects produced by the coupon were still in evidence more than seven months later and showed no evidence of abatement. Specifically, the increments remaining after half a year were not smaller than those observed after the first three months. We can, of course, only guess what would have happened if the measurements had been carried out further, say a full year or two, or even longer. To the extent, however, that this guess is based on fitting an exponential decay function, the data support

Figure 26–3
Effect of Coupon over Time
Ten Ad-Weight Studies
$(N' = 60,601, E_t = 1.2 + 3.3e^{-.35t})$

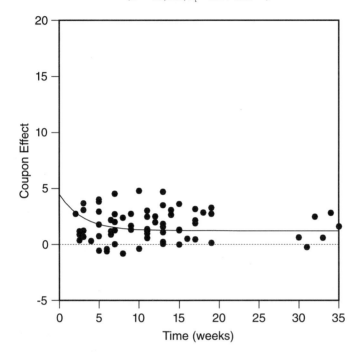

persistence and indicate that the intrinsic effect would still have been there and would have been measurable even later.

The advertising decay data presented above were a by-product of Ad-Weight studies. They were mostly available by virtue of a halfhearted agreement on the part of a few clients to check, for a limited period of time, what would happen to advertising effects after the advertising had stopped. The data for the decay of coupons are even more marginal. The focus was almost entirely on the television advertising and on ascertaining whether that advertising worked "on top of" a coupon. To the extent that conclusions about the persistence of the effect of coupons emerged as by-products, they were of course accepted, but they were not central questions and did not influence the design of the studies to begin with. One might say that whatever interest there may have been in decay of coupons was subordinated to other objectives, and had to make do with the analytic power that was left over after those other objectives had been satisfied.

EMA did, however, conduct one major study for the express purpose of measuring sample and coupon decay. After some urging, I finally persuaded a client that the issue was an important one. The study, which I will call the *Decay* study, provided four randomly equivalent experimental groups, two of which were further split into two subgroups, as follows:

1. *Control.* This group received nothing.
2. *One-Pack.* This group received one package of the test brand as a free sample. Half of the group also received a reply card asking them to report back whether they had liked the product.
3. *Two-Pack.* This group received two packages of the test brand. Half of this group also received the reply card.
4. *Coupon.* This group received a coupon for a free sample of the test brand.

Households were randomly selected from telephone households in the Harrisburg, Pennsylvania, market area and were randomly allocated to the four groups.

Telephone interviews were conducted with approximately 200 respondents per group (100 per subgroup) per biweekly wave. Each interviewing wave used new respondents. The criterion variable was share of reported purchasing. This was measured by asking whether the respondents had bought any brand in the category during the previous week (seven days), if so which brands, and, for each brand, the number of packages. These questions were repeated to elicit purchasing during the prior week. The total number of packages reported for the two-week period for all brands was used to generate the test brand's share of purchasing. The interviews started approximately four weeks after the samples and coupons were sent out.

Since the study design called for drawing the total sample of names initially and allocating fresh respondents to each wave, it was necessary to decide at the outset how long the study was to last. This generated some discussion. How long was long enough? In theory, the answer was forever, or at any rate until the effect disappeared, until the curve touched the *x*-axis, so that we would be sure that we had gotten "all" of the effect and that we were not missing additional sales that would trickle in after we had, as it were, closed the books. In practice, of course, it was not possible to measure anything forever. Instead, we picked a time period that seemed like forever to me and certainly to the practical marketer eager to get on with it and to arrive at a conclusion without excessive nitpicking and fine tuning: ten biweekly waves, covering twenty weeks. Since the first wave was conducted four weeks after the sample/coupon mailing and respondents were questioned about their purchasing during the prior two weeks, the first wave was treated as Week 2, so the test covered a twenty-two-week period.

At the time of designing the study, which was before I had seen any of the Ad-Weight data, I was so convinced that the effects would decay in a few weeks that ten biweekly waves of interviews, covering a period of up to twenty-two weeks after the initial sample delivery, appeared to be extravagant. But we provided for this amount of time because we wanted to make "absolutely" sure that our measurements would extend beyond the time when the effects would be gone. Upon discovering that we had nevertheless underestimated the resilience of the effects, we decided to conduct three additional waves of interviews. By this time, the sample of respondents had been used up. Accordingly, the three additional biweekly waves were collected during Weeks 27–32 by reinterviewing the respondents who had been interviewed during Weeks 1–6.

Altogether the test covered a thirty-two-week period. The upper panel of Figure 26–4 shows the share of purchasing effect of the One-Pack sample relative to the control group over the course of the thirty-two weeks. It is obvious by inspection that while some of the early points are higher than the later points, reflecting decay, there is substantial persistence of the effect. Eleven out of the thirteen data points are positive, including all three of the last three. Fitting the best exponential to the data, we obtain a curve that shows a nonzero asymptote, an intrinsic effect of 3.1 share points. The middle panel of Figure 26–4 shows the effect for the Two-Pack sample. Again, both decay and persistence are obvious by inspection. Dramatically, the effects in this group are generally higher than in the One-Pack group. All thirteen of the points are positive, and the last three points during Weeks 28–32 are at just about the same level as the three points during Weeks 10–14. Fitting the best exponential to these points gives an intrinsic effect of 5.8 share points. Since there is an obvious difference between the One-Pack and Two-Pack groups, we wonder to what extent this *difference* decays or persists. The bottom panel of Figure 26–4 shows the difference in effect between the Two-Pack and the One-Pack. Ten out of the thirteen differences are positive. Fitting an exponential, we obtain an intrinsic difference of 2.8 share points.

The question may be raised whether fitting the exponentials properly captures the real information in the data. How coherent are these curves? We have found an intrinsic effect of 3.1 share points for the One-Pack sample. We have also found an intrinsic effect of 2.8 share points for the difference between the Two-Pack and the One-Pack. Adding the two implies that the Two-Pack should have an intrinsic effect of 3.1 + 2.8 = 5.9 share points. The actual intrinsic effect of the Two-Pack, obtained

Figure 26–4
Effect of Sample over Time
Decay Study
$(N_{1\text{-Pack}} = 2,704,\ N_{2\text{-Pack}} = 2,717,\ N_{\text{Control}} = 2,561)$

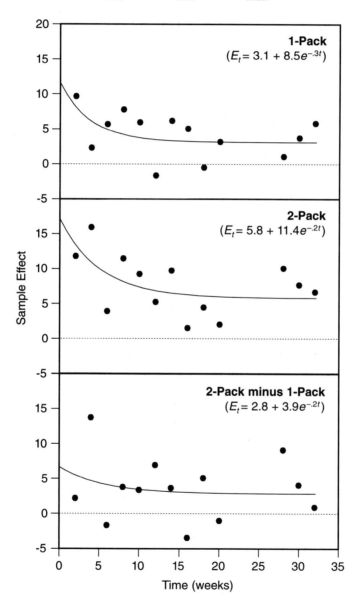

from the direct fitting of the exponential to the Two-Pack data, is 5.8, almost precisely as predicted. This is not merely an artifact or a necessary arithmetic truism but an important finding in its own right. The points in the three panels of Figure 26–4 show a great deal of variability; they fluctuate over a wide range. Fitting the exponential curves to them looks like a precarious business. Do these curves and their parameters capture real information? Or are they merely the product of a capricious mathematical exercise? The consistency of the intrinsic effects addresses this question. If the curves and their parameters were only arbitrary representations, they would not be internally consistent. Exploring this question even further, we put both curves, the exponential for the One-Pack and the exponential for the Two-Pack, on the same chart. This is done in the upper panel of Figure 26–5. The two curves are substantially

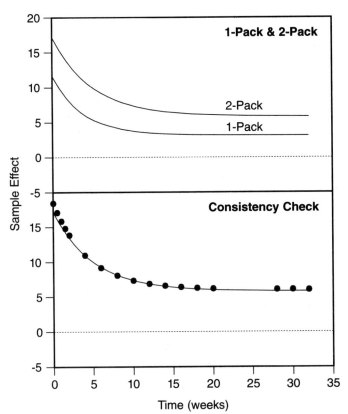

Figure 26–5
Comparison of Effects of Different Samples
Decay Study

Figure 26–6
Effect of Coupon and Card over Time
Decay Study
$(N_{Coupon} = 2{,}626, N_{Card} = 2{,}639, N_{Control} = 2{,}672)$

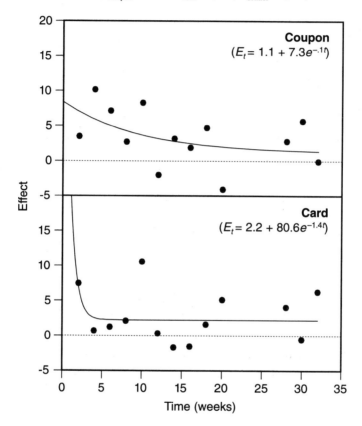

"parallel" to each other. Finally, we test the internal consistency of the curve fitting by checking how well the curves "add back" in their entirety. The lower panel of Figure 26–5 shows a line and some points. The line is the exponential curve for the Two-Pack, just a copy of the curve shown in the upper panel. The points in the panel represent the curve obtained when the difference curve is added to the One-Pack curve. The correspondence is almost perfect. Thus the internal consistency is not limited to the intrinsic effects, but holds along the entire range of the data.

The decay study affords two more comparisons, which are shown in Figure 26–6. The upper panel shows the effect of the coupon. This effect is generally lower than the effect of the sample, but again there is evidence of persistence. Ten of the thirteen points are positive. The exponential fit shows an intrinsic effect of 1.1 share points. Finally, we can break out the effect of the card. The lower panel of Figure 26–6 shows the difference between the groups that received samples *with* the card and those that received samples *without* the card. This effect too shows persistence. The intrinsic effect of the card is 2.2 share points. Although this break makes use of some of the same respondents as the samples, it provides an additional independent comparison. Thus the Decay study is not merely saying but is shouting that the persistence hypothesis is sustained. There is an intrinsic effect. The effect is internally consistent and it lasts.

I have presented the results of the Decay study in detail because this study provides a particularly striking demonstration of the phenomena studied. To get the most comprehensive picture, we put all the available data together. This is done in Figure 26–7. The upper panel shows the

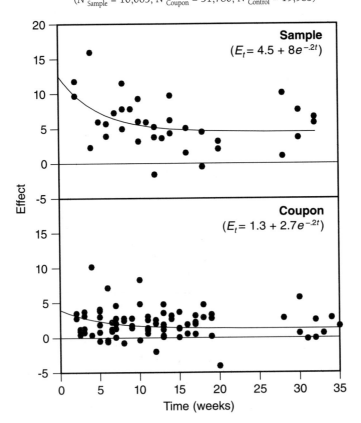

Figure 26–7
Effect of Sample and Coupon over Time
Consolidated
(N'_{Sample} = 10,063, N'_{Coupon} = 31,780, $N'_{Control}$ = 19,983)

Sample
(E_t = 4.5 + 8$e^{-.2t}$)

Coupon
(E_t = 1.3 + 2.7$e^{-.2t}$)

Effect

Time (weeks)

effect of sampling, a consolidation of the data from the two groups of the Decay study, One-Pack and Two-Pack, and the data for the effect of a sample from one of the Ad-Weights. The lower panel shows the effect of a coupon, a consolidation of the coupon effect from the Decay study, and the coupon effects from ten Ad-Weight studies. These charts are just a summary of what we have already seen. Both curves have a nonzero asymptote, a positive intrinsic effect. This effect is 4.5 share points for the sample and 1.3 share points for the coupon. The decay rate is .2 for both curves.

For the sample, 15 out of 16 points obtained more than three months after sample delivery are positive. For the coupon, 30 out of 34 are positive. This could have come about by chance with a probability of less than .00026 for the sample and of .00000 for the coupon. We also see that the effect is in full evidence beyond half a year. Six data points were collected more than half a year after the sample mailing. All six of these are still positive at that time. Nine data points were collected more than half a year after the coupon mailing. Eight of these are still positive at that time. The ninth is just barely below zero. There is no evidence of further abatement of the effects, either for the coupon or for the sample.

The cumulative thrust of the data lends overwhelming support to the persistence hypothesis for advertising, for sampling, for couponing, and, in principle, for any message. We have known that messages produce measurable effects, and have assumed that these effects decay over time. Now we also know that this decay is limited. The effects do not go rapidly to zero, but persist. All of this is summarized in the Third Law of choice.

THE THIRD LAW: THE LAW OF PERSISTENCE
The effect produced by a message is made up of two components: a transient effect and an intrinsic effect. The transient effect decays rapidly. The intrinsic effect lasts indefinitely.

Have I exceeded the bounds of the available data in formulating the Third Law this way? I don't believe so. It is certainly true that the studies I have drawn on covered time periods of eight months at most. Should I have been more circumspect? Should I have said, more conservatively, that the intrinsic effects may last around eight months? I believe the data warrant a stronger statement than that. It is true that we don't know empirically how long the effects may remain detectable, and it is certainly not forever, whatever that may mean. But considering the incessant flow of messages, the veritable bombardment from advertising, couponing, point-of-sale displays, special sales, and product experience itself, even six months is a very long time. Furthermore, the data warrant projection. The increments drop initially, but remain essentially flat thereafter. It is difficult to imagine that, having remained constant between three months and six months after delivery of the message, the effect will suddenly drop precipitously during the subsequent three months. Well, perhaps not pre-cipitously, but how about gradually? How gradually? To controvert the law, there would have to be a drop. But in view of what we have seen, such a drop, if any, would have to be so gradual that it would amount to no drop at all for practical purposes.

If the Third Law is true as postulated, then the observed effects should remain essentially constant after some initial period of time. One way of testing whether this is the case is to eliminate the early weeks after mes-sage delivery, say the first eight weeks, and examine the trend from that time forward. For this purpose we abandon the exponential curve and fit a straight line instead, in effect postulating that there is a linear downward trend. If there is gradual erosion of the effects, the least-squares line should have a negative slope and should hit the x-axis at the point in time when all the effect has vanished. Even just formulating the issue this way illustrates how unreasonable the assumption of a linear decline really is. It implies that the effect will decline at some steady rate until it reaches zero and will then suddenly stop declining. It is precisely because this assumption is so implausible that I proposed the more appropriate nega-tive exponential curve to begin with.

Nevertheless, we examine the linear decline hypothesis, playing devil's advocate as it were. Figure 26–8 shows the results from this perspective. The slopes of the least-squares lines are .02 for the sample and -.02 for the coupon, clearly not materially different from zero and compatible with the conclusion that the effects persist indefinitely for all practical purposes.

There is a quasi-tautological protection in the Third Law, a hidden way out should we encounter recalcitrant data bent on breaking the law. Like every self-respecting law, the Third Law has its built-in defense against potential inconsistencies. It refers to an intrinsic effect that lasts indefi-nitely, but it does not say how large that intrinsic effect is. If the data so decree, it may be zero in particular cases. You might say that this is the ultimate evasion. First I assert that there is persistence of effects, and then I take it right back. Doesn't a zero intrinsic effect amount to having said that perhaps there is persistence and perhaps there isn't? And isn't that equivalent to having said nothing at all?

I don't believe it is. The law articulates an important principle and summarizes some important empirical facts. Relying on the law, we may expect in the general case that some portion of the effect of any message will persist for some long period of time. I say indefinitely, which you may take to mean approximately forever for most practical purposes. This has far-reaching implications. For one thing, it absolves us of the need to

Figure 26–8
Effect of Sample and Coupon over Time
Consolidated
$(N'_{Sample}>7,000, N'_{Coupon}>22,000, N'_{Control}>13,000)$

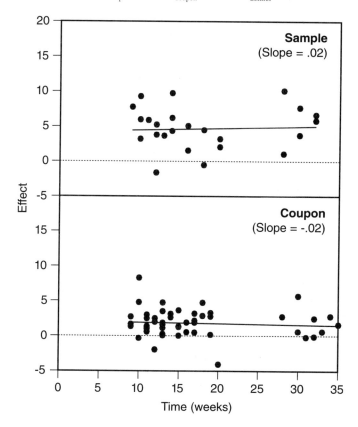

measure every message over time. If we measure it at one point in time only, as we do in Product-STEP for example, say three or four weeks after product delivery, presumably long enough for the transient effect to have vanished and for the measured effect to have reached the intrinsic effect, we don't need to measure it again repeatedly. Relying on the Third Law, we are entitled to assume that the effect will still exist in essentially undiminished form long afterwards. And this will be true generally, even if some particular message or product produces no effect at all or produces an effect that happens to have an intrinsic component of zero.

If all this is so, you may ask, why don't we end up with 100% or at least very high market shares in short order? Nature provides a balance of its own. Your messages' effects are not the only ones that persist. Every other brand is sending messages, dropping coupons, delivering product. All of those messages too have intrinsic effects. And those too persist. You may find your market share unchanged over a six-month period. Looking only at the final result, it may appear that nothing has happened in the interim. But based on what we now know, nothing could be further from the truth. A great many messages were received, produced effects, persisted, and were counteracted by other messages, which in turn produced effects, which also persisted, resulting in a steady-state balance that hides most of what is going on. But it only hides it. It does not obliterate it. And we can render it visible to the naked eye by delivering a single message, say an ad or a sample or a coupon, simultaneously to all respondents in one group, and comparing that group's behavior with a randomly comparable control group that did not receive the message. When that is done, the effect of the message suddenly comes to light, not only during the first few weeks after delivery but also, as we have seen, for a long time afterward.

CHAPTER 27

Budget Allocation Across Brands

Throughout this book, we have dealt with marketing strategy for single brands. Occasionally, as in discussions of line extensions, this has spilled over into consideration of how to optimize offers of several brands in the same product category. But the expansion has stopped there. By their very nature, STEP, Ad-STEP, and Product-STEP have seemed limited to *within-category* problems. But are they?

The most basic *across-categories* problem confronting the multibrand marketer is how to allocate resources. This problem can be articulated as follows: "Given several brands in several product categories, which brands should be left alone? Which brands should be supported? And by what means, by distribution-building efforts, by advertising, or by promotion?" It turns out that a combination of STEP, Ad-STEP, and Product-STEP can address this global intercategory strategy problem.

The following generic *Strategic Potential* test requires three test groups per brand. Group 1 receives a STEP booklet. Group 2 receives a Universal Ad for the test brand, followed by a STEP booklet. Group 3 receives a free sample of the test brand, followed by a STEP booklet. This yields four shares for the test brand, as follows:

> *M:* Market share, from external sources or estimated from usage share in the STEP group.
> *S:* STEP share in the STEP group.
> *U:* STEP share in the Universal Ad group.
> *P:* STEP share in the Product-STEP group.

This set of shares, which will generally be of increasing magnitude, defines the latent potentials of the test brand.

If the STEP share *S* is larger than the market share *M*, this indicates an accessibility deficiency, most likely a deficiency in distribution. It says that the brand has untapped goodwill and that by just putting it on the shelf, or by just giving it parity with the competition on the shelf, gains in share will be produced, raising the share from the market share to the STEP share.

Ad-STEP, using the Universal Ad, measures the advertisability of the brand. It measures whether and to what extent the brand has latent, untapped goodwill that can be exploited by advertising. If U is larger than S, this means that by running advertising for the brand, simply reminding customers that the brand exists, a gain in market share equal to the difference between U and S can be produced.

To say that Share U, generated by the Universal Ad, represents the contribution of advertising is obviously an oversimplification. It is possible that someone will come up with a brilliant campaign that will produce effects way beyond those produced by the Universal Ad. On the other hand, it is possible that actual ads will fall short of what the Universal Ad produces. The Universal Ad simply estimates how easy it is to produce effective advertising for the brand, assuming otherwise comparable creative ingenuity and skill. If Brand X turns out to be more "advertisable" by this yardstick than Brand Y, we can bet that, other things being equal, we have a better chance of developing effective advertising for Brand X than for Brand Y.

Product-STEP measures the total potential of the brand, the share the brand would command if 100% of customers were given product experience with it. If P is larger than S, this means that by just putting the product into the hands of customers, gains can be produced, potentially raising its share by $P - S$ on top of M. Such product experience could be generated by sampling, by couponing, or by other means.

We may think of the difference between the brand's Product-STEP share P and its market share M as the maximum untapped potential of the brand. And we may think of the intervening measures S and U as partitions of that total potential into three components that are potentially achievable by distribution, advertising, and promotion.

Figure 27–1 shows this partition for three real brands in three different product categories, all marketed by the same company. The chart has major strategic implications. Brands A and B happen to have approximately equal current shares (11.0 and 9.7), yet their potentials are very different. Even with 100% product experience, Brand B gains only 3 share points (12.0 - 9.0) over its STEP share. It is a brand that enjoys an acceptable share but has consummated all of its latent potential. Neither advertising nor promotion will do much more for it. Brand A, on the other hand, has four times the potential of Brand B (23.2 - 11.3 = 11.9) and is susceptible to either advertising or promotion. Other things being equal, we expect to generate a much larger number of incremental share points per marketing dollar spent on Brand A than spent on Brand B. Brand C,

Figure 27–1
Strategic Potential Test for Brands from Three Different
Product Categories Marketed by the Same Company
(N = 6,569)

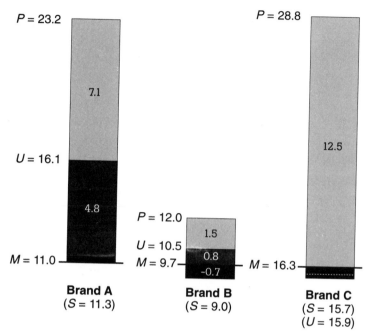

finally, has a share that is approximately 50% higher than those of Brands A and B. It also has a lot of latent potential (28.8 - 15.7 = 13.1), but this potential is contingent on actual product experience. Our best estimate is that advertising alone will not do much for it, unless it succeeds in inducing prospects to try the brand. Accordingly, marketing dollars should be allocated to Brand C, but should be earmarked for consumer promotions designed to put the product into the hands of customers.

Thus a marketer with responsibility for several brands can use the Strategic Potential test, conducted for each of her brands, as a basis for budget allocations among brands and across product category lines. Budget allocations need no longer be left to judgment alone. They can be supported by solid empirical evidence.

SUMMING UP

This is partly an overview of the basic concepts I have dealt with and partly their final synthesis. It is not meant to stand alone. It will serve as a reminder of the ground that has been covered—useful to those who have read the book but, I fear, of limited value to others.

Summing Up

This book has identified the basic problems with which every marketer must deal. It has specified the core variables for studying the customer. It has presented principles for conducting research, for understanding choice, and for formulating marketing strategies. And it has proposed a theory of choice, built on three laws, that has concrete, practical applications. The problems, core variables, principles, and laws are summarized in turn.

The Problems

I said in the Preface that there are only three problems in marketing research. Three sounds good, but I can be flexible. On the one hand, we may want to coalesce two of these into a single one. On the other hand, we may want to add an additional problem. Perhaps I should have said: three problems, give or take one. The point is that the number is small, and that many problems that have traditionally been thought of as different are really the same. This book has dealt with them.

The first problem involves the content of messages. Much of the marketer's work consists of sending messages to prospective customers. The most fundamental of these is the product itself, which can be thought of as a message delivered to the relevant senses of the customer by sight, sound, touch, smell, and taste. This is supplemented by messages addressed to the belief system of the customer, covering characteristics the customer cannot verify by direct observation but accepts because they have presumably been verified by others, for example, the caloric content of foods. This is further supplemented by associative emotional appeals in words, pictures, and music. Each of these messages produces an effect that influences the customer's probability of choosing the brand. This effect can be thought of as the "value" of the message. This value may be expressed as a deserved share if we are dealing with a brand, or as a potential penetration or potential usage if we are dealing with a product category.

Globally, we may speak of the value of an "offer," that is, of an integrated collection of information elements, consisting of product experience, name, package, and advertising. But we may also speak of the value of individual elements of that offer, down to the finest minutiae, such as the color of the brand name on the package. Each of these has a value, and the marketer needs to know what these values are. This defines the first problem: to measure the value of an integrated collection of information elements. This first problem takes in a lot of ground. Concept tests, theme tests, logo tests, price tests, product tests, advertising copy tests can all be thought of as special cases of this problem. If we know how to measure the value of any information element, we know how to measure all. I believe that the optimal method for doing this is STEP for a brand, and VEST for a product category.

STEP and VEST deal with cases in which the options are pre-defined. The marketer asks: Should I use this ingredient or that, this package or that, this brand name or that? Although there is no inherent limit to how many such options can be considered, the number is usually small. There are times, however, when the problem takes on a marginally different form. The marketer still wants to know what messages to send, but poses the question open-endedly. Instead of furnishing the options, she asks: "What options should I consider, and how much is each of them worth?" This question defines the second major problem. It is similar to the first. It can be translated into the first, at least on a conceptual plane. A purist might insist that it is not a separate problem at all. But I believe it is.

When the marketer indicates that she is not prepared to identify the options, she implicitly requires that we create a map designed to enumerate "all," or at least a large number, of her options. That number, defined by the map, usually runs into the millions. We can, of course, imagine creating a huge STEP test, consisting of millions of cells, and argue that we are still dealing with Problem 1. As a practical matter, however, there is a discontinuity that turns the quantitative difference into a qualitative one. Once the number of options has become large enough, a new solution is needed, which results in a subtle retroactive change in the way the problem should have been posed in the first place, elevating it to the status of a separate problem. It can be formulated this way: to measure the value of a synthesized collection of information elements, more specifically, of a synthesized collection of perceived attributes of a brand or product category. I believe that the optimal method for doing this is SUMM.

Both Problems 1 and 2 involve estimating the value of offers. The former measures the deserved share of integrated offers experimentally. The latter estimates the deserved share of synthesized offers by simulation. By contrast, the third problem does not deal with *what* to say but with *how often* to say it. We may know the right message but may nevertheless fail to produce the desired results if we don't deliver that message often enough, or too often, or at insupportable cost. Thus, the third problem addresses the cost efficiency of message delivery. I believe that the optimal methods for doing this are real-life experiments of sampling and couponing, and Ad-Weight for television advertising.

In addition to the questions covered by the basic three problems, the marketer needs factual data pertaining to the state of her business: financial data on revenues, expenses, and profits; manufacturing data on time and cost of production; distribution data on number and location of outlets that carry various brands; sales data on number of units sold at various prices; and customer data on awareness, desirability, and choice. All of these can be grouped under the broad heading of tracking, that is, measuring how these variables change over time.

Tracking could be identified as the fourth problem. I have refrained from doing so because some aspects of tracking, for example, an analysis of manufacturing or sales costs, seem to me to fall clearly outside the boundaries defined by the interface between the marketer and the customer, while others, for example, tracking STEP share, seem to me to fall under the heading of one or another of the basic three problems. Suppose the marketer observes that distribution of her brand is low and that an effort to increase it is in order. Such an effort would certainly entail costs, which raises the question whether the net return would justify these costs. To answer this question she needs to estimate how large a share the brand would command if it were made available to customers in stores that don't carry it now. On closer examination, this turns out to be just another case of Problem 1. By the same token, the tracking of awareness, beliefs, desirability of attributes, and choice at regular intervals may raise questions, but won't answer them. To obtain answers, it will be necessary to evaluate potential courses of action, which again brings us squarely back to one or another of the basic three problems.

I have taken the middle ground of conceding that factual tracking is a valid function, but have not elevated it to the status of a full-fledged "problem." Instead, I have assigned it a peripheral place on the boundaries of Choice Research, where it may from time to time call attention to questions without itself playing a part in answering these. This position is negotiable. Push me hard, and I may agree that Problems 1 and 2 are one and the same at the core. Push me hard, and I may agree that tracking should be treated as a separate problem. Hence my approximate statement that Choice Research deals with three problems, give or take one. The three problems are:

Problem 1: To measure the value of an integrated collection of information elements.

Problem 2: To estimate the value of a synthesized collection of information elements.

Problem 3: To measure the value of delivering a message with some specific frequency.

The Core Variables

All theories use two kinds of variables: *core variables,* which are measured directly and are operationally defined by those measurements, and *construct-variables,* which are defined as functions of the core-variables. It is possible to create an almost unlimited number of construct-variables, but the number of core-variables is usually small. I have used five.

1. *Beliefs.* This covers how the respondent relates to cognitive statements about the world. The measurement consists of asking the respondent whether she believes a statement to be true or false, assigning a 1 or a 0 to it. More generally, the respondent may be asked to assign a probability to the statement. Such a probability can have one of two meanings. The respondent may be uncertain about the truth of the statement, even when the statement is objectively true or false, and may be asked to express this uncertainty as a probability. Or the statement may be only approximately true or false, and the respondent may be asked to express her judgment of that approximation as a probability. In either event, the general measurement of beliefs consists of assigning subjective probabilities to the relative truth of statements. Absolute true-false judgments are only a special case. Sometimes the respondent is given a list and is asked to select the one statement that she judges to be most nearly true. This is equivalent to asking her to assign a probability to each of the statements and to identify the one that received the highest probability.

2. *Desirability.* This measures what the respondent wants. By definition, she wants whatever she says she wants. To be sure, she may lie or may not be consciously aware of her wants. For that reason, some researchers seek to infer what she "really" wants from other evidence. Such inferences, however, lead to construct-variables that must ultimately be defined as functions of other core-variables. I have treated desirability exclusively as a core-variable in its own right. It can be measured by asking the respondent whether she likes or dislikes an object, assigning a +1, 0, or -1 to the object. It may be measured by asking her to use a verbal scale or a bounded numerical scale (for example, a scale between +10 and -10). In

the most general case, she is asked to use the unbounded write-in scale, which I believe to be the optimal instrument for measuring desirability.

3. *Choice.* This variable is closely related to desirability but is not desirability. It is the consequence of the relative desirabilities of different objects. It is measured by asking the respondent to select one object from a set of objects, based on how much she wants or likes or is likely to buy these objects, in effect assigning a 1 to the selected object and a 0 to all others. More generally, choice is measured by asking the respondent to allocate finite resources among the objects of a set, as when she is asked to distribute a number of stickers among the brands of a product category, in effect assigning a probability between 0 and 1, inclusive, to each object. In my view, this is the optimal instrument for measuring choice.

4. *Awareness.* This involves choice of a different kind. Again the respondent is asked to select one object from a set of objects, but this time the selection is based not on what she wants but on her ability to evoke the object when presented with a label that identifies the set. For example, she is asked to name a flower, a tree, a brand of coffee, and so on. This measures the strength of association in her mind between the set and the objects in the set, the psychological accessibility of these objects.

5. *Factual reports.* These deal with the objective world. The respondent is asked to report when she shopped last, what brand she bought, how many packages she bought, what brand of PC she owns, etc. To the extent these reports are intended as stand-ins for the underlying facts, they are subject to error and distortion.

It is possible to devise measuring instruments that are composites of the core-variables. This may be done deliberately or by inadvertence. In particular, every open-ended question generates a composite variable that necessarily has an awareness component. For example, the question, "Which brand of fax machine has the fastest transmission speed?" is a composite of awareness and belief. The question, "Which New York restaurant do you like best?" is a composite of awareness and desirability. And the question, "On which airline did you fly last?" is a composite of awareness and factual report. I believe that, when composites are desired, it is preferable to measure each core-variable separately and to combine two or more of them analytically. For this reason, I have used only the five listed core-variables in my work. Minimally, I can say that this has been sufficient for my purposes. But I also believe that these variables represent a broader taxonomy of everything that needs to be measured, or *can* be measured, when one engages in the peculiar exercise of asking questions and getting answers.

The Principles

The principles are suggested rules of conduct and modes of thought for the researcher and the marketer. They are not exhaustive. The list could be expanded many times over. Nor can they necessarily be demonstrated empirically. To a large degree, they are a matter of definition and temperament, guidelines I have used in my efforts to devise strategies for extracting truth from data, for rendering conscientious service to the clients who hired me. If you are in my line of work, I commend them to you as tools. They have served me well.

Principles Dealing with Discipline in Research

THE INDEPENDENT ANALYSIS PRINCIPLE
The analysis must be completed before the data are collected.

THE SINGLE-CRITERION PRINCIPLE
The analysis must use only a single criterion, and only a single measure for any variable.

THE JUDGMENT-SEPARATION PRINCIPLE
The researcher must adhere to the principles of Choice Research even if his client, the marketer, exercises her right to violate them.

Principles Dealing with the Structure of Choice

THE QUESTION-ANSWER PRINCIPLE
A question is a persuasive message, which triggers an answer, which is a choice.

THE VARIABLE-IDENTIFICATION PRINCIPLE
The measured variable is defined not by the words in the questionnaire, but by the task the respondent is asked to perform.

THE ORGANIC RESPONSE PRINCIPLE
Responses to questions are largely impervious to instructions designed to override the organic way respondents approach tasks.

THE CONGRUENCE PRINCIPLE
The main concern of Choice Research is the congruence between the choice situation in the questionnaire and the choice situation in the world.

THE DESERVED SHARE PRINCIPLE

Measuring the deserved share of an offer amounts to measuring the value of a collection of information elements.

THE ANTECEDENT EFFECT PRINCIPLE

When two products are measured in succession, the measurement of the second product contains a component that is an additional measurement of the first product, an effect that cannot be removed by rotation.

THE LOGIC PRINCIPLE

That which is logical is not necessarily psychological.

THE DESIRABILITY PRINCIPLE

Desires are unlimited; choices are finite.

THE EXPONENTIAL PRINCIPLE

Share of choice decreases exponentially with increasing desirability-rank.

Principles Dealing with Marketing

THE SELLING STRATEGY PRINCIPLE

Explicitly or implicitly, every brand has a selling strategy that consists of the same universal syllogism: Because my brand has attributes A,B,C, . . . , it will satisfy your desires X,Y,Z, . . . better than any other brand.

THE UNIVERSAL MARKETING PRINCIPLE

In a market in which a small number of brands are competing for a large number of customers, most of whom have different desires, the universal marketing question is: Which promises will induce the largest possible number of customers to choose my brand?

THE CUSTOMER SATISFACTION PRINCIPLE

Customer satisfaction is nothing but a brand's deserved share among its own customers.

THE DIFFERENTIATION PRINCIPLE

In a differentiated product category, the optimal strategy is to develop unique product offers. In an undifferentiated product category, the optimal strategy is to focus on image and to proliferate brand names and labels.

THE PRICE-SENSITIVITY PRINCIPLE
Price-sensitivity is independent of price level. On the average, price-sensitivity is the same whether we are dealing with a $1 item or a $1,000,000 item.

THE PRICE EFFECT PRINCIPLE
On the average, a price increase of ten percent will produce a share decrease of around nine percent, but there is a great deal of variability in this result. One time in five the loss will be much larger, and one time in five there will be no loss at all.

THE PROMISES PRINCIPLE
For consumables, only specific features are likely to matter. General promises won't. For durables, both specific features and general promises are of major importance.

THE NAME PRINCIPLE
A name is worth money. For durables, a good name may permit charging as much as twenty percent more for the brand, on the average; in some cases, as much as fifty percent more. It can also be of comparable value for consumables, but only rarely.

THE IMAGE PRINCIPLE
A brand's future is built on its past. It is easier to give a brand the right image in the first place than to change a wrong image once it has taken hold.

THE IMPROVEMENT PRINCIPLE
Excise the word *improvement* from your vocabulary. Think instead of whether you want to *change* your established brand.

THE CHANGING PRINCIPLE
Don't change a successful brand unless you are absolutely sure. The chances are you'll lose more than you'll gain.

THE LINE-EXTENSION PRINCIPLE
Provided you can get your line extension into the stores, a good line extension is likely to do more for you than a positioning change in one of your brands.

THE COMPARISON PRINCIPLE
Beware comparisons. If you don't win, you lose.

THE IDENTIFICATION PRINCIPLE
Don't keep secret which brand you are advertising.

THE GLITTER PRINCIPLE
Good looks aren't everything. They may not be anything. Just because an ad looks better doesn't mean it will sell better.

THE ADVERTISING EFFECTIVENESS PRINCIPLE
Advertising is a game of chance. Even if you are a major marketer, served by a major advertising agency, you have around a 50% chance of running advertising that won't do anything for you and in some cases will actually hurt your brand.

The Laws

I have formulated three laws of choice. I have called them "laws" because I believe that they are true—almost tautologically true—but they are not really tautological. They are subject to empirical verification. And though at least two of the laws may seem self-evident, prevailing practice demonstrates that many practitioners do not know these laws, or do not appreciate their full implications, or just do not act consistently with them. To this extent, then, there is not only theoretical but also practical value in articulating them formally. Here they are:

THE FIRST LAW: THE LAW OF CONGRUENCE
Congruent choice situations have equal choice vectors.

THE SECOND LAW: THE LAW OF PRIMACY
An individual for whom, at the moment of choice, n brands are tied for first place in brand strength, chooses each of these n brands with probability $1/n$.

THE THIRD LAW: THE LAW OF PERSISTENCE
The effect produced by a message is made up of two components: a transient effect and an intrinsic effect. The transient effect decays rapidly. The intrinsic effect lasts indefinitely.

A Closing Comment

Two themes have run through my professional life: the ambition to craft a theory of choice, and the ambition to develop parsimonious methods of measurement. These seemingly separate efforts have been intimately intertwined. When I started, I had an intuition, a belief that somewhere in the business of asking questions and getting answers truths were hidden, principles about aspects of human nature. But I was unable to imagine the form these truths would take, let alone articulate any of them explicitly. The intuition remained an intuition and nothing more.

In the meantime, I was drawn into the business world. I abandoned my search for abstract principles and began to work on practical problems, seeking to help my clients and to advance my business. Toward that end, I spent much time on particulars of study design, focusing on concrete matters, on measurements and techniques. From time to time, this seemed like a digression from my original purpose. But far from being a digression, it proved to be an essential step in its pursuit. The result was that I developed not only specific techniques but also a general theory.

Talking about this theory recently, a colleague of mine pointed a finger at me and said, "*You* will never know whether your theory is worth anything." I accept this verdict. I will never know. For me personally, the work I have done has been a source of great satisfaction. It has therefore been worthwhile in and of itself. That is enough. But I must confess that, in the back of my mind, I nourish the belief that the laws I have formulated are relevant and will pass the test of time.

APPENDIX

This entire book was originally written as a single, continuous narrative. In the end, I transferred the more technical sections into this appendix in order to streamline the main text. The specialist should treat this appendix as an integral part of the book. Ideally, its various sections will be read in conjunction with the chapters that refer to them.

Computation of VEST Penetration

Table A–1, using hypothetical data for one respondent, illustrates how the VEST data for durables are scored and interpreted. The first column lists all the categories of the reference frame, excluding any test categories, arranged in order of their "want to own" rank, from Rank 1, the category the respondent wants to own most, to Rank 20, the category she wants to own least. For analytic purposes, phantom ranks "0" and "21" have been added to the table. The second column (A) shows a 1 or 0 for each category, indicating whether the respondent currently owns the category or not. The total number of categories this respondent owns is 9. Columns P and Q show the cumulative number of categories owned and not owned, respectively, by all ranks lower in the table.

The score assigned to a test category is a function of the ranks between which that test category is inserted. The test category is not assigned a numeric rank of its own but is identified as having *test rank i* if it is inserted between Ranks i and $i+1$. P_i is defined as the number of owned categories that are below Rank i in the table, and Q_i is defined as the number of nonowned categories that are above Rank $i+1$ in the table. The preliminary score (t_i) assigned to a test category with Test Rank i is

$$t_i = \frac{P_i}{P_i + Q_i}$$

Columns 3, 4, and 5 of Table A–1 show P, Q, and t for every test rank a test category could have.

Consider, for example, a test category that might be inserted between Ranks 7 and 8 of the reference categories. We see that such a category would beat 13 reference categories (Categories 8–20). Most of these, however, are of no significance. Saying that the respondent wants to own the test category more than Categories 9–10, 13–16, and 18–20 does not prove anything, since she does not own any of these categories. Accordingly, we eliminate these categories from consideration. We do, however,

Table A–1
Illustrative Durables VEST Analysis
for One Hypothetical Respondent

				Penetration			
Want to Own	Currently Owns			Prelim. Test	Test	Prelim. Ref.	Ref.
Rank	A	P	Q	t	T	r	R
0		9	0	100	100		
1	1	8	0	100	100	100	100
2	1	7	0	100	100	100	100
3	1	6	0	100	100	100	100
4	0	6	1	86	85	93	92
5	1	5	1	83	82	85	83
6	1	4	1	80	79	82	80
7	0	4	2	67	65	73	72
8	1	3	2	60	58	63	61
9	0	3	3	50	47	55	53
10	0	3	4	43	40	46	44
11	1	2	4	33	31	38	35
12	1	1	4	20	18	27	24
13	0	1	5	17	15	18	16
14	0	1	6	14	12	15	13
15	0	1	7	13	11	13	11
16	0	1	8	11	9	12	10
17	1	0	8	0	0	6	4
18	0	0	9	0	0	0	0
19	0	0	10	0	0	0	0
20	0	0	11	0	0	0	0
21		0	11	0	0		
	9					9.265	9.000

regard it as relevant that the respondent wants to own the test category more than Categories 8, 11, 12, and 17, because these are categories the respondent does own. Presumably these ratings reveal a level of interest that might translate itself into ownership. Turning to the other end of the continuum, we note that the respondent does not want to own the test category as much as Categories 1–3 and 5–6, all of which she currently owns. This does not necessarily constitute adverse evidence for the test category. But she also wants to own the test category less than Categories 4 and 7, which she does not own. This implies that she might end up not owning the test category either.

Altogether, we have identified six comparisons that provide some information concerning what the respondent is likely to do. In four cases, she wants to own the test category more than categories she owns, indicating a potential for acquiring the test category. In two cases, she wants to own the test category less than categories she does not own, indicating a potential for *not* acquiring it. Taking the data in their entirety, we may say that, based on the rankings she has given as calibrated against her actual prior behavior, her probability of acquiring the test category is $(4)/(4 + 2) = 67\%$, shown in the Rank 7 line of column t, which represents a preliminary estimate of the test category's penetration. By the same token, a test category ranked between Categories 2 and 3 would be scored 100%, while a test category ranked between Categories 17 and 18 would be scored 0%.

A particularly attractive aspect of VEST is that it is self-calibrating and self-checking. The logic used for calculating the test category's score can be used to calculate a score for each reference category. Basing the calculation on the preliminary test scores (t), we define the corresponding preliminary reference category score (r) for any reference category as the average of the scores that would have been obtained by two test categories—one inserted immediately above and the other immediately below that reference category:

$$r_i = \frac{t_i + t_{i-1}}{2}$$

These scores (r) are shown in the next-to-the-last column of the table.

Adding all the r scores, we obtain a total, $B = \Sigma r_i$. For the twenty reference categories in the example, $B = 9.265$. But the total number of categories currently owned (A) is 9. Thus, for this particular respondent, the estimating procedure has yielded a higher estimate of the potential number of reference categories owned than the actual number owned. It could also yield a lower estimate for another respondent. Our first impulse may be to adjust the estimates by multiplying each r by A/B (9.0/9.265), which would render the total estimated number of categories owned equal to the total actual number of categories owned. This adjustment procedure, however, runs into difficulties for patterns for which the adjustment factor A/B is larger than 1. In those cases, the adjustment would attribute probabilities larger than 1.0 to some of the categories, an unpalatable result. Accordingly, we look for another device to accomplish the same objective. Raising all r's to some power k will do just that. Since all the r's are probabilities and as such range from 0 to 1, raising them to a power will generate numbers ranging from 0 to 1. Specifically, we look for a constant k for the respondent such that

$$\Sigma r_i^k = A$$

This constant can be found by computational approximation. For the particular pattern illustrated in Table A–1, k turns out to be 1.07725. Raising all r's to this power generates the final VEST penetration scores (R) for the reference categories, $R_i = r_i^k$. By the same token, our best estimate of the VEST Potential (T_i) of a test category with Test Rank i becomes $T_i = t_i^k$.

Table A–2 shows hypothetical data for one respondent to illustrate how the VEST data for consumables are scored and interpreted. The categories are arranged from Rank 1, the category the respondent expects to use most frequently, to Rank 20, the category she expects to use least fre-

Table A–2
Illustrative Consumables VEST Analysis
for One Hypothetical Respondent

Want to Use Rank	Usage U	Non-Usage X	P	Q	Usage Occasions			
					Prelim. Test t	Test T	Prelim. Ref. r	Ref. R
0			243	0	35	33		
1	30	5	213	5	34	32	35	32
2	35	0	178	5	34	32	34	32
3	28	7	150	12	32	30	33	31
4	30	5	120	17	31	29	32	29
5	14	21	106	38	26	24	28	26
6	20	15	86	53	22	20	24	22
7	16	19	70	72	17	15	19	18
8	4	31	66	103	14	12	15	14
9	12	23	53	126	11	9	12	11
10	6	29	48	155	8	7	9	8
11	8	27	40	182	6	5	7	6
12	3	32	37	214	5	4	6	5
13	12	23	25	237	3	3	4	4
14	5	30	20	267	2	2	3	2
15	8	27	12	294	1	1	2	1
16	3	32	9	326	1	1	1	1
17	4	31	5	357	0	0	1	1
18	2	33	3	390	0	0	0	0
19	1	34	2	424	0	0	0	0
20	2	33	0	457	0	0	0	0
21				0				
	243						265	243

quently. The next column shows the number of actual past usage occasions (U) for each of the categories. In the general case, the number of usage occasions will not necessarily be monotonically decreasing with increasing rank. But we translate each rank into a best estimate of the number of usage occasions that corresponds to it.

Scanning the number of usage occasions for the twenty categories, we note that Category 2 has the maximum number of usage occasions (M), which happens to be 35. Using this number as the base, we may think of each category as having 35 usage opportunities, some of which are converted into usage occasions and some into nonusage occasions. The number of nonusage occasions X is defined as $X = M - U$, and is shown in column 3. Column 4, headed P, shows the cumulative number of usage occasions, putting into each line the sum of all usage occasions below that line. Column 5, headed Q, shows the cumulative number of nonusage occasions, putting into each line the sum of all nonusage occasions on or above that line. The remainder of the analysis is analogous to the analysis for the durables case. If a test category is ranked between Category 7 and Category 8, it beats all usage occasions that are lower in the table. That number is shown in column P as 70. At the same time, it is beaten by all nonusage occasions that are above it in the table. That number is shown in column Q as 72. Accordingly, we estimate that this category will achieve $(35)(70)/(70 + 72) = 17$ usage occasions, which is the preliminary estimate in column t. By the same token, column T shows the final estimate, and columns r and R show the preliminary and final estimates for the reference categories.

Formally, the number of estimated usage occasions for the test category is

$$t_i = M \frac{P_i}{P_i + Q_i}$$

which is shown in column t of Table A–2. The consumables case is then treated with precisely the same logic that was used for the durables case. In particular, the definitions are:

$$r_i = \frac{(t_i + t_{i-1})}{2}$$

$$\sum_i r_i^k = U$$

$$R_i = r_i^k$$

$$T_i = t_i^k$$

The Variance and Sensitivity of STEP and First-Choice Share

Since first-choice is based on a single observation from each respondent, and STEP can be thought of as the summary of ten observations from each respondent, we expect the variance of STEP shares to be lower than the variance of first-choice shares. Consider the distribution of scores obtained for a brand in a first-choice measurement. This distribution is concentrated at two points: 0 and 1 (100%). The percentage of respondents at these points defines the variance. If we now imagine a distribution of STEP scores having the same mean, the observations of this distribution are no longer concentrated at the two extremes of 0 and 100%. Some observations will have moved out of the zero category toward the mean into the 10% (one sticker), 20% (two stickers), and other categories. Others will have moved out of the 100% category toward the mean into the 90% (nine stickers), 80% (eight stickers), and other categories, bringing all scores closer to the mean, which results in lower variability around the mean and hence a lower variance and standard deviation.

Figure B–1 shows the relationship between the standard deviations of first-choice share and the standard deviations of STEP share for the ten product categories discussed in Chapter 13. Although the standard deviation of any brand depends on the specific distribution of the scores of that brand, we can say, by way of a rule of thumb, that the standard deviation of a STEP share is approximately half the standard deviation of the corresponding first-choice share. This, however, does not necessarily guarantee that STEP share will be more sensitive in discriminating among different message elements than first-choice share, since the differences in first-choice share generated by such message elements will also be commensurately larger. To test the extent to which this is the case, we need a study in which a substantial number of test items were measured both by STEP and by first-choice. The Spectrum study, described in Chapter 19,

Figure B–1
**Standard Deviation of STEP Share versus Standard Deviation of
First-Choice Share for Ten Product Categories**
(N = 8,546, r = .91, m = .48)

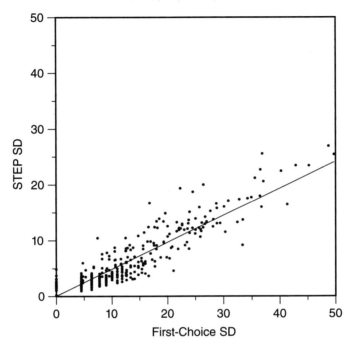

is such a study. It provided for testing sixteen different variants of a product in a decoy label, using a sample of sixteen randomly equivalent groups of approximately 400 respondents. Each of these groups was further divided into two randomly equivalent subgroups to which the decoy brand was presented at a high and a low price, respectively. Figure B–2 shows the relationship between the first-choice shares and the STEP shares for these thirty-two test variants.

The first-choice shares show a wider range than the STEP shares. But which measure is more sensitive? To assess the relative sensitivity of the two measures, we consider all possible pairs of the thirty-two variants. There are (32 x 31)/2 = 496 such pairs. If we divide the share difference of each pair by the standard error of that difference, we obtain its *critical ratio*. By chance alone, only 32% of these critical ratios should be larger than 1, only 4.5% should be larger than 2, and only .2% should be larger than 3.

The upper panel of Figure B–3 shows the percent distribution of the

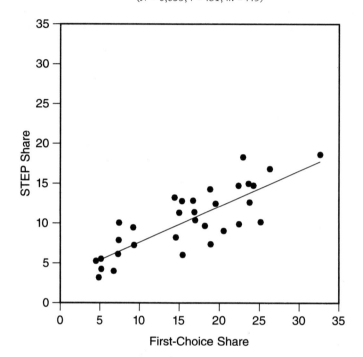

Figure B–2
STEP Share versus First-Choice Share
for Thirty-two Variants in Spectrum Study
($N = 6{,}633, r = .81, m = .45$)

496 critical ratios for first-choice. Clearly, the thirty-two variants were very different from each other. By chance, we would have expected only 32% of the critical ratios to be larger than 1, but empirically 72% were larger than 1. The average critical ratio was 2.43. This means that the average difference would have been statistically significant at better than the 95% confidence level.

The lower panel of Figure B–3 shows the same distribution for the STEP shares. The distribution indicates that, though the absolute STEP shares were smaller than the absolute first-choice shares, the STEP shares were more sensitive statistically in discriminating among the test variants. Twenty-eight percent of the first-choice differences would have been judged to be approximately the same (critical ratio less than 1) but only 20% of the STEP differences. At the upper end, 7.5% of the STEP differences had critical ratios over 6, compared to 1.6% of the first-choice differences. The average critical ratio of the STEP difference was 2.83

Figure B–3
Percent Distribution of Critical Ratios of 496 Differences
between 32 Variants in Spectrum Study
(N = 6,633)

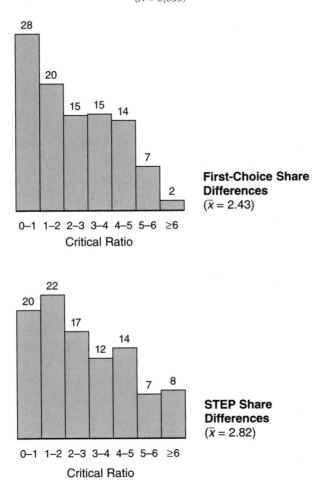

compared to 2.43 for first-choice. This difference implies that, for this data set at least, the STEP test would have required less than 75% of the sample size that would have been required for the first-choice test in order to achieve comparable statistical discrimination among the test variants.

The Tie-Share Vector
and the Frequency Vector

Referring to the matrix in Table 14–1, f_1 percent of the respondents give all their tie scores to the brand in column 1, f_2 percent give half their tie scores to that brand, and so on. The total share of tie scores given to the brand in column 1 is therefore

$$x_1 = \frac{1}{10}(10f_1 + 5f_2 + 3.3f_3 + \ldots) = f_1 + \frac{f_2}{2} + \frac{f_3}{3} + \ldots$$

or, in the general case,*

$$x_i = \frac{1}{10} \sum_{j=1}^{n} f_j\, a_{ij}$$

where a_{ij} is the tie score in row i and column j of the tie matrix.

There is a simple relationship between the frequency vector and the tie-share vector. Consider the tie-score shares x_1 and x_2. Each was calculated by adding a set of elements. These sets are identical except for $f_1 a_{11}$. Expressed as a share on a base of 10, $a_{11} = 1$, $f_1 a_{11} = f_1$. Accordingly, we can subtract column 2 from column 1 to obtain

$$x_1 - x_2 = f_1$$

Similarly, x_3 and x_2 consist of identical elements, except for $f_2 a_{22}$ which, on a share basis is equal to $f_2/2$. By similar subtraction of column 3 from column 2, we obtain

$$x_2 - x_3 = \frac{f_2}{2}$$

---

*Formally, we may say that the tie-score vector (X) is the product of the frequency vector (F) and the tie matrix (T): $X = FT$. Although the frequency vector F is intended to be treated as a row vector mathematically, its elements have been arranged in a column at the left of the tie matrix in order to make the computation more intuitively obvious. For the same reason, the elements of the row vector X have been placed underneath the tie matrix.

And in the general case,

$$x_i - x_{i+1} = \frac{f_i}{i}$$

$$f_i = i\,(x_i - x_{i+1})$$

the nonexisting x_9 term at the end being set equal to 0.

Implications of the STEP-SUMM Slope

The SUMM shares received by the decoy brand were generally higher than the corresponding STEP shares. Why is that so? Conceptually, SUMM and STEP should measure the same thing, as is indeed the case when judged by the dynamic correlations between them. Nevertheless we can hardly regard the observed result as an aberration, since it is reflected in the collective structure of thirty-two independent samples of approximately 200 respondents each. This must mean something. In an effort to find out what it means, we turn to Figure D–1. The top panel shows the relationship between STEP and SUMM for the nine brands comprising the competitive frame. For this purpose, all respondents are used, and the thirty-two different variants of the decoy brand are consolidated into a single "brand." The relationship is represented by an almost perfect curve, the central portion of which is a straight line coinciding with the 45-degree diagonal $y = x$, and flattening at both ends to form a gentle S, with STEP shares approximately 2 points higher than SUMM shares for low-share brands and approximately 3 share points higher than SUMM shares for a high-share brand. There is one blatant exception, the decoy brand, which has been circled on the chart for emphasis; it stands alone, aloof, far from the curve, clearly manifesting something special.

Our first instinct is to look for an artifact. We know that the decoy brand is a "new" brand and that the respondents have recently received a free sample of the decoy brand. This must have something to do with it. Whatever the effect, artifactual or meaningful, it must be rooted in the coming together of the decoy brand and SUMM, for it affects STEP and SUMM differentially. It does not interfere with SUMM's ability to measure reactions to the decoy brand, or with its ability to distinguish among different variants of the decoy brand. But it magnifies these effects while preserving their relative standing. This magnification operates selectively for the decoy brand in SUMM. It must therefore be traceable to some difference between STEP and SUMM that manifests itself only or especially for the decoy brand.

Figure D–1
STEP versus Three SUMM Measures
Nine Brands of Spectrum Study
(N = 6,633)

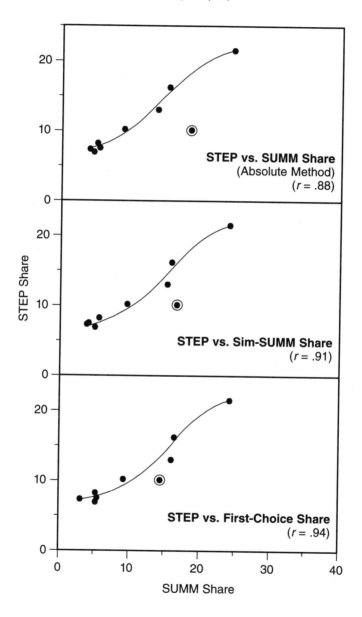

The first and most obvious difference between STEP and SUMM is that whereas STEP shares reflect a single measurement, SUMM shares are derived from the accumulation of many measurements. Does this accumulation result in an exaggeration of scores conveying special benefits on the most recently experienced brand? Fortunately, the Spectrum study included an overall desirability score for each brand, using the same unbounded write-in scale used in the measurement of the desirability of the attributes. We may think of this desirability score as the SUMM score that would have been generated if we had used the most general map of all, one consisting of a single global topic. This score should therefore contain the same information about the brand as the SUMM score and should be conceptually equivalent to it. We may think of it as a stand-in for the SUMM score.

Just as the percentage of respondents who gave a brand a higher SUMM score than they gave any other brand is defined as the SUMM share of the brand, so we define the percentage of respondents who gave a brand a higher overall desirability score than they gave any other brand as the *Simulated-SUMM share* of the brand—or just the *Sim-SUMM share* for short. The relevance of the Sim-SUMM share for the present purpose is that whereas the SUMM share is based on many separate measures, the Sim-SUMM share is based on a single measure. It follows that if this difference is responsible for the nontypical behavior of the decoy brand, the decoy brand should move in line when the relationship between STEP share and Sim-SUMM share is plotted. But it moves only part of the way, as shown in the second panel of Figure D–1. Accordingly, we cannot attribute the observed pattern just to the fact that SUMM employs many measures.

The next hypothesis is that the anomalous behavior of the decoy brand may be traceable to the fundamental difference in the structure of the SUMM and STEP measurements. Whether SUMM measurements are based on the desirability of many topics or on a single topic, they are absolute measurements, which are turned into choice by subsequent analytic conversion. In STEP, the respondent makes direct behavioral choices. Given that the decoy brand has received high exposure among the respondents, perhaps the respondents are more willing to rate the decoy brand favorably on an absolute scale than in a choice that compels them to confront this brand and its competitors simultaneously. Since the respondents were also asked to rank the brands directly, we can examine the relationship between STEP share and first-choice share, both of which are direct measures of choice. This relationship is shown in the third panel of Figure D–1. The decoy brand has moved closer but still generates a higher first-choice share than STEP share, so this does not explain the phenomenon fully either.

It appears that we have eliminated all differences between the measures except one. SUMM share, Sim-SUMM share, and first-choice share, directly or by implication, all require the respondent to make a single choice among the brands, simulating the one next choice the respondent is most likely to make. STEP, on the other hand, requires the respondent to make not one but ten separate choices, simulating the choices the respondent is most likely to make over the course of time. But the decoy brand is distinguished from the other brands in that all of the respondents have had recent exposure to and experience with this brand, creating a resonance of sorts. If we hypothesize that recent exposure to a brand increases the likelihood that people so exposed will choose the brand next, but is not ordinarily sufficient to induce them to forswear the use of other brands permanently, then it is understandable that when they are asked to make *one* choice, the percentage of respondents choosing the decoy brand next (simulated by all the first-choice measures we have examined) will be relatively large, but when requested to make a number of choices, ten in particular, the respondents' prior experiences, habits, and loyalties will assert themselves and will be reflected in the STEP share, which measures their probable choices over the course of time.

The Sensitivity of the Integrated and Absolute Methods

How sensitive are the Integrated and Absolute methods in discriminating among topics? This is central to the practical applications of SUMM, which usually revolve around a search for those topics that hold the greatest promise of share gains for the test brand. The fully-modeled analysis presented in Chapter 19 demonstrated that, taking all topics into account, the Integrated and Absolute methods are about equally effective in predicting changes in STEP shares. But suppose we were interested in comparing the relative potential of different topics, would this hold true?

The relative potential of the different topics for a given brand is usually assessed by a *sensitivity analysis*. Typically, a sensitivity analysis consists of two games per topic for a particular brand, the target brand. For each topic, all respondents are shifted to the attribute that results in the largest share gain for the target brand, and then to the attribute that results in the largest share loss for the brand. This yields two share increments. The positive increment is the maximum gain achievable by the target brand from this topic without help from other topics. The negative increment is the maximum loss the brand could suffer from this topic alone. Since the Spectrum study has twenty-five topics, a full sensitivity analysis consists of fifty games: one positive and one negative one for each of the twenty-five topics.

Once again, we begin by eliminating the decoy brand, which leaves a single SUMM study of 6,633 respondents. One brand is selected to be the target brand, and the sensitivity analysis is run for that brand, using the Integrated and Absolute methods, respectively. Figure E–1 shows the relationship between the increments obtained by the two methods. The share changes range from 23 to -12 for the Integrated method, and from 30 to -11 for the Absolute method. The correlation is .96. The two methods are equivalent.

Figure E–1
Integrated Method versus Absolute Method: Sensitivity Analysis
Twenty-five Top Attributes and Twenty-five Bottom Attributes
Spectrum Study
($N = 6,633$, $r = .96$, $m = 1.03$)

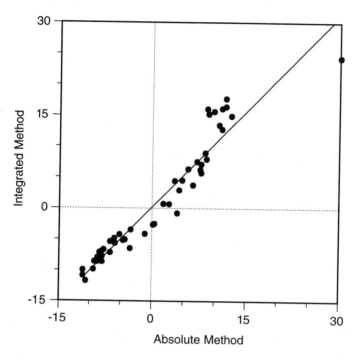

Variants of SUMM

Hierarchical SUMM

A concern that arises as soon as one begins to construct a map is the obvious imbalance in the level of detail with which different subjects are covered. Typically, we are interested in many aspects of the physical product—for example, in the thickness, strength, absorbency, and so on of a paper towel. These physical characteristics occupy a lot of space in the map and require a substantial number of topics for full coverage. As a result, we may construct a map of twenty-five topics, one of which deals with price and twenty-four with various physical characteristics of the product. We may also deliberately give short shrift to characteristics we know to be important in order to concentrate more heavily, or even exclusively, on some particular aspect of the product that happens to be of special interest, for example, its styling. The desire to compensate for these tendencies gives rise to the idea of a hierarchically structured map, appropriately implemented through a hierarchically structured measurement system. Thus, hierarchical SUMM is undertaken either because we are afraid that we may, by inadvertence, create some major imbalance in the construction of the map or because we intend, in full knowledge and with malice aforethought, to create just such an imbalance in pursuit of some special purpose.

Typically, a hierarchical SUMM first breaks choice into a few major components, one or more of which is then broken further into specific topics. In theory, this process can continue through many levels. In practice, we have kept the number of levels to a minimum, both for conceptual and mechanical reasons. Whatever the ultimate structure, we always start at the most general level, the level of the primary topics: product, branding, price, and familiarity. Since the only purpose of the primary topics in this method is to allow a proper reweighting of the specific topics, it is sufficient to measure the desirability contributions of the primary topics directly. Specifically, we ask the respondent to consider the characteristics of the product, the reputation of the brand, the price, and her familiarity with the brand, and to use the unbounded write-in scale to write L's and D's to tell us how much she likes or dislikes each of these aspects of Brand A, Brand B, and so on. This measurement is analogous to the Absolute method. But instead of measuring desirability and beliefs separately, the desirability contribution of each primary topic to each brand is measured in a single step. Appropriately, the method is called the *Topic Contribution method*. Because this measurement takes very little space, it can when appropriate be incorporated into a STEP booklet, which is then called *enhanced STEP*.

The SUMM scores of the brands are defined as the average of the primary topic contributions. Since these topics are few in number and close to what we judge to be the axiomatic structure of the choice process, we assume that the distortions in this first level of measurement are minimal and that the primary topics will yield good approximations of first-choice, or certainly approximations as good as or better than any we are likely to come up with. The next tier, which is usually also the final tier, serves as the elaboration, explanation, or partition of the primary topics. The topics comprising this level are called the *specific topics*. Although the specific topics do not make any contribution to the SUMM score until games are run, they occupy the bulk of the space in the questionnaire and ultimately provide the useful detail for which the study was undertaken.

Imagine a two-tier hierarchical SUMM that uses four primary topics (measured with the single phrases specified in Chapter 17) and fifteen specific product topics (measured in the standard way). Because we are relying on the primary topics to provide the proper relationship between the relative contributions of product and price, we accept the scores obtained from the primary topic measurements at face value. Let the desirability contribution to Brand i of the primary product topic be P_i. Let the contribution to Brand i of some particular specific product topic j be S_{ij}. And let the average of the contributions to Brand i of all the specific product topics be S_i. The quantities P_i and S_i are measures of the same thing—the desirability contribution of Brand i's product component—but they will not in general be numerically equal. First, we do not expect separate measurements of even the same variable to be exactly equal. Second, the primary topic measurement is a summary measure, whereas the specific topics measurement is an average of many specific topics. The desirabilities of the specific topics must therefore be adjusted to add to the appropriate primary topic, so that games using the specific topics will make commensurate contributions to the SUMM scores. Let P and S be the averages of the primary topic contributions and specific topic contributions for all brands:

$$P = \frac{1}{b} \sum_i P_i$$

$$S = \frac{1}{bt} \sum_i \sum_j S_{ij}$$

where t is the number of specific product topics and b is the number of brands. The necessary adjustment can then be accomplished by multiplying every desirability value of every specific product topic by the ratio P/S, leaving the desirabilities of the primary topics, and therefore the SUMM scores, unchanged. The consequences are:

1. The relative desirabilities of all attributes of all specific product topics are preserved, since all of them have been multiplied by the same constant.
2. The SUMM scores of the various brands are preserved at the values assigned to them by the primary topics.
3. The desirability contributions of the specific product topics are scaled properly, since the average of all of them for all brands is exactly equal to the average SUMM score of all brands.

Topic-SUMM

In the early hierarchical studies, before the Topic Contribution method was developed, desirability and beliefs of the primary topics were measured separately. The desirability of the primary topics was measured by asking the respondents to allocate stickers to indicate how much they wanted each of the following:

- A product with physical characteristics that are just right for me.
- A brand that has a reputation that suits me.
- A price that suits my needs.
- A brand I know well and feel comfortable with.

Beliefs were measured by asking the respondents how "true" (0–100%) each of these statements was for each brand. This measurement system was called *Topic-SUMM* because it used a single phrase to represent the entire topic. In this measuring system, the SUMM score of a brand ranges from 100, when the respondent gives the brand maximum credit (100% true) for all topics, to 0, when the respondent gives the brand minimum credit (0% true) for all topics.

I developed Topic-SUMM for use in hierarchical SUMM, and abandoned it later in favor of the Topic Contribution method. By that time, however, Topic-SUMM had acquired a life of its own. Hardly had it been introduced, when the idea arose to use it not merely as a calibrator but as a tool in its own right. In this incarnation, Topic-SUMM no longer serves as a refinement of SUMM but as a shortcut that comes into demand as a means of saving money, a purpose it serves well in a few instances, but which is often illusory because the method is predicated on some stringent assumptions that must be honored scrupulously if the analysis is to remain meaningful.

Topic-SUMM uses no separately defined attributes. Each topic is represented by a single phrase. And that gives rise to a problem. The standard *Attribute-SUMM,* in which each topic is defined by several mutually exclusive attributes, does not require a single continuum, or any continuum at all. A topic can be defined by coalescing two dimensions, for example:

- It is wide and high.
- It is wide and low.
- It is narrow and high.
- It is narrow and low.

It can also be defined by mutually exclusive attributes that do not constitute a continuum at all, for example:

- It is red.
- It is blue.
- It is yellow.

And it can cover objective as well as subjective descriptions of a brand.

In Topic-SUMM these options must be sacrificed. Because each topic is represented by a single phrase, the topic must represent a continuous variable. The single phrase that defines the topic must represent the point of maximum desirability on the continuum. All other points on the continuum must, by definition, represent decreasing levels of desirability for every respondent. Topics cannot therefore be purely objective. For example, in studying ice cream, the phrase, "It is very sweet," cannot be used to define a topic. For even if many respondents like very sweet ice cream, this will not necessarily represent the level of maximum desirability for all respondents. This means that Topic-SUMM's ability to investigate objective dimensions is limited. Only if the objective core of these dimensions is excised by value language does the topic become usable. Thus, the topics cannot read, "It is very sweet" or "It is very soft," but could read, "It has the sweetness I like most" or "It has the softness I like most."

A major tendency when flirting with Topic-SUMM is to acknowledge its limitations in words while ignoring them in fact, saying: "I understand that Topic-SUMM will not tell me whether I should make my brand sweeter or not, softer or not, but it can tell me which of these dimensions is more important. If I find greater potential gains from improvements of sweetness than from improvements of softness, I will know that I need to concentrate on this dimension even if I won't know precisely how to change it. It will therefore at least point me in the right direction."

This is a trap. Topic-SUMM will not allow even this minimal conclusion. To be sure it may tell us that sweetness is "important." But it will not tell us what level of sweetness the respondents had in mind, nor will it alert us to the possibility that though sweetness may appear to be "important," it may be totally impossible to achieve any gains by changing sweetness because such changes could lose as many potential customers as they would gain. This does not mean that Topic-SUMM is totally useless. It has some valid applications, provided the following requirements are met rigorously:

1. Each topic must be a one-dimensional continuum.
2. Desirability must decrease in the same direction all along the continuum for 100% of the respondents.

The following topics, for example, could be used in a Topic-SUMM for a food product:

- It is very convenient.
- It is very healthy.
- It tastes very good.

Presumably all respondents would want as much of each of these attributes as they could get, and it might be useful to find out which of these topics has the largest potential. In most practical situations, however, strict adherence to these rules places such severe limitations on the end user that there is considerable pressure to relax the requirements. This leads either to compromising the quality of the conclusions or to a search for a less restrictive measurement system.

Bipolar-SUMM

The logical next step is to ask whether there is a way to secure the benefits of Topic-SUMM without the onerous requirement that desirability be uniformly monotonic for all respondents, a requirement that automatically eliminates almost all objective dimensions. The middle ground is achieved by a measurement system called *Bipolar-SUMM*. As the name implies, each topic is defined by two poles of a single dimension, such as:

Very big	Not big
Very sweet	Not sweet
Very attractive	Not attractive

In order to capture different shapes of the desirability curve, it is desirable to insert an intermediate point between these poles. This gives rise to a search for appropriate language. What lies between "Very strong" and "Not strong"? How do we keep that intermediate point comparable for different topics? And what specific words will be well understood by the respondents? In the end we concluded, and confirmed in pretests, that the simplest way is the best. We sidestepped the issue altogether and used the vague phrase "in between" for all topics.

Accordingly, Bipolar-SUMM measures desirability for three attributes per topic:

- Very big
- In between
- Not big

- Very sweet
- In between
- Not sweet

- etc.

For each of these attributes, the respondent uses the unbounded write-in scale, writing L's and D's to indicate how much she likes or dislikes the attribute. Bipolar-SUMM's measurement of the desirability of the attributes is identical to that employed in a standard Attribute-SUMM except that the map is simpler, each topic consisting of three attributes that are fully defined by a single adjective or phrase. In this respect, Bipolar-SUMM is closer to Topic-SUMM than to Attribute-SUMM. Unlike Topic-SUMM, however, Bipolar-SUMM does not require an assumption of monotonic desirability and can be used for all kinds of dimensions, including objective ones, provided they are continuous. In particular, it allows the respondents to register different patterns of desirability, as illustrated in the hypothetical examples in Table F–1.

Beliefs about the brands are collected by means of the eleven-point scale illustrated in Figure F–1. For each brand, the respondent checks the

Table F–1
Hypothetical Desirability Patterns

Desirability Pattern	Not Sweet	In Between	Very Sweet
Increasing monotonically	0	3	6
	3	6	6
	3	3	6
Inverted V-shaped	3	6	3
	0	6	4
	4	6	0
Flat	3	3	3
U-shaped	6	0	6
	4	2	6
	6	2	4
Decreasing monotonically	6	3	0
	6	6	3
	6	3	3

one box she believes describes the brand best. The three attributes (Very sweet, In between, Not sweet) for which desirability ratings are explicitly obtained are analytically expanded into eleven attributes by linearly interpolating desirability levels between "Very sweet" and "In between," and between "In between" and "Not sweet." This interpolation certainly involves approximation, but the precision of this type of measurement is limited anyhow, so we don't lose much, while we gain the potential discriminating power afforded by the full eleven gradations.

For analytic purposes, Bipolar-SUMM is a full-fledged Attribute-SUMM and is interpreted and used precisely the same way. Games are played; shares are estimated; diagnostics are constructed. Apart from the fact that some of the desirability scores that would have been collected

Figure F–1
Belief Measurement in Bipolar-SUMM

Table F–2
Comparison of Capabilities of Three Types of SUMM

Type of Topic	Attribute SUMM	Bipolar SUMM	Topic SUMM
One-dimensional topics	x	x	x
Continuous variables	x	x	x
Subjective topics	x	x	x
Objective topics	x	x	
Multidimensional topics	x		
Unordered attributes	x		

empirically in an Attribute-SUMM are computed by interpolation in Bipolar-SUMM, the computer does not know whether it is processing an Attribute-SUMM or a Bipolar-SUMM. The principal difference between the two is in the construction of the map. In exchange for the elegance and simplicity of Bipolar-SUMM, we accept the limitation that each topic must consist of a single continuous variable. If this requirement can be tolerated, Bipolar-SUMM offers an excellent middle ground between the simplicity of Topic-SUMM, which is so confining that it is useful in only the rarest of applications, and the greater complexity and cost of Attribute-SUMM. Table F–2 summarizes the capabilities and limitations of the three measurement systems. The Spectrum study, incidentally, was a combination of Attribute-SUMM and Bipolar-SUMM.

Sim-SUMM

So far, our discussion of SUMM has dealt exclusively with what may be called well-defined product categories, categories like airlines, personal computers, paper towels, and so on. The brands of these categories differ in the degree to which they possess various characteristics, but they generally share a single set of topics and attributes. Not all directly substitutable options, however, lend themselves to this treatment. Suppose we want to study how people spend an evening. They have the choice of going to an opera or to a basketball game. How shall we construct a map for this "product category"? We might be tempted to limit ourselves to topics that are applicable to both of these options, for example: The event starts at 7:00 P.M., 7:30 P.M., 8:00 P.M. The travel time is fifteen minutes, half an hour, three-quarters of an hour. And so on. These topics, however, will be too general for most practical purposes. The decision whether to go to the opera or to the basketball game may depend on some topics that apply only to operas, such as whether it is a Verdi or Puccini opera, and on some topics that apply only to basketball games, such as whether Michael Jordan is playing. This leads to an entirely different view of the process. We have been thinking of topics and attributes as being defined for "product categories." When the various brands of a product category happen to be sufficiently similar, this is indeed so. Otherwise, a separate set of topics and attributes is necessary for each brand. In the general case, therefore, topics and attributes are defined for brands, not for product categories.

At first glance, this seems to give rise to insurmountable problems. Life was difficult enough when we needed to construct only one set of topics and attributes for the entire product category. How can we possibly hope to implement a test using different topics and attributes for each brand? Fortunately, there is a simple solution. It involves focusing on one "test brand," the brand in whose behalf the model is constructed, and to simulate the SUMM scores for the remaining brands. Provided it is not necessary to run SUMM games for these remaining brands, their SUMM scores serve only as a yardstick, defining the desirability level that needs to be exceeded to turn a respondent into a chooser. Accordingly, it should be possible to use a single overall measure of the desirability of a brand as a stand-in for the SUMM score of the brand. Ideally, this overall measurement should be equal to, or roughly equivalent to, or at least well correlated with, the SUMM score, except, of course, that the single measure is likely to be less stable and more afflicted by measurement error, while the SUMM score is likely to be more subject to distortions due to shortcomings of the map.

Since the SUMM score is composed of an aggregation of desirability contributions, each measured by means of the unbounded write-in scale, the most consistent approach is to use the same scale to measure how much the respondent likes or dislikes the brand in its entirety, "all things considered." This generates the single overall score that has been called the *brand desirability*. When this score serves as a substitute for the SUMM score, it is called the *Sim-SUMM score* (Simulated SUMM score) to keep its function clearly in mind. Thus, a Sim-SUMM score is nothing but an overall brand desirability score used as a stand-in for a SUMM score.

We collect Sim-SUMM scores for all brands in the competitive frame, including the test brand. But we construct topics and attributes only for the test brand, and we collect beliefs about these attributes only for the test brand. Thus *all* brands are represented by their Sim-SUMM scores. In addition, the test brand is also represented by its SUMM score. If there are n topics, this SUMM score consists of the average of n measurements, while the Sim-SUMM score consists of a single measurement. One way of looking at this is to say that, in the case of n topics, we have in effect asked the respondent to rate how she feels about *n* self-weighted aspects of the test brand. If the model is good, we expect the average of these *n* ratings to be equal to, or at any rate close to, the single overall rating of the brand, namely its Sim-SUMM score.

How good is the assumption on which the substitution of the SUMM score for the Sim-SUMM score is based? To begin with, we want to make sure that the two are highly correlated and that they discriminate comparably among brands. For this purpose, we need a study in which both SUMM scores and Sim-SUMM scores are available. This is not usually the case. Regular SUMM studies don't ordinarily provide for the collection of Sim-SUMM scores, and Sim-SUMM studies, by definition, collect SUMM scores for only a single brand. The Spectrum study, however, has both. Figure F–2 shows the relationship between the average SUMM score and the average Sim-SUMM score for the nine brands of that study. The Sim-SUMM scores are systematically higher than the SUMM scores, as reflected in the slope of the line, but the correlation is .99, indicating that, in the aggregate at least, the two do indeed measure the same thing.

Figure F–2
Average Sim-SUMM Score versus Average SUMM Score
for Nine Brands of Spectrum Study
($N = 6,633, r = .991$)

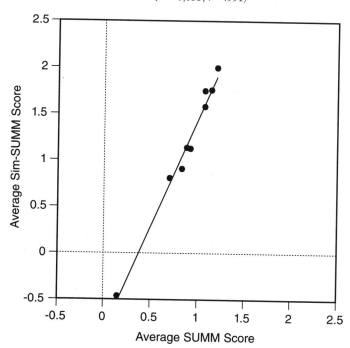

Although this relationship between the SUMM and Sim-SUMM scores is good enough to justify using the Sim-SUMM scores as a reasonable stand-in for the unavailable SUMM scores, the question arises whether we can do better. Can we adjust the attribute desirabilities to yield a SUMM score for the test brand that will not merely be approximately the same as, or highly correlated with, the test brand's Sim-SUMM score but will be literally equal to it? SUMM scores that are computed this way are called *K-SUMM scores*.

Figure F–3
Percent Distribution of Sim-SUMM Minus SUMM or K-SUMM Score
Spectrum Study
(N = 6,633)

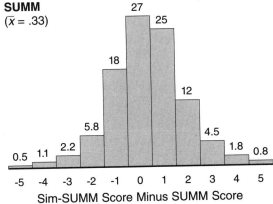

Sim-SUMM Score Minus SUMM Score

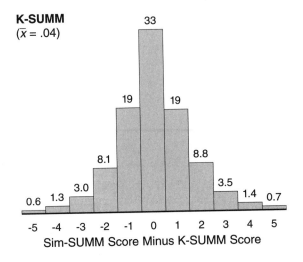

Sim-SUMM Score Minus K-SUMM Score

We begin by looking at the relationship between the SUMM scores and the Sim-SUMM scores in the Spectrum study on an individual basis. We certainly don't expect the SUMM scores and the Sim-SUMM scores to be literally the same, first because we have seen that there is a general tendency for the Sim-SUMM scores to be higher, and second because even if that tendency were corrected, for example by applying a constant multiplier to each SUMM score, we would still be left with the inevitable measurement error in each of the two measurements, which can compound when the two are compared on a score-by-score basis. It is nevertheless instructive to examine the data from that perspective. The top panel of Figure F–3 shows the percent distribution of the differences between the Sim-SUMM scores and the SUMM scores, consolidated for all respondents and all brands. The chart shows that quite apart from the fact that the Sim-SUMM scores are systematically higher, which we know already, around 70% of all the score differences are 0±1.5. We now proceed to adjust the SUMM scores.

Sampling error aside, what does it really mean for the Sim-SUMM score (T) of the test brand to be larger than the corresponding SUMM score (S)? In the general case, the SUMM score is defined as the sum of the desirability contributions of all attributes. Some of these contributions are positive, some negative. One possible way of accounting for the difference between the SUMM score and the Sim-SUMM score is to assume that if the Sim-SUMM score is larger, it means that the desirability contributions of the positive attributes are too small. They therefore need to be increased, while the contributions of the negative attributes need to be decreased. If the SUMM score happens to be larger, the opposite is the case.

Let t be the total number of topics. Let A be the sum of all the positive contributions (a_i) for the test brand, and let B be the sum of all the negative contributions (b_i) for the test brand. Let K be the unknown constant by which the positive contributions need to be enlarged and the negative contributions need to be reduced, or vice versa. If we multiply all positive contributions by K, which will enlarge them (provided K is larger than 1), and if we divide all negative contributions by K, which will reduce them (provided K is larger than 1), we can set the resulting new SUMM score (S) for the test brand equal to the Sim-SUMM score (T) of the test brand. Expressed algebraically, this is:

$$S = AK + \frac{B}{K} = T$$

Solving for K, we obtain

$$AK^2 - TK + B = 0$$

$$K = \frac{T + \sqrt{T^2 - 4AB}}{2A}$$

$$K = \frac{T + \sqrt{T^2 - 4(\Sigma a_i)(\Sigma b_i)}}{2\Sigma a_i}$$

We can now multiply the desirabilities of all topics that made a positive contribution to the SUMM score of the test brand by K, and divide the desirabilities of all topics that made a negative contribution by K. When that is done and we compute the new SUMM score of the test brand, based on the new desirabilities, this score (the calibrated SUMM score, or the *K-SUMM score* for short) will be exactly equal to the Sim-SUMM score of the test brand. We have therefore accomplished several things. First, all comparisons among the brands have been put on the same basis: They are all based on the Sim-SUMM score. All games can be run in the same units, in the sense that the base case adds exactly to the Sim-SUMM score. All relationships among the topics that contributed positively have been maintained unchanged because they were all multiplied by the same constant (K), and all relationships among the topics that contributed negatively have been maintained because they were all multiplied by the same constant ($1/K$). The only thing that has been changed is the relative contribution of the positives and the negatives. These have been modified to add to the Sim-SUMM score.

The adjustment yields a new set of calibrated SUMM scores, the K-SUMM scores. The lower panel of Figure F–3 shows the percent distribution of the differences between the Sim-SUMM score and the K-SUMM score. The differences do not favor either SUMM or Sim-SUMM anymore. The mean of the distribution is substantially zero (.04), indicating that the bias is gone, and the distribution of differences is slightly more concentrated. This benefit is small but translates into a closer correspondence between Sim-SUMM and SUMM games.

To evaluate the K-SUMM adjustment, we ask whether games run after the adjustment are more likely to give the right answer than corresponding games before the adjustment. Ordinarily, we have no way of checking this. But we can check it in this case, because of the redundant luxury of having both SUMM scores and Sim-SUMM scores for all brands in the Spectrum study. This allows us to rephrase the question as follows. Given the fact that the K adjustment (based on a single test brand) brought the SUMM score of that brand in line with its Sim-SUMM score—in fact made the scores equal—how did that adjustment affect the other brands? More important, what impact, if any, did the adjustment have on the outcome of games? In

Figure F–4
Sim-SUMM versus SUMM Game Results
Making Test Brand Like Another Existing Brand, Spectrum Study
(*N* = 6,633)

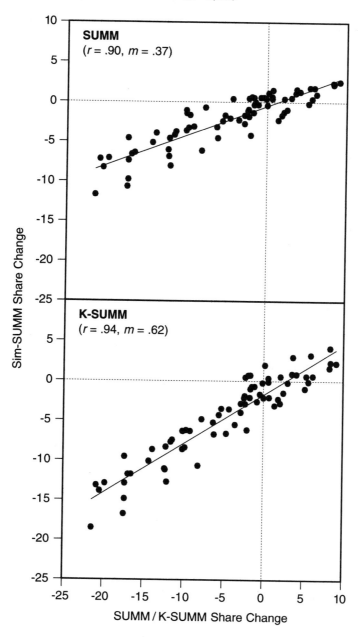

other words, was the adjustment a genuine improvement, or was it illusory?

To answer this question, we designate one brand as the test brand. We run a SUMM game, making the test brand's beliefs identical to those of one of the other brands (the target brand). We add the resulting increment to the Sim-SUMM score of the test brand, compute an estimated share of the target brand, and compare it to the actual Sim-SUMM share of the target brand. Since the Spectrum study has nine brands, 9 x 8 = 72 such comparisons are possible.

The upper panel of Figure F–4 shows the results of seventy-two games, using the unadjusted SUMM scores, in predicting the observed Sim-SUMM shares. The correlation is .90, indicating that the games do quite well, though they generate systematic overestimates of the corresponding Sim-SUMM share differences, as reflected in the slope. The lower panel of Figure F–4 shows the same relationship when the adjusted (K-SUMM) scores are used. The K-SUMM adjustment, derived from the data for the test brand only, has brought about a closer match between the SUMM and Sim-SUMM shares of *all* brands, as reflected in the higher slope (.62 as compared to .37) and in the slightly higher correlation (.94). Thus the K-calibration is not merely illusory, but has enabled us to use the data of one brand to improve the correspondence between the SUMM shares and the Sim-SUMM shares of all brands.

The Game-Simulator

The controlled experiment, for example STEP, is the ultimate gold standard for diagnostic systems. It can tell us definitively which aspect of a stimulus is producing which effect. But when this ultimate diagnosis is too cumbersome or too costly, the next best thing is a model like SUMM that estimates the outcomes of experiments by simulation. From this perspective, every request for diagnostic help should be translatable into an appropriate set of SUMM games, and no diagnostic devices that are not conceptually equivalent to SUMM games should be either possible or necessary. This is approximately but not completely true. In practice, some problems are either sufficiently large in scope or sufficiently unique in application to require special analytic techniques. These techniques use the same underlying assumptions, the same theory, and the same database as SUMM. They are not alternatives to SUMM but expansions of its analytic power.

Suppose a marketer has understood and accepted the theory behind SUMM, has authorized a SUMM study, and is ready to start using it. She appreciates that her connection to the database is through SUMM games, and she accepts the discipline this implies. She may, however, have undertaken the inquiry out of a vague need for help in planning marketing strategy, and she may now say to the researcher, "You have convinced me that I should put all my questions into the form of SUMM games, and I am willing to do this, but I don't know where to begin. I am concerned about missing opportunities, about asking the wrong questions. Perhaps there are games I ought to run that I have not thought of. What can you do to put me on the right track, so I don't overlook something important the data can teach me?" One way, of course, is to run all possible games, or a very large number. But the potential number of games is too large to make this practical, even for the powerful computers at our disposal. So we must look for a way of honoring this request short of brute force. The game-simulator is such a way.

The game-simulator attacks the problem head on. It produces an output that in effect prints out a test brand's share gain or loss produced by every possible game of up to some specified dimensionality (number of topics shifted simultaneously), and it does so in a fairly compact format in a reasonable amount of space. At first glance this promise may sound preposterous. Suppose a study has twenty-five topics and that each of these topics has four attributes. This means that each topic can contribute twelve different belief shifts. Suppose further that we want to list the outcome of all possible eight-dimensional games, that is, of games that consist of eight shifts, one in each of eight topics selected from the twenty-five topics. How many different games does that entail? To begin with, we must select eight topics from the twenty-five. The number of ways this can be done is $25!/(8!\ 17!) = 1,081,575$. But each of these topics can contribute twelve different shifts. Accordingly the total number is $12^{1,081,575}$, which is a pretty large number even as large numbers go.

I have said that we propose to print the game results of all of these games on just a few pages. That is right, or almost right, but you'll have to let me do it my way. In the first place, the results will not be the actual mathematical results that would have been obtained if the games had been run. They will be estimates of these results, as reflected in the name *game-simulator*. A good way to think of it is that just as SUMM is a psychological model of a living population, so the game-simulator is a mathematical model of the psychological model. To be sure, that makes it one step further removed from reality. One might say that it offers an approximation of an approximation. But this is still a good deal. In accepting the approximation, we broaden the range of what we can examine by many orders of magnitude. So even a fairly weak approximation that can cover the entire range of options is a useful starting point. The game-simulator is also subject to instant verification. All we have to do when we spot a promising strategy in the game-simulator is run the relevant game or group of games to check to what extent the game-simulator has pointed in the right direction.

The second limitation is even more modest. Given the almost infinite number of games we propose to cover, we obviously cannot enumerate them in a literal list. But we can do something almost as good, perhaps even better for practical purposes: We can create a simple look-up table from which the relevant estimates can be obtained at a glance or by just adding a few numbers.

We begin by examining the game-simulator's output table. The rows of the table represent all possible one-dimensional shifts arranged by topic. Table F–3 shows two topics from an actual study. Each of these topics has three attributes. We can shift the respondents who have checked Attribute 1 into Attributes 2 or 3. Similarly, we can shift the respondents who have

Table F–3
SUMM Game-Simulator, Net Gains
Excerpt from Output Table

| | Potential Choosers per 1000 for Games of Dimensionality | | | | | | | |
	1	2	3	4	5	6	7	8
Topic 1								
1								
1 – 2	-6	-5	-9	-7	-9	-8	-7	-6
1 – 3	-19	-19	-13	-13	-17	-16	-14	-12
2								
2 – 1	23	21	24	26	23*	20	21*	20*
2 - 3	-14	-13	-21	-18	-16	-17	-17	-17
3								
3 – 1	34	28	27	25	21	22*	20	19
3 - 2	11	23	18	18	16	15	13	13
Topic 2								
1								
1 – 2	-5	-6	-4	-4	-3	-3	-3	-3
1 – 3	-12	-15	-13	-12	-12	-10	-11	-9
2								
2 – 1	16	10	10	11	10	10	10	9
2 – 3	-15	-13	-11	-12	-12	-13	-13	-11
3								
3 – 1	46	43	37	37*	33*	31*	31*	29*
3 – 2	10	27	23	21	19	18	19	18

checked Attribute 2 into Attributes 1 or 3. In general, if a topic has n attributes, the total number of different shifts possible in that topic is $n(n - 1)$. In this case, the total number of possible shifts is 3 x 2 = 6. And though the number of possible shifts certainly increases substantially as the number of attributes per topic becomes larger, the order of magnitude of these shifts is usually quite manageable. For example, if a study happens to have a total of twenty-five topics—three with eight attributes, six with six attributes, ten with four attributes, and ten with three attributes—the total number of lines required to list all possible one-dimensional shifts will be 3 (8 x 7) + 6 (6 x 5) + 10 (4 x 3) + 10 (3 x 2) = 528, a number that can be accommodated on a ten-page output. I am mentioning this only to indicate that, considering the assignment, the size of the table is modest.

The table applies to a specific brand, known as the target brand. The entries of the table are choosers per 1,000. The columns of the table are headed 1 to 8. The columns represent the dimensionality of the game. The numbers in column 1 show the share gain for the target brand for every possible one-dimensional shift. In other words, if the number in the line Topic 1, 2–1, in column 1 is 23, this means that if all respondents who currently believe that Attribute 2 of Topic 1 best describes the target brand were shifted to Attribute 1 of Topic 1, the target brand's share would increase by 23 per 1,000 or by 2.3 percentage points. The numbers in column 1 are not modeled but are the exact changes obtained when the specified game is run. Thus column 1 offers no more than a systematic census of the outcome of all one-dimensional games. That is not so for the other columns of the table. Those columns don't provide actual game results, only more or less accurate estimates of what the games might yield if they were run.

Column 2 provides estimates of all possible two-dimensional games, that is, games defined by making simultaneous shifts in two different topics. Suppose we want to estimate the result of shifting respondents from Attribute 3 to Attribute 1 of Topic 1 *and* from Attribute 2 to Attribute 3 of Topic 2. We look for the table entries in those two lines in column 2. These are 28 and -13, respectively. Adding the two numbers gives an estimate of the outcome of this particular two-dimensional game, 15 per 1,000 or 1.5%. Results of games of higher dimensionality are estimated analogously. Choose any five entries in column 5, and add them to obtain an estimate of the game result. In general, choose any n entries in column n and add them. The "optimal" shifts, that is, the n largest shifts in column n, have been asterisked for easy reference, though results that represent mathematical optima may turn out to be inconsistent, or simply impossible to achieve. Thus the game-simulator should be thought of as a tool for identifying sensible strategies rather than as a blind mechanical guide.

The game-simulator is constructed as follows. Consider one respondent who happens to be a chooser of some brand C, other than the target brand. The SUMM scores of target brand T and of the chosen brand C are D_T and D_C, respectively. Now consider row r of the game-simulator matrix. This row represents a shift from some attribute, say, Attribute i, to some other attribute, say, Attribute j of the same topic. The desirability contribution of Attribute i is d_i, and the desirability contribution of Attribute j is d_j. Accordingly, the change in desirability of the target brand produced by shifting the respondent's belief from Attribute i to Attribute j is $d_r = d_j - d_i$.

The difference in SUMM score between the chosen brand and the target brand is $D = D_C - D_T$. To capture the respondent we must produce a shift large enough to wipe out this advantage of the chosen brand, namely, a shift for which $d_r > D$. For any row for which $d_r > D$, we enter a "1" in column 1, indicating that this shift alone is sufficient to capture the respondent. By the same rule, we enter 1/3 into column 3 of the matrix for each row for which $d_r > D/3$. In general, the entry (e_{rk}) for row r of column k is given by this rule:

$$\text{If } d_r > \frac{D}{k} \text{ then } e_{rk} = \frac{1}{k} \text{, otherwise } e_{rk} = 0.$$

The entire matrix is calculated, one respondent at a time, and divided through by the total number of respondents to express the final output in permil terms, that is, number of respondents per thousand potentially captured by the target brand.

The above explanation has dealt with gains only. To consider losses, we examine all respondents who are currently choosers of the target brand relative to its principal competitor, that is, the competitor whose SUMM score is closest to the target brand. The entire analysis is repeated, generating a game-simulator for losses of current choosers. The two game-simulators can be kept separate or can be superimposed to generate a single net estimate, though that consolidation may obscure what is going on.

It is easy enough to focus on the assumptions and approximations that have gone into the game-simulator algorithm and on the many ways in which it could, indeed should, break down. But such conceptual reservations are beside the point. We knew before we started that we were constructing a model that aspired to provide useful approximations at best. Accordingly, we can retreat to the position that the proof of the pudding is in the eating. We can examine empirical cases and assess how well or poorly the simulator predicts the outcome of games, and we can validate and re-validate the simulator for each new database. If it works well, if it provides useful approximations, we can use it. If it does not, we can discard it—and without unreasonable costs in time or money.

Figure F–5
Game Increments versus Game-Simulator Increments
for Each of Nine Target Brands of Spectrum Study
(*N* = 6,633)

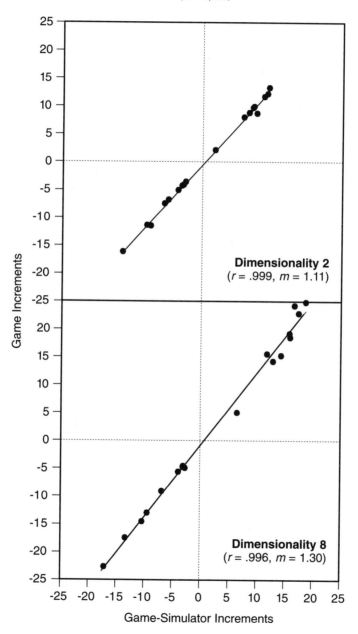

Let us consider such a test for the Spectrum study. We can treat each of the study's nine brands in turn as the target brand. This produces nine different game-simulators. For each target brand, we identify the two-dimensional game that produces the largest positive increment. We also identify the two-dimensional game that produces the largest negative increment, that is, the largest loss for the target brand. This defines two games per brand, or eighteen two-dimensional games for the nine brands of the study. We repeat the process for eight-dimensional games. I have chosen Dimensionality 8 because this is the largest dimensionality that is ordinarily printed out when the game-simulator is run. Figure F–5 shows plots of the increments produced by the game-simulator versus the corresponding increments produced when the games defined by these shifts are actually run. The two-dimensional case has a correlation of 1 (.999) and a slope of 1.1. The eight-dimensional case is a hairsbreadth weaker, with a correlation of .996 and a slope of 1.30. Thus the game-simulator predicts almost perfectly when we examine the most extreme games. It will generally contain more error for more realistic, intermediate games, but it can provide quick answers to complex problems by serving as a look-up table. That, of course, is exactly what it was designed to do.

You might be tempted to say, "The relationship is good enough. I will just use the game-simulator itself." This would be a mistake. The simulator provides only an estimate of the SUMM game, and it is no trouble to run the actual games once we know which ones to run. Properly used, the game-simulator serves as a first screen. It identifies the games that should be run. The games themselves can then be thought of as the second screen. They identify the most promising strategic options. These can finally be tested in STEP to obtain definitive behavioral measures of effects.

Competitive Frame Reduction

I first confronted the need to remove one or more brands from the competitive frame in STEP in connection with testing a reformulation of an established brand. In order to avoid confusion between the standard product and the new product, the respondent received the new formulation of Brand A, labeled "New Brand A," followed by a STEP booklet that contained two pages for the brand—a page for the standard brand and a page for the new brand. Since the purpose of the test was not to evaluate a line extension in which the standard and the new product would coexist in the market but the probable effect of replacing the standard product with the new product, the share of the standard brand had to be removed analytically. This led to the development of enhanced STEP.

In enhanced STEP the three sensitizing questions on the pages of the STEP booklet are replaced with three or four primary-topic questions (see "Topic Contribution Method" in Appendix F). These questions yield a primitive primary SUMM score for each brand. Tie scoring is used to reconcile and synthesize the data. Replacing the STEP scores with the tie scores does not distort the STEP scores, but once tie-score share has become the criterion, we can run a SUMM game to eliminate standard Brand A and determine what share the test brand would receive by itself. Tie-SUMM, of course, is not the only way in which such a reallocation can be made. The following line-extension study enables us to compare three possible ways of making the reallocation.

The study had a control group, representing the current market, and a test group, which received a booklet containing two additional line-extension brands. If we set the shares of these two line-extension brands to zero and reallocate them analytically, each of the remaining brands receives some increment. These increments can then be compared to the corresponding empirical increments (the control group shares minus the test group shares). We must keep in mind, however, that the numbers are small. The sum of all the increments is only 12%. Accordingly, chance errors are commensurately large.

Figure G–1
Empirical versus Analytical Increments for
Reallocation of Two PC Line-Extension Brands
(N = 1,574)

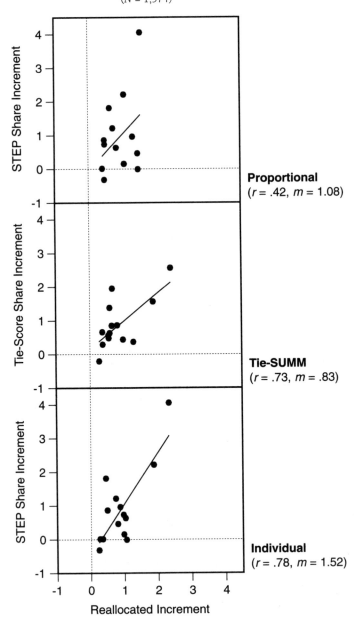

The top panel of Figure G–1 shows a plot of the empirical STEP share increments versus the increments obtained when the shares are simply reallocated proportionately. The correlation is low (.46). As expected, simple proportional reallocation does not do a very good job. We next use a SUMM game with tie scoring to reallocate. The middle panel of Figure G–1 shows the result of this reallocation. The correlation is higher (.73). The tie-scored SUMM game has come closer to predicting the empirically observed increments. At first, I believed that the separate SUMM questions were essential. But I discovered later that a shortcut was almost as good. We can reallocate the STEP stickers proportionately on a respondent-by-respondent basis. This type of reallocation is called individual reallocation. The bottom panel of Figure G–1 shows the relationship between the empirical increments and the individual reallocation increments. Individual reallocation does about as well as Tie-SUMM. Its correlation is marginally higher, but Tie-SUMM's slope is closer to 1. By treating the STEP data as they would have been treated in SUMM, namely one respondent at a time, we have in effect captured the spirit of SUMM analytically without collecting data beyond the STEP stickers themselves. The enhanced STEP may, however, be needed anyhow, notably for hierarchical SUMM and/or Sim-SUMM, discussed in Appendix F.

Share and Countershare Partition

Table H–1 illustrates the logic of Share Partition, applied to a single respondent. The rows of the table represent the attributes, arranged in order from Topic 1, Attribute 1 to the last attribute of the last topic. The columns of the table represent the brands of the competitive frame, arranged in rank order of their SUMM scores, from the highest SUMM score to the lowest SUMM score. In the example, the target brand T (the brand for which the Share Partition is performed) has the third highest SUMM score and is therefore in the third column. The body of the table contains the desirability contributions of the various attributes. One desirability contribution is shown for each topic and each brand in the row corresponding to the attribute the respondent believes best describes the brand. All blank cells have contributions of 0.

The SUMM score of each brand, which by definition is the sum of the desirability contributions for the brand, is shown below. The target brand has a SUMM score of 55. Underneath the SUMM scores are the STEP scores for the brands. Given these scores (3 2 4 0 1 0), we can see by inspection that this respondent is a Tie-Type 3. In other words, the observed STEP scores are "closer," in the least-squares sense, to Tie-Type 3 (3.3 3.3 3.3 0 0 0) than to either Tie-Type 2 (5 5 0 0 0 0) or to Tie-Type 4 (2.5 2.5 2.5 2.5 0 0). Accordingly, the total choice of this respondent is allocated equally among the first three brands (A, B, and T), yielding the SUMM shares: 33 33 33 0 0 0. Brands that have a positive SUMM share are called *strong brands*. Brands that have SUMM shares of 0 are called *weak brands*. For this particular respondent, the target brand is a strong brand.

We now proceed to determine how much the various attributes contribute to the target brand's SUMM share. To do so, we compute the target brand's "advantage" for each topic. This is a vector whose elements are the desirability contribution of the target brand minus the desirability contribution of another brand. For example, the target brand's contribution for Topic 1 is 15. The contributions of the other brands for Topic 1

Table H–1
Illustrative Share Partition for One Respondent

		Attribute Desirability d_{rij}	Desirability Contribution (C_{ijk}) to Brand						Target Brand Positive Advantage P_{rij}	Share Component Z_{rij}
			A	B	T	C	D	E		
Topic 1										
Attribute	1	15			15	15			30	9.4
	2	18		18		18	0			
	3	0	0							
Topic 2										
Attribute	1	62								
	2	60	60							
	3	20		20	20	20			30	9.4
	4	10					10			
	5	0				0				
Topic 3										
Attribute	1	0								
	2	5	5			5	5			
	3	20		20	20	20			45	14.2
SUMM score			65	58	55	43	35	15		
STEP score			3	2	4	0	1	0		
SUMM share			33	33	33	0	0	0	105	33

are 0 18 18 15 0. Accordingly, the target brand's advantage vector for Topic 1 is 15 -3 -3 0 15. Similarly, the target brand's advantage vector for Topic 2 is -40 0 0 20 10 and for Topic 3: 15 0 15 0 15.

We assume that the target brand's share is produced by the positive advantage elements and that the other brands' shares are produced by the negative advantage elements. Since we are, for the moment, interested only in a Share Partition of the target brand, we count only the positive advantage elements. These elements add to 30, 30, and 45 for Topics 1, 2 and 3, respectively, for a total of 105. Percentaging the Topic 1 advantage on that sum and multiplying by 33% yields (30)(33%)/105 = 9.4%, which is the contribution of Topic 1 to the SUMM share of the target brand. By the same token, the contributions of Topics 2 and 3 are 9.4% and 14.2%, respectively. The analysis confirms what is obvious by inspection: Of the three topics, Topic 3 makes the biggest contribution, since it

Table H–2
Illustrative Countershare Partition for One Respondent

		Attribute Desirability d_{rij}	Desirability Contribution (C_{ijk}) to Brand						Target Brand Negative Advantage N_{rij}	Countershare Component Z_{rij}
			A	B	T	C	D	E		
Topic 1										
Attribute	1	15			15	15			−3	4.6
	2	18		18		18		0		
	3	0	0							
Topic 2										
Attribute	1	62								
	2	60	60							
	3	20		20	20	20			−40	62.4
	4	10						10		
	5	0					0			
Topic 3										
Attribute	1	0								
	2	5	5			5		5		
	3	20		20	20		20			
SUMM score			65	58	55	43	35	15		
STEP score			3	2	4	0	1	0		
SUMM share			33	33	33	0	0	0	−43	67

has the largest advantage over the other brands. Topics 1 and 2 also make some positive contributions, though smaller ones.

We now consider the converse of Share Partition. If U_t is the SUMM share of the target brand, we define $1 - U_t$ as the *Countershare* of the target brand, that is, the aggregate share of all the target brand's competitors. And just as the Share Partition of the target brand indicates why respondents choose the target brand, so the Countershare Partition of the target brand indicates why respondents do *not* choose the target brand.

The Countershare Partition of the target brand is similar in structure to the Share Partition of the target brand. It makes use of the identical concepts, but the 180-degree turn, from reasons for choosing to reasons for not choosing, gives rise to one small difference, which is illustrated by computing a Countershare Partition of the target brand for the hypothetical respondent of Table H–1. The basic data portion of that table is reproduced in the left section of Table H-2.

As before, we start by considering the target brand's advantages relative to competitive brands. Now, however, we consider only the strong brands, that is, the brands with nonzero SUMM shares. Since we want to determine the reasons why respondents do *not* choose the target brand, the only advantages that are relevant are advantages with respect to those brands they *do* choose. Advantage is defined as before: the desirability of the target brand minus the desirability of another brand. Only two competitive brands, A and B, have nonzero SUMM shares. Accordingly, the target brand's advantage vector for Topic 1 is 15, -3; for Topic 2: -40, 0, and for Topic 3: 15, 0. This time, we are interested only in the negative advantages, since only these contribute to the respondent's *not* choosing the target brand. The sum of negative advantages is placed in the line that corresponds to the attribute the respondent chose as characterizing the target brand best. Thus, an entry in a line means that the strong competitors are more desirable than the target brand by virtue of this attribute, or, turning it around, that this attribute of the target brand contributes to the strong competitors' being chosen, and hence to the target brand's being *not* chosen.

As in the positive case, we percentage all the advantages, but this time on the sum of the negatives, and multiply by the countershare of the target brand. This yields (-3)(67%)/(-43) = 4.6% for Topic 1 and 62.4% for Topic 2. These share components add to the countershare (67%), and once again the analysis confirms what is intuitively obvious: This particular respondent did not choose the target brand mainly because the target brand has Attribute 3 of Topic 2.

The computations of the Share Partition and Countershare Partition are formally specified as follows: Let d_{rij} be the desirability of Attribute j of Topic i for Respondent r. Let $b_{rijk} = 1$ if j is that attribute of Topic i which the respondent believes describes Brand k best, and let $b_{rijk} = 0$ if j is any other attribute. The desirability contribution (C_{rijk}) of Attribute j of Topic i to Brand k is

$$C_{rijk} = b_{rijk}\, d_{rij}$$

The advantage of the target brand t relative to any other brand k, $(k \neq t)$ is

$$A_{rijk} = b_{rijt}\left(C_{rijt} - \sum_{j} C_{rijk}\right)$$

The positive advantages are

$$P_{rijk} = A_{rijk} \quad \text{if } A_{rijk} \geq 0$$

$$P_{rijk} = 0 \quad \text{otherwise}$$

We define

$$P_{rij} = \sum_k P_{rijk}$$

$$P_r = \sum_i \sum_j P_{rij}$$

Then the share-component (Z_{rij}) for Attribute j of Topic i is

$$Z_{rij} = \frac{P_{rij} U_{rt}}{P_r}$$

where U_{rt} is the SUMM share of the target brand. And the share-component (Z_{ij}) of Attribute j of Topic i, for the entire sample of n respondents, is

$$Z_{ij} = \frac{1}{n} \sum_r \frac{P_{rij} U_{rt}}{P_r}$$

Note that when we sum all the share-components, we obtain

$$Z = \sum_i \sum_j Z_{ij} = \frac{1}{n} \sum_r \sum_i \sum_j \frac{P_{rij} U_{rt}}{P_r} = \frac{1}{n} \sum_r U_{rt} = U_t$$

which is the SUMM share for the target brand. Thus, the analysis has partitioned the SUMM share of the target brand into share-components contributed by the various attributes.

Countershare Partition is defined analogously. The advantage of the target brand t relative to any strong competitive brand s $(s \neq t)$ is

$$A_{rijs} = b_{rijs} \left(\sum_j C_{rijt} - C_{rijs} \right)$$

The negative advantages are

$$N_{rijs} = A_{rijs} \quad \text{if } A_{rijs} < 0$$

$$N_{rijs} = 0 \quad \text{otherwise}$$

The share-component (Z_{rij}) for Attribute j of Topic i is

$$Z_{rij} = \frac{N_{rij} U_{rs}}{N_r}$$

and the share-component (Z_{ij}) of Attribute j of Topic i for the entire sample is

$$Z_{ij} = \frac{1}{n} \sum_r \frac{N_{rij} U_{rs}}{N_r}$$

The Television Version of the Universal Ad

In the television version of the Universal Ad, the product is on a platform in a darkened space. A spotlight is turned on. The voice-over announcer says: "What do you look for in a _____?" The camera moves in toward the product as the announcer reads the copy of the Universal ad. The camera stops when the product fills the screen, about two seconds before the announcer finishes reading the copy. Figure I–1 shows the frequency distribution of effects produced by twenty Universal Ads. Fifteen of these produced positive effects. The average effect was 1.75.

Figure I–1
Frequency Distribution of TV-STEP Share Increments
Produced by Twenty Universal Ads
$(N = 22{,}002, \bar{x} = 1.75)$

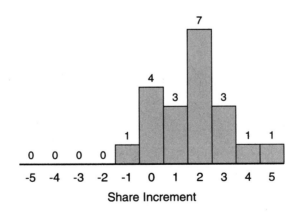

Share Increment

The Contaminated Criss-Cross Tests

In the spring of 1971, EMA was given the assignment to measure the effectiveness of some commercials that were to be shown on several television programs. One brand in each of four product categories was included: napkins, facial tissue, bathroom tissue, and paper towels. Because there was a possibility that any commercial for any of these brands might have some impact on the others, it was necessary to measure all four categories for each program, regardless of which brands were advertised. To include all four categories in the before measure of one sample, and to create a different group of four dummy categories for the other sample, would have lengthened the interview substantially and might have rendered it difficult to implement. To limit each interview to only two categories, offset by two dummy categories, and then duplicate the entire design for the other two categories would have doubled the total sample size required, which was already large by conventional standards. It was a classical study-designer's trap.

Goaded by the need to be operationally effective, by the desire to be economically efficient, seduced by the fact that the design called for two "dummy" categories in any event, I grasped the opportunity to kill two birds with one stone, to split the four categories between the two forms of the questionnaire, and to allow each pair to serve as the dummy pair for the other, in effect enlisting all portions of the questionnaire to earn their keep and contribute productively. It seemed like a good idea, and it would have been a good idea if the four categories had indeed been independent and if there had been no risk that the very presence of some of the questions in the before interview would have an impact on the responses to some of the questions in the after interview.

Looking at it in retrospect, the risk should have been obvious. The very rationale employed in advocating the Criss-Cross design cautioned against before-after designs with the same people, on the ground that the first interview might taint the second. What I had actually done was almost as bad. Although the different product categories, say, bathroom tissue in the before interview and paper towels in the after interview, were in theory different categories, comprising different brands, many of these brands had the same or similar brand names in both categories. To the extent this was so, the after interview on bathroom tissue, for example, became in effect a partial repeat of the before interview on paper towels, and vice versa.

The result of this contamination did not become apparent immediately. I realized what had happened only later. Fortunately, the built-in control of the Criss-Cross design provided an automatic correction for the bias, but the bias itself was real and is clearly visible. Accordingly, I am presenting these tests separately. They serve to illustrate that when it comes to research design, cleanliness is next to godliness.

Figure J–1 shows the average awareness and attitude changes produced by the twenty-six contaminated Criss-Cross tests. The first thing that strikes us in this chart is the major negative awareness change among the nonviewers, which is -4.7%, close to 6 standard errors below zero, a real effect if ever there was one. But what does it mean? Why should the awareness levels of the nonviewers, of all people, have dropped so precipitously from the before to the after interview? Could it be chance? Hardly. The odds of obtaining such a result are less than 1 in a million. Could it be competitive advertising that happened to run on another channel at the same time? Hardly. The data come from six different programs. A competitor would have had to advertise in precise synchroniza-

Figure J–1
Awareness and Attitude Changes among Viewers and Nonviewers in Twenty-six Contaminated Criss-Cross Tests
(*N* = 3,592)

Awareness — SE

		SE
Viewers	-2.2	1.0
Nonviewers	-4.7	.8
Effect	2.5	1.0

Attitude

		SE
Viewers	1.6	.8
Nonviewers	.3	.5
Effect	1.3	.7

tion with the test advertising, and if that had been the case, the effect should have shown up in the attitude changes as well as in the awareness changes. But it did not. The attitude changes among the nonviewers are very close to zero, .3%, which amounts to .4 standard errors, and in the positive direction at that. Could it have been a global effect of some kind, something that happened during the interval between the before and after interviews? Hardly. To be sure, the Criss-Cross design provides for subtracting out effects among nonviewers precisely because it contemplates that such global effects might occur. But in this case, the global effect would have had to be in the same direction time after time, always selectively penalizing the advertised brand, whether that happened to be a bathroom tissue, a paper towel, a napkin, or a facial tissue. It is difficult to imagine such a global effect. But even if we could hypothesize one, such an effect should have cumulated, making the before awareness levels progressively lower over the course of time, and this was not the case. The before awareness levels among the nonviewers are quite stable over the period from March 1971 to May 1971, when the bulk of these tests were conducted: 37, 40, 33, 36, 41, and 37. This leaves the possibility that we are dealing with an artifact. An artifact, in this context, would be a global effect all right—not one attributable to events in the outside world, but brought about entirely by the measurement process itself.

If we focus on that process and on how it translated into the respondent's experience, we note the following sequence. The respondent was asked awareness questions for the two before categories, followed by attitude questions for the two before categories. In the course of asking the attitude questions, all the brands in the category were read to the respondent. This reminded the respondent of some brands she might have been less likely to think of on her own. In the conventional Criss-Cross design this would have been perfectly all right, since the follow-up (after) interview would have covered only a dummy category before the viewing information was collected. In view of the overlap of the brand names in the before and after product categories, however, the normally innocent before attitude questions had the capacity, in this instance, to affect the awareness responses of the after interviews.

To the present day, I don't know precisely why the effect should have been as sweeping as it was, but I had certainly warned against the possibility of just such effects when I developed the Criss-Cross design and should not therefore be unduly surprised or chagrined that, having ignored my own warning, I fell victim to the very risk I had attempted to avoid. If this explanation is correct, there should have been no impact on the attitude measurements in the after interviews, since the competitive frame was presented to the respondents as an integral part of these measurements in any case. And that, of course, is precisely what happened. The artifact affected awareness but not attitude.

On balance, we may say that the phenomenon was due to a global effect after all, though one introduced by the measurement process itself. The Criss-Cross design should have removed this artifact, which presumably operated equally among viewers and nonviewers, by subtracting out the nonviewer changes.

Figure J-2 shows the distributions of the awareness and attitude effects for the contaminated tests. There is, of course, no a priori reason why these tests as a group should have produced the same results as the uncontaminated tests presented previously. There are ample substantive reasons, independent of artifacts, why they could or even should have differed. Most prominent among these is that the contaminated tests were for four paper product categories conducted over a three-month period,

Figure J–2
Frequency Distributions of Net Effects
Twenty-six Contaminated Criss-Cross Tests

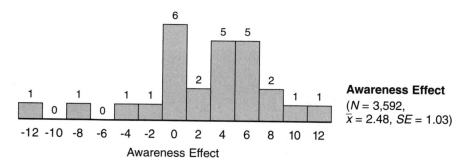

Awareness Effect
(N = 3,592,
$\bar{x}$ = 2.48, SE = 1.03)

Awareness Effect

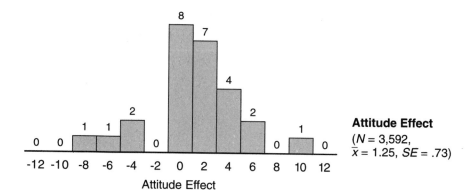

Attitude Effect
(N = 3,592,
$\bar{x}$ = 1.25, SE = .73)

Attitude Effect

while the other tests span several years and cover a wider range of brands in different product categories. Nevertheless, once the net effects have been computed by subtracting the changes among the nonviewers from those among the viewers, as provided by the Criss-Cross design, the two sets of data are remarkably similar. The average attitude changes are almost identical, 1.22 and 1.25, respectively, and the two distributions are not statistically different. The critical variable, of course, is awareness. This difference (4.3 among the noncontaminated, 2.5 among the contaminated) is 1.2 standard errors. It could have been exceeded by chance approximately one time in four. Putting it all together, we may conclude that the contamination certainly had a major impact on the absolute awareness differences among the viewers, but that the nonviewer control built into the Criss-Cross design was probably sufficient to correct for this effect and to yield final net scores not materially different from what they might have been if the contamination had never occurred.

The data underscore the importance of purity on two counts. They illustrate, on the one hand, how easy it is to fall into a trap. And they illustrate concurrently that there is virtue in providing conservative controls, in this instance the subtraction of the nonviewer changes, which may bail us out under unforeseen circumstances.

The Collection and Analysis of Ad-Weight Data

The early Ad-Weight studies provided for two telephone interviews with each respondent. The first interview covered only the criterion variable, for example, purchasing of brands in the product category during the prior two weeks. At the end of the advertising period, all respondents were contacted a second time, and retrospective reports of viewing patterns during the advertising period were obtained. This refinement was intended to make sure that all respondents, regardless of when their criterion variable data had been collected, would be classified into viewing groups on the basis of viewing data collected in the same way at the same time. However, a methodological study conducted in 1976 convinced me that this refinement was not necessary and that if respondents were asked for their "usual" viewing behavior at the time of the original interview, they could be classified into viewing groups in essentially the same way as when the classification was based on data collected during a reinterview.

Figure K–1 summarizes the results of that study for news programs. There were twenty-three waves of interviews altogether. Wave 14 served as the *media-week*. During that week, all respondents, both those who had been interviewed previously and those scheduled to be interviewed subsequently, were called and asked how many times per week they usually viewed each news program. This allowed us to classify all respondents into one of six viewing groups for each news program (0, 1, 2, 3, 4, 5). The respondents were also asked the same question at the end of the criterion-variable interviews during Waves 1–23. The chart shows seven-week moving averages of the weekly viewing reports for each of the six media-week viewing groups. It indicates that, apart from the expected regression to the mean, the weekly data discriminated among the viewing groups in the same way as the media-week data. Based on these results, the second call was eliminated, and both the criterion and viewing information were collected in the same interview thereafter.

Figure K–1
Moving Averages of Weekly Viewing Reports
for Each of Six Media-Week Viewing Classifications
(N = 10,548)

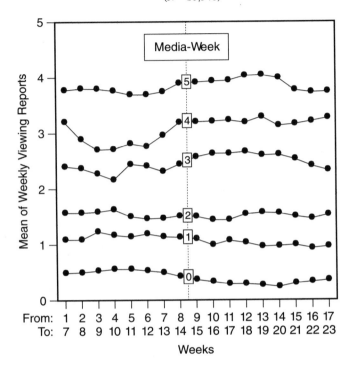

The manner in which the viewing data were obtained also evolved. Originally, when the interviews were conducted by telephone, respondents were asked to report directly how many times per week they had watched each of the relevant programs. Once the change to mail was made, the viewing questions were changed as well and have since been collected in a manner analogous to STEP. The respondents receive ten stickers for each time slot and are asked to allocate them on the basis of how many days in a two-week (ten-day) period they are likely to view various programs or not view television at all.

The Ad-Weight analysis consists of generating a viewing-by-exposure matrix and of computing increments of the criterion variable, stratified by viewing, as shown in Figure K-2. The first row of the figure has only one entry, C_{00}, the criterion variable for people who viewed 0 programs. The next row deals with respondents who viewed only 1 program per week in the relevant time slots. Their exposure can therefore only be 0 or 1. The next row covers respondents who viewed two programs per week in the

Figure K–2
Viewing-Exposure Matrix

	E_0	E_1	E_2	E_3	....	E_i
V_0	C_{00}					
V_1	C_{10}	C_{11}				
V_2	C_{20}	C_{21}	C_{22}			
V_3	C_{30}	C_{31}	C_{32}	C_{33}		
$\vdots$						
V_i	C_{i0}	C_{i1}	C_{i2}	C_{i3}	....	C_{ii}

relevant time slots. Their exposure can therefore be only 0, or 1, or 2. Each respondent qualifies as a *viewer* if she viewed a program in the relevant time slot in any of the markets, but qualifies as *exposed* only if the program she reported viewing happens to have carried the test commercial in accordance with the Ad-Weight schedule.

We now compare criterion-variable differences between respondents exposed to 0 commercials per week and respondents exposed to 1 commercial per week, holding constant their viewing. Conceptually this amounts to saying: We have two equivalent groups of respondents, subject to the assumptions of the Latin Square. Both groups did the same amount of viewing. But some of these respondents viewed on channels that, by virtue of our scheduling, happened to carry a commercial for the test brand, while others viewed on channels that, by virtue of our scheduling, did not happen to carry a test commercial. If we now find that viewers exposed to one commercial bought more than viewers not so exposed, we will credit that buying difference to the commercial.

To estimate the incremental value of one exposure per week compared to 0 exposures, we start by crediting the difference $C_{11} - C_{10}$ of respondents who viewed one relevant program. Analogously, we credit the difference $C_{21} - C_{20}$ of respondents who viewed two relevant programs, and so on. We next need to consolidate the data. In doing so, we take into account the fact that some of the cells in the matrix have substantially larger sample sizes than others. Let n_{ij} be the sample size of the cell in row i, column j. The stability of the difference $(C_{11} - C_{10})$ is a function of the two sample sizes n_{11} and n_{10} and is heavily governed by the smaller of the two. In particular, the *effective* sample size for purposes of gauging the stability of the difference $(C_{11} - C_{10})$ is $N_{11} = n_{11} n_{10} / (n_{11} + n_{10})$. Regardless of how large one of the two cells is, if the other cell shrinks to some small number, the effective sample size becomes approximately equal to that small number. For example, if the sample of one cell is 100 and the other is 1, the effective sample size for assessing the stability of the difference is $(100) \times (1)/101 = .99$. Weighting the increments by their effective sample sizes, the final estimate for the incremental difference (D_{10}) between respondents who received 1 exposure per week and respondents who received 0 exposures per week is

$$D_{10} = \frac{\sum\limits_{i} N_{i1} (C_{i1} - C_{i0})}{\sum\limits_{i} N_{i1}}$$

Continuing in this fashion, we calculate all the increments. If we take the value of the criterion variable in the 0-exposure group (C_{00}) as the base, we may define the corresponding values of the criterion variable for the various exposure groups, by cumulatively adding the increments. In particular, C_i, the value of the criterion variable at i exposures, is

$$C_i = C_{00} + D_{10} + D_{21} + \ldots + D_{ii-1}$$

This is the advertising-response curve. Equipped with it, we can calculate the potential value of any schedule for which the reach-frequency vector is known. That vector tells us what percentage of respondents see 0, 1, 2, 3 . . . commercials per week.

INDEX

Page numbers shown in boldface point to pages on which the term is defined or described.